EUROPEAN ENERGY LAW REPORT XII

Energy & Law Series

European Energy Law Report I, Martha M. Roggenkamp and Ulf Hammer (eds.)
The Regulation of Power Exchanges in Europe, Martha M. Roggenkamp and François Boisseleau (eds.)
European Energy Law Report II, Martha M. Roggenkamp and Ulf Hammer (eds.)
European Energy Law Report III, Ulf Hammer and Martha M. Roggenkamp (eds.)
European Energy Law Report IV, Martha M. Roggenkamp and Ulf Hammer (eds.)
A Functional Legal Design for Reliable Electricity Supply, Hamilcar Knops
European Energy Law Report V, Martha M. Roggenkamp and Ulf Hammer (eds.)
European Energy Law Report VI, Martha M. Roggenkamp and Ulf Hammer (eds.)
Electricity and Gas Supply Network Unbundling in Germany, Great Britain and The Netherlands and the Law of the EU, Eckart Ehlers
Legal Design of Carbon Capture and Storage, Martha M. Roggenkamp and Edwin Woerdman (eds.)
European Energy Law Report VII, Martha M. Roggenkamp and Ulf Hammer (eds.)
European Energy Law Report VIII, Martha M. Roggenkamp and Ulf Hammer (eds.)
European Energy Law Report IX, Martha M. Roggenkamp and Olivia Woolley (eds.)
EU Regulation of Cross-Border Carbon Capture and Storage, Marijn Holwerda
The Non-Discrimination Obligation of Energy Network Operators, Hannah Kruimer
European Energy Law Report X, Martha M. Roggenkamp and Henrik Bjørnebye (eds.)
A Legal Framework for a Transnational Offshore Grid in the North Sea, Hannah Katharina Müller
Prevention and Compensation for Transboundary Damage in Relation to Cross-Border Pipelines, Mehdi Piri Damagh
Handbook of Shale Gas Law and Policy – Economics, Access, Law and Regulation in Key Jurisdictions, Tina Hunter (ed.)
European Energy Law Report XI, Martha M. Roggenkamp and Catherine Banet (eds.)
European Energy Law Report XII, Martha M. Roggenkamp and Catherine Banet (eds.)

EUROPEAN ENERGY LAW REPORT XII

Edited by
Martha M Roggenkamp
Catherine Banet

intersentia
Cambridge – Antwerp – Chicago

Intersentia Ltd
Sheraton House | Castle Park
Cambridge | CB3 0AX | United Kingdom
Tel.: +44 1223 370 170 | Fax: +44 1223 370 169
Email: mail@intersentia.co.uk
www.intersentia.com | www.intersentia.co.uk

Distribution for the UK and Ireland:
NBN International
Airport Business Centre, 10 Thornbury Road
Plymouth, PL6 7PP
United Kingdom
Tel.: +44 1752 202 301 | Fax: +44 1752 202 331
Email: orders@nbninternational.com

Distribution for Europe and all other countries:
Intersentia Publishing nv
Groenstraat 31
2640 Mortsel
Belgium
Tel.: +32 3 680 15 50 | Fax: +32 3 658 71 21
Email: mail@intersentia.be

Distribution for the USA and Canada:
Independent Publishers Group
Order Department
814 North Franklin Street
Chicago, IL 60610
USA
Tel.: +1 800 888 4741 (toll free) | Fax: +1 312 337 5985
Email: orders@ipgbook.com

The Energy & Law Series is published in parallel with the Dutch series Energie & Recht.

European Energy Law Report XII

ISBN 978-1-78068-672-1
D/2018/7849/104
NUR 828

British Library Cataloguing in Publication Data. A catalogue record for this book is available from the British Library.

PREFACE

The editors are very pleased to present the *European Energy Law Report XII*. The *European Energy Law Report* is an initiative taken by the organisers of the European Energy Law Seminar, which has taken place on a regular basis in the Netherlands since 1989. The aim of this seminar is to present an overview of the most important legal developments in the field of international, EU and national energy and climate law. Whereas the first seminars concentrated on the developments at European Community (EC) level, which were the result of the establishment of an Internal Energy Market, the focus has now gradually switched to the developments at national level following the implementation of the EU Directives on internal electricity and gas markets, promoting renewable energy sources, mitigating climate change and securing energy supply. This approach can also be found in these reports.

Similar to the previous *European Energy Law Reports*, this book includes chapters based on papers presented at the 28th European Energy Law Seminar, which was organised on 23 and 24 January 2017 and which examined a wide range of issues involving the promotion of renewable energy sources and the need to secure a regular and reliable energy supply. The book consists of five parts: 'Developments in the EU and EU Energy Law'; 'Promoting Renewable Energy Production: Cross-border Projects and Dispute Settlement'; 'Energy Consumers as Renewable Energy Producers: The Concept of Prosumers'; 'Balancing Renewable Electricity Production with Supply Security: National Experiences with Capacity Mechanisms'; and 'Promoting the Use of Sustainable Gas and Security of Gas Supply'. Where necessary, the chapters have been updated up to June 2018.

We are grateful for the support of the speakers at the seminar and their cooperation in rewriting their papers for the purpose of this book. We also would like to thank the authors and co-authors who did not speak at the seminar but who were willing to participate in this project so that we could provide you with a 'complete' picture of all the topics discussed. Finally, we would like to acknowledge the help and support of the publisher in publishing this book. We are confident that these reports will be part of an important and long-lasting tradition in this field.

Martha M Roggenkamp and Catherine Banet
Groningen/Oslo, 15 June 2018

CONTENTS

PART II. PROMOTING RENEWABLE ENERGY PRODUCTION: CROSS-BORDER PROJECTS AND DISPUTE SETTLEMENT

LIST OF ABBREVIATIONS

ACER	Agency for the Cooperation of Energy Regulators
ANODE	*Association nationale des opérateurs détaillants en énergie* (National Association of Energy Retail Operators)
BAT	Best available techniques
BDEW	*Bundesverband der Energie- und Wasserwirtschaft e.V.*
BEB	*Balgarska energiyna borsa*
BEIS	Department for Business, Energy and Industrial Strategy
BImSchG	*Bundesimmissionsschutzgesetz*
BIT	Bilateral investment treaty
BMWi	*Bundesministerium für Wirtschaft und Energie*
BNetzA	*BundesNetzAgentur*
CA	Cooperation Agreement
CCGT	Combined cycle gas turbine
CEF	Connecting Europe Facility
CFD	Contracts for difference
CH_4	Methane
CHP	Combined heat and power
CJEU	Court of Justice of the European Union
CM	Capacity market
CMU	Capacity market unit
CO_2	Carbon dioxide
CRE	*Commission de Régulation de l'Energie* (French energy regulator)
CSP	Concentrated solar power
DEA	Danish Energy Agency
DECC	Department of Energy and Climate Change
DEFRA	Department for Environment Food and Rural Affairs
DSO	Distribution system operator
DSR	Demand-side response
E-Act	Electricity Act (Dutch)
EC	European Commission
E-Control	Austrian Energy Regulator
ECT	Energy Charter Treaty
EdF	*Electricité de France*
EEA	European Economic Area
EEAG	Environmental and Energy State Aid Guidelines

EEG	*Erneubare Energien Gesetz* or Renewable Energy Sources Act
EEPR	European Energy Programme for Recovery
EEZ	Exclusive Economic Zone
ENEA	Polish State-owned Electricity Company
ENTSO-E	European Network of Transmission System Operators for Electricity
ENTSO-G	European Network of Transmission System Operators for Gas
EnWG	*Energiewirtschaftsgesetz*
EU	European Union
EU ETS	EU emission trading system
Euratom	European Atomic Energy Community
FCC	Fluid catalytic cracker
FCEV	Fuel cell electric vehicles
FET	Fair and equitable treatment
FiT	Feed-in tariff
FTA	Free trade agreement
FQD	Fuel Quality Directive
GATT	General Agreement on Tariffs and Trade
GB	Great Britain
GCG	Gas Coordination Group
GGETA	Greenhouse Gas Emissions Trading Act
GO	Guarantees of origin
GSE	*Gestore dei Servizi Energetici* S.p.A.
GW	Gigawatt
ICSID	International Centre for Settlement of Investment Disputes
IEM	Internal energy market
IFA	Interconnexion France-Angleterre
IGA	Intergovernmental Agreement
KapResV	*Kapazitätsreserveverordnung*
KDT	Polish Electricity Act
kV	Kilovolt
Kw	Kilowatt
LEC	Local energy community
LOLE	Loss of load expectation
LPG	Liquefied petroleum gas
MEA	Ministry of Economic Affairs and Climate (The Netherlands)
MPE	Minister of Petroleum and Energy (Norway)
NAFTA	North American Free Trade Agreement
MFN	Most favoured nation
MRP	Market reference price
MW	Megawatt
NBP	National balancing point
NetzResV	*Netzreserveverordnung*

NGET	National Grid Electricity Transmission plc
NGG	National Grid plc
NRA	National Regulatory Authority
NVE	Norwegian Water Resources and Energy Directorate (regulator)
NEW	North-Western Europe
O_2	Oxygen
Ofgem	Office of Gas and Electricity Markets
OPAL	*Ostsee-Pipeline-Anbindungsleitung*
PCA	Postal code area
PCC	Precipitated calcium carbonate
PCI	Projects of common interest
PEM	Polymer electrolyte membrane
PGNiG	*Polskie Górnictwo Naftowe i Gazownictwo*
PP	Peak period
PPA	Power purchase agreements
PSO	Public service obligations
PPE	*Programmation pluriannuelle de l'énergie* (Multiannual Energy Programme)
PV	Photovoltaic
RAIPRE	*Registro administrativo de instalaciones de producción de energía eléctrica*
RES	Renewable energy sources
ROW	Rest of the world
RTE	*Réseau de Transport d'Electricité*
SCC	Stockholm Chamber of Commerce
SEM	Single electricity market
SONI	System Operator for Northern Ireland
TFEU	Treaty on the Functioning of the European Union
TPA	Third party access
TSO	Transmission system operators
TTF	Title transfer facility
UK	United Kingdom
UNCITRAL	United Nations Commission on International Trade Law
UNCLOS	United Nations Convention on the Law of the Sea
UNFCC	United Nations Framework Convention on Climate Change
VKU	*Verband kommunaler Unternehmen e.V.*
VoLL	Value of lost load
WTO	World Trade Organization

LIST OF CONTRIBUTORS

Catherine Banet
PhD, Associate Professor, Scandinavian Institute of Maritime Law, Petroleum and Energy Law Department, Oslo, Norway. Email: catherine.banet@jus.uio.no

Lea Diestelmeier
PhD researcher, Groningen Centre of Energy Law, University of Groningen, Groningen, The Netherlands. Email: l.diestelmeier@rug.nl

Dijana Dmitruk
Advisor, Centre for Energy Resources, Danish Energy Agency, Danish Ministry of Energy, Utilities and Climate, Copenhagen, Denmark. Email: ddm@ens.dk

Berend Jan Drijber
Advocate General at the *Hoge Raad*, the Dutch Supreme Court. Until 1 October 2017 he was a partner with Pels Rijcken & Droogleever Fortuijn N.V. in The Hague, The Netherlands. Email: B.Drijber@HogeRaad.nl

Ruven Fleming
PhD, Assistant Professor of Energy Law, Groningen Centre of Energy Law, University of Groningen, Groningen, The Netherlands. Email: r.c.fleming@rug.nl

Emma France
Lawyer, Herbert Smith Freehills, Paris, France. Email: Emma.France@hsf.com

Silke Goldberg
Partner, Herbert Smith Freehills LLP and PhD researcher at the Groningen Centre of Energy Law, London, United Kingdom. Email: Silke.Goldberg@hsf.com

Christina Heber
PhD, Associate, Linklaters LLP, Berlin, Germany. Email: christina.heber@linklaters.com

Thomas Herman
Associate, Herbert Smith Freehills, Paris, France. Email: Thomas.Herman@hsf.com

Dirk Kuiken
PhD researcher, Groningen Centre of Energy Law, University of Groningen, Groningen, The Netherlands. Email: d.kuiken@rug.nl

Matthias Lang
PhD, Partner, Bird & Bird, Düsseldorf, Germany. Email: Matthias.Lang@twobirds.com

Nikos Lavranos
PhD, Independent Legal Advisor for Investment law & Arbitration, NL-Investmentconsulting, Haarlem, The Netherlands. Email: contact@nl-investmentconsulting.com

Ceciel Nieuwenhout
PhD researcher, Groningen Centre for Energy Law, University of Groningen, Groningen, The Netherlands. Email: c.t.nieuwenhout@rug.nl

Kai Uwe Pritzsche
PhD, LL.M. (Berkeley), partner of Linklaters LLP, Germany. Email: kai.pritzsche@linklaters.com

Julian Roberts
Senior economist, Office of Gas and Electricity Markets (Ofgem), London, United Kingdom. Email: julian.roberts@ofgem.gov.uk

Martha M Roggenkamp
PhD, Professor of Energy Law and Director of the Groningen Centre of Energy Law, University of Groningen, Groningen, The Netherlands. Email: m.m.roggenkamp@rug.nl

Cees Verburg
PhD researcher, Groningen Centre for Energy Law, University of Groningen, Groningen, The Netherlands. Email: c.g.verburg@rug.nl

INTRODUCTION

Martha M Roggenkamp and Catherine Banet

The *European Energy Law Report XII* (EELR XII) presents an overview of the most important developments in the field of international, EU and national energy and climate law as discussed at the 28th European Energy Law Seminar, held on 23 and 24 January 2017 in The Hague, the Netherlands. Although a wide range of topics and developments were discussed at the seminar, we recognise that the common thread is the promotion of renewable energy sources (RES) and how this affects the need to secure a regular, reliable and affordable energy supply. This is thus also the common theme of this book but, in order to make the information accessible, we have divided the topics into separate sub-themes. With this in mind, the book has been divided into five parts, with each part covering a different development. The order and content of these sections do not necessarily correspond to those of the papers presented at the seminar.

DEVELOPMENTS IN THE EU AND EU CASE LAW AND THEIR IMPACT ON THE ENERGY SECTOR

The first part of this book opens with two chapters examining issues which are relevant to the shaping of the EU and EU energy law. These chapters present the withdrawal of the UK from the EU (Brexit) and recent EU case law respectively. Although this grouping involves two different issues, both are relevant for shaping EU energy law.

Chapter I starts with a highly topical examination of the future of the EU by discussing the impact of Brexit on the energy sector. Although Brexit features on an almost daily basis on television and in the newspapers, its impact on the energy sector has so far hardly been discussed. Silke Goldberg attempts to fill this void with a chapter called 'Pulling the plug? Brexit and its impact on the Energy Sector'. She begins by first presenting the background to Brexit and the legal measures taken by the UK Government to initiate it, as well as the possible alternative pathways for a post-Brexit UK-EU relationship (hard vs soft Brexit). How this may impact the energy sector is then highlighted by way of a discussion of the impact of the UK's withdrawal on cross-border energy trade with the EU, as Brexit may result in import/export tariffs on energy and the construction and use of interconnectors between the UK and the EU. As a result, Brexit may have a negative impact on the UK's supply security. Of special interest in this regard is the energy relationship with Ireland; can the UK (including Northern Ireland) and the Republic of Ireland continue to operate a single electricity market or does Brexit bring an end to this important process of energy market integration? The author then moves on to a discussion of the UK's position in Euratom; given the separate legal nature of Euratom, it is questionable whether Brexit also means that the UK has withdrawn from the organisation. Despite this uncertainty it is questionable whether the UK Government is willing to address this sensitive issue before Brexit takes place on 29 March 2019. The chapter concludes with a brief analysis of Brexit's impact on climate change. As the UK is also a party to the United Nations Framework Convention on Climate Change and the Paris Agreement and already has some strict national targets in place, Brexit may also have an impact on the future relationship between the UK and the EU should the former decrease its climate change ambitions.

The next chapter presents an overview of EU case law that is relevant for the energy sector. Berend Jan Drijber first discusses case law relating to the rules governing the internal energy market. These cases involve, inter alia, the extent to which France (*Anode* case) is entitled to regulate gas supply tariffs at retail level; the ECJ ruled in accordance with the earlier *Federutility* case (see EELR IX) that this requires proof that such price intervention is necessary and proportional. The *Eni & Uprigaz* case is also about consumer protection but in relation to Regulation (EU) 994/2010 governing security of gas supply (see also Chapter XIII of this book) and addresses, in particular, the definition of 'protected customers' in relation supply standards. Under the heading of 'capacity allocation', the author discusses two cases, *E-Control v ACER* and *PGNiG v Commission*, involving capacity allocation on interconnectors. The first case is surprising as the Austrian regulator (E-Control) lodged an appeal against ACER. The second case involved the extent to which long term capacity allocation may impact supply security and cause irreparable harm. Thereafter, the author discusses several cases dealing with the free allocation of CO_2 emission allowances. As Directive 2009/29/EC gradually limits the free allocation of these allowances, the Court has had to answer questions from several national courts regarding the transitional period and decide on some technical issues relating to the free allocation of emissions allowances. Under the heading 'renewables', three different cases are discussed: *Essent Belgium*, *E.ON Biofor Sverige* and *J.D (Poland)*. Whereas the first case raises the issue of discriminatory treatment of renewables on the basis of the origin of (green) electricity, the second case is about 'green' gas and the scheme supporting the cross-border transport of biomethane. The third case involved the interpretation of the definition of 'energy from renewable resources', ie whether hydropower from renewable sources should be limited to natural waterfalls or whether it could be extended to artificial water flows. The last section of this chapter presents case law involving

State aid rules, ie the *PGE* case involving long-term power purchase agreements, the *ENEA* case involving support for electricity produced by cogeneration and case law on the German financial support scheme EEG. State aid law is becoming increasingly important for the energy sector, as is also illustrated by some of the other chapters in this book (see, for example, Chapters V, VI, IX, X and XI).

PROMOTING RENEWABLE ENERGY PRODUCTION: CROSS-BORDER PROJECTS AND DISPUTE SETTLEMENT

Part II of EELR XII presents three important developments regarding investments in renewable energy projects in the EU. Currently the EU is bound by the so-called '20-20-20 goals', which prescribe a target of 20 per cent gross renewable energy consumption by 2020.[1] Individual national targets and the legal instrument through which to achieve them are incorporated in Directive 2009/28/EC. This Directive provides two important instruments designed to reach these targets. First, it facilitates the establishment and use of national support schemes in order to compensate for any additional costs relating to 'green' energy in comparison to traditional 'grey' energy. Second, it recognises that some Member States may not be in a position to reach these targets by themselves and therefore, in the spirit of solidarity, should be able to achieve these targets collectively via a joint support mechanism, joint projects or statistical transfer of specified amounts of renewable energy sources. The Directive offers little guidance regarding the way in which Member States should design their national support schemes. Consequently, some of these schemes have proven to attract considerable foreign investments.

Chapter III examines this issue of foreign investments in renewable energy projects in the EU and, in particular, the disputes that have arisen following changes in national RES support schemes. Perhaps surprisingly, these disputes are not dealt with via national or EU law mechanisms but are increasingly resolved by making use of the Energy Charter Treaty (ECT). Nikos Lavranos and Cees Verburg analyse some central disputes that have arisen under the ECT in their chapter entitled 'Renewable Energy Investments Disputes – Recent Developments and the Way Forward'. In order to do so, they first describe the regulatory changes that led to the ECT disputes. They then proceed to examine the various arbitral awards. Although investors in various other EU Member States, such as the Czech Republic, Bulgaria and Greece have also been confronted with regulatory changes to RES support schemes, this chapter focuses on the ECT awards involving Spain and Italy, as these are currently the only available examples of RES awards under the ECT. Moreover, with regard to

1 Following the 2030 Climate & Energy Framework an overall new target of 27% applies to the consumption of renewable energy sources. See http://ec.europa.eu/energy/en/topics/energy-strategy-and-energy-union.

Spain in particular and, to a lesser extent, Italy, these are the countries that have been faced with the highest number of investment treaty claims.

Investments in renewable energy projects depend on the type of renewables available in each Member State. Coastal states that are densely populated, like many North Sea countries, increasingly look offshore for developing wind energy projects. So far these projects have tended to be national in scope, resulting in park-to-shore connections (see also EELR XI). From an energy trade and internal market perspective, it makes sense to develop cross-border connections and, subsequently, an offshore grid. Ceciel Nieuwenhout addresses the development of such offshore hybrid grid infrastructure in Chapter IV and raises the issue of whether there is a need for a new interpretation or for new terminology in order to provide investors with sufficient regulatory certainty and achieve this goal. For this purpose, she first examines the relevant provisions under international law relating to jurisdiction over (hybrid) offshore electricity cables. This is followed by a discussion of EU law regulating such cables. Thereafter, she discusses the regulatory practice of the Kriegers Flak combined grid solution. The latter example demonstrates the need for greater clarity and regulatory certainty, especially in taking into account the long-term ambitions for offshore wind energy.

The last chapter in this part involves another example of the promotion of cross-border energy projects. Dijana Dmitruk presents in Chapter V the 'Danish-German Cooperation Agreement on the first Cross-Border Tenders of Support for Renewable Electricity – A Blueprint for Future Cross-Border RES Projects?'. This cooperation agreement makes use of the possibility provided in Directive 2009/28/EC of establishing a regime of statistical transfer between Member States. This particular example involves an agreement between Germany and Denmark regarding a pilot project concerning two tenders for support schemes (price premium) for electricity produced by solar PV. Following a presentation of the background for this cooperation agreement, the author discusses the national legal bases in Germany and Denmark and the conditions for opening up the national support schemes. The author then presents the contents of the cooperation agreement. This includes an analysis of the tender design, the exchange and verification of information concerning the installations on each side of the border, the statistical transfer and the way in which risk and liability is dealt with in order to safeguard and protect the investors. The chapter concludes with an analysis of the first two tenders and the extent to which this pilot project may provide a blueprint for other cross-border projects.

ENERGY CONSUMERS AS RENEWABLE ENERGY PRODUCERS: THE CONCEPT OF PROSUMERS

Whereas part II focused on 'traditional' investors in renewable energy projects, a new type of developer is gradually emerging. This is the case of existing consumers who start to produce electricity from renewable energy sources, by making use of solar PV for example. This new type of producer is often referred to as 'prosumer' and is examined in this part of this book. There is thus far no EU law regulating 'prosumers' but their advent is the result of structural changes that the energy sector has sought. The gradual emergence of these prosumers is illustrated by three different examples of national approaches to their regulation, each national example presenting a different perspective and background to the trend.

Matthias Lang first presents, in Chapter VI the example of 'prosumers' legislation in Germany. The concept is closely linked to the process of energy transition (*Energiewende*) and the subsequent need to increase the levels of generation from renewable energy sources. Because renewable energy installations are usually not developed and owned by traditional energy supply companies, a new type of developer has emerged. In German law, these developers are dealt with under the heading of 'self-supply' (*Eigenversorgung*). This concept was initially introduced in the Feed-in Act of 2012 and continued to be present in the Renewable Energy Sources Acts (EEG) of 2014 and 2017. The concept of 'self-supply' refers to the situation where a natural or legal person consumes electricity themselves instead of feeding the electricity into the grid. The primary, original incentive for becoming a self-supplier in Germany is to be found in the EEG, as these self-suppliers were exempted from paying the EEG surcharge which is usually charged to customers in order to cover the costs of the feed-in tariffs. This regime has incentivised self-supply for large consumers and this chapter discusses the background, introduction and design of this regime. It then goes on to present the amendments that have been introduced in order to limit the number of customers that could be exempted from the EEG surcharge and the extent to which these exemptions are to be considered as State aid (see also Chapter II). As a result, the current regime governing self-supply is no longer a financial incentive to becoming a prosumer.

Chapter VII presents the legal framework for prosumers in the Netherlands. As in Germany, the term 'prosumers' is not defined by law but is enabled by some provisions in secondary legislation. In practice, the concept primarily applies to small/household consumers. Under Dutch law, it is nevertheless possible to identify two categories of prosumer: individual prosumers and collective prosumers. The latter category also enables those who cannot place solar panels on their roof to still reap the benefits associated with being a prosumer if they form part of a collective (eg a house owners' association). Lea Diestelmeijer and Dirk Kuiken first present the background and the relevant legal provisions that apply in the Netherlands. They then discuss the category of 'individual' prosumer. As, in essence, prosumers under Dutch law cannot sell their electricity to other household consumers, their choices are limited to either consuming all of their electricity themselves or selling it to a supplier and feeding it into the grid. In order to facilitate the latter, the Netherlands applies a regime of 'net-metering'. This may change if 'smart meters' are installed throughout the Netherlands, as these are capable of communicating meter readings between consumers and system operators or suppliers in real time. In order to assist persons who do not have the necessary means to become prosumers, Dutch law allows for collective organisations to engage in electricity generation. This can be based on either a postal code area agreement, which was introduced in 2014 and provides those participating in the scheme with similar financial incentives as individual prosumers, or on the Decree governing experiments with decentralised renewable electricity generation, which provides some exemptions from the Electricity Act in order for collectives to generate electricity from renewables. There follows a discussion of these individual and collective prosumers and, at the end of the chapter, the authors briefly examine the concept of the 'active customer' introduced in the EU's Clean Energy Package of 2016 and how this could affect the Dutch regime of prosumers.

A third example is presented in Chapter VIII in analysing the position of 'prosumers' in Norway. The situation in Norway differs in many ways from the two above. First, in Norway there is no need to incentivise the production and use of renewable energy sources as electricity generation is already almost totally based on renewable energy sources. Second, Norway has revised its legislation on 1 January 2017 to provide a clear legal basis (including a definition) for the governance of the activities of this specific market player, which, in fact, focusses on residential prosumers. In contrast to the two examples above, the Norwegian regime does not provide for specific financial incentives. Consequently, other arguments serve as the relevant motivation for becoming a prosumer in Norway. Catherine Banet discusses the manner the concept has evolved in Norway and the applicable legal framework. She also addresses some future developments, such as grid tariff regulation and the need to amend the regime in order to facilitate collective prosumers.

BALANCING RENEWABLE ELECTRICITY PRODUCTION WITH SUPPLY SECURITY: NATIONAL EXPERIENCES WITH CAPACITY MECHANISMS

The increasing share of renewable energy sources has an impact on the need to ensure the security of energy supply. Due to the intermittent character of renewables and the necessity to balance demand and supply, there is a need to have available a sufficient 'traditional' generation capacity. As such, this raises the question of who is willing to invest in new and/or modern generation capacity when there is uncertainty regarding the extent and frequency of its use and when electricity prices remain quite low? This concern is referred to as 'generation adequacy'. Therefore, there may be a need to adopt new measures to supplement the energy-only markets. These measures have often taken the form of so-called 'capacity remuneration mechanisms', which can be distinguished into three main types:

(i) capacity payments: where generators receive a fixed compensation;
(ii) capacity market: the creation of a new market in which energy capacity is traded via certificates;
(iii) strategic reserves: where generating units are kept exclusively available for emergencies (eg when the market is not able to cover demand) and are called upon by an independent body (eg the Transmission System Operator).

Although capacity remuneration mechanisms have existed in the EU since the 1990s, their use has been gradually increasing. Given the potential impact on market liberalisation, the European Commission started to review the different national capacity mechanisms and launched, in April 2015, a State aid sector inquiry which assessed eleven Member States and revealed some 35 capacity mechanisms already in place. The sector inquiry concluded that capacity mechanisms could be an adequate measure to ensure the security of supply, but that Member States need to make a detailed assessment of their need. Part IV of this book examines three examples of such mechanisms from countries being reviewed, namely the UK, Germany and France.

First, Julian Roberts presents in Chapter IX the regime governing the capacity market in the United Kingdom. Discussions about the introduction of a capacity market began in 2009 as the country had to face important changes in its electricity system. It was confronted with: (i) the closure of many end-of-life coal and nuclear-based generators; and (ii) the increasing use of renewable energy sources (constituting some 25% of total generating capacity at the time of writing). Replacing the old power plants with low carbon generation capacity requires major investment. Since new generation would not be able to replace the closing power plants fast enough, the Government anticipated falling capacity margins and introduced a capacity mechanism. The legislation was amended in 2013 and 2014 to enable the introduction of a capacity market and, in parallel, the capacity market was designed. Instead of a strategic reserve, the Government opted for a capacity market, ie a market-based approach. This chapter begins by discussing the background, legal framework and State aid approval necessary to introduce the capacity market. This is followed by a brief introduction of the economic theory explaining the rationale of creating a capacity market. Thereafter, the author discusses the design of the market, which basically consists of six stages: analysis, prequalification, auction, payments and penalties, delivery and trading. The chapter concludes with an analysis of the results so far (with lower prices than expected) and the challenges lying ahead.

Chapter X then looks at the way in which Germany is using capacity mechanisms; this mechanism is based on a different approach as it makes use of capacity reserves. Also, in Germany, the process of energy transition (*Energiewende*) is the main reason for introducing such a mechanism. Due to the large scale introduction and use of intermittent renewable energy sources, conventional power plants cannot be operated economically because, under the merit order system, these power plants are not operating for a sufficient number of hours per year. Therefore, the operators need to set very high peak prices to cover their fixed costs. In order to address this problem, Germany introduced its first reserve mechanisms in 2012. This regime has subsequently been amended due to the abovementioned European Commission's Sector Inquiry, among other things. Kai Pritzsche and Christina Heber present in this chapter the background for introducing capacity mechanisms in Germany and how the regime has evolved. There are currently four mechanisms in place: (i) the network reserve (*Netzreserve*); (ii) the capacity reserve (*Kapazitätsreserve*); (iii) the security stand-by mode (*Sicherheitsbereitschaft*); and (iv) the network stability plants (*Netzstabilisierungsanlage*). The authors assess each of these in detail and conclude with the assertion that energy transition involves a constant market restructuring. As such, changes can be expected to the current market design.

In Chapter XI, Thomas Herman and Emma France assess the way in which France has applied a capacity mechanism regime. The introduction of such a regime had been discussed since 2010 and led to the adoption of a detailed regime and set of rules governing the capacity market in 2015. Security of supply in a market subject to a process of energy transition is also the main driver for the introduction of a capacity market. Through the adoption of its capacity market mechanism, France applies a market-based, country-wide and decentralised approach. The chapter first describes the evolution of the legislative and regulatory framework governing the French capacity market and related litigation. Thereafter, it presents the existing regime based on a system of trade in capacity guarantees and the modifications that were made to it following the European Commission's decision that the initial French regime (providing capacity certificates free of charge and without cross-border participation) would constitute a State aid measure not compatible with the EU State Aid Guidelines. It goes on to provide an overview of the market practices and it concludes with some outlooks from the authors.

PROMOTING THE USE OF SUSTAINABLE GAS AND SECURITY OF GAS SUPPLY

In the last part of this book – Part V – the focus switches to gas. The gas market is facing similar challenges as the electricity sector, ie climate change and supply security. These concerns could have an impact on the gas sector and result in new sustainable gas sources being developed. These range from the use of biogas to enabling a process called power-to-gas, which refers to the use of electricity as the input for the production of hydrogen and oxygen through the decomposition of a water molecule by way of electrolysis. This process may be considered as sustainable if intermittent renewable energy sources like wind and solar are used. Power-to-gas may then serve as a storage option but also creates some sort of 'green' product, eg 'green' hydrogen. In the longer term, the use of power-to-gas and 'green' hydrogen may play a role in securing EU security of gas supply. Currently, however, the EU legislator is opting for a different solution as it limits its focus to natural gas only.

The development of green hydrogen is discussed by Martha M Roggenkamp in Chapter XII and, in particular, in relation to the use of power-to-gas in refineries, from EU and German perspectives. Refineries are large CO_2 emitters and the use of green hydrogen may reduce the level of CO_2 emissions. Another issue is the impact of the use of green hydrogen on the refineries' end-product: transport fuels. After a general introduction to the topic and the reasons for its discussion from EU and German law perspectives, the chapter presents the refineries sector and the refinery process. It then outlines the concept of power-to-gas and how this can be used in the refinery process. The focus then turns to the legal frameworks in the EU and Germany respectively. These range from the rules governing the use of the refineries' energy consumption, which include the application of the EU Emissions Trading Scheme and the rules on CO_2 emissions trading, to the rules governing the refineries' products, eg transport fuels. One of the issues discussed is the Fuel Quality Directive and the extent to which the life-cycle approach envisaged in this directive impacts fuel quality. In other words, does the use of green hydrogen result in more sustainable transport fuels?

The last chapter of this book, Chapter XIII, presents the new EU security of gas supply Regulation or Regulation (EU) 2017/1938. This Regulation is the successor to Regulation 994/2010 and is supposed to address some of its shortcomings. It should be noted that the new Regulation does not consider other or renewable gasses as a means to guarantee supply security. The focus is entirely on natural gas and how the EU as a whole should ensure the security of gas supply. The chapter concentrates on the main novelty of the Regulation, the imposition of obligatory 'solidarity' between Member States in a gas crisis. According to the Regulation, this has to be achieved by two means. First, by clustering directly connected (neighbouring) Member States into so-called 'risk groups'. Second, the Regulation provides for a new Article 13 which spells out concrete solidarity measures that Member States have to take in case of an emergency. This can be seen as a clear example of the solidarity principle, which, among other things, has been included in Article 194 TFEU. Ruven Fleming begins this chapter by providing the background to the Regulation, as well as its structure and aims. Thereafter, he analyses its main novelties: the development of risk groups and the solidarity mechanism. He concludes that with regard to this Regulation the proof of the pudding is in eating; in other words, it remains to be seen how Member States will respond in case of a gas crisis.

PART I

DEVELOPMENTS IN THE EU AND EU ENERGY LAW

CHAPTER I

BREXIT AND ITS IMPACT ON THE ENERGY SECTOR

Pulling the Plug?

Silke GOLDBERG

1. INTRODUCTION

Following the referendum on 23 June 2016 and the subsequent General Election in June 2017, the nature of the UK's future relationship with the EU remains uncertain. It seems more likely than not, however, that the status quo of remaining within the internal energy market is unfeasible.

Yet, the prevailing mood in the UK energy sector seems to be that a divorce of sorts, ie a complete physical separation of the UK[1] and EU electricity markets, is undesirable. Commercial incentives to sustain, and nurture, further market integration between the UK and the EU by way of interconnectors (both in the electricity and gas industry) seem to remain strong; as are concerns about the knock-on effects of Brexit for the security of energy supply and regulatory uncertainty.

The current negotiation timetable, however, does not seem likely to produce anything tangible for the sector until later in the Brexit negotiations as energy is not one of the high priority areas to be dealt with early on in the negotiations.

This is likely to result in prolonged - and unprecedented - regulatory uncertainty across the energy sector. Comments from some EU companies have suggested they too hoped that pragmatism might trump politics in the energy sector.[2]

---

1 Covering both the British and Northern Irish electricity markets.

2 A WARD, 'Ireland weighs post-Brexit energy security options', *Financial Times*, 26 July 2017, available at: https://www.ft.com/content/51c5a4a8-6d2c-11e7-b9c7-15af748b60d0.

This chapter will provide a brief overview of key themes for the energy sector which are likely to be affected by Brexit as well as a brief outlook for the immediate future as the Brexit negotiations take shape in a more tangible way:

The areas discussed in this chapter include:

- tariffs on energy imports/exports by the UK as a non-EU state;
- interconnectors;
- security of energy supply post-Brexit;
- the Isle of Ireland and its Single Electricity Market (SEM);
- the UK's membership of the European Atomic Energy Community (Euratom); and
- the UK's commitments to climate change targets and the EU emissions trading system (EU ETS).

By necessity, as the negotiations are a moving feast, this chapter comments on general themes affecting the Brexit negotiations and the likely post-Brexit relations between the EU and the UK as applied to the energy sector, rather than providing a detailed commentary on the progress, or otherwise, of the ongoing Brexit negotiations.

For the purposes of this chapter, the author has adopted a 'hard Brexit' scenario as the assumed outcome of the current negotiations. Throughout this chapter, 'hard Brexit' is to be understood as the result where the UK not only leaves the EU, but also the internal market, the customs union with the EU and Euratom.

Alternative models for the post-Brexit UK–EU relationship exist, but seem increasingly improbable. These options include:

- the continued membership of the Internal Energy Market (IEM), similar to Norway's current arrangements,[3] ie implementation of the EU's energy market regime and payment into the EU with no voting rights on the relevant legislation;
- a series of sector-specific bilateral arrangements similar to the EU–Swiss arrangement as alternatives to or in addition to free trade agreements with specific jurisdictions outside the EU; and
- tracking of the EU legislative and regulatory regime without any formal arrangement (any trade occurring in these circumstances would be subject to the rules of the World Trade Organization (WTO) once Britain becomes a fully fledged member in its own right).

[3] Although Norway is not a member state of the European Union, it is part of the European Economic Area (the EEA). As such, it has access to the European internal market and can freely trade its goods and service within the EEA territory, subject to compliance with the relevant EU legislation.

Although the UK Government's pronouncements to date have not commented specifically on the prospect of remaining in the IEM, this is not likely in view of the Government's firm opposition to arrangements that involve acceptance of EU legislation, such as the relevant European Energy Directives and Regulations, to remaining part of the relevant EU institutions (such as ACER, ENTSO-E and ENTSO-G) and to the Court of Justice of the European Union (CJEU) having superior jurisdiction to that of national courts.

Conversely, if Brexit were to result in exit from the IEM, the UK would likely be excluded from the benefits of market integration initiatives, such as market coupling, cross-border balancing and capacity market integration.

Each variation of the above may involve some degree of acquis of EU law, the UK acceptance of the jurisdiction of the CJEU and the four freedoms, including the free movement of people. These issues are not considered in detail in this chapter.[4]

In any event, in the immediate future, and probably during the two years in which the UK negotiates its exit agreement with the EU, Brexit may have little or no impact on interconnectors. Thereafter, the extent to which the UK will develop its own energy regulations independent from the EU is as yet unclear.

2. WITHDRAWAL BILL

One of principal areas of uncertainty for all sectors is the continued application (or otherwise) of EU law by the UK post-Brexit (until 29 March 2019, the likely date of the formal exit of the UK from the EU, the UK remains bound by the acquis communautaire).

The British Government published the European Union (Withdrawal) Bill in July 2017 ('Withdrawal Bill')[5] and this was intended as the key piece of UK domestic legislation that will implement Brexit. The principal purpose of the Bill is to repeal the European Communities Act 1972, which gives effect and priority to EU law in the UK, thereby formally reasserting the sovereignty and independence of domestic law.[6]

---

4 See, for instance, http://ukandeu.ac.uk/fact-figures/what-effect-would-brexit-have-on-free-movement/ or https://www.anothereurope.org/wp-content/uploads/2017/09/aeip-free-movement-final-web.pdf for further details on free movement related issues.

5 The latest version of the Withdrawal Bill as well as information on the current status of the Bill is available at: https://services.parliament.uk/bills/2017-19/europeanunionwithdrawal.html.

6 The Long Title of the Withdrawal Bill identifies its purpose as a bill to 'repeal the European Communities Act 1972 and make other provision in connection with the withdrawal of the United Kingdom from the EU'.

So as to avoid a legal vacuum in UK law when EU law ceases to apply, the Withdrawal Bill is also intended to preserve and convert into domestic law, the whole body of EU law applying to the UK at the time it leaves the EU.

Whilst there are a number of legal and political issues with the Withdrawal Bill, a detailed critique of these is outside the scope of this chapter. For present purposes, it is suffice to note that the actual language used in the draft Bill is considerably less clear than the accompanying Explanatory Notes, and will require attention on its passage through Parliament if legal clarity and certainty are to be achieved.

From an EU law perspective, the draft is concerning as a provision in Schedule 1 of the Withdrawal Bill seems to remove virtually all of the UK courts' ability to give effect to general principles of EU law, such as proportionality and legal certainty, potentially even in cases about pre-Brexit matters. This would change the rules of public law enforcement significantly and may limit the ability of the courts to apply EU case law more generally.[7]

It is likely that the Withdrawal Bill (and the implications as to the non-application of future EU law) will elicit a reaction from the EU during the negotiations. For now, it represents merely the domestic policy view of the UK Government on the future application of EU law in all sectors. The consequences of this approach in relation to the energy sector will be discussed as part of this chapter.

3. TARIFFS

3.1. INTRODUCTION

Perhaps the single most important issue for the energy sector post-Brexit is the question of trade tariffs. If trade tariffs[8] were to be imposed on electricity, oil and gas by the UK and the EU, there would be economic consequences affecting both physical supply of energy to and from the UK and trading arrangements between the UK, the EU and third-party countries. Likewise, tariffs imposed on key pieces of equipment used in the energy sector could also have an impact on the sector.

In the UK and EU, gas and electricity markets would be affected and the underlying economics of EU–UK interconnectors would need to be re-evaluated. It is likely that the consumer benefit analyses routinely undertaken at the request

---

7 See also Institute for Governance, 'Brexit and the European Court of Justice', June 2017, pp 4, 7 and 8, accessible at: https://www.instituteforgovernment.org.uk/sites/default/files/publications/IfG_Brexit_Euro_Court_Justice_WEB.pdf.

8 Trade tariffs in the customs and excise sense, not to be confused with the transportation tariffs that are applied by transmission system operators.

of national regulatory authorities for each interconnector project would be less positive than in a scenario without such a tariff or other trade barriers being imposed.

3.2. TARIFFS WITHIN THE EU

As an EU Member State, the UK is a member of the European internal market and the customs union, it enjoys the following advantages:

- UK goods currently benefit from tariff-free access to the EU market and vice versa; and
- the UK, along with all other EU Member States, applies a common customs tariff to all third-country goods imported from outside the EU. Once third-country goods are admitted upon payment of the common customs tariff, these goods then benefit from tariff-free circulation within the EU, including between the UK and other EU Member States.

The EU's common customs tariff is known as the EU's 'most favoured nation tariff' because, as a WTO Member, the EU must apply the same most favourable tariffs to products from all other WTO Members.

The position post-Brexit will depend on the parameters of the new UK–EU trade relationship. However, given the complexity and timing of the Brexit negotiations, and the possibility of the UK remaining in the IEM, visibility on this point seems unlikely to be available for some time.

In a 'hard Brexit' scenario (ie the UK leaves both the EU internal market and customs union, without a new free trade agreement (FTA) with the EU in place, and can no longer benefit from preferences in the EU's existing FTAs):

- UK exports to the EU would become subject to the EU's MFN tariff;
- EU exports to the UK would become subject to the new MFN tariff that the UK itself adopts post-Brexit – on the basis of UK Government statements, it seems likely that the UK will seek to replicate the EU's MFN tariff so far as possible in order to minimise disruption;
- UK exports to the rest of the world (RoW) would become subject to the third country's applicable MFN tariff; and
- RoW exports to the UK would become subject to the UK's new MFN tariff.

3.3. THE WTO

At present, import duties on electricity are not allowed to be imposed by the EU, as the EU (along with its Member States including the UK) has legally committed to a 'bound' tariff rate of zero on electricity in its WTO goods schedule. A 'bound' tariff rate is the highest tariff rate that can be imposed by a WTO Member without risking a finding of a legal violation and related trade repercussions.

While bound rates define maximum tariff rates, bound tariff rates can change. Pursuant to Article XXVIII GATT,[9] WTO Members generally have a right to, inter alia, modify the bound rates set out in their goods schedules. In exchange for this, they must provide benefits in other areas (eg reduce a tariff on another product of similar importance in trade terms) or face modification or withdrawal of substantially equivalent concessions from certain other interested WTO Members (eg an increase of bound duties on a number of products). In practice the main participants in such a negotiation on electricity would be the EU and the UK, since there is (presumably) little cross-border trade in electricity with other non-EU/EEA countries, with the possible exception of Switzerland.

Under the EU's current schedule, the bound tariff rate for electricity and crude oil is 0%, whilst tariffs slightly vary for other energy-related products; the tariff for natural gas is set at 0.7%, certain light oil blends at 4.7%, liquid paraffin at 3.7%, lithium-ion for use in battery manufacture at 2.7%, wind turbine blades at 2.7%, etc.[10] In a post-Brexit world, goods entering the UK or the EU from third countries will no longer benefit from free circulation between the UK and EU as part of the EU customs union. For natural gas, for instance, this means that the EU – and the UK, should it adopt the same schedule – can apply an MFN tariff of up to 0.7% on natural gas.

It is important to note that the modification described above does not require unanimous agreement. If the EU or the UK wanted to make such a modification they would have to agree 'compensatory trade benefits' with the 'other side', the UK or the EU. If an agreement could not be reached, the EU or the UK could make such modifications without agreement but the 'other side' could then itself remove trade benefits in order to 'restore the balance'. In other words, a WTO Member that wants to change its tariff obligations can ultimately do this on a quasi-unilateral basis but will have to accept a form of 'trade retaliation' from other WTO Members whose trade is negatively impacted.

WTO Members can invoke emergency or exemption clauses to restrict imports or exports of electricity (such as Article XI:2(a) GATT or XX GATT), provided there is a degree of objective justification.

---

9 General Agreement on Tariffs and Trade 1994.

10 Herbert Smith Freehills, the Boston Consulting Group and Global Counsel, 'Strong Currents: Navigating the Post-Brexit Energy Market' (2017) pp 8 and 9, download available at: https://www.herbertsmithfreehills.com/latest-thinking/strong-currents-navigating-the-post-brexit-energy-market.; the WTO website for the European Union allows to download the Bound Tariff schedule for the EU here: http://stat.wto.org/TariffProfiles/E28_e.htm.

At present, the EU and the UK share a single WTO goods schedule. Following Brexit, the UK will have to define a goods schedule for itself. It is likely that the UK will largely retain the same conditions, especially regarding bound tariff rates, as contained in the current EU schedule. It is also likely that the EU will retain the fundamental aspects of its goods schedule, at least with respect to bound tariffs. If both the EU (on behalf of its Member States) and the UK do not modify the current bound rate of zero on electricity, then they will be legally prohibited from imposing import duties on electricity. Whilst the UK and any parties investing in its energy sector may, to some extent, rely on the principles in the Energy Charter Treaty in relation to investment protection and the transit of energy across the territory of the UK, the tariff provisions of the WTO will apply regardless.

3.4. OTHER IMPORT AND EXPORT RESTRICTIONS

Export duties are not bound in the EU WTO goods schedule and are further permitted by Article XI:1 GATT. Consequently, the EU is free to impose export duties. Post-Brexit, the same right would probably apply to the UK, as it does to most WTO Members, subject to some exceptions.

The ability to impose other import and export restrictions such as quotas and other non-tariff measures is mainly governed by Article XI:1 GATT. This provision prohibits all such restrictions on imports and exports, other than duties, taxes or other charges. This legal obligation is in principle not subject to negotiation and therefore would continue to apply in the same manner following any type of Brexit (hard or soft).

4. INTERCONNECTORS

4.1. A BRIEF INTRODUCTION

Interconnectors were originally introduced to assist with the security of energy supply. In addition to this prevailing purpose, they also facilitate European energy integration by enabling energy to be traded throughout the EU. Due to their economic and social importance, interconnectors receive funding from the EU and are also heavily regulated.[11] It is this importance for the integration of the European energy markets that also makes them particularly vulnerable to

11 See, for instance, P Trichakis and V Parail, 'Obstacles to Interconnectors', *Utility Week*, 11 October 2013, available at: https://utilityweek.co.uk/obstacles-to-interconnectors/.

Brexit-related risks. Interconnectors are, in more than one sense, at the heart of both the future Energy Union and the energy-related Brexit negotiations.

The UK's interconnectors are necessary for its energy security and the development of its energy market, both of which will most likely be affected by Brexit. This impact is largely dependent on the regulation the UK adopts regarding its interconnectors, the trade deals it enters into with the EU and countries beyond the EU, the funding for which the UK's interconnectors will be eligible, and the contribution the UK's interconnectors make to the energy security of EU Member States.[12]

In the absence of new gas fired power stations and a capacity market which successfully encourages the building of new generation facilities,[13] the UK is likely to face a generation gap following the closure of coal fired power stations and the steady decline of North Sea oil and gas production by 2020.

Against this backdrop, electricity interconnectors provide important additional capacity to the UK electricity market:[14]

- Currently, there are four interconnectors in operation (IFA1 (France), Moyle (Ireland), BritNed (The Netherlands) and EWIC (Ireland)) which provide around 4GW of capacity.
- Further planned projects (Nemo (Belgium), Eleclink (France), Aquind (France), GridLink (France), IFA2 (France), FABLink (GB/France/Alderney), NSN (Norway), Viking (Denmark) and Greenlink (Ireland) will assist by bringing up to 14 GW of additional capacity to the UK's supply portfolio.

The UK interconnector regime is unique in the EU in that it specifically allows for, and encourages merchant interconnectors to be developed by, private investors.[15] In contrast, other jurisdictions tend to look to incumbent transmission system operators (TSOs) for development of interconnectors. For instance, the French energy code provides that Réseau de Transport d'Electricité (RTE) (the electricity TSO) is the sole entity with responsibility for interconnection with the grids of other European countries.

---

12 S Muter Goldberg, 'Brexit & Interconnectors' (2017) OGEL 2, available at: https://www.ogel.org/article.asp?key=3680.

13 See Chapters X and XI of this volume on capacity mechanism.

14 At present, there are no new gas interconnectors planned between the UK and continental Europe, so the impact of Brexit on new gas interconnectors is being set aside for the purpose of this chapter.

15 See also EERL Report IV, Part IV: 'The Establishment of Cross-Border Subsea Interconnectors – the Norned Cable', EERL Report X, Part I, Chapters II and III.

4.2. POTENTIAL POST-BREXIT UK–EU ELECTRICITY ARRANGEMENTS

Given that the UK electricity market is highly interconnected, its being reliant upon electricity flows from the continental market – in particular France (from where the UK is importing up to 2GW) – and already established important trading patterns with the EU electricity market, physical disconnection of the two markets is generally seen as highly unlikely. That being said, Brexit may still negatively impact on energy trading – and therefore on UK energy security – as the UK is a net importer of electricity.

Of course, the overall framework of the future relationship between the UK and the EU post-Brexit will to a large extent determine Brexit's impact on the UK's energy sector. Possible models for that relationship include:

- continued membership of the IEM, similar to Norway's current arrangements, with the implementation of the EU's energy market regime and payment into the EU with no voting rights on the relevant legislation;
- tracking the EU legislative and regulatory regime without any formal arrangement; or
- a series of sector-specific bilateral arrangements similar to the EU–Swiss arrangement as alternatives for or in addition to free trade agreements with specific jurisdictions outside the EU.

If Brexit were to result in an exit from the IEM, the UK would probably be excluded from the benefits of market integration initiatives, such as market coupling, cross-border balancing and capacity market integration.

UK Prime Minister Theresa May, in her speech on 17 January 2017, announced a 'hard Brexit' strategy which is intended to result in the UK leaving not only the EU but also the internal market, the customs union and Euratom. Nevertheless, the White Paper released by the UK Government[16] emphasises that it is considering all options for the UK's future relationship with the EU on energy, with particular focus on avoiding disruption to the all-Ireland Single Electricity Market (see below). The White Paper underlines that:

> coordinated energy trading arrangements help to ensure lower prices and improved security of supply for both the UK and EU Member States by improving the efficiency

16 'The United Kingdom's Exit from, and New Partnership with, the European Union', White Paper, available at: https://www.gov.uk/government/publications/the-united-kingdoms-exit-from-and-new-partnership-with-the-european-union-white-paper/the-united-kingdoms-exit-from-and-new-partnership-with-the-european-union--2.

> and reliability of interconnector flows, reducing the need for domestic back-up power and helping balance power flows as we increase the level of intermittent renewable electricity generation.[17]

Although UK Government statements to date have not commented specifically on the prospect of remaining in the IEM, it is uncertain whether this could be accommodated in spite of its (apparently) firm opposition to:

- arrangements that would involve post-Brexit acceptance of EU legislation (such as relevant European Energy Directives and Regulations);
- remaining part of EU-wide institutions (which would include the Agency for the Cooperation of Energy Regulators (ACER), the European Network of Transmission System Operators for Electricity (ENTSO-E) and the European Network of Transmission System Operators for Gas (ENTSO-G)); and
- the CJEU having superior jurisdiction to that of the UK's national courts.

4.3. THE IMMEDIATE IMPACT OF BREXIT ON INTERCONNECTORS

The increasing use and role of interconnectors between the UK and the EU energy market speaks to a level of interdependency between the electricity markets, and the UK Government is generally supportive of interconnectors. As a result, during the two years in which the UK negotiates its exit agreement with the EU, Brexit may not unduly impact on existing projects. However, there are some concerns amongst investors that the economic case for new interconnectors may be affected if, for example, the UK is not part of the IEM or electricity imports/exports are made subject to trade tariffs.

Ultimately, the likely result and impact of Brexit will not be fully known until 2019 (at the earliest). Commentators have suggested that projects which are already under construction, or which have reached financial investment decisions, are likely to be less affected.[18] However, the discomfort for investors, sponsors and European regulators alike may lead to delays for projects unless pragmatic long-term solutions can be found. The continuing – and unprecedented – uncertainty (including the extent to which the UK will develop its own energy regulations independent from the EU – requiring negotiation of an alternative, reliable regime) will inevitably start to have an effect on interconnector projects, both current and in the pipeline.

17 Ibid, para 8.28.

18 Frontier Economics, 'The Effects of Brexit on the UK Power Market', available at: https://www.frontier-economics.com/documents/2016/07/effects-brexit-uk-power-market-part-one_frontier-lcp-brexit-briefing.pdf.

European energy regulators are watching Brexit-related developments and their impact on the internal energy market closely. CRE, the French energy regulator, when conducting its consultation[19] on IFA2, specifically raised the issue of Brexit, stating that:

> [t]he outcome of the British referendum hence raises two questions. First, one has to check that the project is interesting for the European electricity system, even in a situation where the United Kingdom would no longer be a member of the European Union and an active member of the internal market. Second, a specific analysis of the risks raised by the consequences of the British referendum, and the measures taken to mitigate such risks, is needed.

In its decision[20] in support of the IFA2 project, the CRE concluded that whilst 'there is no visibility on the future operating conditions of these interconnectors following the British referendum, the CRE considers that the treatment of these projects is an issue of European importance'. The CRE also emphasised that it intended to engage Ofgem and other counterparts to develop a common understanding of UK–EU interconnectors. It could be inferred from this that European regulators may be willing to take a pragmatic approach to Brexit-related regulatory issues in order to find workable solutions for interconnectors.

As the politics and policies around Brexit continue to evolve, operators and sponsors of interconnector projects will need to keep an active watching brief on developments. To the extent that they engage in dialogue with the UK Government, they may wish to consider suggesting that remaining in the IEM is likely to provide more security – not only for their relevant projects, but also for the energy sector as a whole.

4.4. THE LIKELY IMPACT OF BREXIT ON THE REGULATORY FRAMEWORK

4.4.1. The Role of European Bodies

ACER is a decentralised EU agency set up by the EU to help ensure that the single European market for gas and electricity functions properly. Its regulatory activities are overseen by a Board of Regulators, composed of

[19] Public consultation of 1 December 2016–3 January 2017 by the Commission de Regulation de l'Energie, France. The consultation document is available at: http://www.cre.fr/en/documents/public-consultations/the-interconnector-ifa2-between-france-and-great-britain/download-consultation.

[20] http://www.cre.fr/en/documents/deliberations/decision/interconnector-ifa2-project.

senior representatives of the national regulatory authorities for energy, of the 28 Member States. Its administrative and budgetary activities fall under the supervision of an Administrative Board, whose members are appointed by European institutions.[21]

There is no concept of 'associated membership' or 'observer status' within ACER. Its primary function is the monitoring, implementation and, in some limited circumstances, enforcement of EU legislation. With the UK's departure from the EU and (potentially) the IEM, its participation in the functions of ACER will cease.[22]

The situation is however different in relation to the ENTSOs, which, whilst creations of European Regulations, are in essence non-governmental organisations set up as international non-profit associations under Belgian law. They have full members (ie the TSOs from EU Member States) as well as observer and associated members from outside the EU. ENTSO-E, for instance, has 43 member TSOs from 36 countries.[23]

To the extent that the UK remains part of the IEM, it would also likely remain subject to the relevant European Energy Directives and Regulations and part of the institutions (such as ACER, ENTSO-E, and ENTSO-G) regulating the IEM.[24]

Conversely, following a full exit from the IEM, a new forum would need to be founded to address the relevant aspects of the regulatory regime (eg market coupling, capacity allocation, balancing, treatment of interconnection point and tariffs). The European network codes that define interconnectors' operating rules may also not be enforced in the UK anymore, raising uncertainties regarding future capacity allocation rules.

It may be possible for the relevant UK companies NGET (electricity system operator for Great Britain, NGG (gas system operator for GB) and SONI (the electricity system operator for Northern Ireland)) to continue to participate in the ENTSOs as an observer or under another, specially negotiated status. However, it is likely that such a status would diminish British influence on EU network codes as the British TSOs would be unlikely to have full participation rights. Should the British TSOs not be part of the ENTSOs in any capacity following a 'hard Brexit' scenario, this issue would be exacerbated.

---

21 ACER, 'Organisation and Bodies', available at: https://acer.europa.eu/en/The_agency/Organisation/Pages/default.aspx.

22 ACER, 'Revised Programming Document 2018–2020', January 2018, pp 13 and 14, available at: https://acer.europa.eu/en/The_agency/Mission_and_Objectives/Documents/ACER%20Programming%20Document%202018-Revised%20Jan%202018.pdf.

23 Entso-E, 'ENTSO-E Member Companies', available at: https://www.entsoe.eu/about-entso-e/inside-entso-e/member-companies/Pages/default.aspx.

24 S Muter Goldberg, 'Brexit & Interconnectors', above n 12.

In view of the need to find a pragmatic solution for the treatment of interconnection points as to capacity allocation, tariffs, quality and so on, it is likely that a form of arrangement between the British TSOs and the ENTSOs will be found. The change in status will increase the importance of robust and flexible interconnector agreements as well as IGAs.

4.4.2. Different Rules for Existing and Future Interconnectors

The Third Electricity Directive[25] defines interconnectors as 'equipment used to link electricity systems' which would have meant that UK interconnectors fell within the scope of this definition. However, Regulation 714/2009[26] (the 'Electricity Regulation') amends that definition to restrict interconnectors to mean a 'transmission line which crosses or spans a border between Member States and which connects the national transmission systems of the Member States', which would exclude EU–UK interconnectors.

This restrictive definition is identical to that in the Third Gas Directive,[27] which defines interconnectors as 'a transmission line which crosses or spans a border between Member States for the sole purpose of connecting the national transmission systems of those Member States'.

Whilst technically the EU unbundling regime, introduced as part of the Third Energy Package, will no longer apply in the UK, the relevant provisions have already been transposed into UK legislation, which will continue to apply unless Parliament makes the policy choice to amend it post-Brexit. This would appear to be unlikely given that the unbundling regime has, at its core, the liberalisation of the British energy sector: the EU regime is partly based on the UK model and is firmly rooted in the Electricity and Gas Acts as well as the relevant licensing regime (although derogations in specific cases could potentially be implemented through unilateral UK legislative changes). The UK will thus be unable to untangle itself entirely from the EU energy legislation, which means that parts of the EU regime, particularly unbundling, will continue to affect the UK post-Brexit.

It is likely that the exemption regime pursuant to Article 17 of the Electricity Regulation and Article 36 of the Third Gas Directive (under which new infrastructure can be exempted from the ownership unbundling, revenue investment, third party access and revenue investment regimes) would no longer be available to new interconnectors.

---

25 Directive 2009/72/EC concerning common rules for the internal market in electricity and repealing Directive 2003/54/EC.

26 Regulation 714/2009 on conditions for access to the network for cross-border exchanges in electricity and repealing Regulation (EC) No 1228/2003.

27 Directive 2009/73/EC concerning common rules for the internal market in natural gas and repealing Directive 2003/55/EC.

4.4.3. *The Applicability of the Projects of Common Interest (PCI) Regime to Future UK Interconnectors*

If UK interconnectors do not qualify as interconnectors for the purposes of EU legislation, this may also have implications for the ease with which future UK interconnector projects are able to achieve PCI status.[28]

The PCI list was initially set out in 2013 in Annex I to Regulation 347/2013.[29] The revised list was published on 18 November 2015 and contains 195 key projects that are seen as fundamental to achieving the energy objective of completing the Energy Union and Europe benefitting from affordable, secure and sustainable energy. PCIs can benefit from:

- accelerated planning and permit granting;
- a single national authority for obtaining permits;
- aligned regulatory conditions; and
- lower administrative costs due to streamlined environmental assessment processes.

Interconnectors feature heavily in this list as they are a fundamental aspect in achieving the objective of an Energy Union. Most importantly, interconnectors support the low carbon agenda by providing cheap access to low carbon electricity, supporting the market viability of intermittent generation by facilitating market balancing, and reducing European decarbonisation costs.

In the UK, the NEMO, Greenlink, Viking, Icelink, NSI West Electricity, Aquind, FAB, IFA2, Gridlink, and ElecLink interconnectors as well as the Moffat reverse flow projects have obtained PCI status. Several other interconnector projects are understood to have applied for PCI status.[30]

Whilst it is not entirely clear whether an interconnector project will remain eligible for PCI status after the UK exits the EU, there are strong arguments in

---

28 PCIs are key (cross-border) infrastructure projects which connect the intra-EU energy systems. Their aim is to support the EU's energy policy, climate objectives and the Internal Energy Market. Every two years, the Commission draws up a new list of PCIs which includes the projects that have met the various relevant requirements. In order to qualify as a PCI, a project has to have a significant 'impact on energy markets and market integration in at least two EU countries, boost competition on energy markets and help the EU's energy security by diversifying sources, and contribute to the EU's climate and energy goals by integrating renewables'; further detail on PCIs can be found at: https://ec.europa.eu/energy/en/topics/infrastructure/projects-common-interest.

29 Regulation 347/2013 on guidelines for trans-European energy infrastructure and repealing Decision No 1364/2006/EC and amending Regulations (EC) No 713/2009, (EC) No 714/2009 and (EC) No 715/2009.

30 For a complete list of PCI projects as of April 2018, please see here: https://ec.europa.eu/energy/sites/ener/files/documents/memberstatespci_list_2017.pdf.

favour of maintaining that status in relation to the relevant projects on the basis that:

- it is located on the territory of one Member State (the relevant non-UK EU Member State, in relation to which there would be no change following Brexit); and
- it will have a 'significant cross-border impact' because it will continue to contribute to cross-border grid transfer capacity on the corridor by at least 500 MW, thus affecting the supply security of EU Member States.

In addition, there are examples of PCIs connecting the EU with third countries, such as the EuroAsia Interconnector, which runs between Israel, Cyprus and Greece. This interconnector includes three separate PCIs, one of which is the interconnection between Hadera (Israel) and Kofinou (Cyprus).[31]

4.4.4. The Availability of European Project Funding Sources

In addition to funding available for PCIs, the Commission has listed the indirect financial benefit of increased viability for investors and the direct benefit of access to the CEF. This is a fund of €5.35 billion to be invested in connectivity projects covering the IEM by 2020. A variety of financial instruments are also used to fund projects, such as guarantees and project bonds, as this will aid in attracting private sector investment into the projects funded by the CEF.

The CEF estimates that the upgrading, development and construction of adequate energy transmission infrastructure of European importance will require investments of about €140 billion in electricity and at least €70 billion in gas. The objective of CEF is to facilitate this and it is not the only source of European Funding that can be called upon.

It is likely that access to the CEF will fall away for UK projects in a 'hard Brexit' scenario. In addition, there would be long-term funding implications for new projects given that access to European Investment Bank loans may be cut off by Brexit.

However, in relation to UK–EU interconnectors, there are good arguments that access to CEF support should be maintained even in a post-Brexit scenario, as the non-UK section of the interconnector continues to remain in the UK, and the relevant interconnector will continue to make a positive contribution to the IEM.

[31] For a complete list of PCI projects as of 2015, please see: http://eur-lex.europa.eu/legal-content/EN/TXT/PDF/?uri=OJ:JOL_2016_019_R_0001&from=EN. This list is currently under review, with an updated list expected for late 2017.

4.5. POSSIBLE MITIGANTS FOR REGULATORY RISK

4.5.1. Intergovernmental Agreements

Project risk, including political and regulatory risk, for international infrastructure projects such as interconnectors is sometimes mitigated through a package of host government agreements for each host state and/or an intergovernmental agreement (IGA) between, or among, host states. IGAs are usually treaties entered into under local and international law and are ratified or enacted into domestic law accordingly.

Typically, the project sponsors are the beneficiaries of the governmental commitments as the government-to-government undertakings address the political and regulatory risks associated with the project. To the extent that they have not done so, developers and operators of interconnector projects will want to ensure that their interests are represented in any such agreements and promote political support for the relevant project's objectives and plans.

The European Commission will necessarily have some involvement with any IGA; pursuant to the Treaty of Lisbon, IGAs in the energy sector between EU and EU non-Member States will trigger the involvement of the EU both in the negotiations, through representatives of the European Commission, and as a party to the IGA itself. As such, the EU as a whole will influence the future regime applicable to energy sector arrangements between the EU and individual Member States, including the role of interconnectors.

Recent experience of IGAs in relation to EU–third country gas pipelines has shown that the European Commission will approach any such IGA strictly in line with the current EU regulatory regime.

4.5.2. Interconnector Agreements

The running of interconnectors and the necessary cooperation between TSOs is usually governed by interconnector agreements (or joint operating agreements) which set out the governance and operational principles of the relevant interconnector.

Accordingly, some of the economic, regulatory and trade issues discussed in this chapter could be addressed at sub-legislative level in interconnector agreements between the relevant TSOs, including the treatment of interconnection points and the cooperation of TSOs with the relevant regulators.

A key advantage of this type of agreement is that they are bilateral as between the relevant TSOs; for electricity interconnectors, Member States are not normally a party to such agreements (the situation can be different for gas interconnectors which are, for reasons stated above, outwith the scope of this chapter). Interconnector agreements therefore do not require legislation nor, in most cases, governmental involvement, nor the approval of the remaining 27 EU Member States.

TSOs of existing interconnectors, as well as the relevant adjacent TSOs, may wish to carefully examine any existing interconnector agreements as to whether amendments might be required in light of the changing regulatory landscape in any Brexit scenario.

There will potentially be two or even three regulatory regimes to take into account (UK, EU and relevant Member State) when drafting post-Brexit interconnector agreements. Further, interconnector agreements cannot fully replicate a regulatory regime, even if they can build upon ones which are not fully aligned in order to make the structure work.

5. SUPPLY SECURITY

5.1. ELECTRICITY

Any disruption of electricity trade between the UK and the EU in the form of tariffs, or as a result of diverging regulatory regimes, is likely to lead to increased costs which in turn will make it more difficult to insulate UK customers from higher utility bills. The reason for this is that demand for electricity in the UK is rising, thus reducing the UK's spare capacity and increasing the price of electricity. Interconnectors are vital to protecting supply security and increasing capacity.

Research by Enappsys[32] has shown that, on the basis of the winter's electricity demand in 2015/16, there will be

- 85 hours this winter when spare capacity falls below 2GW;[33] and
- roughly 12 hours when demand will exceed standard capacity.

This means that last-resort measures (eg restarting large power plants which have been mothballed, firing up small, inefficient diesel and gas engines, and even paying large consumers to use less at peak times) will be required.[34]

Whilst such measures are rarely used, they are cost intensive. In 2015/16, wholesale power prices rocketed to £2,500 per megawatt-hour, up from a going rate of £60. Restarting mothballed power plants this winter would cost at least £3,000 per MWh.[35]

32 'GB Electricity Market Summary: Second Quarter 2016 Apr to Jun', available at: https://docs.wixstatic.com/ugd/42d1d7_f659613405074b4993a3b40c4dac5a37.pdf.

33 Ibid.

34 'Britain told to brace itself for power shortages', available at: https://www.ft.com/content/2c1f71c6-2ef7-11e6-bf8d-26294ad519fc.

35 'GB Electricity Market Summary: Second Quarter 2016 Apr to Jun', above n 32.

Electricity imported through subsea interconnectors has become an important source of power for the UK, accounting for 6.6% of supplies last year. As further interconnection projects come on stream, this proportion is expected to increase.

Interconnectors are also likely to play a part in lowering consumers' utility bills. In 2013, the then Department of Energy and Climate Change[36] commissioned a study by Baringa which showed that depending on the adopted scenario, level of interconnection and countries to which the interconnection is made, UK consumers could see benefits of up to £9 billion (net present value) in the period up to 2040.[37]

5.2. GAS

As between the UK and the EU, gas markets are physically already well integrated through three interconnectors (IUK,[38] BBL[39] and Moffat[40]) with only small wholesale price differences and little congestion.[41] Subject to any drastic changes in energy policy by the UK Government, the gas sector is therefore unlikely to suffer following Brexit. Structurally, any EU27–UK gas interconnectors will be affected by the same type of issues as the electricity interconnectors.

The Brexit negotiations coincide with (i) the end of the initial long-term gas interconnector contracts (IUK 2018, BBL 2022) and therefore greater pressure on gas hubs like the National Balancing Point in the UK (NBP) and the Title Transfer Facility in the Netherlands (TTF) and (ii) the EU's review of its gas security strategy.

In respect of the replacement of the IUK and BBL contracts, whilst the NBP–TTF spread – a mathematical indicator showing the delta of the gas price in the Netherlands and the UK – provides the direction for gas to flow, shippers

---

36 Now part of the Department for Business, Energy and Industrial Strategy.

37 'Department for Energy and Climate Change: More Interconnection: Improving Energy Security and Lowering Bills', December 2013, available at: https://www.gov.uk/government/uploads/system/uploads/attachment_data/file/266460/More_interconnection_-_improving_energy_security_and_lowering_bills.pdf.

38 The IUK interconnector is a 235-km pipeline between Zeebrugge (Belgium) and Bacton (UK) which started operations in 1998. It is the only bi-directional gas pipeline between continental Europe and the UK.

39 The BBL interconnector is a 235-km pipeline between the Netherlands and the UK; see also EERL Report II, Chapter 11: 'Establishment and Role of the Bacton- Balgzand Pipeline within the Internal Gas Market'.

40 The Moffat interconnector is a one-way pipeline from Moffat (Scotland) to the Republic of Ireland by way of which the UK exports gas to Ireland.

41 See also Ofgem, 'Wholesale Energy Markets in 2016', available at: https://www.ofgem.gov.uk/publications-and-updates/wholesale-energy-markets-2016.

will take other factors into account, such as the cost of the service provided by the IUK and BBL interconnectors compared to alternatives such as LNG.

The UK gas market is amongst the most mature and liquid gas markets in Europe. Brexit may, however, contribute to a shift towards other EU markets (particularly TTF in the Netherlands, which outranked the UK as the most liquid market in 2015) and change expectations in respect of future infrastructure investments.[42]

As the EU is currently undergoing a review of its gas supply security arrangements, including Regulation 994/2010,[43] Brexit could increase the UK's supply security risk, as the UK might be excluded from the 'solidarity principles', in accordance with which European nations agree to supply gas to their neighbours in the event of a gas supply crisis. Conversely, as Ireland is largely dependent on GB gas imports (see below), it is possible that the EU tries to intervene in the form of a solidarity mechanism for Ireland.

6. IRELAND AND THE SINGLE ELECTRICITY MARKET

Brexit will also have an impact on the energy sector in Ireland, perhaps more so than on any other EU country, as part of the UK (Northern Ireland) is currently operating a single electricity market (SEM) with the Republic of Ireland.

SEM was established in 2007 with the aim of improving the competitive structure and efficiency on the energy markets of both Northern Ireland and the Republic of Ireland. SEM fully links both jurisdictions, creating an integrated market with its own set of market rules in form of the Trading and Settlement Code.[44] Every entity that wishes to become active on the market – for example, market operator, system operators, generators and interconnector owners – has to comply with the Code and in turn the EU regulatory regime. In May 2018, SEM will become iSEM, the integrated single energy market built on the EU electricity target model, which in turn is based on bilateral trading, market coupling and uniform gate closure across the EU.[45]

Although compliant with the EU's Third Energy Package (but not yet the Target Model), the Code is not based on European legislation; this is due to the fact that the bilateral agreement on the establishment of SEM predates the Third Energy Package. Instead, it derives its raison d'être from a bilateral

42 Ibid.

43 See Chapter XIII of this Volume.

44 The Trading and Settlement Code can be accessed at: http://www.sem-o.com/MarketDevelopment/Pages/MarketRules.aspx.

45 EirGrid Group (2016), 'Quick Guide to the Integrated Single Electricity Market: The I-SEM Project', Version 1, p 3, available at: http://www.eirgridgroup.com/__uuid/f110639e-9e21-4d28-b193-ed56ee372362/EirGrid-Group-I-SEM-Quick-Guide.pdf.

cooperation agreement between Dublin and Westminster. The effects of Brexit are therefore unlikely to be felt immediately after the UK's departure, but may become apparent in the medium to long term.

SEM is regulated by the Irish Commission for Energy Regulation which, as the Irish National Regulatory Authority for both the Republic of Ireland and Northern Ireland, is subject to the EU energy sector regime. If SEM were maintained post-Brexit, a part of the UK would therefore continue to be subject to EU law.

Brexit, if not carefully managed with a solution which specifically addresses the SEM issue, would effectively reverse a decade's worth of progress in energy integration on the island of Ireland. There are a number of possible post-Brexit arrangements and solutions to this issue:

- Designate Northern Ireland a special zone where EU law remains applicable. This may cause tension though if the UK's energy policy were to diverge from European provisions in the future. One key point must be considered. If EU legislation continued to apply in Northern Ireland, the UK Government would have to accept that regulatory divergence could occur in the UK itself, ie between Northern Ireland and Great Britain. This may in turn create the constitutional challenge of how to transpose EU legislation that requires domestic implementation. So far this power has not been devolved to the Stormont assembly, but remains securely with Westminster.
- Create a special status for SEM which, whilst compliant with EU law, would not subject Northern Ireland to the jurisdiction of the European institutions (ie an 'EU-compatible' solution). Like option one, this arrangement would raise implementation issues and would equally require a new jurisdictional forum to assume the former responsibilities of the European institutions.
- Unwind SEM entirely which is unlikely to be politically palatable in either the Republic or Northern Ireland.
- Alternatively, and perhaps the most straightforward solution (from a UK domestic perspective), the EU might grant the Republic of Ireland the right to conclude a bilateral agreement with the UK to address the future workings of SEM (or indeed iSEM). This option is politically outside the gift or influence of the UK Government as it is dependent both on the political will of the EU27 as well as the Irish Government. As there are many Brexit-related issues that impact the island of Ireland directly and more immediately than any other EU27 country, any bilateral deal between the UK and Ireland, if entered into, is likely to cover a wide range of issues. Such issues include border control and freedom of movement, as well as energy, and look set to be rather complex.

Irish gas supply security is heavily dependent on the UK and specifically on the Moffat interconnector. According to the winter outlook document produced by Gas Networks Ireland,[46] 96.3% of annual Irish gas supply requirements in 2014/15 came from British imports via the Moffat interconnector. Whilst the Corrib gas field is anticipated to improve Ireland's security of supply, it is anticipated that even at full operational capacity, it will only meet approximately 56% of Gas Networks Ireland System's annual forecast; leaving Ireland's supply security reliant on UK gas imports and accordingly exposed to Brexit risks.

The issue of Irish security of supply is therefore likely to be a key feature on the agenda during the energy sector-related Brexit negotiations, as the current arrangements through the Moffat interconnector are the 'cheapest way to provide security of supply to Irish consumers'.[47] If it is not possible to maintain the current arrangements regarding the Moffat interconnector, it is conceivable that Ireland may need to build a dedicated LNG terminal with regasification facility.[48]

Issues pertaining to the Irish energy market seem to be an important factor for the Government in considering the UK's future relationship with the EU energy sector as it is the only sector in relation to which the White Paper specifically states that the UK would explore 'all options'[49] regarding its future relationship with the EU; not least to avert disruption to SEM as both Northern Ireland and the Republic of Ireland rely on its functioning for their supply security.

7. EURATOM

7.1. EURATOM'S INSTITUTIONAL RELATIONSHIP TO THE EUROPEAN UNION

Established in 1957 via the Euratom Treaty, Euratom is a separate entity from the EU with its own legal personality.[50] The Euratom Treaty has not seen any major changes ever since it took effect six decades ago.[51] Whilst structurally

---

46 Gas Network Ireland (2015), Winter Outlook 2015/16, available at: http://www.gasnetworks.ie/Global/Gas%20Industry/18444_GNI_WinterOutlook_15-16_v9.pdf.

47 'Brexit and Security of Supply for UK and Ireland Gas Supply Security', newsletter by the Oxford Institute for Energy Studies, January 2017, available at: https://www.oxfordenergy.org/wpcms/wp-content/uploads/2017/01/Brexits-impact-on-gas-markets-OIES-Energy-Insight.pdf.

48 S Muter Goldberg, 'Brexit & Interconnectors', above n 12.

49 'The United Kingdom's Exit from, and New Partnership with, the European Union', above n 16, para 8.28.

50 The Euratom Treaty can be accessed at: http://eur-lex.europa.eu/legal-content/EN/TXT/PDF/?uri=CELEX:12012A/TXT&from=EN.

51 It has been pointed out that 'the Euratom Treaty has largely been left behind in the development of the European Community and European Union Treaties', in C True, 'Legislative Competences of Euratom and the European Community in the energy sector: The Nuclear Package of the European Commission', (2003) 28 EL Rev 684.

sharing the same institutional framework as the European Union, Euratom also comprises two further exclusive bodies:

- The Supply Agency, which has both the exclusive permission to enter into contractual agreements with respect to ores, source materials and special fissile materials originating from within or outside of the Euratom area, and a general right of option in relation to ores, source materials and special fissile materials produced within the Member States; and
- The Safeguards Office, which guarantees that nuclear material is not diverted for unintended purposes and that all safeguarding duties, relevant to nuclear material, are adequately complied with.

As indicated, both Euratom and the EU use the European Commission, Council and Parliament, as well as the CJEU. Legally speaking, however, Euratom is a distinct entity from the Union, having been established under the separate Euratom Treaty (as opposed to the European Treaties – currently in form of the Treaty on European Union (TEU) and the Treaty on the Functioning of the European Union (TFEU)). This separate identity has been highlighted in various instances, amongst others, in the context of the changes introduced by the Treaty of Lisbon. Whilst this legislation materially amended the institutional arrangements in relation to the EU, Euratom was mostly unaffected 'by the European Union construct stricto sensu'.[52]

Both the European Treaties and the Euratom Treaty set out the competencies of their respective institutions, ie in relation to the EU and Euratom. However, rather than replicating the text of the institutional provisions as included in the European Treaties, Article 106a of the Euratom Treaty simply contains references to all the relevant provisions in the European Treaties, deeming them similarly applicable to Euratom.[53] The European Treaties only apply insofar as they do not derogate from, or conflict with, anything set out in the Euratom Treaty.[54]

One such 'assumed' competence, for instance, is the withdrawal mechanism contained within Article 50 TEU. Should the UK wish to leave Euratom it can therefore do so; however, this is not effected by way of Article 50 itself, but by the separate provision set out in Article 106a of the Euratom Treaty.

---

52 I Cenevska, 'The European Parliament and the European Atomic Energy Community: a Legitimacy Crisis?' (2010) 35 EL Rev 424.

53 S Muter Goldberg and S Sumit, 'Withdrawal of the United Kingdom from Euratom' (2007) OGEL 2, available at: https://www.ogel.org/article.asp?key=3684.

54 See Art 106a(3) of the Euratom Treaty. See also E Ameye and I Arregui, 'National Nuclear Third Party Insurance Pools Revisited from a European Union Competition Law Perspective' (2012) 30 J Energy & Nat Resources L 274.

7.2. THE UK'S WITHDRAWAL: MANDATE, CHALLENGES AND CONSEQUENCES

Due to this inherent separate nature, an important issue to consider is whether the referendum to leave the EU even provided the UK Government with a mandate to withdraw from Euratom. The referendum never expressly enquired whether the British people wished to exit Euratom (nor is the author aware of Euratom ever being mentioned in this context in any relevant publications or consultations by the Government).

Furthermore, in order to withdraw from Euratom effectively, a notice in accordance with Article 106a of the Euratom Treaty (and not Article 50) must be made. As the UK's Withdrawal Notice[55] purported to be 'in accordance with Article 50(2) as applied by Article 106a', however, the author considers it arguable that it did not meet the formal requirements of an effective notice. This issue may seem technical, but could have practical ramifications, as the two-year notice period for Euratom only commences on the date of the notice. If no effective notice has been given, the clock has not yet started ticking.

In light of these issues, there are several grounds on which the UK's exit from Euratom could be challenged before the British courts:

- as it is uncertain whether the Withdrawal Bill actually bestowed on the Government the right to depart from Euratom, the legal argument could be made that the Government has no mandate to proceed with the departure;
- whilst leaving the EU does not equate to exiting Euratom, by law doing so may have material ramifications for the civil nuclear generation sector and consumers; and
- arguably, an exit from Euratom would infringe the property rights of members of the British nuclear market, as the departure may deprive them of the rights they currently enjoy (eg access to the nuclear common market or nuclear supply chain arrangements).

Whilst no challenges have been brought so far and it is not yet possible to say with certainty whether any legal challenges may be brought, successfully or not, it is nevertheless useful to be aware of the potentially impending risks.

Irrespective of the issue of effective notice, the UK's withdrawal from Euratom will have significant practical consequences. As explained, the 'exit clock' starts ticking from the moment the Government serves its notice. Unless it is granted an extension, the UK will need to agree replacement arrangements alongside all

[55] Prime Minister's Letter to Donald Tusk Triggering Article 50, 29 March 2017, available at: https://www.gov.uk/government/uploads/system/uploads/attachment_data/file/604079/Prime_Ministers_letter to_European_Council_President_Donald_Tusk.pdf.

other Brexit aspects within the two-year window (assuming that Brexit applies to the UK's Euratom membership).

Such negotiations would need to be carried out on multiple parallel tracks:

- negotiating any Brexit-related terms and substitutional arrangements for the UK;
- negotiating any Brexatom-related terms and substitutional arrangements for the UK;
- meetings with Euratom and non-Euratom countries for the purposes of negotiating any bilateral substitutional arrangements;
- discussions regarding the new security and safeguarding provisions that the UK will have to adhere to after leaving Euratom (it is unlikely that any states would consent to new cooperation or trade agreements, without having the reassurance of an adequate regime);
- considering the more universal effects of leaving Euratom seeing as that it also forms part of other instruments, including the Treaty of Almelo (establishing the enrichment company Urenco)[56] and Euratom Directives (eg the Radioactive Waste and Spent Fuel Management Directive);[57] and
- preparing for the improbable and undesirable version of Brexatom in which the UK departs after the two-year notice period, without having agreed any replacement arrangements. To cater for such an outcome, the Government may be advised to take account of more practical responses, such as increasing the existing stocks of fuel, potentially expending current storage facilities or alternative generation capacity.

Given the potential timing issue in simultaneously progressing (and concluding) all these multiple tracks of discussion until March 2019 (or the end of a potential transition period), Tom Greatrex, the Chief Executive of the Nuclear Industry Association (the trade association of the UK civil nuclear industry) has flagged that it is 'vital' for transitional arrangements to be put in place 'to give the UK time to negotiate and complete new arrangements with EU member states and third countries including the US, Japan and Canada who have Nuclear Cooperation Agreements within the Euratom framework'.[58]

Where no such agreement is reached when the UK exits Euratom, nuclear industry imports and exports do not simply become more expensive, but illegal. This will materially affect the civil nuclear generation sector (and consumers),[59]

56 Treaty of Almelo, 4 March 1970, http://fissilematerials.org/library/urenco70.pdf.

57 Council Directive 2011/70/EURATOM, 19 July 2011, http://eur-lex.europa.eu/legal-content/EN/TXT/PDF/?uri=CELEX:32011L0070&from=EN.

58 European Union (Notification of Withdrawal) Bill (HL Bill 103 of 2016–17), House of Lords Library Note, 15 February 2017, http://researchbriefings.files.parliament.uk/documents/LLN-2017-0009/LLN-2017-0009.pdf.

59 See the evidence given before the Business, Energy and Industrial Strategy Committee; 'Leaving the EU: Energy and climate negotiation priorities, Business, Energy and Industrial

as well as other nuclear industries such as the nuclear decommissioning and those that use radioactive materials (eg automobile, aeronautics and mining). In this light, the author notes that it is inconceivable that the Government would not secure adequate replacement arrangements (or transitional agreements) to Euratom (though, in order to do so, the Government may have to relent on certain other matters in the wider Brexit negotiations).

In a statement to the House of Commons on 31 January 2017, Mr Davis noted that the UK 'will maintain the closest possible nuclear cooperation with the European Union', though that 'relationship could take a number of different forms and will be of course subject to negotiation'.[60] At the same time, Mr Davis has also confirmed that the Government has been planning for a scenario where it is unable to agree an exit deal and that it has 'been planning for the contingency – all the various outcomes, all the possible outcomes of the negotiations'.[61]

7.3. THE ROAD TOWARDS BREXATOM

As highlighted above, the author considers that the Government's decisions (i) to exit Euratom and (ii) to do so without having secured replacement arrangements, are predominantly motivated by politics and not legally necessary. If the UK had chosen to retain its Euratom membership for the time being – even though proceeding with Brexit – it would undoubtedly have faced a certain degree of complexity, but primarily in relation to technical aspects. The key advantage of remaining within Euratom on a temporary basis would, of course, have been that it would not have been pressured to achieve any agreements within the prescribed two-year window alongside the separate Brexit negotiations. Instead, the Government could have provided its withdrawal notice at a point in the future once all the relevant Brexit arrangements had been reached.

That being said, whilst the Government theoretically has the option to withdraw its notice to exit Euratom (and re-submit it at a later stage after all Brexit-related terms have been agreed):

- there are currently no provisions in either of the treaties (relating to Euratom or the European Union) that would set out how a Member State may withdraw its notice of withdrawal from Euratom (or the EU); and

Strategy Committee', 28 February 2017, http://www.parliamentlive.tv/Event/Index/54352a9b-ac49-44a8-8fab-25c533571ca6.

60 Opening statement on Second Reading of EU (Notification of Withdrawal) Bill, 31 January 2017, https://www.gov.uk/government/news/opening-statement-on-second-reading-of-eu-notification-of-withdrawal-bill.

61 Britain has a Brexit backup plan if talks fail, says David Davis, Reuters, 13 March 2017, http://uk.reuters.com/Article/uk-britain-eu-idUKKBN16J0JN.

- the Government could run the argument that a party may withdraw an offer at any point before the relevant acceptance occurs. As such, there is, generally speaking, nothing that should stop the Government from withdrawing its notice (whilst still continuing with its departure from the EU).

Another factor that may support this approach is that neither the European Council,[62] nor its President, Mr Donald Tusk,[63] have acknowledged the UK's decision to leave Euratom in their respective responses to the Article 50 Notice (or addressed the existence of Article 106a). However, such a decision would naturally be subject to political consideration by the British Government and, at the time of writing, this seems unlikely as the May administration remains committed to a joint Brexit/Brexatom exit from the EU.[64]

8. CLIMATE CHANGE

Even if the UK were to leave behind the EU Climate Change Package, it would still have to comply with the very stringent UK targets, as well as any commitments arising from international agreements such as the Paris Agreement and the UNFCCC.[65]

UK regulations of many energy topics, including carbon capture and storage, implement the relevant Directives of the Climate Change Package and therefore conscious decisions would need to be taken to move away from them through new regulation.

8.1. THE EU'S EMISSION TRADING SYSTEM

Brexit may also have an impact on the future of the EU's carbon market and weaken the current structure of the EU ETS. The UK is the EU's second-largest emitter of greenhouse gases (after Germany),[66] with its utility companies being among the largest buyers of carbon allowances for the EU ETS.

---

62 Statement by the European Council (Art. 50) on the UK notification, 29 March 2017, available at: http://www.consilium.europa.eu/en/press/press-releases/2017/03/29-euco-50-statement-uk-notification/.

63 Remarks by President Donald Tusk following the UK notification, 29 March 2017, available at: http://www.consilium. europa.eu/en/press/press-releases/2017/03/29-tusk-remarks-uk-notification/.

64 S Muter Goldberg and S Sumit, 'Withdrawal of the United Kingdom from Euratom', above n 53.

65 The UK is a separate party to both the Paris Agreement and the UNFCCC and therefore will be bound by its obligations under these agreements post-Brexit.

66 Eurostat, 'Total Greenhouse Gas Emissions by Countries (Including International Aviation and Indirect CO_2, Excluding LULULCF), 1990–2015 (Million Tonnes of CO_2 Equivalents)

On the day after the referendum, prices for EU ETS allowances fell by more than 10% to their lowest level since March 2016.[67] Brexit occurring before the end of Phase III (2013–20) may be highly disruptive to the smooth functioning of the system. The author notes, however, that there might be room for the UK to continue its participation in the EU ETS until 2020 or even thereafter as part of the possible transition period (subject, of course, to the outcome of the ongoing negotiations). At the time of writing (February 2018), the UK Government is considering a two-year transition period post-2019; whilst this is not driven by EU ETS related concerns but rather overall policy issues pertaining to the post-Brexit arrangements of the UK, such a transition period would help to keep the current commitment phase of the EU ETS intact.[68] Whilst this is not a policy that is fully accepted by the entire British Cabinet and would – obviously – also require EU consent, such a transitional period would, among other things, successfully address the issues arising from a UK exit from the EU ETS mid-compliance period.

Furthermore, the supply/demand dynamics of the EU ETS and the market reforms for the period after 2020 (when the current commitment period of the EU ETS expires) could be affected. The UK's departure has the potential of shifting the existing balance towards lower ambition for further reforms of the EU ETS ahead of Phase IV (2021–30);[69] thus weakening the decarbonisation element of the system.

As an alternative to a full exit, it is possible that the UK might continue to participate in the EU ETS without being an EU member, and follow a similar path to Norway, whose companies participate in the scheme despite not being an EU member;[70] in this case, any impact on the EU ETS is likely to be of a short-term nature only.

Updated', available at: http://ec.europa.eu/eurostat/statistics-explained/index.php/File:Total_greenhouse_gas_emissions_by_countries_(including_international_aviation_and_indirect_CO2,_excluding_LULUCF),_1990_-_2015_(million_tonnes_of_CO_2_equivalents)_updated.png.

67 See: http://markets.businessinsider.com/commodities/historical-prices/co2-emissionsrechte/EURO/1.3.2016_27.6.2016.

68 For more on the EU ETS and Brexit, see, for instance, A Froggatt and G Wright, Chatham House, and S Goldberg, Herbert Smith Freehills, 'Crunch Time on Brexit and Climate Policy', available at: http://eciu.net/blog/2018/crunch-time-on-brexit-and-climate-policy.

69 For more information on Phase IV of the EU ETS, see: https://ec.europa.eu/clima/policies/ets/revision_en.

70 The EEA-EFTA states (Norway, Iceland and Liechtenstein) joined the EU ETS scheme in its Phase II; Directive 2008/101/EC amended the original EU ETS directive to include all flights to, from and within all EU countries and Norway, Iceland and Liechtenstein are covered under the EU ETS.

8.2. INTERNATIONAL CLIMATE COMMITMENTS

In the past, the UK has been a driving force in the EU's involvement in international climate negotiations.[71] This role emerged in part due to the UK's own high level of ambition in this area as well as its capacity to conduct international climate diplomacy.

With its departure, the EU's overall level of ambition may well decrease which, in turn, could affect the upcoming review cycles for updated nationally determined contributions under the Paris Agreement in 2018 (for 2020), 2023 (for 2025) and 2028 (for 2030).[72] The author considers it likely that, whilst the UK and EU will remain important players on the international climate scene, Brexit will dampen the voices of both during future negotiations.

9. OUTLOOK

It is too early yet to estimate the shape of the future EU–UK relations post-Brexit as a whole, or specifically in relation to the energy sector. Whilst there are economic (and perhaps common sense) indicators that would suggest that strong relations and indeed (inter-)connections will remain between the two jurisdictions post-29 March 2019, the Brexit negotiations are an intensely political process which may yet hold surprises for the sector.

As mentioned in the introduction, the Withdrawal Bill will transpose any part of the acquis communautaire that is not already part of UK legislation into UK law on 29 March 2019. However, the implementation of the Withdrawal Bill is also likely to mark the end of automatic tracking of EU legislation in the UK.

For the energy sector, the Clean Energy Package (or Winter Package) proposed by the European Commission may be the first significant EU energy legislation that might not be implemented in the UK. At the time of writing, this is somewhat unclear as it will in part depend on the timing of the adoption of the Clean Energy Package (if adopted by the EU legislators prior to 29 March 2019, the UK would technically be obligated to transpose and implement it) as well as on practical issues that will arise from certain aspects of the Clean Energy Package such as, for instance, the governance of the Energy Union in relation to the GB and Northern Irish energy markets.

---

71 See, for instance, Clean Energy News, 'UK to Ratify Paris Agreement by the End of Year Pledges May', September 2016, available at: https://www.cleanenergynews.co.uk/news/efficiency/uk-to-ratify-paris-agreement-by-the-end-of-year-pledges-may; UK Government, 'UK Ratifies the Paris Agreement', November 2016, available at: https://www.gov.uk/government/news/uk-ratifies-the-paris-agreement.

72 EELR XI, Chapter IV, 'The Paris Agreement to the UNFCCC: Underlying Dynamics and Expected Consequences for the Energy Sector'.

At present, anecdotal evidence suggests that there is no 'Brexit effect' in relation to private investments in the UK energy sector. However, as the negotiations progress, there is a real risk of a private sector investment hiatus as Brexit approaches, particularly in respect of pre-financial close and pre-Final Investment Decision (FID) developments unless the negotiations send signals of stability and an outline of the framework for future EU–UK relations soon.

As it seems likely that further clarity regarding the energy sector will only emerge at some point in 2018, when negotiations have moved on from the so-called 'first tier' issues, the next year will be both a year of uncertainty and – perhaps – more clarity as to future EU–UK relations post-Brexit.

CHAPTER II
EU CASE LAW AND THE ENERGY SECTOR

Berend Jan DRIJBER

1. INTRODUCTION

This contribution reviews the case law of the Luxembourg-based European Court of Justice (ECJ or the Court) regarding the energy sector from mid-2016 to the turn of 2017/18. Most decisions are preliminary rulings at the request of a national court of one of the EU Member States (Article 267 of the Treaty on the Functioning of the European Union (TFEU)). The ECJ also hears cases brought by the European Commission (the Commission) against one or more Member States (Article 258 TFEU), as well as appeals against rulings of the General Court on points of law (Article 263 TFEU). The General Court hears at first instance the administrative law appeals against decisions of EU institutions and EU agencies.

The chapter is organised as follows. It starts by discussing cases concerning certain internal market rules (section 2). It goes on to look at two cases involving a dispute on capacity allocation (section 3). The next topic is a series of cases regarding free CO_2 emission allowances (section 4). Subsequently, the chapter discusses cases relating to renewables that reflect the energy transition from fossil sources to renewable energy (section 5). Finally, it deals with disputes involving the rules on State aid, which is an area of growing importance for the energy sector (section 6).

2. INTERNAL MARKET

2.1. *ANODE*[1]

In a liberalised market, prices are set by the free play of supply and demand in the market. For social reasons a Member State may wish to protect certain categories of end users, such as households, against increases in energy prices.

---

1 ECJ 7 September 2016, Case C-121/15, *Association nationale des opérateurs détaillants en énergie (ANODE) v Premier Ministre a.o.*, ECLI:EU:C:2016:637.

This French case concerns the regulation of prices for the supply of natural gas to consumers in order to protect security of supply and territorial cohesion.[2] Energy suppliers have a statutory obligation to apply tariffs calculated in accordance with cost-based criteria drawn up by public authorities. ANODE, an association of suppliers operating at retail level, challenged the compatibility of this tariff regulation with the public service provisions in Article 3 of the Directive 2009/73, the Third Gas Directive and the general provision on services of general economic interest laid down in Article 106(2) TFEU. In essence, ANODE argued that these rules do not provide a proper justification for rules restricting the free play of market forces.

As in previous cases involving regulation of consumer energy prices, the Court took a very critical stand.[3] It found that the French price intervention constituted by its very nature an obstacle to the achievement of a competitive market in natural gas at retail level. With regard to the question of whether or not such obstacle can be justified on the basis of the protection of public service the Court underlined that Member States have a wide margin to define the notion of public service enshrined in Article 3(2) of Directive 2009/73/EC. However, for a restrictive measure to be justified on that basis, it must meet all the requirements set out in that provision (one which is the condition of non-discrimination), and it must also be proportionate in terms of scope and duration.

In this particular case, the Court held that Article 3(2) of Directive 2009/73/EC does not *a priori* preclude a particular method of determination of prices based on taking costs into consideration, provided that such method does not give rise to consequences that go beyond what is necessary for achieving the objectives of general economic interest pursued.[4] The Court carefully avoided saying directly that the French measure had disproportionate effects but it gave the referring court a significant amount of scope to end up with a negative verdict.[5]

---

2 ‘*Cohésion territoriale*’ normally refers to the concept of universal service: in each part of the national territory, including in the more remote areas, consumers must have access to an essential service at an affordable price.

3 ECJ 20 April 2010, Case C-265/08, *Federutility and Others v Autorità per l'energia elettrica e il gas*, ECLI:EU:C:2010:205. See T Deruyter and F Vandendriessche, ‘State Regulation of Supply Prices for Electricity and Gas’ in MM Roggenkamp and O Woolley (eds), *European Energy Law Report IX*, Intersentia, Cambridge 2012, pp 23–43. The other case is ECJ 10 September 2015, Case C-36/14, *Commission v. Poland*, ECLI:EU:C:2015:570. See BJ Drijber, ‘EU Case Law and the Energy Sector’ in MM Roggenkamp and C Banet (eds), *European Energy Law Report XI*, Intersentia, Cambridge 2017, para 3.2.

4 Case C-121/15, para 73, second indent.

5 The Court uses, in para 54, a standard phrase to express the idea that it is formally the referring court that must decide: ‘While it is for the referring court to assess in the main proceedings whether that requirement of proportionality is satisfied, it is, however, for the Court to provide that court, on the basis of the information available, with all the necessary indications for that purpose from the point of view of EU law (see, to that effect, judgment of 20 April 2010, *Federutility and Others*, C-265/08, ECLI:EU:C:2010:205, paragraph 34).’

In sum, this judgment does not add a great deal to the earlier *Federutility* case. The message is that the Member State in question has a heavy burden to show that price intervention is necessary and proportionate.

2.2. *ENI & UPRIGAZ*[6]

The first common legal framework to safeguard security of gas supply in the event of supply disruption was established in 2004 (Directive 2004/67/EC). The Russian–Ukrainian gas crisis in January 2009 caused an unprecedented disruption of gas supplies in the EU. This crisis led the EU legislator to adopt Regulation (EU) 994/2010,[7] which establishes gas infrastructure standards in order to improve security of gas supply and lays down harmonised security of supply standards. These latter standards include an obligation to ensure gas supply to 'protected customers'. Article 8 of this regulation provides that natural gas undertakings must ensure gas supply to protected customers in extreme situations. To that end, gas suppliers must hold gas stocks for a prescribed minimum period. Member States may under certain conditions impose stricter supply standards. France takes the opportunity to go beyond the standards set in the regulation. The question is whether it has gone too far.

First, a French Decree has extended the obligation to hold gas stocks to other categories of customers than the 'protected customers' as defined in Regulation (EU) 994/2010.[8] The Decree also covers all non-domestic customers connected to a distribution network and who have not contractually accepted an interruptible supply. The Decree therefore also includes users who do not have the same degree of vulnerability as the category of users defined in the regulation, such as companies that are not a small or medium enterprise. The French gas sector was unhappy with these additional requirements, presumably because gas suppliers had to keep larger gas stocks.

In its ruling, the Court does not categorically exclude that Member States use a wider definition of 'protected customers' as a means to set stricter standards. However, Regulation (EU) 994/2010 mentions a number of conditions that must

6 Judgment of 20 December 2017, Case C-226/16, *Eni & Uprigaz v Premier Ministre*, ECLI:EU:C:2017:1005.

7 Regulation (EU) 994/2010 concerning measures to safeguard security of gas supply and repealing Council Directive 2004/67/EC (OJ 2010, L 265, p 1).

8 By virtue of Article 2(1)(a) of Regulation (EU) 994/2010 'protected customers' means 'all household customers connected to a gas distribution network and, in addition, where the Member State concerned so decides, may also include: (a) small and medium-sized enterprises, provided that they are connected to a gas distribution network, and essential social services, provided that they are connected to a gas distribution or transmission network, and provided that all these additional customers do not represent more than 20% of the final use of gas.'

be met for those purposes. It is for the national court to verify whether these conditions are met. In the case at hand, it seems unlikely that they have been met. As it often does, the Court answers the question whether stricter rules are permitted by 'yes, provided' (which sounds slightly more friendly than 'no, unless', but the effect is the same). In that respect, the approach followed is similar to that in cases involving the regulation of market prices, such as *ANODE*.

The French Decree moreover requires suppliers to hold sufficient stocks of natural gas *in France*. Such a geographic requirement is, however, incompatible with Article 8(5), 2nd sentence of Regulation (EU) 994/2010 which expressly prohibits the making of the obligation to keep gas stocks being based on infrastructure located within the territory of the Member State.

This case illustrates that the internal market today is much more than an area of free trade. The internal market is also about protection of vulnerable consumers, security of supply, and solidarity between the EU Member States. This judgment also shows that national governments have a narrower margin of discretion with regard to choice of measures for safeguarding security of supply than they had under Directive 2004/67/EC. An EU regulation is directly applicable in Member States which means that it does not need to be transposed into national law. A regulation is therefore, generally, the appropriate legal instrument to impose precise obligations on EU Member States as well as on the industry. However, Regulation (EU) 994/2010 also states that increased solidarity 'does not affect the sovereign rights of Member States over their own energy resources'.[9]

2.3. *BEB*[10]

This case involves a dispute between Bulgarian company BEB and the Bulgarian Energy Regulator (KEVR). BEB had applied for a licence for electricity transmission and balancing group coordinator. KEVR rejected that application on the ground that national law provides for a single licence and that such licence had already been granted to an entity named ESO.

The Bulgarian court asked whether the provisions on ownership unbundling in Article 9(1) of Directive 2009/72/EC (Third Electricity Directive) precludes a TSO and a major supplier of electricity having a *common* shareholder (it does not say who this common shareholder is but one may presume that this is the Bulgarian State). In its ruling, the Court declined to answer that question because Bulgaria has used the option not to apply the obligation of ownership unbundling. Bulgaria applies the alternative option of designating an

---

9 See recital 39 of Regulation (EU) 994/2010.

10 Judgment of 26 October 2017, Case C-347/16, *Balgarska energiyna borsa AD (BEB) v Komisia za energiyno i vodno regulirane (KEVR)*, ECLI:EU:C:2017:816.

Independent Transmission Operator (ITO) as referred to in Article (9)(8)(a) of Directive 2009/72/EC. A preliminary question concerning the interpretation of the unbundling regime was therefore theoretical only.

The Bulgarian court also asked whether it is lawful to designate a single TSO/ITO for the whole of the national territory. The unsurprising answer to that question was that a monopoly is not as such contrary to Directive 2009/72/EC. Indeed many Members States have a national or regional monopoly.[11]

A final question relates to the compatibility of this monopoly with the EU competition rules. That question too was regarded by the Court as inadmissible. The order for reference of the Bulgarian court did not provide sufficient information to enable the Court to answer that question properly.

In sum, the answers given by the Court are rather disappointing.[12]

3. CAPACITY ALLOCATION

3.1. *E-CONTROL v ACER*[13]

Ever since the liberalisation of the electricity markets the allocation of capacity on interconnectors has been a source of litigation in the national courts or arbitration proceedings. The Third Package has transferred control over capacity allocation on interconnectors to the EU level.[14] In some situations, this has given rise to tension between national regulators or between Member States. It is submitted that this phenomenon shows that it was right to lift decision making to the European level.

The Austrian Energy Regulator E-Control was unhappy with an opinion by ACER, the European Agency for the Cooperation of Energy Regulators based in Ljubljana (Slovenia), on the methods of capacity allocation in the Central-East European region. E-Control took the surprising step of challenging this opinion in court, or to be more precise: it lodged an appeal to the General Court against the decision of the Board of Appeal of ACER holding that an appeal against an opinion of ACER is inadmissible. The Czech Republic and Poland supported ACER, revealing the political dividing line that appeared to surround this matter.

The General Court confirmed the decision of the Board of Appeal. Under the EU system of judicial protection non-binding acts such as opinions are not

11 Case C-347/16, para 50.

12 The case was decided without an opinion of the Advocate General.

13 Judgment of 29 June 2017, Case T-63/16, *E-Control v ACER*, ECLI:EU:T:2017:456. See BJ Drijber, 'EU Case Law and the Energy Sector' in MM Roggenkamp and C Banet (eds), *European Energy Law Report XI*, Intersentia, Cambridge 2017, pp 29–44, at 2.3, for the summary proceedings in this matter.

14 See Article 39 of Directive 2009/72/EC.

subject to judicial review since they do not produce legal effects. This outcome was foreseeable for those who are familiar with the rather strict system of judicial protection in the EU.

3.2. *PGNiG v COMMISSION*[15]

The next case on capacity allocation is an application for interim measures to the President of the General Court. The case concerns the OPAL pipeline (Ostsee-Pipeline-Anbindungsleitung) which, in the north, is connected to the Nordstream pipeline. It runs roughly along the eastern border of Germany and transports Russian natural gas into the Czech Republic to an exit point at Brandov.

The Third Gas Directive makes it possible for owners of new interconnectors to apply for an exemption from the obligation to grant TPA in order to encourage investments in interconnectors.[16] Exemptions are granted by the national regulator, under the control of the Commission, which has the power to withdraw the exemption. The powers of the Commission have been strengthened compared to the regime under the Second Gas Directive.

In 2009, the German Regulator BundesNetzAgentur (BNetzA) accorded such an exemption to OPAL, on the condition that a dominant firm and its group companies (meaning Gazprom and Wingas) cannot reserve more than 50% of the capacity. In 2016, BNetzA decided that the other 50% capacity, so far unused, was to be made subject to TPA through a transparent and non-discriminatory auction. The Commission approved that decision while adding conditions with regard to the auction in order to ensure that users other than Gazprom would have a fair share of the 'liberalised' capacity. Amongst other things, the Commission raised the ceiling concerning the freely attributable interconnection capacities.

The Polish electricity company Polskie Górnictwo Naftowe i Gazownictwo (PGNiG) found that in spite of the amendments required by the Commission, this decision did not give it sufficient protection against Gazprom's presumed dominance. PGNiG claimed that, as a result of the decision, Gazprom would be able to take at least 80% of the capacities of the pipeline which are subject to the bidding procedure. PGNiG argued that, as a result, it would lose access to diversified supply sources or that it would continue to have such access but at higher costs. In both cases this could affect the security and continuity of supplies to end users in Poland which it was for PGNiG to guarantee under the Polish Energy Law. PGNiG also claimed that Gazprom's long-term reservation

---

15 President of the General Court, Order of 21 July 2017, Case T-130/17R, ECLI:EU:T:2017:541, *Polskie Górnictwo Naftowe i Gazownictwo v Commission.*

16 Article 36 of Directive 2009/73/EC.

of the additional transport capacities would have irreversible effects on the downstream contracts concluded by operators involved in the transport and distribution and delivery of gas supplies by Gazprom. For those reasons, PGNiG applied for a stay of the execution of the Commission's decision.

This application was dismissed. The President of the General Court held that the immediacy of the alleged harm had not been demonstrated. Statistically this outcome is not at all surprising because, save as for situations of bankruptcy or near bankruptcy, it is almost impossible to satisfy the condition that execution of a decision causes *irreparable* harm. PGNiG did not appeal the decision of the President of the General.[17]

4. CO_2 EMISSION ALLOWANCES

4.1. *BOREALIS POLYOLEFINE, OMV REFINING & MARKETING, DOW BENELUX AND ESSO ITALIANA*[18]

The basis for the granting of greenhouse gas emission allowances is Directive 2003/87/EC, as amended by Directive 2009/29/EC.[19] Under the European Emissions Trading Scheme (EU ETS), the amount of allowances allocated free of charge is gradually decreasing. In the period under consideration, the Court has answered questions from several national courts with regard to both the transitional rules for harmonised allocation of the allowances which are laid down in Commission Decision 2011/278/EU[20] and the national implementation measures for the transitional free allocation of allowances which are laid down in Commission Decision 2013/448/EU.[21]

The multiple references for a preliminary ruling all turn around the cross-sectoral 'correction factor' that causes a gradual reduction across-the-board for all greenhouse gas-emitting operators. The correction factor is referred to in

17 At the time of writing there was not yet a ruling in the main proceedings, Case T-130/17.

18 ECJ 28 April 2016, joined cases C-191/14, C-192/14, C-295/14, C-389/14 and C-391/14 to C-393/14, *Borealis Polyolefine GmbH and Others v Bundesminister für Land- und Forstwirtschaft, Umwelt und Wasserwirtschaft and Others*, ECLI:EU:C:2016:311.

19 Directive 2003/87/EC of the European Parliament and of the Council of 13 October 2003 establishing a scheme for greenhouse gas emission allowance trading within the Community and amending Council Directive 96/61/EC (OJ 2003 L 275, p 32), as amended by Directive 2009/29/EC of the European Parliament and of the Council of 23 April 2009 (OJ 2009, L 140, p 63).

20 Decision 2011/278/EU of 27 April 2011 determining transitional Union-wide rules for harmonised free allocation of emission allowances pursuant to Article 10a of Directive 2003/87/EC of the European Parliament and of the Council (OJ 2011, L 130, p 1).

21 Decision 2013/448/EU of 5 September 2013 concerning national implementation measures for the transitional free allocation of greenhouse gas emission allowances in accordance with Article 11(3) of Directive 2003/87/EC of the European Parliament and of the Council (OJ 2013, L 240, p 27).

Article 10a(5) of Directive 2003/87/EC. It is expressed in a percentage to be determined in accordance with Article 15(3) of Decision 2011/278/EU. The actual annual percentages (a list in decreasing order) are set out in Annex II to Decision 2013/448/EU. National emission trading authorities are bound by this correction factor when they calculate the maximum annual amount of allowances free of charge. This explains why questions of validity of these EU law provisions may arise in appeal proceedings against a decision of the national authority fixing this maximum amount.

In preliminary references from Austrian, Dutch and Italian courts similar questions were raised on the validity of a number of provisions that constitute the basis for determining the maximum annual amount. The first provision under scrutiny was Article 15(3) of Commission Decision 2011/278/EU, insofar as that provision precludes *emissions from electricity generators* from being taken into account in the determination of the maximum annual amount. The Court held that this provision is not unlawful because the exclusion of electricity installations results directly from Article 10a of Directive 2003/87/EU and does not go beyond the scope of the powers delegated to the Commission to adopt implementing measures.

The amount of allowances allocated free of charge is based on previous activity levels of an installation. As from 1 January 2013 onwards, the scope of application of Directive 2003/87/EC has been broadened so as to include emissions from the production of aluminium and of certain sectors of the chemicals industry, referred to as 'the added installations'. The Court was also asked to rule on the validity of Article 4 of and Annex II to Commission Decision 2013/448/EU, according to which the Commission, when establishing the maximum annual amount, shall take into account emissions generated by 'the added installations prior to 1 January 2013'. As a result of this provision, the historic data of the emissions before that date were being input for the calculation of the correction factor. The Court held that Article 4 of and Annex II to Commission Decision 2013/448/EU are not compatible with Article 10a(5) of Directive 2003/87/EC, since that hierarchically superior provision stipulates that for added installations only emissions *from* 1 January 2013 could be taken into account.[22] In that respect the ruling is favourable for the gas-emitting companies.

The Court, however, limited the temporal effect of its own declaration of invalidity, 'so that, first, that declaration does not produce effects until 10 months following the date of delivery of this judgment so as to enable the Commission to adopt the necessary measures and, second, measures adopted during that period on the basis of the invalidated provisions cannot be called into question'.[23] The Court did so for reasons of legal certainty. Not only would

22 Joined cases C-191/14 a.o., para 95.
23 Joined cases C-191/14 a.o., para 111.

the annulment of the correction factor be 'capable of calling into question all of the final allocations made prior to this judgment in the Member States prior to be valid, having serious repercussions on a large number of legal relations established in good faith',[24] but national authorities, in the absence of an applicable correction factor, would also be prevented from allocating allowances during the period following this judgment. A temporary legal vacuum could 'jeopardise the implementation of the allowance trading scheme put in place by Directive 2003/87 and, consequently, the attainment of the objectives pursued by it. Indeed, any interruption of the allowance trading scheme would go against the main objective of that directive, namely to protect the environment by reducing greenhouse gases …'.[25]

In a number of cases where the temporal effects of a judgment were limited so as to exclude claims over past situations the Court excluded from that limitation the parties who had filed applications or equivalent complaints prior to the delivery of the judgment concerned.[26] In this case, however, the Court did not make such an exception for the applicants in the various national proceedings.[27] A possible explanation for withholding these applicants the benefit of their success in court could be that otherwise national authorities would be forced either to grant retroactively extra allowances free of charge or to provide for some other form of appropriate compensation. This outcome is understandable but not entirely satisfactory. On this basis, the Dutch Council of State dismissed the appeal by Dow Benelux and others against decisions of the national trading emission authority NEA, holding that in these decisions the maximum annual amount for each applicant had been set in accordance with Decision 2013/448/EU which was to be regarded as valid (and hence binding) at the moment the decision on the allocation of emission allowances was adopted.[28]

4.2. OTHER CASES RELATING TO THE FREE ALLOCATION OF CO_2 EMISSION ALLOWANCES

In a second series of cases, that were not joined, the Court had to decide a number of technical issues relating to the free allocation of emission allowances.[29]

---

24 Joined cases C-191/14 a.o., para 105.

25 Joined cases C-191/14 a.o., para 106.

26 The Court decides on a case by case basis whether declaration of invalidity has an effect *ex nunc*.

27 The Court decides on a case by case basis whether the parties who started proceedings are excluded from the limitation of the effects in time. See K Lenaerts, I Maselis and K Gutman, *EU Procedural Law*, OUP, Oxford 2013, §10.23.

28 Dutch Council of State 31 August 2016, ECLI:NL:RVS:2016:2354.

29 In all cases the French judge J-C Bonichot was the reporting judge and the Court dispensed with an opinion of the Advocate General.

In *Vattenfall*,[30] the Court answered the questions (i) which installations are covered by the EU ETS and (ii) when the emissions trading obligations start to become binding for a gas-emitting company. The emissions trading obligation of an installation for the generation of electricity 'starts on the date of the first emissions of greenhouse gases, and thus potentially before the date of the first generation of electricity'.[31]

E.ON Kraftwerke[32] concerns a dispute on the permitted scope of the obligation to provide information on changes to capacity and activity of installations. Companies that are subject to the EU ETS system and receive a free allocation of allowances may be required 'to provide information relating to all planned or effective changes to the capacity, activity level and operation of an installation, without limiting that requirement solely to information relating to changes that would affect the allocation'.[33]

In *Borealis Sweden*,[34] the Court decided amongst other things that it is lawful to exclude from free allowances heat that is exported to private households so as to avoid double counting. The Court also addressed a number of other technical matters. For the remainder this judgment too confirmed the ruling in *Borealis Polyolefine*.

In *Yara Suomi*,[35] the Court once more confirmed *Borealis Polyolefine*. Besides that, it held that the correction factor may be applied to installations in sectors exposed to a significant risk of carbon leakage.

4.3. *SCHAEFER KALK*[36]

This case raises the issue of the validity of a provision of Commission Regulation (EU) 601/2012 on the monitoring and reporting of greenhouse gas emissions.[37] Pursuant to Article 49(1) of that regulation, CO_2 which is not emitted but transferred to (i) a capture installation, (ii) a transport network or

---

30 ECJ 28 July 2016, Case C-457/15, *Vattenfall Europe Generation AG v Bundesrepublik Deutschland*, ECLI:EU:C:2016:613.

31 Case-457/15, para 43.

32 ECJ 8 September 2016, Case C-461/15, *E.ON Kraftwerke GmbH v Bundesrepublik Deutschland*, ECLI:EU:C:2016:648.

33 Case C-461/15, para 40.

34 ECJ 8 September 2016, Case C-180/15, *Borealis AB and Others v Naturvårdsverket*, ECLI:EU:C:2016:647.

35 ECJ 26 October 2016, Case C-506/14, *Yara Suomi Oy e.a. v Työ-ja elinkeinoministeriö*, ECLI:EU:C:2016:799.

36 ECJ 19 January 2017, Case C-460/15, *Schaefer Kalk GmbH & Co. KG v Bundesrepublik Deutschland*, ECLI:EU:C:2017:29.

37 Regulation (EU) 601/2012 of 21 June 2012 on the monitoring and reporting of greenhouse gas emissions pursuant to Directive 2003/87/EC of the European Parliament and of the Council (OJ 2012 L 181, p 30).

(iii) a storage is to be subtracted from the emissions of that installation. The German authorities had refused to apply that provision and refused to allow Schaefer Kalk to subtract from the emissions subject to the monitoring obligation the carbon dioxide generated in an installation for the calcination of lime transferred to a precipitated calcium carbonate (PCC) installation. Such an installation does not qualify as a capture installation, a network or a storage.

The Court held that this limitation to these three categories is too narrow. Other emissions that are not released into the atmosphere should be treated in the same manner. This is to be done, for example, when CO_2 is chemically transformed into a new, stable chemical in which the CO_2 is bound, which is what Schaefer Kalk was doing. Accordingly, the provisions of Regulation (EU) 601/2012 are invalid insofar as they systematically include in the emissions of an installation the CO_2 transferred from that installation into another installation, regardless of whether or not that CO_2 is actually released into the atmosphere.

In reaching this conclusion the Court also referred to the 'sub-objectives' of the EU ETS: 'although the principal objective of the scheme for greenhouse gas emission allowance trading is to reduce emissions of such gases substantially, one of its sub-objectives is to preserve the integrity of the internal market and of conditions of competition'.[38] In this case, the difference between an operator who releases greenhouse gases and an operator who avoids such emissions does not allow the second operator to hold onto a greater allowance than the first. The difference in treatment cannot be regarded as distorting competition between those two operators.[39] One may even wonder whether it would not be discriminatory if, in spite of objective difference(s), the two operators were treated in exactly the same manner.

5. RENEWABLES

5.1. *ESSENT BELGIUM*[40]

In 2016, the Court had to decide a second *Essent Belgium* case. The first one, in 2014, concerned the treatment of guarantees of origin originating from other Member States for the purposes of a national support scheme

---

[38] The Court referred in that context to its judgments of 29 March 2012, Case C-505/09P *Commission v Estonia*, ECLI:EU:C:2012:170, para 79, and of 22 June 2016, Case C-540/16P, *DK Recycling und Roheisen v Commission*, C-540/14P, ECLI:EU:C:2016:469, paras 49 and 50.

[39] Case C-460/15, para 47.

[40] ECJ 29 September 2016, Case C-492/14, *Essent Belgium NV v Vlaams Gewest a.o.*, ECLI:EU:C:2016:732.

for electricity from renewable resources.[41] The second case raises another problem of discriminatory treatment on the basis of the origin of (green) electricity. Around 2004, a regional rule in Belgium provided that electricity produced from renewable energy is exempted from distribution fees, insofar as the electricity is fed directly by generating installations into the regional distributions systems (and subsequently into the distribution systems at national level). As a result of this condition, imported electricity was not able to take advantage of an exemption from the distribution fee. Although prima facie it is fairly obvious that this legislation should fall foul of EU law, the best angle for tackling the issue is less obvious.

The Court found first of all that a differential treatment in the access of suppliers to the distribution systems, as in the case at hand, does not fall to be assessed under Directive 2009/28 on the promotion of electricity produced from renewable energy sources,[42] but under both the internal market directives[43] and the general rules on the free movement of goods (Article 34 TFEU). Referring to older case law relating to the First Electricity Directive 96/92/EC, the Court found that, contrary to Article 16 of Directive 96/92/EC and Article 20(1) of Directive 2003/54/EC, the legislation results in electricity suppliers being treated differently, depending on the origin of the green electricity being marketed by those suppliers.[44]

The Court then proceeded to a lengthy analysis of the possible justification for such a difference in treatment. In Directives 96/92/EC and 2003/54/EC a specific provision justifying a difference in treatment between suppliers of green energy is lacking; there is only a provision allowing that system operators may be required to give priority, when dispatching generating installations, inter alia, to installations producing green electricity.[45] At the same time, the Court noted the legitimacy of the objective of the legislation at issue, namely promoting the production of green electricity. The Court subsequently turned to the public service obligations in Article 3 of Directives 96/92/EC and 2003/54/EC. It rehearsed the conditions that are to be met for a national measure to qualify as 'public service obligation', including the principle of proportionality, without however drawing a conclusion as to the justification of the measure at issue.

---

41 ECJ 11 September 2014, Case C-204/12 to C-208/12, ECLI:EU:C:2014:2192). That judgment confirmed the Court's ruling of 1 July 2014, Case C-573/12, *Ålands Vindkraft AB v Energimyndigheten*, ECLI:EU:C:2014:2037. See BJ Drijber, 'EU Case Law and the Energy Sector' in MM Roggenkamp and C Banet (eds), *European Energy Law Report XI*, Intersentia, Cambridge 2017, at 4.3.

42 At the relevant time, Directive 2001/77/EC was still in force. That directive was repealed, from 1 January 2012, by Directive 2009/28/EC (OJ 2009 L 140, p 16).

43 At the relevant time, Directive 2003/54 (OJ 2003, L 176, p 37) was still in force.

44 Case C-492/14, para 82.

45 Ibid, para 83, referring to Article 11(3) of Directive 96/92 and Article 14(4) of Directive 2003/54.

The Court extended its analysis to the Treaty rules on the free movement of goods 'with which the public service obligations established under Article 3(2) of each of the Directives 96/92 and 2003/54 must also apply'.[46]

In the end, the Court held that the difference in treatment was not justified because it is uncertain whether the green electricity *producers* (as opposed to the electricity suppliers), and hence the production of green electricity, actually have the benefit of this advantage. In other words, there is no (sufficient) causal link between the effect of the measure and the objectives it pursues. The Court held that the Treaty rules on free movement of goods (at the time: Article 28 and 30 EC) and several provisions of Directive 96/92/EC, Directive 2003/54/EC and Directive 2001/77/EC, 'read together', preclude the Belgian measure.

The author's reading of the judgment is that the Court implicitly held that the conditions for access to the network have not been the subject of exhaustive harmonisation at EU level. Indeed, where the EU legislator has opted for exhaustive harmonisation, a national measure relating to the harmonised matter must be assessed in the light of the provisions of that harmonising measure and not in the light of primary law (ie the TFEU).[47] This is interesting because ECJ's ruling of 7 June 2005 in *VEMW* suggested that the rules regarding the non-discriminatory access to networks are fully harmonised.[48]

5.2. *E.ON BIOFOR SVERIGE*[49]

Like *Essent Belgium*, this Swedish case is an example of a case in which the Court simultaneously applies provisions of a harmonisation directive and the Treaty provisions on free movement of goods. This case is about the import of biogas, which is only used for the transport sector, from Germany into Sweden through an interconnected network. Article 18(1) of Directive 2009/28/EC on the promotion of the use of energy from renewable sources[50] stipulates that a certain method must be used to verify whether biofuels are in compliance with the sustainability criteria. For the purposes of these verifications, national authorities shall require economic operators to use a so-called 'mass balance system'.

---

46 Case C-492/14, para 95.

47 See eg Case C-573/12, *Ålands Vindkraft AB v Energimyndigheten*, ECLI:EU:C:2014:2037, para 57.

48 ECJ 7 June 2005, Case C-17/03, *VEMW v Directeur DTe*, ECLI:EU:C:2005:362. The Court refused to consider Article 106(2) TFEU (Article 86(2) EC) as a possible objective justification for a priority right to interconnection capacity for a company entrusted with tasks of general economic interests. See paras 89 and 90 of that judgment.

49 ECJ 22 June 2017, Case C-549/15, *E.ON Biofor Sverige AB v Statens energimyndighet*, ECLI:EU:C:2017:490.

50 OJ 2009, L 140, p 16.

A German sister company of E.ON Sverige adds consignments of biogas to the German gas distribution network. E.ON Sverige transports these consignments via the German and Danish gas networks to Sweden. The gas is covered by a German sustainability certificate issued in accordance with the German national mass balance verification system. The Swedish Energy Regulator, however, ordered E.ON Sverige to modify its verification system as regards the sustainability of the imported biogas in order to ensure that the mass balance was achieved 'within a location with a clear boundary', as required by Swedish law. The effect of this order was that gas certified as 'biogas' in Germany could not be classified as 'sustainable' in Sweden. It followed that the biogas in question could not benefit from reductions of CO_2 and energy taxes. E.ON sought annulment of the Energy Regulator's order. The Swedish court asked for a preliminary ruling.

The Court first held that Article 17 of Directive 2009/28/EC seeks to ensure that biofuels may be taken into account by the Member States for three environmental purposes, provided that they fulfil the sustainability criteria. One of the purposes mentioned is 'the eligibility for financial support for the consumption of biofuels and bioliquids'.[51] Article 17 seeks to facilitate trade in sustainable biofuels but it does not as such regulate imports nor, particularly, does it require Member States unconditionally to authorise imports from other Member States. It follows that Article 18(1), which requires operators to use a mass balance system having certain technical characteristics 'does not place an obligation on the Member States to authorise imports of sustainable biogas via their interconnected national gas networks'.[52] This does not answer the question of whether the additional requirements imposed by Swedish law, as enforced by the Energy Regulator, are compatible with EU law.

The same goes for the second preliminary question asked by the Swedish court. That court wanted to know whether Article 18(1) of Directive 2009/28/EC is legally valid in the light of Article 34 TFEU. The Court rehearsed the case law on the interpretation of Article 34 TFEU and on the scope of Article 114 TFEU, which is the legal basis for legislative measures aimed at achieving the European internal market. The Court noted that where sustainable biogas is transported between Member States via interconnected national gas networks, Article 18(1) allows for the sustainability of that gas to be recognised in the Member State of import for the purposes set out in Article 17(1). Article 18(1) of Directive 2009/28/EC is therefore not invalid.[53]

Finally, the Court answered the question that the Swedish court had not asked but should have asked: whether Article 34 TFEU (free movement of goods) precludes the contested order of the Energy Regulator. In line with the opinion

---

51 Article 17(1)(c) of Directive 2009/28.

52 Case C-549/15, para 42.

53 Ibid, para 71.

of Advocate General Campos Sánchez-Bordona, the Court gave an affirmative answer to that question.

5.3. *J.D. (POLAND)*[54]

This case relates to a technical question of interpretation of Directive 2009/28 in proceedings between a company operating in the electricity generation sector and the Polish Energy Regulator. The latter had refused to grant an extension of a licence to produce electricity in a small-scale hydropower plant located at the point of discharge of waste water from another plant. The company (referred to as J.D.) held a licence authorising it to produce electricity from renewable sources in two small-scale biogas plants and a small-scale hydropower plant, the latter being located at the point of discharge of industrial waste water from another plant not involved in electricity production.

The question submitted to the Court concerned the definition of 'energy from renewable sources' mentioned in Article 2(2)(a) of Directive 2009/28/EC. More precisely, the question is whether hydropower from renewable sources is to be interpreted narrowly (meaning that it is limited to power generated from natural waterfalls) or whether it should have a broad interpretation so as to include hydropower provided from an artificial water flow.

In answering this technical question the Court opted for the wider interpretation of 'hydropower'. That interpretation is supported by the objectives pursued by Directive 2009/28/EC. It follows from Article 1 of this directive that it seeks to promote the production of energy from renewable sources. The opposite interpretation could reduce the amount of hydroelectric energy capable of benefiting from measures promoting the production of energy from renewable sources which the Member States are to implement and could therefore undermine the full achievement of the objectives of that directive.[55]

6. STATE AID

6.1. INTRODUCTION

The number of State aid rulings in the energy sector is increasing. This is hardly surprising. Transitions in the energy sector normally require support schemes from government in order to compensate for competitive disadvantages resulting from this transition. In the days of liberalisation of the energy markets

54 ECJ 2 March 2017, Case C-4/16, *J.D. v Prezes Urzędu Regulacji Energetyki*, ECLI:EU:C:2017:153.

55 Case C-4/16, paras 34–37.

(around 2000 in Western Europe), many producers of electricity were faced with costs of investments or commitments with a guarantee of sale which they were unable to recoup, the so-called 'stranded costs'. In 2001, the Commission published an analytical method for assessing the compatibility of financial compensation for stranded costs with the EU State aid rules (Articles 107 and 108 TFEU).[56]

More recently, the transition to energy from renewable sources has caused Member States to subsidise the production of clean energy. The support schemes are normally intended to help producers of energy from renewable sources to finance the investments in infrastructure such as pipelines or windfarms and/or to enable them to offer their product at competitive prices. Many of these support schemes have been declared compatible with the internal market pursuant to Article 107(3) TFEU. Thus, billions of subsidies have gone and are still flowing to producers of energy from renewables. It seems that, meanwhile, we have reached the point where the tail is wagging the dog. In some regions of the EU, the production of subsidised green electricity is reaching such volumes that conventional production installations, which have higher marginal costs, are structurally loss making and now suffer from a competitive disadvantage. This is in particular so for gas-fired power stations. Since approximately 2012, market wholesale prices have generally been at such a low level that gas-fired power stations are not profitable when dispatched. That is why many power stations are 'mothballed' or even abandoned altogether. Fossil fuelled power stations will nonetheless continue to have an essential function for the security of supply, in particular on days that there is no sunshine and little wind. In the near future, a case may be made for entrusting operators of power stations, in particular of gas fuelled power stations, with a service of general economic interest (Article 106(2) TFEU), thus providing a possible justification for State aid.

The section turns to ECJ judgments involving questions of State aid in the period under consideration.

6.2. *PGE*[57]

Like Hungary, Poland decided in the 1990s to modernise its electricity infrastructure by concluding long-term power purchase agreements (PPAs). In Poland, these PPAs were agreed with a number of national electricity generators. Under these agreements, the electricity generators concerned undertook to set up new generation facilities, modernise their equipment and supply to PSE a fixed minimum volume of electricity, produced at specific plants. For its part,

56 Communication of 26 July 2001 relating to the methodology for analysing state aid linked to stranded costs.

57 ECJ 15 September 2016, Case C-574/14, *PGE Górnictwo i Energetyka Konwencjonalna S.A. v Prezes Urzędu Regulacji Energetyki*, ECLI:EU:C:2016:686.

PSE undertook to purchase at least the agreed minimum volume of electricity, at a price based on the principle of passing all costs on to the consumer. PSE's purchase commitments gave the generators the necessary certainty to make the investments needed to modernise the sector.

Following the entry into force of Directive 96/92/EC in Poland, the Polish Electricity Act (KDT) provided the generators concerned with the option of terminating the PPAs. In particular, KDT introduced for those generators who terminated those agreements at their own initiative a right to compensation of stranded costs. Electricity generators which were parties to PPAs could benefit from such compensation each year for a period of time corresponding to the time the PPA terminated early.[58] In 2007, that scheme was approved by the Commission as lawful aid.[59]

The Energy Regulator establishes the amount of annual compensation for each generator. The amount thus fixed constitutes the basis for adjusting the amount that had been paid by way of advance payment. The case at hand concerns a dispute about the amount of aid paid to generator PGE in 2009. The Energy Regulator had fixed that amount by taking into account that in 2009 another generator, ELB, belonged to the same group as PGE, which it did not at the time PGE concluded the commitments that had given rise to the stranded costs. The Polish Supreme Court asked the ECJ whether changes in the ownership structure had to be taken into account when fixing the annual amount of compensation. In that regard, the Court held that the relevant point in time is the current situation (in the year for which the annual amount is fixed) and not the past situation (at the time the Commission assessed the stranded costs). It is submitted that it makes sense that one has to look at the existing and not at the past structure of the group and its financial results.

The Polish Supreme Court also referred a preliminary question of an institutional nature. It asked whether the national authorities (both administrative and judicial authorities) are precluded from reviewing, at the stage of the implementation of a State aid scheme, whether that scheme complies with the Commission's methodology for stranded costs if that scheme has already been approved by the Commission under the State aid rules. This question led the Court to rehearse its case law on the respective roles of the Commission and the national courts. In conclusion the Court held that 'where the Commission has assessed a State aid scheme in light of the Stranded Costs Methodology and classified it as being compatible with the internal market

58 Case C-574/14, paras 11–14.

59 Commission Decision 2009/287/EC of 25 September 2007 on State aid awarded by Poland as part of Power Purchase Agreements and the State aid which Poland is planning to award concerning compensation for the voluntary termination of Power Purchase Agreements (OJ 2009, L 83, p 1).

before its implementation, the national authorities and courts are precluded from reviewing in turn, at the time the State aid in question is implemented, whether it is consistent with the principles set out in that methodology'.[60]

6.3. *ENEA*[61]

This case is another example of an intervention by the Polish Energy Regulator. For the period from 1 January 2003 to 1 July 2007, the Polish Law on energy provided for a support scheme for electricity produced by cogeneration. The support consisted in an obligation for undertakings selling electricity to end users, including intermediaries, to ensure that 15% of their total sales of electricity be produced by cogeneration. In addition, the maximum tariffs for sale of electricity *to end users* were regulated by the Energy Regulator.

ENEA produces and sells electricity. For the year 2006, ENEA did not entirely fulfil its quota obligation to purchase electricity produced by cogeneration, which led the Energy Regulator to impose a financial penalty on ENEA. On appeal ENEA, an electricity company wholly owned by the Polish State, argued that the obligation to purchase electricity produced by cogeneration constitutes State aid in favour of the producers of such electricity. The Polish Supreme Court asked the Court the interesting question whether a public company, which is 'treated as an emanation of a Member State', may invoke an infringement of Article 107 TFEU. There was unfortunately no need to answer that last question since the Court held that there is no State aid to the producers of the electricity cogenerated with heat: the obligation on both private and public undertakings to purchase electricity produced by cogeneration with the production of heat does not constitute an advantage *through State resources*.

That answer is not as self-evident as it may seem. In earlier cases an obligation to purchase electricity from renewable sources has been qualified as State aid even if there was no transfer of money from the State's budget to the producers of such electricity.[62] The key differences with these previous cases are: (i) the Polish scheme was not financed through compulsory contributions but by own financial resources; and (ii) the purchase obligation applied equally to private and public suppliers. If only suppliers owned by the State or other public entities had this obligation the outcome of the case could have been different.

---

60 Case C-574/14, para 41. This conclusion is based on an interpretation of Article 107(1) TFEU (the prohibition of State aid) and Article 4(3) TEU (the general duty of sincere cooperation), read together with Article 4(2) of Decision 2009/287/EC.

61 ECJ 13 September 2017, Case C-329/15, *ENEA v Prezes Urzędu Regulacji Energetyki*, ECLI:EU:C:2017:671.

62 For example, ECJ 17 July 2008, Case C-206/06, *Essent Netwerk Noord*, ECLI:EU:C:2008:413, and ECJ 19 December 2013, Case C-262/12, *Association Vent De Colère!*, ECLI:EU:C:2013:851.

There is a large amount of similarity between this ruling and the *Preussen Elektra* case of 2001.[63] Curiously, this precedent is not mentioned in the reasoning of the Court. Ever since the *Preussen Elektra* judgment the Commission has played down the importance of that ruling in an attempt to regain full control over national measures that favour suppliers of green energy through compulsory purchases at prices above market prices.

6.4. CASE LAW ON THE GERMAN EEG

In Germany, substantial financial support to electricity production from renewable sources is paid for by all electricity consumers on the basis of the so-called 'EEG-surcharge'. 'EEG' stands for the *Erneubare Energien Gesetz*. Energy-intensive industries are entitled to a reduction of the EEG surcharge. By its decision of 25 November 2014, the Commission qualified these reductions as State aid within the meaning of Article 107(1) TFEU, which it declared compatible with the internal market (and hence lawful) in accordance with Article 107(3) TFEU.[64]

Germany challenged this decision, arguing that the reduction does not entail State aid. First, it does not confer an advantage; it compensates for a competitive disadvantage. Second, the reduction for energy-intensive industries does not involve State resources. The General Court dismissed the appeal.[65] In light of existing case law on both the issues of advantage and State resources that should hardly come as a surprise.[66]

The next edition of the EEG (EEG 2014) provides, amongst other things, for an exemption of the surcharge for auto-generators of electricity. By its decision of 23 July 2014,[67] the Commission held that this exemption constituted a selective advantage and hence a State aid which it also approved in accordance with Article 107(3) TFEU. In spite of this positive outcome, German heavy industries and their associations challenged the decision because they were opposed to the label 'State aid'. The General Court dismissed the appeal as inadmissible for lack of interest.[68] One should nonetheless be aware of the practical relevance of that

63 ECJ 13 March 2001, Case C-379/98, *PreussenElektra*, ECLI:EU:C:2001:160.

64 The Commission defined a number of limits but what matters is that the scheme was approved.

65 General Court 10 May 2016, Case T-47/15, *Germany v Commission*, ECLI:EU:T:2016:281.

66 Germany has lodged an appeal at the ECJ; Case C-405/16P (pending at the time of writing).

67 The EEG 2014 was approved before the earlier EEG was, because the latter had initially not been notified to the Commission. For a period of time therefore, the reduction of the surcharge had been illegal State aid which did not need to be recovered from the companies that benefited from the reduction.

68 General Court 22 September 2016, Case T-750/15, *Mitteldeutsche Braunkohlengesellschaft a.o. v Commission*, ECLI:EU:T:2016:534.

argument for the industries benefiting of the exemption of the surcharge: if there is no aid, there is no need to notify the measure to the Commission.

7. CONCLUSION

The objective of a survey of case law is not to give a scientific answer to a research question. By way of summary two trends may be highlighted. One is that the transition to clean energy generates many questions of a financial nature, in particular on the State aid aspects of a support scheme and, in the near future, possibly on fresh stranded costs issues. Another observation is that, in spite of detailed directives and regulations, the Court is still called upon to interpret provisions of the TFEU. There is a clear need for modernised and more precise legislation. The Energy Union, proposed in February 2015, is however progressing slowly.[69]

[69] See Third Report on the State of the Energy Union of 23 November 2017 (COM (2017) 688 final).

PART II

PROMOTING RENEWABLE ENERGY PRODUCTION: CROSS-BORDER PROJECTS AND DISPUTE SETTLEMENT

CHAPTER III

RENEWABLE ENERGY INVESTMENT DISPUTES

Recent Developments and Implications for Prospective Energy Market Reforms

Nikos LAVRANOS and Cees VERBURG

1. INTRODUCTION

There has always been a strong relationship between investment disputes in the energy sector and international investment law, with the former often contributing to the development of the latter.[1] Historically, most of the energy-related investment cases concerned the mining sector or the conventional electricity sector.[2] In recent times, an increasing number of cases concern disputes that have arisen in the renewable energy sector.

Over the last few decades States, including Member States of the European Union (EU), have increasingly acknowledged the importance of renewable energy sources (RES) for a variety of reasons, including climate change mitigation and the reduction of energy dependency. In order to increase RES energy production, EU Member States have adopted support schemes aimed at incentivising RES investments.

In some countries, these initiatives were so successful that the States were subsequently confronted with guaranteed payments to RES producers at such high levels that – in the eyes of those States – the support schemes became

---

1 P CAMERON, *International Energy Investment Law – The Pursuit of Stability*, OUP, Oxford 2010, pp vii, 145–52; K SCHEFER, *International Investment Law – Text, Cases and Materials*, Edward Elgar Publishing, Cheltenham 2016, p 217; A SINCLAIR, 'The Origins of the Umbrella Clause in the International Law of Investment Protection' [2004] 20 Arbitration International 411, 412; A SABATER and M STADNYK, 'International Arbitration and Energy: How Energy Disputes Shaped International Investment Dispute Resolution' in K TALUS, *Research Handbook on International Energy Law*, Edward Elgar, Cheltenham 2014.

2 P CAMERON, *International Energy Investment Law – The Pursuit of Stability*, OUP, Oxford 2010, pp 145–46.

untenable when the financial crisis, starting in 2008–09, hit many EU Member States. Consequently, several EU Member States adopted measures which reduced payments or fundamentally altered remuneration parameters – sometimes even with retroactive effect.

Unavoidably, this has resulted in an unprecedented high number of investment disputes. Besides numerous court proceedings before domestic courts, international RES investment disputes have arisen under the Energy Charter Treaty (ECT), the North American Free Trade Agreement (NAFTA) and several bilateral investment treaties (BITs).

Moreover, since many investment disputes have been brought by European investors against EU Member States, the European Commission (EC) has regularly intervened as *amicus curiae* in support of the EU Member States claiming that arbitral tribunals lack jurisdiction since EU law supersedes the ECT and BITs. Accordingly, the EU – through the EC – is also involved as a non-disputing party in these disputes.

The increased levels of RES production are confronting the energy markets, especially the electricity market, with challenges – of a technical, organisational and legal nature.[3] Therefore, the EC took the first steps in late 2016 to reform the energy markets within the EU in order to facilitate a transition to sustainable, well-functioning and liberalised energy markets.[4]

The proposed reforms of the EC are also aimed at reducing the risk of investment treaty claims being brought by RES investors. Given the fact that market reforms might adversely affect certain market players, the implications for investors are highly relevant in order not to undermine investor confidence. After all, a successful transition to a sustainable energy supply system will require billions in investments in the EU for decades to come, the majority of which will have to be made by the private sector.

This chapter analyses some central RES disputes that have arisen under the ECT, most notably those involving Spain and Italy. Section 2 starts by describing the regulatory changes that led to the ECT disputes. Section 3 continues with an examination of the various arbitral awards. Although investors in various other EU Member States, such as the Czech Republic, Bulgaria and Greece have also been confronted with regulatory changes to RES support schemes, this chapter focuses on the ECT awards involving Spain and Italy as these are currently the only available RES awards under the ECT. Moreover, in particular Spain and to a lesser extent Italy are the countries that have been confronted with the highest number of investment treaty claims.

---

3 M KEAY, 'Electricity Markets are Broken – Can They be Fixed?' (2016) Oxford Institute for Energy Studies, available at: https://www.oxfordenergy.org/wpcms/wp-content/uploads/2016/02/Electricity-markets-are-broken-can-they-be-fixed-EL-17.pdf.

4 See for more information: https://ec.europa.eu/energy/en/news/commission-proposes-new-rules-consumer-centred-clean-energy-transition.

Further, this chapter puts the various ECT awards in perspective with the energy market reforms proposed by the EC in the 'Clean Energy for All Europeans' package, also often referred to as the 'Winter Package'. More specifically, it analyses to what extent these reforms may affect RES investors and identifies potential investment disputes that may arise.

2. BACKGROUND FOR THE PAST RENEWABLE ENERGY INVESTMENT DISPUTES

Since most of the RES investment cases have arisen against EU Member States and have been (at least partly) the result of measures adopted on the basis of EU law, the main aspects of EU RES law and policy will be introduced first.

Subsequently, and on that basis, the relevant legislative RES framework of Spain and Italy will be shortly outlined in order to provide the background for the analysis of the RES investment treaty disputes which have been decided so far and are publicly available.

2.1. THE EU LEGISLATIVE FRAMEWORK

The promotion of RES generation and use has long been a policy objective of the EU which resulted in the adoption of harmonised provisions in secondary EU law.[5] Today, the Renewable Energy Directive 2009/28/EC (RES Directive) provides for the main legal framework 'driving the development of renewables' in Europe.[6] This Directive sets mandatory RES targets for the Member States. These targets vary per EU Member State, ranging for example from 14% of RES for the Netherlands to 49% for Sweden. Meanwhile, the EU and its Member States have committed themselves to increase the RES level to 30% of total consumption in 2030. From an investor's perspective, two elements of the RES Directive are of particular interest.

First, the RES Directive allows Member States to adopt financial support schemes in order to reach their national targets by 2020.[7] Financial support can be given in a variety of ways, such as tax breaks, green certificates and direct support, either in the form of a feed-in tariff (FiT) or feed-in premium (FiP) or

---

5 H VEDDER, A RØNNE, MM ROGGENKAMP and I IÑIGO DEL GUAYO, 'EU Energy Law' in MM ROGGENKAMP, C REDGWELL, A RØNNE and I IÑIGO DEL GUAYO, *Energy Law in Europe – National, EU and International Regulation*, OUP, Oxford 2016, p 318.

6 Ibid, p 320; Directive 2009/28/EC of the European Parliament and of the Council of 23 April 2009 on the promotion of the use of energy from renewable sources and amending and subsequently repealing Directives 2001/77/EC and 2003/30/EC [2009] OJ L140/16.

7 Article 3, Directive 2009/28/EC of the European Parliament and of the Council of 23 April 2009 on the promotion of the use of energy from renewable sources and amending and subsequently repealing Directives 2001/77/EC and 2003/30/EC [2009] OJ L140/16.

a combination thereof.[8] Despite the fact that the RES Directive explicitly allows for financial support, it should be noted that the rules regarding State aid are fully applicable. As becomes clear from the Commission's State aid guidelines for the period 2014–20, financial support should increasingly be awarded on the basis of a competitive process; such as tenders or auctions.[9]

Secondly, EU law provides RES installations priority or guaranteed access to the electricity grids.[10] This gives RES generators certainty in relation to two things. First, that they will be physically connected to the grid, and second, that their renewable energy will be dispatched in priority. This is a clear derogation from the principle of non-discriminatory access to the grids and ensures that 'when dispatching electricity generating installations, transmission system operators shall give priority to generating installations using renewable energy sources in so far as the secure operation of the national electricity system permits'.[11]

2.2. THE SPANISH LEGISLATIVE FRAMEWORK

Spain had enacted a special regime for inter alia solar energy producers, mainly through two Royal Decrees (Nos 661/2007 and 1578/2008). Under this framework (the 'Initial Framework'), RES producers benefitted from a FiT for a 25-year period. In addition, most plants would receive 80% of that tariff after the initial 25-year period. The level of remuneration depended on the plant's installed capacity, among other criteria. In order to benefit from this special regime, RES investors had to register their facilities in a public registry (*Registro administrativo de instalaciones de producción de energía eléctrica*, RAIPRE) within a peremptory deadline. From 2010 onwards, Spain modified the Initial Framework (the 'Modified Framework') on several occasions after it became apparent that the Initial Framework became financially unsustainable. The consequences of the Modified Framework were as follows:

- elimination of the FiT after the start of the plant's 26th year (later, 30th year) of operations;

---

8 H VEDDER, A RØNNE, MM ROGGENKAMP and I IÑIGO DEL GUAYO, 'EU Energy Law' in MM ROGGENKAMP, C REDGWELL, A RØNNE and I IÑIGO DEL GUAYO, *Energy Law in Europe - National, EU and International Regulation*, OUP, Oxford 2016, p 322.

9 Communication from the Commission - Guidelines on State aid for environmental protection and energy 2014–2020 (2014/C 200/01), para 109.

10 Article 16(2), Directive 2009/28/EC of the European Parliament and of the Council of 23 April 2009 on the promotion of the use of energy from renewable sources and amending and subsequently repealing Directives 2001/77/EC and 2003/30/EC [2009] OJ L140/16.

11 Ibid, Article 16(2)(c). Note, this requirement does not apply to renewable gas sources. H VEDDER, A RØNNE, MM ROGGENKAMP and I IÑIGO DEL GUAYO, 'EU Energy Law' in MM ROGGENKAMP, C REDGWELL, A RØNNE and I IÑIGO DEL GUAYO, *Energy Law in Europe - National, EU and International Regulation*, OUP, Oxford 2016, p 327.

- requirement of certain plants to take measures to be able to react to voltage dips;
- capping the amount of equivalent operating hours subject to the special regime (and thus, subject to the tariff); and
- establishing a transmission charge of EUR 0.55/MWh.

Finally, in 2013 and 2014, Spain went one step further by abolishing the Initial Framework for all RES producers.[12] As the arbitral tribunal in *Eiser v Spain* noted, these measures essentially replaced the old support scheme with a completely new one, on the basis of which the remuneration parameters are fundamentally different and to a large extent based on hypothetical assumptions that do not take into account the actual and individual characteristics of the projects.[13] Also, this new regime was applied to existing facilities. For existing investments that deviate from the hypothetical assumptions on which the new remuneration scheme is based, the consequences were very significant.[14] These last drastic steps have resulted in nearly 40 RES investment treaty disputes, which is an unprecedented high number for one State.

2.3. THE ITALIAN LEGISLATIVE FRAMEWORK

In 2005, Italy introduced a number of measures to incentivise investment in the renewable PV electricity sector. The legal framework for these measures is referred to as '*Conto Energia*'.

The principal incentive contemplated by *Conto Energia* takes the form of a FiT; a guaranteed subsidy paid on the basis of the amount of solar electricity fed into the grid. Under *Conto Energia* the amount of the specific guaranteed FiT is determined by the Italian Regulatory Authority for Electricity, Gas and Water on a case by case basis considering a number of specific criteria based on the technical characteristics of the PV power plant. Among the assessment criteria are: whether the installation is ground-fixed, rooftop, integrated or non-integrated, and the nominal capacity of the PV plants.

In addition, the FiT scheme under *Conto Energia* has the following characteristics:

- The relevant FiT level applicable to a specific PV power plant is guaranteed for 20 years from the date of connection of the PV power plant to the national grid;

---

12 These measures include: Royal Decree Law 2/2013, Royal Decree Law 9/2013, Law 24/2013, Royal Decree 413/2014 and Ministerial Order IET/1045/2014.

13 *Eiser Infrastructure Limited and Energía Solar Luxembourg S.à r.l. v Kingdom of Spain*, ICSID Case No. ARB/13/36, Final Award, 4 May 2017, para 148.

14 See section 3.1.3 below.

- FiTs are paid, on a monthly basis, in direct proportion to the amount of energy generated by the PV power plant and fed into the national grid;
- FiTs are to be paid by the *Gestore dei Servizi Energetici* S.p.A. (GSE), which is a State-owned company whose remit consists of promoting and supporting renewable energy sources in Italy; and
- PV energy producers conclude an agreement with the GSE that, among other things, guarantees the relevant FiT level for 20 years.

From 2010 onwards, the incentives set out in the *Conto Energia* scheme have been reduced through several government decrees – in particular, the so-called *Terzo Conto Energia*, the *Quarto Conto Energia* and the *Quinto Conto Energia* – in order to keep up with the falling costs of PV energy. Although these measures had an impact on the PV sector, importantly, they did not affect the level of the FiT.

The situation has changed due to the latest measures contained in an Act approved by the Italian Parliament on 11 August 2014.[15]

Departing from earlier amendments to the FiT scheme, the Act reduces the FiT levels guaranteed to PV power plants already connected to the national grid and that were subject to agreements between PV electricity producers and the GSE. In this sense, the measures contained in the Act are retrospective in nature.

The Act only applies to PV power plants with a nominal capacity exceeding 200 kW. It gives the owners of affected PV power plants three options to be made by 30 November 2014:

- A FiT reduction ranging between 17% and 25%, which applies on a sliding scale depending on the number of years of FiT remaining. Under this sliding scale, PV power plants that had the lowest possible amount of years of FiT remaining (12 years) will see a 25% reduction. At the other end of the spectrum, PV power plants that have 19 or more years of FiT remaining will suffer a reduction of 17% in FiTs. With a view to assuaging PV electricity producers, these cuts are coupled with a four-year extension of the 20-year FiT scheme. However, this extension of time is unlikely to offset the loss arising from the FiT cuts, particularly in relation to the older PV power plants that will suffer the heaviest reductions.
- The Act states that the owners of a PV installation may choose to maintain the 20-year duration of the FiT, but subject to a variable reduction in the

15 See Law 11 August 2014, No 116, published in the *Italian Official Gazette* No. 192/2014 on 20 August 2014 that ratified the decree issued by the Italian Government on an urgent basis on 24 June 2014, the so-called '*Decreto taglia bollette*' (DL No 91, published in the *Italian Official Gazette* No. 144/2014 on 25 June 2014) (the Act).

first period of residual FiT, with an equal increase in the second period. Unfortunately, the Act does not provide any guidance on the operation of the above-mentioned mechanism, which was intended to be implemented by means of a decree to be issued by the Italian Ministry for Economic Development by 1 October 2014. Ultimately, the harm caused by choosing this option would depend on the terms of the implementing decree. What is clear, however, is that this option will have an impact on the cash flows expected by owners of PV plants, which, in turn, will make it more difficult for them to service their debt.

- Maintaining the 20-year duration of the FiT, but suffering a reduction on the applicable FiT determined on the basis of the nominal capacity of the relevant plant.

If a choice is not made by the plant owner within the stated deadline, the third option described above will apply automatically. The reductions apply from 1 January 2015 onwards. In addition, the Act changes the mechanism under which the GSE pays the FiTs to PV electricity producers. From the second quarter of 2014, the GSE will only remunerate the owners of PV power plants – irrespective of their size – with fixed monthly instalments equal to 90% of the PV power plant's estimated annual electricity production, based on GSE's historic records. The balance between the PV power plants' estimated annual electricity production and the actual production in a given calendar year will be paid by GSE by 30 June of the following calendar year. This will have an obvious impact on the cash flow of the owners of the affected PV power plants. This, in turn, may prevent owners of PV plants from complying with relevant loan agreements. The effects of the Act, in particular the retrospective application of reductions in FiTs, have resulted so far in eight investment treaty claims against Italy by aggrieved RES investors.

2.4. INVESTMENT PROTECTION UNDER THE ENERGY CHARTER TREATY (ECT)

The ECT, which was adopted in 1994 and entered into force in 1998, is a multilateral trade and investment agreement with more than 50 Contracting Parties, including the EU and all of its Member States except Italy, which terminated the ECT as of 1 January 2016.[16] The ECT's investment chapter can be

[16] It should be noted that despite the termination of the ECT, Italy remains bound by the ECTs 'sunset-clause' of Article 47(3) ECT. This means Italy continues to be subject to investment treaty claims based on the ECT regarding RES investments for another 20 years, which predate the termination date.

invoked by investors whose investment is 'associated with an economic activity in the energy sector.'[17] As such, it unquestionably covers RES projects.

The ECT's investment chapter contains various standards of investment protection that regulate the relationship between the foreign investor and the host State by prescribing the rule of law. Amongst others, its legal regime provides for non-discrimination, no expropriation without compensation, the obligation of the State to observe commitments entered into with investors and the obligation to provide fair and equitable treatment (FET).[18] Arbitral practice under the ECT firmly establishes that this latter notion includes the protection of legitimate expectations of investors.[19]

In addition to these substantive guarantees, Article 26 ECT contains an investor–State dispute settlement clause which directly allows investors to initiate dispute settlement procedures against the host State. In practice, the preferred avenue of investors to settle investment disputes is through international arbitration, on the basis of either the ICSID Convention, the ICSID Additional Facility Rules, the SCC Arbitration Rules or the UNCITRAL Arbitration Rules.[20] At the time of writing, there were 118 known ECT arbitration cases, making the treaty the most often invoked investment treaty in existence, well ahead of NAFTA.[21]

3. ARBITRAL AWARDS

This section analyses the first publicly available RES awards against Spain and Italy.

---

17 Article 1(6), the Energy Charter Treaty (adopted 17 December 1994, entered into force 16 April 1998).

18 Ibid. Articles 10(1), 10(7) and 13.

19 *Plama Consortium Limited v Republic of Bulgaria*, ICSID Case No. ARB/03/24, Award, 27 August 2008, paras 176 and 219; *Electrabel S.A. v Republic of Hungary*, ICSID Case No. ARB/07/19, Decision on Jurisdiction, Applicable Law and Liability, 30 November 2012, paras 7.74–7.79; *Electrabel SA v The Republic of Hungary*, ICSID Case No. ARB/07/19, Award, 25 November 2015, para 155; *AES Summit Generation Limited and AES-Tisza Erömü Kft v The Republic of Hungary*, ICSID Case No. ARB/07/22, Award, 23 September 2010, paras 9.3.8–9.3.17; *AES Corporation and Tau Power B.V. v Republic of Kazakhstan*, ICSID Case No. ARB/10/16, Award, 1 November 2013, paras 291, 397–412; *Anatolie Stati, Gabriel Stati, Ascom Group SA and Terra Raf Trans Traiding Ltd v Kazakhstan*, SCC Case No. V (116/2010), Award, 19 December 2013, para 941; *Mamidoil Jetoil Greek Petroleum Products Societe S.A. v Republic of Albania*, ICSID Case No. ARB/11/24, Award, 30 March 2015, paras 705–12.

20 Article 26(4), the Energy Charter Treaty (adopted 17 December 1994, entered into force 16 April 1998).

21 For a list of known ECT investment dispute settlement cases, see: http://www.energycharter.org/what-we-do/dispute-settlement/all-investment-dispute-settlement-cases/. Note, not all of these cases concern RES projects.

3.1. THE SPANISH CASES

3.1.1. Charanne v Spain

On 21 January 2016, the first award of the more than 30 RES investment treaty arbitrations against Spain was issued in *Charanne v Spain*.[22] From the outset it should be pointed out that this first arbitration case challenged only the 2010 measures and did not concern the 2013 and 2014 measures, which were significantly more severe for RES investors. Accordingly, the takeaways from this award cannot simply be applied automatically and fully to the other RES disputes. Nonetheless, the analysis of this arbitral tribunal and its conclusions serve as important signposts.

In 2009, the claimants – Charanne B.V., a Dutch company, and Construction Investments S.à.r.l., a Luxembourgish company – acquired shares in Grupo T-Solar Global, S.A. (T-Solar), which indirectly owned 34 solar plants. After mergers and share transfers over the course of 2011 and 2012, the claimants held an interest in T-Solar through two further companies (jointly, Isolux). The *Isolux* case is discussed separately in section 3.1.2 below.

The claimants claimed 'less than 10 million euros' for violations of the ECT.[23] The EC filed an *amicus curiae* brief.[24] The Stockholm Chamber of Commerce (SCC) Arbitration Institute administered the arbitration under its 2010 Arbitration Rules, with Madrid as the seat of the arbitration. The tribunal comprised Alexis Mourre (President), Guido Santiago Tawil (claimant's appointment) and Claus von Wobeser (respondent's appointment). Arbitrator Tawil appended a partial dissenting opinion[25] to the Final Award.[26]

3.1.1.1. The ECT Remains Available for Intra-EU Disputes

At the jurisdictional level, one of the main arguments brought forward by Spain is that – for various reasons – European investors would be prohibited from relying on the ECT to bring claims against EU Member States. This argument has also been used by other EU Member States which have been confronted with ECT claims – strongly supported by the EC.

---

22 *Charanne and Construction Investments v Spain*, SCC Case No. V 062/2012, Final Award, 21 January 2016.

23 Ibid, para 563.

24 An *amicus curiae* brief is submitted by a party, in this case the EC, that has an interest in the outcome of the proceedings, with the aim of influencing the decision of the tribunal. An investment tribunal usually has a certain margin of discretion when deciding whether or not to accept such submissions.

25 *Charanne and Construction Investments v Spain*, SCC Case No. V 062/2012, Dissenting Opinion of Prof Dr Guido Santiago Tawil, 21 December 2015.

26 *Charanne and Construction Investments v Spain*, SCC Case No. V 062/2012, Final Award, 21 January 2016.

More specifically, Spain argued that Article 344 of the Treaty on the Functioning of the EU (TFEU) prevented European investors from bringing a claim against an EU Member State. The arbitral tribunal rejected this argument. For the tribunal, Article 344 TFEU '[l]iterally' refers to inter-State disputes, rather than to disputes between EU Member States and private persons.[27] The numerous domestic court disputes that concern the interpretation of EU legislation belie Spain's thesis that only EU institutions should have jurisdiction over disputes concerning EU law.[28] For the tribunal, EU Member States could agree to arbitrate disputes that 'may involve' EU law issues.[29] Moreover, relying on the *EcoSwiss* case, the tribunal considered it 'universally accepted' that arbitral tribunals have both the ability and the duty to apply EU law.[30] Citing the *Electrabel v Hungary* award, the tribunal construed Article 344 TFEU as a guarantee that the Court of Justice of the EU has the final say on EU law in order to ensure its uniform interpretation. Also, citing *Electrabel* again, the tribunal underscored that the EU accepted the possibility of investor-State arbitration under Article 26 ECT when it became a party to that treaty, which does not admit reservations.[31]

In short, all the arguments claiming that EU law somehow prohibits European investors from using the ECT to bring claims against EU Member States were fully rejected. This is an important conclusion as the arbitral tribunal explicitly accepted that the ECT is available for intra-EU disputes.

3.1.1.2. Broad Definition of 'Investor' is Maintained

Spain also argued that the claimants were not investors under Article 1(7) ECT. For Spain, the claimants were 'empty shells' ultimately controlled by two Spanish nationals.[32] Access by these individuals to the tribunal would also violate the Spanish Constitution, Spain argued, as most Spanish citizens would not enjoy such access.

The arbitral tribunal dismissed this objection. The tribunal assessed its jurisdiction in light of the ECT, rather than Spain's domestic laws. Moreover, the tribunal held that Article 1(7)(a)(ii) ECT simply requires that a company be

27 Ibid, para 441.

28 See for a discussion of the Spanish jurisprudence: P HOLTROP, 'A Turn on Spanish Jurisprudence on Retroactivity?' Blogpost, 22 February 2011, available at: http://holtropslp.com/holtropblog/index.php?option=com_content&view=article&id=106:a-turn-in-spanish-jurisprudence&catid=35:articles&Itemid=83.

29 *Charanne and Construction Investments v Spain*, SCC Case No. V 062/2012, Final Award, 21 January 2016, para 443.

30 Ibid.

31 Article 46, the Energy Charter Treaty (adopted 17 December 1994, entered into force 16 April 1998).

32 *Charanne and Construction Investments v Spain*, SCC Case No. V 062/2012, Final Award, 21 January 2016, para 412.

'organised in accordance with the law applicable' in a Contracting Party to be recognised as an investor of that party.[33] The claimants met this test.

More importantly, the tribunal refused to analyse the nationality of ECT investors through 'economic' criteria as suggested by Spain. The tribunal found it significant that the benefits of the ECT could only be denied to companies controlled by nationals of ECT parties (or 'third State' nationals) under Article 17 ECT. The tribunal stated that Spain's argument would also deny benefits to companies controlled by host State nationals, a possibility it said had been rejected by the drafters of the ECT. In appropriate circumstances, the tribunal would have considered (but Spain did not adduce) arguments on lifting of the corporate veil, such as fraudulent corporate structures or in cases of 'fraud to jurisdiction' (eg a transfer of the assets that comprise the investment after a dispute has arisen). Accordingly, the arbitral tribunal applied the broad definition of 'investor' by simply analysing whether or not the claimants had fulfilled the formal condition of being organised in accordance with the applicable law in a Contracting Party of the ECT.

Again, this is an important conclusion for investors who have structured their investments in such a way to obtain maximum investment protection through the ECT.

3.1.1.3. No Violation of the ECT (Articles 13 and 10(1))

At the merits level, the claimants argued that the Spanish measures constituted an 'indirect expropriation' and thus violated Article 13 ECT. They also claimed that the measures were in violation of Article 10 ECT, in particular the FET standard.[34]

---

33 Ibid, para 116.

34 Article 10 ECT defines the fair and equitable treatment standard (FET) standard as:

> 'Each Contracting Party shall, in accordance with the provisions of this Treaty, encourage and create stable, equitable, favourable and transparent conditions for Investors of other Contracting Parties to make Investments in its Area. Such conditions shall include a commitment to accord at all times to Investments of Investors of other Contracting Parties fair and equitable treatment. Such Investments shall also enjoy the most constant protection and security and no Contracting Party shall in any way impair by unreasonable or discriminatory measures their management, maintenance, use, enjoyment or disposal. In no case shall such Investments be accorded treatment less favourable than that required by international law, including treaty obligations. Each Contracting Party shall observe any obligations it has entered into with an Investor or an Investment of an Investor of any other Contracting Party.' See for a detailed analysis: CH SCHREUER, 'Fair and Equitable Treatment (FET): Interaction with other Standards' in G. COOP and C. RIBEIRO, *Investment Protection and the Energy Charter Treaty*, JurisNet, Huntington 2008, pp 63–155.

(i) Indirect Expropriation (Article 13 ECT)

The claimants argued that the Modified Framework constituted indirect expropriation, as it deprived them of a 'substantial value' of their indirect investment in T-Solar (Article 1(6)(b) ECT). They also argued that the Modified Framework affected their future cash flows and, therefore, their returns, a form of investment according to Article 1(6)(e) ECT.

The arbitral tribunal disagreed. According to the tribunal, a measure constitutes indirect expropriation under international law if it 'substantially affect[s]' the investor's property rights.[35] This can occur when the State effectively takes all or part of the investment, or when the taking causes a loss of such a magnitude that it 'destroys [the] value' of the investment.[36] The parties agreed that Spain had not affected the claimants' shareholder rights and that T-Solar was still in operation, turning a profit and in possession of its assets. Therefore, the claimants actually complained of a reduction in the profitability of T-Solar and, consequently, of the value of their shares. However, the arbitral tribunal concluded that this reduction does not justify an indirect expropriation claim in itself.

(ii) Fair and Equitable Treatment (Article 10(1) ECT)

First, claimants argued the Modified Framework frustrated their legitimate expectations that the Initial Framework would remain stable and that they would receive the FiTs. They argued that Spain enticed the claimants' investments through the Initial Framework and through Government materials that promised up to 15% profitability. They expected to receive FiTs throughout the lifecycle of the plants, which they estimated at 35–50 years (Spain's estimate was 25–30 years). For the claimants, registration with RAIPRE consolidated their right to receive the FiTs.

The arbitral tribunal dismissed this part of the claim. The tribunal accepted that legitimate expectations could be derived both from specific commitments and from the host State's legal system. However, it rejected the notion that both types of expectations were identical. An investor cannot expect that an existing regulatory framework will remain unchanged absent a specific commitment from the host State.[37] Similarly, regulations aimed at a limited number of investors are as 'general' as any statute or regulation and do not create specific commitments vis-à-vis each investor.[38] Accepting the opposite proposition would excessively limit States' ability to regulate their economies.

---

35 *Charanne and Construction Investments v Spain*, SCC Case No. V 062/2012, Final Award, 21 January 2016, para 461.

36 Ibid, para 466.

37 Ibid, para 499.

38 Ibid, para 493.

Furthermore, the tribunal was not persuaded that the claimants had any legitimate expectations that the Initial Framework would not be modified (eg a stabilisation clause or a statement addressed to investors). These expectations should be analysed objectively, rather than on the basis of the investors' subjective beliefs at the time of the investment. The expectations should also be reasonable in light of any representations by the host State. Additionally, in order to frustrate legitimate expectations, the regulatory changes should not have been 'reasonably foreseeable at the time of the investment'.[39] As part of their due diligence, investors in a 'highly regulated sector such as energy' must 'exhaustive[ly]' analyse the applicable legal framework before they make their investment.[40]

In this regard, the tribunal found that:

- Spanish law and jurisprudence that predated the investment allowed Spain to modify its solar energy regulations;
- Spanish Government documents that enticed solar energy investments were not 'sufficiently specific' to create the expectation claimed; and
- RAIPRE registration was an administrative requirement before being able to sell energy, rather than a guarantee to a specific return.

Secondly, the claimants argued that the Modified Framework applied retroactively and thus breached their acquired rights to operate under the Initial Framework. They drew a parallel with Argentina's liability for the 'pesification' of obligations denominated in foreign currencies, notably in *CMS v Argentina*.

The arbitral tribunal dismissed this part of the claim, as it had found no legitimate expectations to a stabilisation of the regulatory framework. Moreover, and unlike the case before it, *CMS v Argentina* involved specific, contractual commitments.[41]

In short, the arbitral tribunal fully rejected the two main complaints of the claimants. Essentially, the tribunal concluded that the deprivation of their investments caused by the Spanish measures was not sufficiently serious enough as to constitute an 'indirect expropriation'. Besides, the majority of the arbitral tribunal concluded that the claimants did not have any legitimate expectations that the regulatory framework would remain stable – even the application of those measures retroactively, ie to existing installations, did not amount to a violation of the FET-standard. However, it should be noted that the claimants' appointed arbitrator Tawil did not agree with the majority of the tribunal.

39 Ibid, para 505.
40 Ibid, para 507.
41 Ibid, para 545.

3.1.2. Isolux v Spain

The *Isolux v Spain*[42] case concerned the same investments as the *Charanne v Spain* case, but whereas *Charanne* challenged the 2010 measures, the *Isolux* case concerned the measures adopted between 2012 and 2014. Isolux B.V. became an investor in the Spanish solar sector only in 2012, after its Spanish and Canadian parents decided to restructure their investments in Spain through the Netherlands.[43] This proved to be a stumbling block for Isolux's claim.

According to the tribunal, which rendered its award in July 2016, the Spanish regulatory framework governing RES had already been modified 'repeatedly' when Isolux decided to invest in 2012.[44] Therefore, the claimant could foresee and should have anticipated that future amendments to the legal framework were likely.[45] As a consequence, 'no reasonable investor could have the expectation that this framework would not be modified in the future and would remain unchanged.'[46] In the end, the majority of the tribunal would dismiss all of Isolux's claims while claimants' appointee Guido Tawil (the same as in the *Charanne* case) disagreed with the tribunal's finding on the FET standard, and instead held that the claimants had a legitimate expectation that the FiT would remain in force unchanged.[47]

3.1.3. Eiser v Spain

In the *Eiser* case, which was decided in May 2017, the claimants are Eiser Infrastructure Limited, a private limited company incorporated under the laws of the United Kingdom, and Energia Solar Luxembourg S.à.r.I., a private limited liability company incorporated under the laws of Luxembourg.

From 2007 onwards, the claimants had invested in concentrated solar power (CSP) plants, which became operational in 2012. Since the historical finance and operational costs of Eiser's investments deviated from the 'hypothetical efficient plant' standard that was employed by the Spanish authorities, revenue was reduced by 66% in comparison to the previous regime, which reduced the value of the investment to €4 million while Eiser had invested almost €130 million.

---

42 *Isolux Netherlands, BV v Kingdom of Spain*, SCC Case No. V 2013/153, Award, 17 July 2016, paras 348–54; *Charanne and Construction Investments v Spain*, SCC Case No. V 062/2012, Final Award, 21 January 2016, para 395.

43 *Isolux Netherlands, BV v Kingdom of Spain*, SCC Case No. V 2013/153, Award, 17 July 2016, para 281.

44 Ibid, paras 781–88.

45 Ibid.

46 Ibid, para 787.

47 See *Isolux Netherlands, BV v Kingdom of Spain*, SCC Case No. V 2013/153, Dissenting Opinion of Arbitrator Tawil, 6 July 2016.

In other words, the changes to the regulatory framework adopted by Spain dramatically reduced the revenues which Eiser had projected on the basis of the previous regulatory regime. Consequently, Eiser argued that Spain breached the ECT.

At the jurisdictional level, the arbitral tribunal – as the *Charanne* tribunal – rejected the EU law arguments raised by Spain and the EC.[48]

At the merits level, the starting point for the Eiser tribunal was clearly different compared to the *Charanne* case, which involved the 2010 Spanish measures complained that had a far less significant impact on the investments than he subsequent measures complained by Eiser.

In substance, the arbitral tribunal thus found that the Spanish measures retroactively prescribed design standards in violation of the FET standard, although the tribunal started its analysis by saying that '[a]bsent explicit undertakings directly extended to investors and guaranteeing that States will not change their laws or regulations, investment treaties do not eliminate States' right to modify their regulatory regimes to meet evolving circumstances and public needs.'[49] However, the tribunal considered that the regulatory changes in this case exceeded the boundaries of fairness and equitableness. In particular, the 'obligation to accord fair and equitable treatment means that regulatory regimes cannot be radically altered as applied to existing investments in ways that deprive investors who invested in reliance on those regimes of their investment's value.'[50]

On the basis of the discounted cash flow method, the arbitral tribunal awarded Eiser damage at €128 million. Hence, *Eiser* is the first case of the more than 30 investment treaty claims currently pending, which Spain has lost. Meanwhile, Spain has successfully applied to vacate the recognition of the ICSID award before a US court, where the investors sought enforcement of the award.[51] In addition, Spain has also requested the annulment of the ICSID award. An ad hoc Annulment Committee has been established at the end of October 2017. Therefore, it remains to be seen whether the *Eiser* award will stand or be annulled.[52] Although most cases against Spain remain pending,[53] the *Eiser* award

---

48 *Eiser Infrastructure Limited and Energía Solar Luxembourg S.à r.l. v Kingdom of Spain*, ICSID Case No. ARB/13/36, Final Award, 4 May 2017, paras 204 ff.

49 Ibid, para 362.

50 Ibid, para 382.

51 *Eiser Infrastructure Limited et al v Kindgom of Spain*, US District Court Southern District of New York, No 17 CV 3808 (LAK), 28 June 2017. See L YONG, 'Spain reverses confirmation of solar award in New York', GAR 17 November 2017, available at: http://globalarbitrationreview.com/article/1150664/spain-reverses-confirmation-of-solar-award-in-new-york.

52 See the ICSID website regarding the *Eiser* case, available at: https://icsid.worldbank.org/en/Pages/cases/casedetail.aspx?CaseNo=ARB/13/36.

53 It should be noted that the arbitral tribunal in the *RREEF v Spain* case has accepted jurisdiction and will decide the case on the merits.

clearly indicates that the more recent and harsher Spanish measures to reduce the financial support by completely altering the remuneration parameters are more likely to breach the ECT obligations of Spain.

3.1.4. Novenergia v Spain

On 15 February 2018, an award was rendered in the case *Novenergia v Spain*. Novenergia, a Luxembourgish company, had invested in various Spanish PV projects from 2007 onwards, a date comparable to the date of investment in the *Eiser* case.[54] The claimants argued that the Spanish measures adopted between 2010 and 2014 violated various standards of treatment contained in Articles 10(1) and 13 ECT. The most important claim in this case was that the Spanish measures frustrated the legitimate expectations of the investors in violation of the FET standard.

As a preliminary remark, it is worth pointing out that the effects of the Spanish measures adopted in 2013 and 2014 on the investments of Novenergia were less harmful than they were on Eiser's investment. In the case of Novenergia, its investment 'showed lower revenues on all of the PV Plants, the majority of which showed a decrease between 24 and 32% between 2013 and 2016.'[55] In fact, Novenergia was still making a profit of approximately 5% post-tax, a number below the target rate of return of the Spanish legislation, which was set at 7.398%.[56]

With regards to jurisdiction, the tribunal rejected the intra-EU objection of Spain although it did accept that it did not have jurisdiction over the claim concerning taxation measures, due to the tax carve out in Article 21 ECT.

On the merits, the tribunal would establish a violation of the FET standard. The *Novenergia* award is noteworthy because it deviates from earlier ECT (RES) awards concerning legitimate expectations claims in two respects.

First of all, an important issue in any claim concerning legitimate expectations is the source of the expectation. In the Spanish RES cases investors like Charanne, Eiser and Novenergia invested in Spain on the basis of RD 661/2007. The question that arises is: can a general regulatory framework, such as RD 661/2007, give rise to legitimate expectations that are protected under the ECT? In the *Charanne* and *Eiser* cases, the tribunals were rather unequivocal: in the absence of a specific commitment by the State to the contrary, a general legal framework cannot give rise to legitimate expectations that are protected under the ECT.[57]

54 *Novenergia II – Energy & Environment (SCA) (Grand Duchy of Luxembourg), SICAR v The Kingdom of Spain*, SCC Arbitration (2015/063), Final Arbitral Award, 15 February 2018, para 539.

55 Ibid, paras 687 and 695.

56 Ibid, paras 824 and 827.

57 *Charanne and Construction Investments v Spain*, SCC Case No. V 062/2012, Final Award, 21 January 2016, para 499. *Eiser Infrastructure Limited and Energía Solar Luxembourg S.à r.l. v Kingdom of Spain*, ICSID Case No. ARB/13/36, Final Award, 4 May 2017, para 362.

However, the *Novenergia* tribunal accepted that RD 661/2007 and several other documents produced by the Spanish authorities concerning its RES policy, none of which were specifically addressed to Novenergia, were a sufficient source to protect Novenergia's expectations.[58] This is a surprising conclusion, especially given the fact that all of these documents were also discussed in the *Charanne* case, where the tribunal held that it 'does not believe that, by themselves, these documents could have generated a legitimate expectation as to the fact that the tariff anticipated at the time of the investment would not be modified.'[59] The *Novenergia* tribunal would acknowledge in its analysis of the umbrella clause claim that 'in the instant case the Claimant made no contract with the Kingdom of Spain and the rights that the Claimant invokes are founded in general regulatory acts enacted by the Kingdom of Spain for a generality of investors in the field of renewable energy. They cannot therefore be equated with … *ad personam* commitments …'.[60] Thus, while the tribunal was aware of the fact that there were no specific commitments made by Spain promising stability to the investors, it did accept general legislation and documents as an appropriate source of a legitimate expectation.

Allowing investors to base a claim of legitimate expectations on a general legal framework in force at the time the investment was made 'greatly expands the potential scope of the doctrine' and disregards recent developments in investment arbitration which generally rejects these claims as evidenced, not only by the other RES ECT awards, but essentially all ECT cases concerning legitimate expectations.[61] In the ECT *AES v Kazakhstan* case, the tribunal held that 'it would require the very clearest of commitments on the part of the State to refrain from adjusting that regulatory framework in some specified manner

58 *Novenergia II - Energy & Environment (SCA) (Grand Duchy of Luxembourg), SICAR v The Kingdom of Spain*, SCC Arbitration (2015/063), Final Arbitral Award, 15 February 2018, paras 667–69 and 681.

59 *Charanne and Construction Investments v Spain*, SCC Case No. V 062/2012, Final Award, 21 January 2016, para 496.

60 *Novenergia II - Energy & Environment (SCA) (Grand Duchy of Luxembourg), SICAR v The Kingdom of Spain*, SCC Arbitration (2015/063), Final Arbitral Award, 15 February 2018, para 715.

61 J BONNITCHA, *Substantive Protection Under Investment Treaties - A Legal and Economic Analysis*, CUP, Cambridge 2014, p 184; *Plama Consortium Limited v Republic of Bulgaria*, ICSID Case No. ARB/03/24, Award, 27 August 2008, para 176; *Electrabel S.A. v Republic of Hungary*, ICSID Case No. ARB/07/19, Decision on Jurisdiction, Applicable Law and Liability, 30 November 2012, paras 7.76–7.78; *Electrabel S.A. v Republic of Hungary*, ICSID Case No. ARB/07/19, Award, 25 November 2015, para 155; *Mohammad Ammar Al-Bahloul v The Republic of Tajikistan*, SCC Case No. V (064/2008), Partial Award on Jurisdiction and Liability, 2 September 2009, paras 200–02; *AES Summit Generation Limited and AES-Tisza Erömü Kft v The Republic of Hungary*, ICSID Case No. ARB/07/22, Award, 23 September 2010, paras 9.3.17–9.3.18; *AES Corporation and Tau Power B.V. v Republic of Kazakhstan*, ICSID Case No. ARB/10/16, Award, 1 November 2013, paras 289–91.

to give rise to any expectation that an investment would be insulated from the effects of normal legal and regulatory evolution.'[62]

A second notable finding of the *Novenergia* tribunal concerns the standard of review applied to the Spanish measures adopted in 2013 and 2014. In the *Eiser* case, the tribunal had held that the FET standard was violated because the radical changes introduced in these years had destroyed the value of the investment.[63] In *Novenergia* it was held:

> The Tribunal disagrees with the approach adopted by the arbitral tribunal in *Eiser*, [...] In the Tribunal's view, the assessment of whether the FET standard has been breached is a balancing exercise, where the state's regulatory interests are weighed against the investors' legitimate expectations and reliance. It is not simply sufficient to look at the economic effect that the challenged measures have had. Destruction of the value of the investment is clearly determinative in the assessment of whether a state has breached Article 13 of the ECT, but it is but one of several factors to consider when determining whether a state has breached Article 10(1) of the ECT. Nevertheless, in the Tribunal's opinion, the economic effect on a claimant's investment is an important factor in the balancing exercise pursuant to Article 10(1) as well, as it can go towards showing a change in the essential characteristics of the legal regime relied upon by investors in making long-term investments.[64]

Instead, the *Novenergia* tribunal held that the 2013 and 2014 measures were so 'radical and unexpected' that they 'fell outside the acceptable range of legislative and regulatory behaviour' and 'entirely transform[ed] and alter[ed] the legal and business environment under which the investment was decided and made'.[65] Consequently, since the measures had a 'significant damaging economic effect' on the investment, the tribunal considered the measures to be 'drastic and unexpected in a manner that is contrary' to Spain's obligation to provide FET to investors.[66] By accepting that 'significant' economic damage suffices to establish a breach of the FET standard, contrary to the complete destruction of value as suggested by *Eiser*, the threshold of liability seems to be lower in the standard of review as applied by the *Novenergia* tribunal. What most likely played a role in this case is the retroactive effects of the various measures that were introduced, as evidenced by the explicit references to this by the tribunal.[67]

---

62 *AES Corporation and Tau Power B.V. v Republic of Kazakhstan*, ICSID Case No. ARB/10/16, Award, 1 November 2013, para 289.

63 *Eiser Infrastructure Limited and Energía Solar Luxembourg S.à r.l. v Kingdom of Spain*, ICSID Case No. ARB/13/36, Final Award, 4 May 2017, para 382.

64 *Novenergia II – Energy & Environment (SCA) (Grand Duchy of Luxembourg), SICAR v The Kingdom of Spain*, SCC Arbitration (2015/063), Final Arbitral Award, 15 February 2018, para 694.

65 Ibid, para 695.

66 Ibid.

67 Ibid, paras 121, 143 and 697.

As in *Eiser*, damages in the *Novenergia* case were quantified on the basis of the discounted cash flow method: €53.3 million. The tribunal considered 'that the DCF-method is considered particularly suitable for valuating income-streams that are regulated', such as FiTs.[68]

3.2. THE ITALIAN CASES

3.2.1. Blusun v Italy

The *Blusun v Italy* case was decided in late 2016 and concerned, besides the general regulatory changes identified in section 2.3 above, measures that specifically affected Blusun's investment without necessarily affecting all RES investors in Italy.[69] For example, the investor was confronted with a municipal stop-work order during construction because the local prosecutor was concerned that the project was not properly permitted.[70] The project also faced regulatory uncertainty because the Italian Government sought to challenge the constitutionality of certain elements of a local law on the basis of which Blusun's project was permitted.[71]

The investors put forward various claims, including a lack of legal stability in violation of Article 10(1) first sentence ECT and a violation of their legitimate expectations as protected under the FET standard of Article 10(1) second sentence ECT.[72]

Before addressing the claims, the tribunal made some general remarks about the proper interpretation of Article 10(1) ECT. Since the *Charanne v Spain* award was the only publicly available RES ECT award when the *Blusun* case was decided, the tribunal devoted special attention to its findings. It is notable that the *Blusun* tribunal explicitly criticised some aspects of the *Charanne* award.

In *Charanne*, the tribunal held that a general support scheme can only give rise to protected legitimate expectations when a specific commitment – which guarantees that the support scheme will not be altered – from the State towards the investor has been made.[73] Nevertheless, the *Charanne* tribunal accepted that the ECT does impose some constraints on the State when it is making regulatory changes: '[A]n investor has a legitimate expectation that, when modifying the

68 Ibid, para 820.

69 *Blusun S.A., Jean-Pierre Lecorcier and Michael Stein v Italian Republic*, ICSID Case No. ARB/14/3, Final Award, 27 December 2016, paras 91–124.

70 Ibid, paras 116–19.

71 Ibid, paras 91–95.

72 Ibid, paras 159–70.

73 *Charanne and Construction Investments v Spain*, SCC Case No. V 062/2012, Final Award, 21 January 2016, para 499.

existing regulation based on which the investment was made, the State will not act unreasonably, disproportionately or contrary to the public interest.'[74]

The *Blusun* tribunal disagreed with the standard of review as proposed by the *Charanne* tribunal:

> Of the three criteria suggested in *Charanne*, 'public interest' is largely indeterminate and is, anyway, a judgement entrusted to the authorities of the host state. Except perhaps in very clear cases, it is not for an investment tribunal to decide, contrary to the considered view of those authorities, the content of the public interest of their state, nor to weigh against it the largely incommensurable public interest of the capital- exporting state. The criterion of 'unreasonableness' can be criticized on similar grounds, as an open-ended mandate to second-guess the host state's policies. By contrast, disproportionality carries in-built limitations and is more determinate. It is a criterion which administrative law courts, and human rights courts, have become accustomed to apply to governmental action.[75]

Subsequently, the tribunal made some general observations on Article 10(1) ECT. The following observation is of particular relevance in RES cases where measures that reduce financial support are at the heart of the dispute:

> In the absence of a specific commitment, the state has no obligation to grant subsidies such as feed-in tariffs, or to maintain them unchanged once granted. But if they are lawfully granted, and if it becomes necessary to modify them, this should be done in a manner which is not disproportionate to the aim of the legislative amendment, and should have due regard to the reasonable reliance interests of recipients who may have committed substantial resources on the basis of the earlier regime.[76]

Thus, the *Blusun* tribunal proposes a proportionality test for cases where FiTs are reduced to analyse whether the international obligations of the State under the ECT have been violated.

Eventually, the tribunal would dismiss all claims. The legal stability claim was rejected because the Italian measures did not completely dismantle the legal framework that was constructed to attract investors.[77] Although the measures did make 'substantial changes to the regime of incentives', 'they did not abolish incentives' for which operators had already qualified.[78] The legitimate expectations claim was rejected on the basis that the *Terzo Conto Energia* of Italy did not constitute a 'special commitment to the Claimants with respect to the extension and operation of FiTs, nor did it specifically undertake that

---

74 Ibid, para 514.

75 *Blusun S.A., Jean-Pierre Lecorcier and Michael Stein v Italian Republic*, ICSID Case No. ARB/14/3, Final Award, 27 December 2016, para 318.

76 Ibid, para 319.

77 Ibid, paras 363–64.

78 Ibid, para 364.

relevant Italian laws would remain unchanged.'[79] Instead, the tribunal identified many reasons why the project failed, many of which would fall squarely within the commercial risk that any investor faces: such as a decision to purchase land at above market prices, a failure to obtain financing and the decision to make creative use of a permitting process.[80]

The final word has not been said in this case since Blusun has filed an application for annulment and an ad hoc Annulment Committee has been established by ICSID.[81] Hence, it remains to be seen whether the Blusun award will stand or not. In the meantime, the project vehicle in which Blusun invested has gone bankrupt.

3.2.2. Eskosol v Italy

Eskosol was an RES project developer. It was established in Italy in 2009 by a Belgian company, Blusun (the same claimant of the case discussed above), and four Italian nationals. Following some changes in the company structure and legal nature, Blusun remained the owner of 80% of Eskosol's shares. The company had been constituted in Italy to carry out the planning, development and building of solar PV power plants and to connect them to the national grid. When the Eskosol's project was launched, the above described FiT system was already in place. Eskosol claimed that through the subsequently adopted measures, the FiT was reduced to a point where the project became economically unviable, which made Eskosol unable to pay its debt. Eskosol claimed that it led to the company being placed under bankruptcy receivership. Pursuant to Italian law, the Italian bankruptcy receiver is the one who has the power to institute proceedings on behalf of Eskosol.

After Eskosol's request for arbitration was registered, Italy filed an application to dismiss Eskosol's claim pursuant to Rule 41(5) of the ICSID Arbitration Rules according to which 'a party [to a dispute] may … file an objection that a claim is manifestly without legal merit'. The arbitral tribunal, however, denied Italy's request in a decision of 20 March 2017.[82]

On 12 June 2017, the arbitral tribunal ruled on a second application by Italy requesting security for costs pursuant to Rule 39(1) of the ICSID Arbitration Rules. Rule 39(1) provides that 'a party [to a dispute] may request that provisional

---

79 Ibid, para 374.

80 Ibid, para 376.

81 On the basis of Article 52 of the ICSID Convention either party to the dispute may request the annulment of the award on one or more of the grounds contained in that provision, which are primarily procedural in nature. The ICSID Annulment procedure is not an appeal mechanism. See the ICSID website on the *Blusun* case, available at: https://icsid.worldbank.org/en/Pages/cases/casedetail.aspx?CaseNo=ARB/14/3.

82 *Eskosol S.p.A. in liquidazione v Italian Republic*, ICSID Case No. ARB/15/50, Decision on Respondent's Application Under Rule 41(5), 20 March 2017.

measures for the preservation of its rights be recommended by the Tribunal'. In its application, Italy argued that there was a 'material risk' that, in the scenario that Eskosol's overall claim and action were denied, the company would not be in a position to comply with a costs award. Italy's application was further substantiated by the fact that Eskosol had recently been declared bankrupt.

In its decision of 12 June 2017, the arbitral tribunal interestingly found, as a threshold matter, that '[r]equests for measures regarding security for costs are … not ipso facto beyond the scope of a tribunal's powers' and that 'nothing in the [ICSID Convention or the Arbitration Rules], addressing an ICSID tribunal's authority to recommend provisional measures, suggests that this authority is limited only to certain types of measures, or alternatively stated, excludes certain types of measures'.[83] In the case at hand, although the tribunal accepted that Eskosol's bankruptcy made it unlikely that the company would be in a position to pay an eventual costs award directly from its own funds, the arbitral tribunal ruled that Italy had not demonstrated that a measure of security for costs was either necessary or urgent. The tribunal was also satisfied by the fact that Eskosol had contracted an insurance agreement with coverage of up to €1 million which rendered the risk of non-payment of costs very low. The tribunal ultimately denied Italy's application for security for costs. The case remains currently pending as to its merits.

Due to the close relationship, the tribunal refers repeatedly to the obvious relevance that the *Blusun* award has for the *Eskosol* case. Indeed, the tribunal points out that Italy is free to argue, later in the case, that the conclusions reached by the *Blusun* tribunal are persuasive and should be followed in the *Eskosol* case. To this end, and should Italy decide to take this course, the Eskosol tribunal ordered the production of the *Blusun* award in full. On this point, two considerations are called for. First, as noted, since the *Blusun* case concerned various measures, including (but not limited to) those complained of in the *Eskosol* case, the findings of the *Blusun* tribunal are certainly relevant to guide the *Eskosol* tribunal. Second, Italy succeeded in raising the important question of legal consistency and certainty in international investment arbitration. Obviously, the danger of two arbitral tribunals issuing contradicting decisions is something that should be avoided.

Thus, the *Eskosol* tribunal will be confronted with issues of systemic importance on the consistency of international investment arbitration.[84]

---

83 *Eskosol S.p.A. in liquidazione v Italian Republic*, ICSID Case No. ARB/15/50, Procedural Order No. 3, 12 June 2017, para 31.

84 G GAGLIANI, 'A first look at *Eskosol v Italy*: Has either party gained the upper hand?' Kluwer Arbitration Blog, 13 June 2017, available at: http://arbitrationblog.kluwerarbitration.com/2017/06/13/first-look-eskosol-s-p-liquidazione-v-italian-republic-either-party-gained-upper-hand/.

3.3. INTERIM CONCLUSION

Although Spain and Italy were initially rather successful in fending off investors' claims, the tide may slowly be turning in favour of the investors.[85] Especially harmful measures that are applied retroactively seem to be reviewed with suspicion. Cases like *Eiser* and *Novenergia* set interesting examples for investors. Indeed, this line of jurisprudence has been confirmed in the two most recent awards, *Masdar*[86] and *Antin*,[87] in which Spain was again found to have breached the ECT by adopting the 2013 and 2014 changes of the FiT support scheme. Spain was ordered to pay €64.5 million and €112 million compensation respectively to the investors. Nevertheless, since investment arbitration is always a fact-specific exercise, one has to be cautious in jumping to conclusions; issues such as the date of the investment and the effects of a measure on the economic viability of an investment may very well differ from case to case.

The *Eiser* and *Novenergia* cases are also of interest because of the quantification of damages. Both tribunals confirm that in cases where FiTs were reduced, the discounted cash flow method is an appropriate manner to quantify damages as the determination of the future income flow requires relatively little speculation. Although not uncommon in investment treaty arbitration, adopting an income-based approach to the quantification of damages deviates from the 'decided preference for asset based methods' as applied by many international courts and tribunals, not being investment tribunals.[88]

---

85 This also holds true for the Czech Republic. Recently, the Czech Republic was successful in a RES investment treaty dispute that was based on the Germany–Czech Republic BIT. This was the first case of seven RES against the Czech Republic. See: *Mr. Jürgen Wirtgen, Mr. Stefan Wirtgen, Mrs. Gisela Wirtgen, JSW Solar (zwei) GmbH & Co. KG v the Czech Republic*, PCA Case No. 2014-03, Final Award, 11 October 2017. However, in January 2018 it was reported that the Czech Republic had also lost a comparable dispute on the merits. See: LE PETERSON, 'Heiskanen, Born and Thomas see some investment treaty breach in Czech solar case, but debate over remedies is held over for separate phase' (IAReporter, 2018), available at: http://tinyurl.com/y79xtkwm>.

86 *Masdar Solar & Wind Cooperatief U.A. v Kingdom of Spain*, ICSID Case No. ARB/14/1, Award, 16 May 2018. Note: the *Masdar* and *Antin* cases were concluded after submission of this chapter.

87 *Antin Infrastructure Services Luxembourg S.à.r.l. and Antin Energia Termosolar B.V. v Kingdom of Spain*, ICSID Case No. ARB/13/31, Award, 15 June 2018. 'Spain suffers fourth solar loss', GAR (19 June 2018), available at: https://globalarbitrationreview.com/article/1170705/spain-suffers-fourth-solar-loss. LE PETERSON, 'Spain suffers another nine figure loss, this time in Zuleta-chaired Energy Charter Treaty arbitration', IAReporter (19 June 2018), available at: https://www.iareporter.com/articles/spain-suffers-another-nine-figure-loss-this-time-at-hands-of-zuleta-chaired-energy-charter-treaty-tribunal/.

88 See Article 36 para 26, Draft articles on Responsibility of States for Internationally Wrongful Acts with commentaries, ILC 2001, p 104.

4. UPCOMING EU REFORMS IN THE ENERGY MARKETS AND EFFECTS ON INVESTMENTS

The Clean Energy for All Europeans package or 'Winter Package', was put forward by the EC in November 2016. It consists of multiple proposals for review of existing EU energy legislation totalling more than 500 pages.[89]

One of the maxims defended by the EC was that the EU should lead the energy transition rather than just adapt to it. Therefore, the package has three main goals: 'putting energy efficiency first', 'achieving global leadership in renewable energies' and 'providing a fair deal for consumers'.[90] Another strong underlying consideration was the fact that electricity markets in the EU are 'broken' in the sense that the existing market design no longer works.[91] The existing financial support schemes in favour of RES in combination with priority access to the grid have often made them insensitive to market-based price signals. As the market share of RES increases, this situation has resulted in a depreciation of electricity prices in Europe due to the low to non-existent marginal costs for RES projects.[92]

The higher the penetration of supported RES in a given market, the more the markets are distorted; especially when one takes into account that the supply and demand of electricity has to be in balance at any given second. It has been said that 'a market like the current version but with very high penetrations of renewable energy could have zero or negative prices for all but a few hours of the year. Under such a market neither renewable energy nor conventional generation will be viable.'[93] This is why the Winter Package aims to move 'towards a new market design of a smart and sustainable energy system in Europe and its Member States.'[94] Smart in the sense that it is aimed at incentivising both the supply as well as the demand side of responding to price signals and sustainable in the sense that it should integrate large quantities of RES in a well-functioning market.

Since investors in RES generation assets are part of the supply side of the electricity market, this section will primarily analyse to what extent the proposed

---

89 K TALUS, 'Old Problems and New Challenges: Will the Energy Union Provide the Answers?' [2017] 2 European Investment Law and Arbitration Review 211, in particular 215 ff.

90 N LAVRIJSSEN and A CARRILLO PARRA, 'Radical Prosumer Innovations in the Electricity Sector and the Impact on Prosumer Regulation,' (2017) 9 Sustainability 1207 at 1208.

91 M KEAY, 'Electricity Markets are Broken – Can They be Fixed?' (2016) Oxford Institute for Energy Studies, available at: https://www.oxfordenergy.org/wpcms/wp-content/uploads/2016/02/Electricity-markets-are-broken-can-they-be-fixed-EL-17.pdf.

92 Ibid, pp 8–15. Also, the fact that wind and solar energy are intermittent and thus less reliable poses challenges in the electricity market.

93 D NELSON, B O'CONNELL, L DE LORENZO and M HUXHAM, 'European Renewable Energy Policy and Investment' (2016) Climate Policy Initiative, p 56, available at: https://climatepolicyinitiative.org/publication/european-renewable-energy-policy-investment/.

94 S LAVRIJSSEN, 'Power to the Energy Consumers' (2017) Tilburg Law School Legal Studies Research Paper Series, No. 09, p 1.

measures of the Commission will affect them and to what extent tension may arise between the proposed measures and the provisions of the ECT.

4.1. FINANCIAL SUPPORT FOR RENEWABLES

Regarding the support to incentivise RES investments, the proposed recast of the RES Directive 2009/28/EC still provides for the possibility of financial support.[95] However, in contrast to the current RES Directive, the new proposal puts much more emphasis on the importance of market-based mechanisms to award financial support, such as tenders and auctions.[96] Although this was already enshrined in the EC's Guidelines on State aid, it is now proposed to be included in the text of the RES Directive.

In order to minimise market distortions due to financial support, the proposed RES Directive also requires support schemes to be 'designed so as to integrate electricity from renewable sources in the electricity market and ensure that renewable energy producers are responding to market price signals and maximise their market revenues.'[97] This clearly reflects the desire to expose RES generators benefitting from support to market signals, thereby adjusting their behaviour which should contribute to a well-functioning market.

The proposed changes to the regime governing guarantees of origin (GO) of energy produced by RES may, however, have an adverse financial impact for existing investors. Currently, the 2009 RES Directive provides that an RES generator that receives financial support may also obtain GOs for the energy produced.[98] These GOs, which by themselves do not 'confer a right to benefit from' support schemes, can subsequently be sold by the generator to anyone who is interested in them, such as electricity suppliers or consumers that claim or desire that their electricity is 'green'.[99] Although the GO market and the 'physical' electricity market are delinked, GOs can create an additional source of income for RES generators.

The proposed RES Directive, however, prohibits GOs being issued to RES generators that benefit from financial support without any transitional

95 Article 4, Proposal for a Directive of the European Parliament and of the Council on the promotion of the use of energy from renewable sources (recast), COM(2016) 767 final/2.

96 Ibid, Article 4(3).

97 Ibid, Article 4(2).

98 Article 15(2), Directive 2009/28/EC of the European Parliament and of the Council of 23 April 2009 on the promotion of the use of energy from renewable sources and amending and subsequently repealing Directives 2001/77/EC and 2003/30/EC [2009] OJ L140/16. This can differ per EU Member State. In Germany, eg GOs cannot be issued to RES generators that benefit from the RES support scheme.

99 H VEDDER, A RØNNE, MM ROGGENKAMP and I IÑIGO DEL GUAYO, 'EU Energy Law' in MM ROGGENKAMP, C REDGWELL, A RØNNE and I IÑIGO DEL GUAYO, *Energy Law in Europe – National, EU and International Regulation*, OUP, Oxford, 2016, pp 325–26.

arrangements for existing investors.[100] This can prove problematic for established investors: will existing power purchasing agreements (PPA) become inoperable when the generators are no longer awarded GOs that they are supposed to transfer on the basis of the PPA?[101] If these RES generators will have to acquire these GOs through an auction in order to comply with their PPA commitments, as proposed by the Commission, this clearly turns an additional source of income into a potential additional source of expense. Although the market of GOs is relatively small if expressed in Euros (approximately €120 million in 2016), it does cover almost one-third of the renewable electricity consumption in the EU.[102] Given the relatively low amount of money involved, it is not very likely however that changes to the GOs will deprive investors of the entire value of their investment.[103]

A final provision regarding financial support that deserves mentioning is Article 6 of the proposed RES Directive which concerns the stability of that support:

> Without prejudice to adaptations necessary to comply with State aid rules, Member States shall ensure that the level of, and the conditions attached to, the support granted to renewable energy projects are not revised in a way that negatively impacts the rights conferred thereunder and the economics of supported projects.

This provision immediately brings to mind the ECT disputes discussed in the previous section. Since a comparable provision was lacking in the 2009 RES Directive, aggrieved investors in various EU Member States had no legal basis on the basis of the 2009 RES Directive to challenge the measures that undermined the stability of financial support on the basis of EU law. If a situation comparable to that in Spain would arise in the future, investors could argue that the State concerned would not only be violating its obligations under the ECT, but also under the amended RES Directive.

In this context, the conflicting positions of the EC are exposed. On the one hand, it intervenes in all RES investment disputes by supporting the Member States, that is against the aggrieved RES investors, while on the other hand, the Commission now explicitly recognises the adverse effects of withdrawing the existing support mechanisms.

---

100 Article 19(2), Proposal for a Directive of the European Parliament and of the Council on the promotion of the use of energy from renewable sources (recast), COM(2016) 767 final/2.

101 See *Detailed Consideration of the Guarantee of Origin Scheme in the 'Clean Energy for all Europeans' Package* (April 2017) Association of Issuing Bodies, p 12, available at: https://www.aib-net.org/documents/103816/-/-/32d0e9ed-32c5-76a3-14e2-cfeb1966bfa8.

102 J JANSEN, 'Does the EU Renewable Energy Sector Still Need a Guarantees of Origin Market?' *(2017)* CEPS, p 2, available at: https://www.ceps.eu/publications/does-eu-renewable-energy-sector-still-need-guarantees-origin-market.

103 *Eiser Infrastructure Limited and Energía Solar Luxembourg S.à r.l. v Kingdom of Spain*, ICSID Case No. ARB/13/36, Final Award, 4 May 2017, para 382.

4.2. REGULATORY SUPPORT: PRIORITY DISPATCH

RES investors should be aware of the potential changes to the regime governing the access and dispatch of RES. Much of Article 16 of the 2009 RES Directive is removed in Article 20 of the proposed RES Directive, including the rules on priority and guaranteed access. This means that the current privilege that RES generators enjoy will disappear and that future RES generators will be subject to the general rules.

As becomes clear from the proposed Electricity Regulation, however, priority dispatch will continue to exist for small projects of less than 500 kW and demonstration projects for innovative technologies.[104] Furthermore, the proposed Electricity Regulation explicitly states that RES generators that are subject to the priority dispatch regime of the current legislation and that have been commissioned prior to entrance into force of the proposed Electricity Regulation 'shall remain subject to priority dispatch.'[105] If the proposal of the Commission is adopted, it would thus constitute the proper way to reform the market: it would affect the situation for future investors but would not affect those already established.

The question is, however, whether the Commission's view will finally be adopted. In May 2017, the Agency for the Cooperation of Energy Regulators (ACER) and the Council of European Energy Regulators (CEER) argued in favour of removing priority dispatch for both new and existing RES generators.[106] Depending on the financial consequences for existing investors, this could lead to new investment treaty disputes, particularly because various ECT arbitral tribunals referred to the importance of priority dispatch in their RES awards.

In *Charanne v Spain*, for example, the tribunal held that investors can legitimately expect that when regulatory frameworks are amended, a State will not act unreasonably, disproportionately or contrary to the public interest.[107] With regard to the proportionality, the tribunal added that 'this criterion is satisfied as long as the changes are not capricious or unnecessary and do not amount to suddenly and unpredictably eliminate the essential characteristics of

---

104 Article 11(2), Proposal for a Regulation of the European Parliament and of the Council on the Internal Market for Electricity (recast), COM(2016) 861 final/2.

105 Ibid, Article 11(4).

106 'Renewables in the Wholesale Market' (2017) European Energy Regulators' White Paper No. 1, available at: http://www.acer.europa.eu/Official_documents/Position_Papers/Position%20papers/WP%20ACER%2001%2017.pdf. The European Federation of Energy Traders also proposed stricter changes to the rules than the Commission, see: 'RES Integration and Market Based Dispatch' (2017) European Federation of Energy Traders, available at: http://www.efet.org/Files/Documents/Downloads/EFET_CEP-amendments_RES-Redispatch_June-2017.pdf, pp 3–4.

107 *Charanne and Construction Investments v Spain*, SCC Case No. V 062/2012, Final Award, 21 January 2016, para 514.

the existing regulatory framework.'[108] The existence of a FiT and 'the possibility to sell their electricity production to the system in priority' were later identified by the tribunal as 'fundamental characteristics' of the existing support scheme.[109] The *Charanne* award therefore not only shows that the arbitrators were aware of the significance of priority dispatch for the economic viability of an RES investment, but they even considered it as a 'fundamental characteristic' of a support scheme.

Likewise, in *Eiser v Spain* the tribunal emphasised the importance of both the FiT and priority dispatch for obtaining external financing for the project:

> The operating companies in which Claimants invested were able to obtain this significant level of non-recourse financing because RD 661/2007 offered predictable subsidized prices for sale of the plants' production (including some electricity generated by gas) and guaranteed priority of access to the grid. These features enabled Claimants, their co-investors, and their lenders to design and finance CSP facilities reasonably anticipated to produce long term revenues sufficient to cover operating and capital costs and provide an acceptable stable return to the investors.[110]

The tribunal subsequently went on to discuss how the Spanish measures affected one of these two pillars; namely the FiT. According to the tribunal, by applying a new remuneration methodology to existing investors, the authorities 'in effect retroactively prescribe design and investment choices that in regulators' view should have been incorporated in plants designed and built some years before.'[111] Depending on the individual circumstances of each investor in case of a removal of priority dispatch, a similar line of reasoning can be adopted if the priority is also removed for existing investors. Those investors that have made preparations for additional storage capacity might be better equipped to adjust to a market without priority dispatch than those that have not.[112]

The *Antin v Spain* tribunal reiterated the findings of the *Charanne* tribunal and held that the contested measures in the case at hand altered the FiT scheme and 'withdrew the right of priority of grid access and priority of dispatch for [renewable energy] installations'.[113] The subsequent considerations of the tribunal, however, exclusively focus on the regulatory changes concerning the FiT and priority dispatch is not mentioned again.

---

108 Ibid, para 517.

109 Ibid, para 533.

110 *Eiser Infrastructure Limited and Energía Solar Luxembourg S.à r.l. v Kingdom of Spain*, ICSID Case No. ARB/13/36, Final Award, 4 May 2017, para 412.

111 Ibid, para 414.

112 Interestingly enough, in *Eiser*, one of the reasons that the claimants CSP plant was not efficient according to the modified Spanish standards was exactly because they incorporated the addition of future capacity possible in their design plans.

113 *Antin Infrastructure Services Luxembourg S.à.r.l. and Antin Energia Termosolar B.V. v Kingdom of Spain*, ICSID Case No. ARB/13/31, Award, 15 June 2018, para. 560.

The *Charanne*, *Eiser* and *Antin* awards thus show that arbitrators are aware of the importance of priority dispatch for the economic viability of an RES project. They have even considered it as a fundamental characteristic of a support scheme. Taking this into account, one has to conclude that the proposed changes to the RES Directive and Electricity Regulation, as made by the EC, concerning priority dispatch are probably the best way forward. By exempting existing investors from the new regime, it cannot be argued that the rules are changed in the middle of the game. Although the proposal might still increase investment uncertainty for some time, especially given the fact that the date of commissioning of a project in relation to the date of entrance into force of the new legislation will determine what rules are applicable, this risk should be sufficiently clear to any future investor.

5. CONCLUSION

This chapter has highlighted the increasing interaction and tension between the promotion of RES in Europe and investment treaty arbitration disputes.

Pushed by the EC and EU legislation, EU Member States have promoted the expansion of RES by various support mechanisms. Some of these support mechanisms have been very successful in achieving a greater market share of RES. However, implementing an energy transition has also proven to be a difficult learning exercise for States: how does one strike a proper balance between controlling the costs of RES production while at the same time creating incentives to encourage the production thereof? Also, the consequences of increased levels of RES are currently showing their effects on the electricity markets, which raises the question of how one incentivises RES generation – which is intermittent in nature and is associated with low marginal costs – in the environment of a well-functioning market where the security of supply is guaranteed?

In some States, such as Spain, one could argue that the legislator did not find a proper balance: the costs of a poorly designed and financially unsustainable support scheme were passed on to RES generators while alternatives were available. It currently seems that States where consumer electricity tariffs are regulated by the government, sometimes in a manner that is far from cost-efficient, are particularly prone to striking the wrong balance. While RES producers could not have reasonably assumed that the support mechanisms would never change, the drastic reduction of support – sometimes by redesigning support schemes with retroactive effect – goes beyond what can be expected from rule of law-based EU Member States. The various cases discussed in this chapter illustrate that there is a fine line between measures that may still be considered to be acceptable and those which breach the investment protection standards guaranteed in the ECT.

In this context, it is laudable that the EC proposes in the revised RES Directive that RES investors must be protected against retroactive changes to the support mechanisms. In other words, in Commission's opinion, retroactive withdrawal of support is considered a no-go. It is desirable that the EU Member States should also recognise this when they adopt the Directive. Although the legislative process is still underway, the European Parliament and Council seem to largely agree with the approach suggested by the Commission, albeit with diverging nuances.[114]

Looking forward, it is beyond doubt that significant challenges lay ahead and it is also clear that the generous support mechanisms of the past will not continue. Instead, the RES market will gradually become subject to the full application of the EU State aid and internal energy market rules.[115] This development will be aided by the rapidly falling price of RES technology and the constantly improving efficiency rates. The emphasis in EU legislation concerning RES will move from maximising RES generation to integrating large quantities of RES in a well-functioning market.

However, creating a functioning and competitive RES market is only one side of the coin. The other side of the coin is to ensure that investments in RES remain sufficiently attractive, so that they will be consistent with the trajectory to meet the targets. This requires that RES investors can be sure of making a reasonable profit out of their investments. That in turn necessitates the creation of a stable legal framework. In other words, legal certainty and foreseeability are and continue to be essential, also for existing RES investors. That is now explicitly recognised by the EC in its Winter Package proposals.

114 See Amendments 132 and 133, Amendments adopted by the European Parliament on 17 January 2018 on the proposal for a directive of the European Parliament and of the Council on the promotion of the use of energy from renewable sources (recast) (COM(2016)0767 – C8-0500/2016 – 2016/0382(COD)). For remarks of the Council, see Proposal for a Directive of the European Parliament and of the Council on the promotion of the use of energy from renewable sources (recast) – General approach, 2016/0382 (COD), 13 December 2017, p 58.

115 I ESPA, 'Promoting Renewables in the Energy Union: Current Strategies and the Challenges Ahead' [2017] 2 European Investment Law and Arbitration Review 225.

CHAPTER IV

OFFSHORE HYBRID GRID INFRASTRUCTURES

The Kriegers Flak Combined Grid Solution

Ceciel NIEUWENHOUT*

1. INTRODUCTION

On a shallow sandbank in the Baltic sea, a challenge to current electricity grid regulation is starting to take shape. The offshore wind farm Kriegers Flak, under Danish jurisdiction, will be connected both to the Danish onshore grid and to two German offshore wind farms, Baltic 1 and Baltic 2, which are already connected to the German coast.[1] Thus, an electrical connection with the name Kriegers Flak Combined Grid Solution with three offshore wind farms in the middle will be constructed between Denmark and Germany. Current electricity grid regulation was not designed with this type of connection in mind. Consequently, several legal uncertainties exist regarding this new development.

First, some attention needs to be paid to terminology. There is not yet a legal or official term that covers the connection between at least two countries and at least one offshore wind farm. Such infrastructure can be used both for electricity trade and for the transport of offshore-produced electricity to the onshore electricity grid. This can thus be seen as a grid connection with hybrid functionality. In this chapter, for clarity's sake, this type of connection will be referred to as 'hybrid' grid infrastructure.[2]

---

* This chapter builds on the presentation of Gert Elze (Energinet.dk) on 'Developing a New Type of Electricity Interconnectors – Combined Grid Solutions' at the European Energy Law Seminar 2017. The research for this paper is based on earlier work funded by PROMOTioN (Progress on Meshed HVDC Offshore Transmission Networks), http://www.promotion-offshore.net. This project has received funding from the EU's Horizon 2020 research and innovation programme under grant agreement No 691714.

1 More technical information about this project can be found at: https://en.energinet.dk/Infrastructure-Projects/Projektliste/KriegersFlakCGS.

2 The adjective 'hybrid' is used more often in the context of offshore electricity cables with two functions (interconnection and offshore wind farm connection). Examples are the

The question of terminology is of further relevance: interpretation of the terminology used in current energy law determines in which 'category' an asset falls. This has direct consequences for the way the infrastructure can be regulated, which in turn influences the profitability of the investment and eventually whether the electricity infrastructure will be constructed or not. For the development of offshore connections in the most cost-effective way, it is essential that there is clarity concerning how hybrid grid infrastructure will be defined and categorised under international, European and national law.

Therefore the terminology and categorisation for hybrid cables should be considered carefully: can hybrid grid infrastructure fit in the definitions and categories contained in the current law, or would the creation of new legal terminology be needed for the development of hybrid offshore grid infrastructure? After giving a short factual background of hybrid grid infrastructure (section 2), this chapter addresses the abovementioned question of terminology and interpretation on the basis of an analysis of international and European law (sections 3 and 4 respectively). Throughout the chapter, the Kriegers Flak Combined Grid Solution will serve as an example of how these issues are dealt with in practice. Although national law influences the regulation of hybrid assets as well, it falls beyond the scope of this chapter to review all the different national laws that are relevant for hybrid assets for both Denmark and Germany.

2. THE NEED FOR HYBRID GRID INFRASTRUCTURES

In the coming years, a high number of offshore wind farms are planned to be constructed. They are located increasingly far off the coast,[3] which makes the connection between the offshore wind farm and the onshore grid longer and thus more expensive. TSOs aim to make these investments more cost-efficient by increasing the usage of the cable,[4] for example by connecting multiple wind farms

---

North Seas Countries Grid Initiative (NSCOGI) WG2 Paper on 'Cost allocation for hybrid infrastructures', 28 July 2014, http://www.benelux.int/files/8414/0923/4156/cost_allocation_paper_final_version_28_July_2014.pdf; NorthSeaGrid study final report, 24 March 2015; PwC, Tractebel Engineering, Ecofys, Study on regulatory matters concerning the development of the North Sea offshore energy potential, January 2016. In the Kriegers Flak Combined Grid Solution, the term 'combined' is used, as opposed to 'separate'. Nevertheless, the Combined Grid Solution is also hybrid grid infrastructure. In the pre-feasibility study, the word 'hybrid' is coined as well, but specifically in the context of a combination of different engineering technologies (HVDC and AC).

3 This is done for several reasons: countries may want to keep their coastline visually clear from wind farms; they may want to use the waters close to the coast for other purposes such as navigation, fishing or tourism; and, generally, countries may plan wind farm areas where the expected yield is the highest, which is often further offshore.

4 For calculations of the utilisation rate of different hybrid assets, see A Flament, P Joseph et al, 'NorthSeaGrid Study Final Report' (2015) (hereinafter: NorthSeaGrid Final Report 2015), pp 43–44.

on one cable or by designing the connection in such a way that it connects the electricity grids of two countries, in other words, a hybrid connection. Another development is that with the increasing amount of renewable energy in our electricity system, interconnection between different electricity systems becomes more important for system stability and security.[5] Additionally, interconnection facilitates trade and brings the costs of electricity down.[6] This provides an extra reason for constructing hybrid connections rather than radial connections.[7]

However, hybrid connections pose several legal, regulatory and technical challenges. This results in a higher perceived risk for investors and thus extra capital costs for the project. Therefore, for every project, the benefits of extra interconnection capacity and cable usage for offshore wind farm connections should be weighed against the extra costs for constructing hybrid infrastructure. The costs and benefits may alter over time as technology progresses and regulatory risks are mitigated. Therefore, the business case for hybrid projects may change significantly during the project development phase.

This is also visible in the case of Kriegers Flak, which has already been under investigation for a decade, with a joint pre-feasibility study including Sweden dating from 2009.[8] Sweden decided not to participate in the project,[9] so the Kriegers Flak Combined Grid Solution is now going ahead with only Denmark and Germany. The Danish and German TSOs, Energinet.dk and 50Hertz, are project developers, owners and operators.[10] The Kriegers Flak Combined Grid Solution was awarded the status of European Project of Common Interest (PCI),[11] meaning that it benefits from procedural streamlining in the planning and permitting phase and from the possibility of financial assistance from the

5 Report of the Commission Expert Group on electricity interconnection targets, 'Towards a Sustainable and Integrated Europe', November 2017, p 12, available at: https://ec.europa.eu/energy/sites/ener/files/documents/report_of_the_commission_expert_group_on_electricity_interconnection_targets.pdf.

6 Ibid, p 11. These benefits are spread over different actors in different countries and do not necessarily lie with the same actors as those who bear the extra costs; NorthSeaGrid Final Report (2015), p 70.

7 Radial connections are connections from offshore wind farms to the coast.

8 Energinet.dk, Svenska Kraftnät, Vattenfall Transmission, 'An Analysis of Offshore Grid Connection at Kriegers Flak in the Baltic Sea' (2009) available at: http://www.svk.se/siteassets/om-oss/rapporter/090507_kriegers-flak-pre-feasibility-report-final-version.pdf.

9 An important difference between Sweden and the other countries in this context is that whereas Denmark and Germany place the connection responsibility of offshore wind farms to the onshore grid with the TSO, Sweden has a system whereby the offshore wind farm owner constructs and operates this connection to the onshore grid. This influences the business case for hybrid infrastructure significantly.

10 Other relevant actors in this context are the connected offshore wind farm owners: for Baltic 1 and 2, this is EnBW. For Kriegers Flak Offshore Wind Farm, this is Vattenfall.

11 Commission Delegated Regulation (EU) 2016/89 amending Regulation (EU) No 347/2013 of the European Parliament and of the Council as regards the Union list of projects of common interest, Annex B, 4.1. The Combined Grid Solution featured on the first list of projects of common interest as early as 14 October 2013.

Connecting Europe Facility (CEF).[12] However, the project did not make use of this possibility. Instead, it received funding via the European Energy Programme for Recovery (EEPR).[13]

Figure 1. Schematic overview of the Kriegers Flak Combined Grid Solution

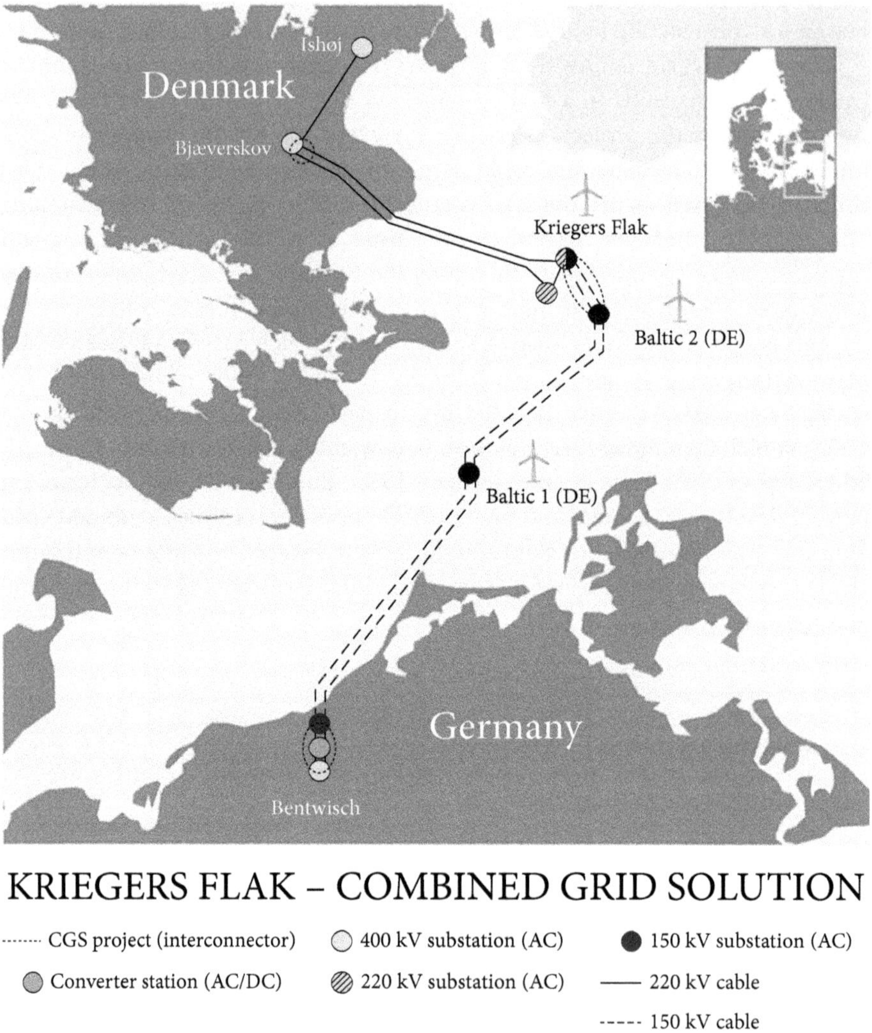

Source: Energinet.dk.

12 The Connecting Europe Facility is established by Regulation (EU) 1316/2013 in order to financially promote projects of common interest in trans-European networks.

13 The total project costs were €900 million, out of which €311 million were EEPR-fundable activities. The project promoters paid €161 million and the EEPR funded €150 million of this sum. See: https://setis.ec.europa.eu/energy-research/sites/default/files/project/docs/baltic-kriegers-flak_en.pdf.

While the Kriegers Flak Combined Grid Solution will be a frontrunner of hybrid grid infrastructure, the project may be used as a model for further connections. A similar structure is being investigated for the connection of 'IJmuiden Ver' and 'East Anglia', a Dutch and an English offshore wind farm.[14] Another example is the COBRA cable, an offshore connection between the Netherlands and Denmark, which received funding for research and development activities related to the possibility of connecting German offshore wind farms to the cable.[15]

The legal challenges discussed in this chapter in relation to the Kriegers Flak Combined Grid Solution are to a large extent also applicable to other potential hybrid projects and in the long term to the development of an offshore electricity grid. Solutions to regulatory uncertainty, reducing the risk and thus the cost of capital of hybrid connections, will therefore not only benefit Kriegers Flak Combined Grid Solution but also other potential projects.

3. INTERNATIONAL LAW RELATING TO JURISDICTION OVER HYDRID OFFSHORE CABLES

3.1. THE QUESTION OF JURISDICTION

For the regulation of offshore electricity cables in general, and for hybrid electricity infrastructures in particular, it is important that states have the right to regulate the construction and usage of these cables as well as to enforce these rules. As these cables are located for the most part outside the states' territories, this right cannot stem from territorial sovereignty. Therefore, the aim of this section is to assess whether and to what extent states have jurisdiction over these cables on another basis, namely on the basis of the law of the sea.[16] The main source of international law addressing the rights and duties of states at sea is

---

14 Dutch Ministry of Economic Affairs, 'Ontwikkelkader Windenergie op Zee' (2016) available at: https://www.rijksoverheid.nl/documenten/kamerstukken/2016/04/28/kamerbrief-met-ontwikkelkader-windenergie-op-zee (in Dutch), p 15. In this policy document of the Dutch Government, hybrid connections to the UK are deemed 'conceivable' (denkbaar) but not concretised any further. The TSO (TenneT) concretises this with a joint investigation with UK stakeholders into this connection: https://www.tennet.eu/our-key-tasks/innovations/north-sea-infrastructure/ (under 'Development').

15 TenneT, 'Business Case Description COBRACable DCI 13-059', December 2013, p 4. Available at: https://www.tennet.eu/fileadmin/user_upload/Our_Grid/Interconnections/CobraCable/DCI-13-059_-__COBRAcable_Business_Case_-_03-12-2103_-_publieksversie.pdf.

16 HK Müller, *A Legal Framework for a Transnational Offshore Grid in the North Sea*, Intersentia, Cambridge 2016, pp 26–27.

the United Nations Convention on the Law of the Sea (UNCLOS).[17] UNCLOS provides that the actual right of a coastal state to regulate a cable depends on the location and on the function of this cable.

Concerning the location of the cable, UNCLOS distinguishes several maritime zones. The territorial zone, reaching up to 12 nautical miles from shore,[18] is considered as an extension of the coastal state's land territory.[19] Therefore, the coastal state has full jurisdiction over all activities in this zone. Beyond the territorial zone lie the continental shelf and the Exclusive Economic Zone (EEZ). On the continental shelf, a natural prolongation of the land under water, coastal states have sovereign rights to explore and exploit natural resources such as oil and gas fields.[20] In the EEZ, which the state has to declare actively through a public declaration and which reaches at most 200 nautical miles from shore,[21] the state also has sovereign rights to exploit the natural resources, both living and non-living.[22] This also includes the production of energy from the 'water, currents and winds'.[23] Accordingly, the jurisdiction of the state in this area is limited to the activities mentioned in UNCLOS.[24] As such, the state only has so-called 'functional jurisdiction'. An important clarification needs to be made regarding functional jurisdiction: countries have the right to regulate, but they have to actively make their law applicable to their activities in the EEZ or on the continental shelf.[25]

With the theory of functional jurisdiction, offshore wind farms fall under the jurisdiction of the coastal state.[26] With regard to the cables needed to connect these offshore wind farms to the shore, the basis for jurisdiction is debated. One possible approach is to say that the cables are indivisible from the wind farm

---

17 United Nations Convention on the Law of the Sea of 10 December 1982, Montego Bay (hereinafter: UNCLOS). This Convention entered into force in 1994 and is ratified by 168 states, including all states bordering the North Sea.

18 Article 3 UNCLOS. The distance of 12 nautical miles equals 22 kilometres approximately.

19 Article 2(1) UNCLOS, although there is a limitation in Article 2(3): the sovereignty over this zone is exercised subject to this Convention and to other rules of international law.

20 Articles 76(1), 77(1) UNCLOS.

21 Articles 55, 57 UNCLOS. The distance of 200 nautical miles equals 370 kilometres approximately.

22 Article 56(1)a UNCLOS. Whereas the sovereign rights over the natural resources in the continental shelf were already adopted in the 1958 Geneva Conventions on the Law of the Sea, the inclusion of sovereign rights over the natural resources in the EEZ was added in 1982 with the drafting of UNCLOS.

23 Article 56(1)a UNCLOS.

24 HK Müller (n 16) pp 31–33.

25 Ibid, p 31.

26 This follows from the coastal states' right to explore and exploit the natural resources in the EEZ (which includes the production of energy from the water, currents and winds) in combination with UNCLOS Article 60(1), which provides that coastal states have the exclusive right to construct and to authorise the construction, operation and use of installations and structures for the purposes provided for in article 56. Offshore wind turbines constitute such installations. See, eg, ibid, p 37.

and that, therefore, they should be interpreted as forming part of the installation or structure needed to exploit the natural resources of the EEZ. However, in most countries, this is not the practice.[27] Another approach is to consider the cables as separate assets, which fall under the category of 'installations or structures'. In UNCLOS, these terms are not defined.[28] Some argue that as cables and pipelines are already clearly addressed elsewhere in UNCLOS,[29] and as states do not have the obligation to remove them after their functional lifetime has ended,[30] they are not intended to fall under 'installations and structures'.[31] A third option entails a teleological approach. This approach is based on the idea that the cables to connect offshore wind farms are an essential part of the exploitation of the natural resources in this case, as states cannot enjoy this exploitation of winds at the EEZ if the electricity never reaches the onshore grid. An argument supporting this approach is that under UNCLOS, states also have an exclusive right to regulate the construction, operation and *use* of, amongst others, installations and structures.[32]

Cables to connect offshore wind farms are not the only electricity cables in the sea. There are also cables used for other purposes, such as to connect the electricity grids of two countries to each other, so-called interconnectors. As part of the doctrine of the free seas,[33] UNCLOS allows all states to lay cables and pipelines on the continental shelf.[34] It also entails that, when a third state wishes to lay a cable, the coastal state may only take reasonable measures with regard to the exploration and exploitation of the natural resources.[35]

27 In Sweden, Norway and the Netherlands before 2015, the legal situation under national law was that the cable was seen as part of the wind farm, ie indivisible from it. However, in many other countries, the cable is owned and operated by another entity (mostly the TSO) as a separate asset from the wind farm itself. This is the case, eg, in Denmark, Germany, the UK, France and the Netherlands after 2015. CT Nieuwenhout, 'WP7.1 Deliverable 1 Legal Framework and Legal Barriers to an Offshore HVDC Electricity Grid in the North Sea' (2017) chapter 5, available at: https://www.promotion-offshore.net/fileadmin/PDFs/D7.1_-_Legal_framework_and_legal_barriers_to_an_offshore_HVDC_electricity_grid_in_the_North_Sea.pdf.

28 G Walker, *Definitions for the Law of the Sea, Terms Not Defined by the 1982 Convention* (Martinus Nijhoff, Leiden 2012) gives some guidance on installations, placing them in the same category as artificial islands, as 'a human-made edifice … which is usually employed to explore or exploit marine resources', p 104. Interestingly, 'structures' are not even addressed in this book that aims to address terms not defined in UNCLOS. It therefore remains a guess as to whether submarine cables can fall under the definition of structures.

29 Namely in Article 79 dealing with the freedom to lay submarine cables and pipelines.

30 This obligation does exist for 'installations and structures'; UNCLOS Article 60(3).

31 HK Müller (n 17) p 37.

32 Article 60(1) UNCLOS; HK Müller (n 16) p 38 (emphasis added).

33 All freedoms of the seas are listed in Article 87 UNCLOS with regard to the high seas, but the doctrine was already developed by Hugo Grotius in his book *Mare Liberum* (1609).

34 Article 79(1) UNCLOS.

35 Article 79(2) UNCLOS. Interestingly, although the Article covers submarine cables as well as pipelines, a differentiation is made with regard to the rights of the coastal state in the context of cable or pipeline laying. In Article 79(2), it is provided that, concerning pipelines,

Regular electricity interconnector cables are not needed for generating energy from 'the waves, currents or winds' and, as such, they are not related to the exploitation of the natural resources of the EEZ. Thus, they cannot fall under the functional jurisdiction states have in the EEZ. Instead, they fall under the freedom to lay cables. This means that, based on UNCLOS, beyond the territorial zone, the coastal state does not have jurisdiction over these cables, regardless of whether they land at the shores of this state or not.[36]

3.2. INTERPRETATION OPTIONS

It is in this context that the question under which regime hybrid assets fall arises. This can be looked at from three different angles.

One option is that the legal regime changes as the function of the cable changes: when the wind does not blow, the cable's function is limited to interconnection, with very limited jurisdiction of the coastal state. When there is offshore electricity generation again, the cable falls under the functional jurisdiction regime again. This option creates a legally untenable situation in which the legal status of the cable and the jurisdiction over it can change almost per second.

A second option is to divide the construction in three (or more) parts, namely, the part from country A to the converter station A (part 1);[37] secondly from this converter station to the converter station B (part 2); and finally from the second converter station to the onshore grid of country B (part 3). If these parts are seen as separate elements, one can argue that only part 2 falls under the freedom to lay cables, as this part is not necessary to enjoy the exploitation of the natural resources in the EEZ, whereas parts 1 and 3 do fall under the functional jurisdiction regime. However, this is also undesirable, as states and developers will probably want legal certainty and clear regulation over the middle part between wind farm A and wind farm B.

---

the coastal state may also take reasonable measures with regard to pollution prevention. Moreover, the coastal state has to consent to the delineation of pipelines according to Article 79(3) UNCLOS. Similar rights are not given to coastal states in the context of submarine cables. This difference can be explained by cables being 'relatively benign' to the maritime environment, whereas pipelines may carry substances that can cause severe pollution. R Beckman and T Davenport, 'The EEZ Regime: Reflections after 30 Years', LOSI Conference paper (2012), p 22.

36 In the past, states have found pragmatic solutions to this lack of jurisdiction by concluding bilateral agreements, eg with regard to oil or gas pipelines. See MM Roggenkamp, 'Petroleum Pipelines in the North Sea: Questions of Jurisdiction and Practical Solutions' (1998) 16 *Journal of Energy and National Resources Law* 98.

37 Converter stations are installations that regulate the voltage, type (AC or DC) and quality of the electricity in the cables it connects to.

Figure 2. Schematic overview of hybrid electricity cable

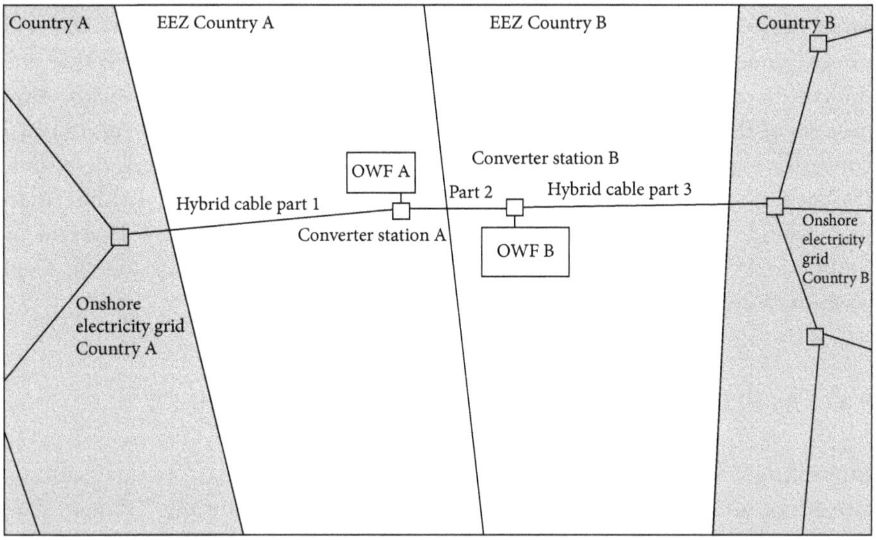

Source: Produced by the author.

A third option is to use a broad interpretation of UNCLOS' terminology. There is some room in UNCLOS for this: according to Article 60.1, the coastal state has exclusive rights over the construction, operations and *use* of installations constructed for the purposes of Article 56 (the exploration and exploitation of resources in the EEZ) 'and for other economic purposes'. In this approach, the focal point is the (two or more) converter stations, installations which are essential for the successful transmission of electricity over long distances in general.[38] One could state that regulation of a cable between the two offshore converter stations is necessary for the *use* of these installations. Then, it also does not matter that they are not solely used for the transmission of offshore-generated electricity but also for interconnection between states, as interconnection, with the purpose of electricity exchange, falls under the 'other economic purposes'. This is also why this approach focuses on the converter stations rather than the wind turbines as installations: the use of wind farms as installations can be served already by single wind farm-to-shore cables, but for converter stations, interconnection as 'other economic purpose' can be included. With this interpretation based on Article 60 UNCLOS, the cable between these converter stations can indeed be seen as falling under the functional jurisdiction of the coastal state.

---

38 Converter stations higher the voltage over long distance cables in order to limit electrical losses during transmission. Without this, electrical losses over long distances are higher than the remaining amount of electricity, meaning that no electricity can be transported at low voltage over long distances.

However, it can be asked whether this broad interpretation of UNCLOS is sufficient in order to reach the desired level of jurisdiction over the entire hybrid asset; some activities concerning the middle part of the hybrid asset will still not fall under the jurisdiction of the coastal state. An example of this is that it is difficult to conclude that the coastal state has jurisdiction over the construction process of the cable or even the delineation of the cable part between the two converter stations based on the regulation of the *use* of the converter stations. If states do regulate this, the coastal state's jurisdiction goes further than that provided by UNCLOS. An alternative is to conclude a new bilateral or multilateral treaty between the relevant states that explicitly elucidates the legal position of hybrid offshore cables.

3.3. APPLICATION TO THE KRIEGERS FLAK PROJECT

Interestingly, the issue of jurisdiction over the cable on the basis of international law is not addressed in the regulatory decision concerning the Kriegers Flak Combined Grid Solution, nor in other regulatory documents about Kriegers Flak.[39] For capacity calculation and system operation issues, the entire asset, from the Danish converter station to the German converter station, is considered to be an interconnector.[40] However, as the majority of the cable is also necessary to connect the offshore wind farms to the onshore grid, it can be claimed that Denmark and Germany have jurisdiction at least over the cables between the wind farms and the shores on both sides. On the part in the middle, between the two wind farms, it is more difficult to establish whether Germany and Denmark have jurisdiction on the basis of the current interpretation of UNCLOS. With the broad interpretation explained above, jurisdiction can be established and this apparently gives Denmark and Germany sufficient certainty about the extent of their jurisdiction. However, for future developments with other configurations, such as interconnectors to which offshore wind farms are connected at a later time,[41] this might not be enough legal certainty to allow for investment. There are several alternatives to using a broad interpretation or ignoring the issue altogether, for example, the coastal states could conclude an agreement under international law or amend existing treaties in order to elucidate the legal position of hybrid assets under international law.[42]

---

39 Such as the joint pre-feasibility study, see n 8 above.

40 Energitilsynet, *Metodegodkendelse af markedsmodel for Kriegers Flak havvindmøllepark – elforsyningslovens §73 a*, 15 January 2014, para 38.

41 HK Müller (n 16) p 17.

42 CT Nieuwenhout (n 27) pp 11–13.

4. EUROPEAN LAW RELATING TO THE REGULATION OF HYBRID ELECTRICITY CABLES

4.1. APPLICABILITY OF EU LAW

A first question is whether EU law is applicable to hybrid electricity infrastructures at all. This is an important question as the current regulation of electricity infrastructures is directed to a large extent by EU energy law. It lays down the rights and duties of transmission infrastructure owners and operators, as well as the rules concerning their income.

A detailed answer to the question of applicability of EU law at sea reaches beyond the scope of this chapter, but is analysed in academic literature.[43] The short answer is that, according to case law of the Court of Justice of the EU (CJEU),[44] EU law is applicable when the Member States themselves have jurisdiction, on the basis of territorial sovereignty or on another basis, such as functional jurisdiction. This again is dependent on international law, where interconnectors fall under the freedom to lay cables, whereas cables to connect offshore wind farms fall under the exclusive sovereign rights of the coastal state, which creates functional jurisdiction. In a relevant case regarding the construction of a submarine telecommunications cable between Sweden and Finland, the CJEU ruled that the Sixth VAT Directive[45] was not applicable to the laying of this cable beyond the territorial waters of Sweden.[46]

One could conclude, by analogy to the telecommunications cable mentioned above, that whereas EU law is applicable to all cables that are used in connection

---

43 For example HK Müller (n 16) pp 68 *et seq.* See also RS Mehta, 'The Continental Shelf, No Longer a Terra Incognita to the EU' (2012) 49 Common Market Law Review 1395–1422.

44 See CJEU Case C-111/05 *Aktiebolaget v Skatteverket* [2007] ECR I-2697; CJEU Case C-286/90 *Anklagemyndigheden v Peter Michael Poulsen and Diva Navigation Corp.* [1992] ECR I-6019; CJEU Case C-6/04 *Commission v United Kingdom* (Habitats Directive) [2005] ECR I-9017; CJEU Case C-347/10 *Salemink v Raad van Bestuur van het UWV* [2012] ECR 2012; CJEU Case C-37/00 *Weber* [2002] ECR I-2013.

45 Sixth Council Directive 77/388/EEC of 17 May 1977 on the harmonisation of the laws of the Member States relating to turnover taxes – Common system of value added tax: uniform basis of assessment (OJ 1977 L 145, p 1), as amended by Council Directive 2002/93/EC of 3 December 2002 (OJ 2002 L 331, p 27).

46 The case concerned the construction of a fibre-optic cable between Sweden and Finland. The VAT directive was applicable to the territory of the Member States. The Court ruled: 'However, the sovereignty of the coastal State over the exclusive economic zone and the continental shelf is merely functional and, as such, is limited to the right to exercise the activities of exploration and exploitation laid down in Articles 56 and 77 of the Convention on the Law of the Sea. To the extent that the supply and laying of an undersea cable is not included in the activities listed in those articles, that part of the operation carried out in those two zones is not within the sovereignty of the coastal State. That finding is confirmed by Articles 58(1) and 79(1) of the Convention, which permit, subject to certain conditions, any State to lay undersea cables in those zones.' CJEU Case C-111/05 *Aktiebolaget*, para 59.

with the economic exploitation of the EEZ, including for the connection of offshore wind farms, EU law is not applicable to electricity interconnectors. For hybrid electricity infrastructure, one can argue that EU law is only applicable to the part of the cable that is used for the connection of offshore wind farms, but with a broad interpretation of international law, it is defendable that EU law is applicable to the cable in its entirety.

In practice, EU law regulates the activities of transmission system operators in general, including their submarine interconnectors.[47] In EU law, no differentiation is made on the basis of whether an interconnector cable is located at sea or not, and if at sea, whether in the territorial waters or in the continental shelf. Thus, the factual situation differs from the formal legal situation, but this has not led to any CJEU court proceedings relating to the regulation of electricity cables so far.

4.2. SUBSTANTIVE EU LAW

Concerning substantive EU law, the question of definitions and interpretation is again pertinent,[48] as it influences which rules are applicable to the infrastructures. In the Electricity Directive, interconnectors are defined neutrally and rather technically as 'equipment used to link electricity systems.'[49] For the purposes of the Regulation on Cross-Border Exchanges in Electricity, this definition is further refined to 'a transmission line which crosses or spans a border between Member States and which connects the national transmission systems of the Member States'.[50] Under both definitions, a hybrid grid solution such as that between Germany and Denmark would fall under the definition of interconnector on the sole basis of crossing a border between EU Member States. However, the difference is already relevant with regard to hybrid grid solutions

47 For example, the income over interconnectors is regulated in Regulation (EC) 714/2009 of the European Parliament and of the Council of 13 July 2009 on conditions for access to the network for cross-border exchanges in electricity and repealing Regulation (EC) No 1228/2003, OJ 211/15, (hereinafter: Regulation (EC) 714/2009), Article 16(6). EU law is also applied in regulatory practice concerning offshore interconnectors: *cf.* Nederlandse Mededingingsautoriteit, Decision 102746/47.BT522, 2007 (in Dutch) gives an explicit overview of applicable EU law: https://www.acm.nl/sites/default/files/old_publication/bijlagen/3826_Besluit_NorNed_2007.pdf, from paras 42–52; ACM Decision 11.0373.52 Besluit Certificering Britned Development Ltd. (in Dutch): https://www.acm.nl/sites/default/files/old_publication/publicaties/13010_besluit-certificering-britned-development-ltd-2014-06-06.pdf, pp 6–7.

48 See for an interpretation of definitions in various instruments of EU law: HK Müller (n 16) pp 265 *et seq.*

49 Directive 2009/72/EC of the European Parliament and of the Council of 13 July 2009 concerning common rules for the internal market in electricity and repealing Directive 2003/54/EC 2009/72/EC, OJ 211/55, Article 2(13).

50 Article 2(1), Regulation (EC) 714/2009.

in which the UK is involved: as the UK has different national rules regarding the connection of offshore wind farms, cables to connect offshore wind farms to the onshore transmission system in the UK EEZ are not deemed to be part of the national transmission system.[51] Rather, they are offshore transmission systems.[52] Therefore, a cable connecting to an offshore wind farm in the UK EEZ is an interconnector under the definition of the Directive, but cannot technically be considered an interconnector under the Regulation.

In addition, the qualification of hybrid interconnectors depends on whether the entire asset is considered as one or whether the asset is split in three, or more, parts. In that case, the middle part could be considered to be an interconnector whereas the other parts could be determined as being part of the national electricity system, which is not further defined in either the Directive or the Regulation.

Because there are specific EU law rules applying to interconnectors, it is important to determine whether the definition of 'interconnector' applies to hybrid infrastructures, in full or in part.

First of all, specific rules apply to the revenues for interconnectors and congestion income. The revenue coming from the congestion over the interconnector is earmarked to be spent on guaranteeing the actual availability of the capacity and/or on 'maintaining or increasing interconnection capacity through network investments, in particular new interconnectors'.[53] There is a possibility of exemption from this rule under specific circumstances. A new interconnector may be exempted from the rules when the level of investment risk is so high that construction would not take place if the normal regime were used. In addition, a number of other criteria must be met, such as that the investment must enhance competition in the electricity supply and that the interconnector must be owned by a person which is separate at least in legal form from the system operators whose systems it connects to.[54] This exemption possibility is used several times, for example in various interconnectors in which the United Kingdom is involved,[55] due to their specific regulation of the transmission grid.[56]

Next is the question of access to the cable for market participants and capacity calculation, especially in relation to the priority access regime for renewables such as offshore wind. In Regulation (EC) 714/2009, there is a fundamental rule that '(t)he maximum capacity of the interconnections and/or the transmission

---

51 CT Nieuwenhout (n 27) pp 123–24.

52 Ibid.

53 Article 16(6), Regulation (EC) 714/2009.

54 Article 17(1), Regulation (EC) 714/2009.

55 A list of all exemption decisions is available at: https://ec.europa.eu/energy/sites/ener/files/documents/exemption_decisions2017_0.pdf.

56 See, in general, H Knops and H de Jong, 'Regulated vs. Merchant Transmission Investment' in MM Roggenkamp and U Hammer, *European Energy Law Report IV*, Intersentia, Antwerpen 2007.

networks affecting cross-border flows shall be made available to market participants, complying with safety standards of secure network operation'.[57] It can be seen from the wording that this basic principle of congestion management applies to hybrid assets too. Here, it does not matter whether these assets are defined as interconnectors or other transmission networks, as both are covered in the provision. In Article 16(1) of the same Regulation, it is provided that congestion issues shall be addressed by market-based solutions on a non-discriminatory basis.[58] However, the Renewable Energy Directive 2009/28/EC defined a regime for priority access and priority dispatch for renewable energy on the electricity grid.[59] This means that, when there is congestion on the grid, other electricity sources will have to be curtailed before the renewable sources are curtailed. This is also the case for offshore wind energy. This rule should also be taken into account for hybrid assets.

Consequently, there seems to be a conflict between the rule that, on the one hand, maximum capacity should be available to market participants and that, on the other hand, priority dispatch on the grid should/shall be provided to renewable energy. This is because a market-based solution with non-discriminatory access is per definition not possible if one source is prioritised over other sources. The two provisions are only reconcilable when they are filled in with a specific interpretation,[60] as will be explained in more detail in the case study for Kriegers Flak below.

The uncertainty surrounding the legal definition and regulation of hybrid assets is detrimental to their development. This weakness was already identified in 2012 by the North Seas' Countries Offshore Grid Initiative (NSCOGI), which concluded that there is no explicit legal framework for hybrid assets. Parties to the NSCOGI recommended, amongst other things, that 'an agreed and compatible approach' to hybrid assets should be developed, and that the consistency between the Renewable Energy Directive and the Regulation on Cross-border electricity supply should be clarified.[61] However, five years later, the issue still remains to be addressed.

The proposals for review of the Electricity Directive and Regulation as part of the 2016 'Clean Energy for All Europeans' package[62] may prove to be the best

57 Article 16(3), Regulation (EC) 714/2009.

58 Ibid, Article 16(1).

59 Directive 2009/28/EC of the European Parliament and of the Council of 23 April 2009 on the promotion of the use of energy from renewable sources and amending and subsequently repealing Directives 2001/77/EC and 2003/30/EC (Renewable Energy Directive), Article 16(2)b.

60 HK Müller (n 16) p 266 gives more information on the interpretation of EU law.

61 NSCOGI, 'Recommendations for guiding principles for the development of integrated offshore cross border infrastructure' Benelux Secretariat (2012), available at: http://www.benelux.int/files/4714/0923/4575/recommendations.pdf, p 2.

62 https://ec.europa.eu/energy/en/news/commission-proposes-new-rules-consumer-centred-clean-energy-transition.

opportunity for a legislative change. If the legislative package is adopted in the form proposed by the European Commission, the contradiction between the legal regimes for priority access for renewable energy and the need to guarantee maximum capacity available to the market will be solved. In the recast Directive on Renewable Energy, the European Commission proposes to remove priority access for renewables.[63]

Opinions vary significantly on this issue.[64] On the one hand, the removal of priority access eliminates the contradiction between different legal provisions and allows for a market model in which the full capacity on a hybrid asset is auctioned on a market. However, it is not favourable for wind farm owners, as they will then have to compete for capacity on the hybrid connection. This results in a less favourable treatment than for other wind farms that are connected radially. Wind farm owners would then probably prefer to be connected to the shore radially, instead of via a hybrid asset. Alternatively, their non-prioritised access and dispatch will be reflected in a higher tender/subsidy price. This effect could be mitigated by having other regulatory arrangements in place, such as compensation payments. However, this is not tenable in the long term, especially when it is not about one asset but about a meshed offshore grid. It is submitted that investigations should be carried out into the feasibility of a dedicated offshore grid regulatory framework.[65] In such a dedicated framework, specific regulatory issues like the question of jurisdiction, coordinated grid development, priority access and market rules can be addressed.

4.3. REGULATORY PRACTICE UNDER THE KRIEGERS FLAK COMBINED GRID SOLUTION

For the Kriegers Flak Combined Grid Solution, the applicability of EU law raises particular issues in relation to the seemingly contradictory requirements of the Renewable Energy Directive and the Regulation on Cross-Border

---

63 COM(2016) 767 (final) Proposal for a Directive of the European Parliament and the Council on the promotion of the use of energy from renewable sources (recast), 30 November 2016, compare Article 16 (old) versus Article 20 (new).

64 In a public consultation for the legislative changes after 2020, stakeholder views varied with 54% stating that the merit order alone would suffice and 46% stating that some form of exemption is still necessary for renewable energy. This is under the heading for priority dispatch, but the entire Article on priority access and priority access is removed. European Commission, Public consultation on the Renewable Energy Directive for the period after 2020, Analysis of stakeholder views, 2016, p 5. Available at: https://ec.europa.eu/energy/sites/ener/files/documents/Summary%20RED%20II%20Consultation.pdf. Analysis flagging priority access as an important issue for hybrid projects: NorthSeaGrid Final Report (2015), p 86.

65 This is addressed in the ongoing project PROMOTioN (2016–20) work package 7 (Regulatory affairs).

Exchanges in Electricity. In the regulatory decision concerning the market model for Kriegers Flak,[66] the Danish Energy Regulatory Authority (DERA, or *Energitilsynet*) addressed this issue in a pragmatic way.

The market model of the project entails that, in principle, transport of electricity from the offshore wind farms to shore has priority on the cable.[67] The Danish wind farm Kriegers Flak sells its electricity on the East Danish spot market.[68] The TSOs forecast the available capacity on the cable by deducting the electricity production on an hourly basis one day ahead.[69] This capacity will be reserved for the wind farms. The remainder of capacity will be made available to the market. Kriegers Flak offshore wind farm thus has the same conditions as other offshore wind farms in East Denmark.[70] The German offshore wind farms (Baltic 1 and 2), constructed several years ago, will keep operating according to the same conditions. The interconnection capacity is then calculated on the basis of what capacity is left after the transport to the shores of Denmark (for Kriegers Flak) and Germany (for Baltic 1 and 2) and based on 'netting' of the electricity flows in the two directions.[71]

The market model for the Combined Grid Solution obviously adheres to Directive 2009/38/EC as it gives the offshore wind farms priority dispatch on the infrastructure towards 'their' coastal state. However, whether it is also compatible with Regulation 714/2009 depends on the interpretation of the terminology in this Regulation. DERA, in consultation with the European Commission,[72] reasons that 'maximum capacity' of the asset is in fact to be interpreted as the capacity that is left after the capacity reserved for the offshore wind farm is subtracted, not as the total available capacity on the cable. In this way, the market model also fulfils the requirements of Regulation 714/2009.[73]

One element that helps in this regard is that the wind farm owners cannot take advantage of their position in the middle of an interconnector cable, as they have to feed the electricity into their 'own' market.[74] This creates a level playing

66 Energitilsynet, 'Metodegodkendelse af markedsmodel for Kriegers Flak havvindmøllepark – elforsyningslovens §73 a', 15 January 2014. Available at: http://energitilsynet.dk/el/afgoerelser/tilsynsafgoerelser/2014/metodegodkendelse-af-markedsmodel-for-kriegers-flak-havvindmoellepark-elforsyningslovens-73-a/.

67 Ibid, para 30.

68 Ibid, para 29 and 31.

69 Ibid, para 30.

70 Ibid, para 31.

71 Ibid, 'Figure 2' on p 7 and para 37. 'Netting' in this context means that the available export capacity of a country is calculated by adding the cable capacity between that country and the offshore wind farm(s) to the current production at the offshore wind farm(s).

72 Ibid, 'Bilag 2'. The Annexes are available at: http://energitilsynet.dk/fileadmin/Filer/0_-_Nyt_site/EL/Tilsynsafgoerelser/2014/KriegersFlak3.pdf.

73 Energitilsynet, 'Metodegodkendelse af markedsmodel for Kriegers Flak havvindmøllepark – elforsyningslovens §73 a', para 100.

74 Ibid, para 101. This means that the operators of the Danish wind farm feed into the Danish market and that the operators of the German wind farms feed into the German market.

field between the concerned offshore wind farm operators and other generators in East Denmark and Germany respectively, which is in the spirit of European law in general.[75] Only the TSOs are able to receive revenues from congestion on the cable,[76] which is then earmarked in conformity with the provisions of the Regulation.[77]

This specific interpretation of EU law works for the Combined Grid Solution, mostly because the wind farms were already planned and even operational in the case of Baltic 1 and 2. The project was designed in order not to interfere with the rights of the wind farm operators compared to the base scenario of radial connections on both sides. This is due to the way in which the project was developed, as the wind farms, especially in the case of Germany, were there first and should not be negatively affected by the new developments. However, when a wind farm is tee-ed in to an existing interconnector, this solution does not necessarily work.

For example, in the case of the COBRA cable,[78] the interconnector between Denmark and the Netherlands will already be constructed before German wind farms are connected to it. These wind farms will not be connected to the German electricity grid directly, only to the grid in the Netherlands and Denmark. Many questions arise in this case. The first is to know whether the wind farm feeds into the German electricity markets, into the Danish or Dutch market or whether this is left to the wind farm owner to decide. Secondly, it should be clarified whether the wind farm has priority on the capacity of the cable or whether the wind farm operator should bid for this capacity as any market participant would do.

These questions are particularly pertinent because the regulatory decisions following these questions may negatively affect the business case of the cable, which is currently constructed on an interconnector business case without offshore wind farm connection. Compensation mechanisms and cross-border cost allocation calculations can be used to mitigate the loss of the original market model, but this will result in very complicated regulation.

---

75 CJEU Case 26/62 *Van Gend en Loos* was the first case in which the Court used an interpretation according to the spirit, general scheme and wording of the European Treaties. Equal market access is one of the principles in the structure of the Treaties. G Beck, *The Legal Reasoning of the Court of Justice of the EU*, Hart Publishing, Oxford 2012, p 320.

76 Energitilsynet, 'Metodegodkendelse af markedsmodel for Kriegers Flak havvindmøllepark – elforsyningslovens §73 a', para 101.

77 Article 16(6), Regulation (EC) 714/2009.

78 The option to connect German offshore wind farms to the existing COBRACable interconnector (between Denmark and the Netherlands) is being investigated thanks to a grant from the European Energy Programme for Recovery. However, the interconnector is initially constructed as a 'normal' interconnector without any hybrid elements. See: http://www.cobracable.eu/.

5. CONCLUSION: NEED FOR NEW INTERPRETATION OR FOR NEW TERMINOLOGY?

Hybrid electricity assets incorporating the connection of offshore wind farms as well as interconnection between different countries' electricity grids challenge current law and regulations, as they fall between different definitions and legal categories. The legal uncertainty as to which regime applies leads to higher risk and thus higher capital costs for the TSOs when dealing with hybrid projects.

In order to facilitate the construction of hybrid assets such as the Kriegers Flak Combined Grid Solution, this chapter concludes that it is necessary to use a wide interpretation of current international and European law in order to make the assets fall within the desired regulatory regime. However, this can only be done to a certain extent without stretching the law too far. With an interpretation of international or European law that is too wide, regulatory uncertainty will increase again. The interpretation will ultimately be subject to judicial review.

With the prospect of more hybrid offshore grid developments, it may be better to change the definitions in the law instead of using a wide interpretation, in order to increase legal certainty and to be sure to cover the entire asset rather than only parts of it. Thus, the development of hybrid offshore electricity infrastructure calls for a review of the current definitions in EU law, to ensure common interpretation, legal certainty and an attractive investment environment.

CHAPTER V

DANISH–GERMAN COOPERATION ON THE FIRST CROSS-BORDER TENDERS FOR RENEWABLE ENERGY

A Blueprint for Future Cross-Border RES Projects?

Dijana Dmitruk*

1. INTRODUCTION

In July 2016, Denmark and Germany concluded a cooperation agreement[1] (CA) on a pilot project allowing the realisation of the two first cross-border tenders of financial support for renewable electricity in Europe. The tenders were technology specific and related to the generation of electricity from solar photovoltaic installations (solar PV). The outcome of the pilot was surprising: solar PV projects with planned locations in Denmark secured all the winning bids in the two cross-border tenders with historical low prices for solar PV in this part of the world.

This chapter provides insight into the legal framework of this pilot cooperation, focusing on certain key elements of the CA. Based on the practical experience gained from the Danish–German cooperation, it also draws some lessons in terms of what to keep in mind when designing these kinds of cross-border projects. Finally, the chapter provides some concluding remarks and

* The views and opinions presented in this chapter are those of the author and do not necessarily reflect the official policy or position of the Danish Government.

1 Agreement between the Government of the Kingdom of Denmark and the Government of the Federal Republic of Germany on the Establishment of a Framework for the Partial Opening of National Support Schemes to Support the Generation of Energy from Solar Photovoltaic Projects and for the Cross-border Administration of such Projects in the Context of a Single Pilot Run in 2016, signed on 20 July 2016 in Berlin, United Nations Treaty Collection, registration no. I – 54273.

reflections for future cross-border initiatives, asking whether this cooperation could serve as a blueprint for future cross-border renewable energy projects.

2. A BRIEF BACKGROUND

In the spring of 2014, when the European Commission was considering the Danish applications on State aid for solar PV and wind electricity, the Commission put the legality of the Danish public service obligation (PSO) charge into question. At that time – and to a certain extent still today – financial support for electricity from renewables in Denmark was mainly financed through a PSO charge. The PSO charge is applied on all electricity bills in Denmark with the purpose of financing public support for renewable electricity.

More precisely, the Commission raised concerns as to whether the PSO charge was in compliance with Articles 30 and/or 110 of the Treaty on the Functioning of the European Union (TFEU). The concern was whether there could be a risk that the charge had a discriminatory effect on imported electricity from renewable sources[2] and thus: 'If domestic electricity production is supported by aid that is financed through a charge on all electricity consumption, including consumption of imported electricity, then the method of financing, which imposes a burden on imported electricity not benefitting from this financing, risks having a discriminatory effect on imported electricity from renewable energy sources and thereby violate Articles 30 and/or 110 of the Treaty.'[3]

With the aim of remedying this potential discrimination, Denmark reached a temporary solution with the Commission for the years 2015 and 2016. Thereafter, the Commission approved the notified aid measures for solar PV and wind electricity in two separate State aid decisions dated October 2014 (State aid decisions of October 2014).[4]

The temporary solution entailed a commitment to open a specified share of the Danish tendered capacity in 2015 and 2016. This temporary solution had to observe point 126[5] of the Guidelines from the European Commission

---

2 Point (54) of SA.36204 (2013/N) – Aid to photovoltaic installations and other renewable energy installations.

3 Point (53) of SA.36204 (2013/N).

4 Commission decision of 24 October 2014 concerning state aid case no. SA.36204 (2013/N) – Denmark – Aid to photovoltaic installations and other renewable energy installations, and Commission decision of 28 October 2014 concerning state aid case no. SA. 37122 (2013/N) – Denmark – Aid to household wind turbines and offshore wind turbines with an experimental aspect. The two decisions were subsequently rectified by the Commission on 18 December 2014.

5 According to point 126 of the EEAG, the pilot tenders organised in 2015 and 2016 needed to cover at least 5% of the planned new electricity capacity from renewable energy sources *cf.* footnote 17 of point (57) of SA.36204 (2013/N).

on State aid for environmental protection and energy (2014–20) (EEAG, or Guidelines):[6] so the specified share would amount to 6% or 2.4 MW (depending on which one of the two figures was highest) of the 5% of the total Danish tendered capacity in 2015 and 2016.[7] The formula chosen for the calculation of the 6% figure reflected Denmark's situation as a transit country for electricity between Scandinavia and central Europe, by only taking into account the share of imported electricity actually consumed in Denmark given that only this share is effectively subject to the PSO charge.[8]

At that time, the size of the pilot tender in Denmark in accordance with point 126 of the EEAG – and thus the 5% of the tendered capacity in 2015 and 2016 – was expected to amount to 20 MW, entailing that the figure of 6% would be fulfilled if Denmark opened 1.2 MW of the 20 MW to installations located in one or more countries of the European Economic Area (EEA). However, Denmark indicated that in order to attract foreign investors, the effective share of tendered capacity for which the investors could bid would amount to a total capacity of 2.4 MW.[9] Since the 2.4 MW proved to be a bigger figure than the 6% of the 5% (20 MW) of all tendered capacity in 2015 and 2016, Denmark had to carry out a pilot tender of 20 MW solar PV of which 2.4 MW had to be opened to installations located in one or more countries of the EEA.

At the same time, Germany experienced similar challenges concerning the finance mechanism for the German national support scheme for renewable electricity. For reasons similar to the Danish case, the Commission was concerned that the financing of the German renewables support scheme via a surcharge to be paid on all electricity consumed in Germany was potentially contrary to the EU prohibition against discriminatory charges. Germany included in its Renewable Energy Sources Act 2014[10] an opening of up to 5% of its newly installed capacity per year to installations located in other Member States from 2017 onwards and to conduct a cross-border pilot tender of support for electricity from solar PV before 2017 in order to secure State aid approval for the Act.[11]

The cooperation between Denmark and Germany was thus born from the circumstance that both countries agreed to open their pilot tenders in order to

---

6 2014/C 200/01.

7 Point (57) of SA.36204 (2013/N).

8 The 6% figure was established as a function of Denmark's total imports of green electricity from the neighbouring countries, Norway, Sweden and Germany divided by the total electricity supply in Denmark and multiplied by the yearly newly installed green electricity capacity. The imports of green electricity have been calculated as the average share of imports (more specifically imports not due to transit, but for consumption in Denmark only) from each of the neighbouring countries multiplied with the renewables share of total electricity production in each of the respective countries *cf.* point (57) of SA.36204 (2013/N).

9 Point (57), footnote 17 of SA.36204 (2013/N).

10 Gesetz für den Ausbau erneuerbarer Energien, 2014.

11 Point (337) of SA.38632 (2014/N) – EEG 2014 – Reform of the Renewable Energy Law.

secure State aid approval for their respective renewables support systems from the Commission.

3. THE EU AND NATIONAL LEGAL FRAMEWORKS

3.1. EU LEGISLATION

The starting point of the cooperation was that Denmark and Germany would conduct two mutually-opened but separate national tenders with individual tender designs.

The overall EU legal framework for the set-up of the two cross-border tenders in the pilot consisted of the TFEU, the EEAG and Directive 2009/28/EC on the promotion of the use of energy from renewable sources (RES Directive).[12] For the Danish tender, the EU legal framework also consisted of the State aid decisions of October 2014 and for the German tender also of the State aid decision for the approval of the German Renewable Energy Sources Act 2014.[13] For the Danish pilot tender, the assessment in Denmark[14] concluded that this tender was not subject to the EU Public Procurement Directive[15] or the EU Utilities Directive.[16] However, since it was also assessed in Denmark that contracts resulting from the tender have a clear cross-border interest, those contracts are subject to the general principles of EU law in the TFEU regarding, among other things, the principle of equal treatment, transparency, proportionality and prohibition of discrimination on grounds of nationality.[17] Furthermore, the tendering procedure was organised in accordance with the EEAG.

The RES Directive establishes a legal framework for the development of renewable energy in the EU until 2020. Article 3 of the Directive sets binding national targets on the share of renewable energy sources in the final energy consumption to be met by the year of 2020.[18] If a Member State fails to achieve its mandatory target, the Commission can start infringement procedures.

---

12 Directive 2009/28/EC on the promotion of the use of energy from renewable sources and amending and subsequently repealing Directives 2001/777EC and 2003/20/EC, OJ L 140/16.

13 SA.38632 (2014/N).

14 See the Conditions for the pilot tendering procedure for a price premium for electricity generated at solar photovoltaic installations, published by the Danish Energy Agency on 11 November 2016, available at: https://ens.dk/en/our-services/current-tenders/pilot-tender-price-premium-electricity-solar-pv.

15 Directive 2014/24/EU of the European Parliament and of the Council of 26 February 2014 on public procurement and repealing Directive 2004/18/EC.

16 Directive 2014/25/EU of the European Parliament and of the Council of 26 February 2014 on procurement by entities operating in the water, energy, transport and postal services sectors and repealing Directive 2004/17/EC.

17 See again the Conditions for the pilot tendering procedure for a price premium for electricity generated at solar photovoltaic installations.

18 The Directive also sets a binding target for renewable energy used for transport.

In order to meet their target, Member States are required to take action and adopt implementation measures,[19] which can take the form of support schemes and/or measures of cooperation between different Member States and with third countries in accordance with Articles 5 to 11 (cooperation mechanisms).[20] The establishment of cooperation mechanisms can help Member States reaching their targets in cooperation with other Member States, including by supporting RES measures in other Member States. The three main cooperation mechanisms in the RES Directive are:

i) *Statistical transfers*[21] where Member States agree to attribute renewable energy produced in one Member State to another in their statistical accounting for target compliance. The transfer, which is done ex-post and virtually, will count towards the national RES target of the latter Member State.[22] This is purely an accounting procedure without transfer of physical energy involved.
ii) *Joint projects*[23] where the renewable energy from a specific project is shared between the Member States, with or without a physical flow of the energy produced.
iii) *Joint support schemes*[24] where Member States co-finance their new renewable energy production independent of its location but within their territories.

The choice of cooperation mechanisms i) – iii) depends on the objectives of the countries involved. For example, the mechanism of Statistical transfers would be the simplest model if the objective is purely lowering costs of target compliance while undertaking technology development and testing; long-term cooperation objectives are more easily achieved with the Joint projects mechanism.[25] In the case of the Danish–German cooperation, the choice was made to apply the cooperation mechanism of Statistical transfers.[26]

Denmark also had to notify the set-up of the Danish pilot tender to the Commission in order to obtain a State aid approval, that was received in

19 Article 3(2), RES Directive.
20 Article 3(3)(a)(b), RES Directive.
21 Article 6, RES Directive.
22 Article 6(1)(a)(b), RES Directive.
23 Article 7, RES Directive. Pursuant to Article 9, RES Directive, joint projects with physical flows can also be arranged with third countries.
24 Article 11, RES Directive.
25 Guidance on the use of renewable energy cooperation mechanism, Commission staff working document, SWD (2013) 440 final, p 5.
26 See on this aspect section 4.4 below.

the autumn of 2016[27] and which was a precondition for the coming into force of the Danish national legal basis for the pilot project.

3.2. THE NATIONAL LEGAL BASIS

The experience from the Danish–German pilot shows that, when working on cross-border tendering procedures, it is important to allocate sufficient time for the screening, drafting and preparation of the national legal basis. The timeframe of course depends on the legal system of the relevant country, but in Denmark at least, this was a time-consuming part of the set-up of the pilot project.

In the spring of 2016, the Danish Parliament passed a bill for the Act on a Pilot Tender for Price Premiums for Electricity Produced by Solar Photovoltaic Installations.[28] This is a project-based Act since it only applies to this one specific cross-border pilot project. In case further cross-border projects on support for electricity from renewable energy sources are decided in Denmark, new legislation would have to be drafted and passed by the Danish Parliament.

On its side, during the summer of 2016, Germany adopted the German Ordinance for Cross-Border Renewable Energy Auctions,[29] which was based on the legal framework and authorisation defined in the German Renewable Energy Sources Act 2014. An important element was the possible extra-territorial nature of some national provisions. Notably, the German legislation included elements which would have effect on the territory of the partner country. For example, solar PV installations financed by Germany have to be ground-mounted, whether they are located in Germany or abroad, which raised the question during the negotiations of whether Denmark could accept that this requirement would apply to installations financed by Germany but located on Danish territory. Ultimately, this was accepted by Denmark.[30]

The lesson learned here was that, when drafting national legislation enabling cross-border participation, there should be as few as possible – if any at all – requirements that could affect the territory of the partner country. Any such requirement stemming from national legislation bears the highest potential for conflicts between parties when negotiating the cooperation agreement. Indeed, the conclusion of a cooperation agreement will be made difficult – and

---

27 Commission decision of 28 September 2016 concerning state aid case SA.44626 (2016/N) – Pilot tender for solar energy.

28 Act no. 261 of 16 March 2016 (*Lov om pilotudbud af pristillæg for elektricitet fremstillet på solcelleanlæg*).

29 Verordnung zur grenzüberschreitenden Ausschreibung der Förderung für Strom aus erneuerbaren. Energien sowie zur Änderung weiterer Verordnungen zur Förderung der erneuerbaren Energien, 11 July 2016.

30 See section 4.2 below.

perhaps even impossible[31] – if a country has already passed national legislation that includes elements which cannot be deviated from when negotiating the cooperation agreement and which have an impact on the way that the partner country wishes to deploy renewables on its own territory. The Danish project-based Act[32] reflects such consideration by providing Denmark with a great deal of flexibility during the negotiations. The Act does not contain conditions for the opening that would affect the territory of the partner country; this is left to the discretion of the negotiating parties.

Another approach could be to start by concluding a cooperation agreement, and make its entry into force conditional upon the respective national legal basis of the participating countries being adjusted accordingly. However, this approach evokes the risk that it may become impossible to succeed in getting the necessary legislation in place for some or all of the negotiated aspects in the respective countries due to political or legal reasons,[33] or that perhaps the legislative process is so lengthy that it may stall the cross-border project.

Obviously, the choice of approach concerning the interaction between the cooperation agreement and the national legal basis will be highly influenced by national circumstances, including the nature of the legal systems and the political situation. The timeframe for completion of the cross-border project will also play a role in the negotiations. In some cases, it may even prove advantageous to work on the cooperation agreement and the national legal basis simultaneously.

Finally, the contractual framework around the tendering process can be used to bring further certainty to the projects. In the Danish pilot tender, the financial support is awarded by contracts concluded between the Danish Energy Agency (DEA) and the winning bidders. One of the reasons for choosing this approach was that this creates a contractual link between the DEA and the winning bidders, including those with planned projects in Germany, and thus eliminates uncertainty related to the non-applicability of Danish legislation to German territory and the payment of support to potential winning bidders with installations located in Germany.

---

31 If an agreement cannot be reached, as a last resort, an attempt may be made to change the national legislation that includes the barrier – if that is politically possible – but in practice this would typically trigger a time-consuming process which could risk stalling the negotiations and thus the cross-border project (this is especially challenging if the completion of the cross-border project is subject to a fixed non-negotiable deadline).

32 The Act on a Pilot Tender for Price Premiums for Electricity Produced by Solar Photovoltaic Installations.

33 Further, maybe for some countries – depending on the national legal system or/and due to political reasons – it may prove impossible to engage in negotiations with the partner country without a legal national basis being in place beforehand.

3.3. THE CONDITIONS IN NATIONAL LAW FOR THE PARTIAL OPENING OF NATIONAL SUPPORT SCHEMES

3.3.1. Denmark

The Danish Act on a Pilot Tender for Price Premiums for Electricity Produced by Solar Photovoltaic Installations provides that there are three conditions for foreign participation in the tender process:[34]

i) the partner country has to be a member of the EEA;
ii) its grid has to be directly connected to Denmark; and
iii) a cooperation agreement has to be concluded.

The reasoning behind the Danish requirement of direct interconnection (ii) is that the potential discrimination connected to the PSO charge is only relevant with respect to those suppliers that deliver electricity for consumption in Denmark and thus only with respect to the EEA countries that the Danish electricity grid is directly connected to. This also reflects the physical import requirement that the Commission permitted Denmark to introduce in the State aid decisions of October 2014, since, without import, no discrimination in the sense of Articles 30 and 110 TFEU would occur in the first place. In practice this meant that Denmark could limit the partial opening of its national support scheme for renewable energy to directly interconnected EEA countries, which, at that time, were Germany, Norway and Sweden.

Due to the complexity of electricity flows, Denmark considered that it is impossible to ensure that the electricity generated from one specific Danish funded installation in a partner country is delivered to Denmark. Consequently, it was concluded that the only manner to document the physical import of electricity from a specific installation abroad was the criterion of direct interconnection. Therefore, the Danish Act contains an interconnection requirement.

The Danish authorities were also against the introduction of excessive requirements of administrative proof, and of mechanisms for the reservation of interconnector capacities. Introducing such mechanisms can alter physical flows between countries and lead to inefficient market results.

Finally, Danish authorities considered that the requirement of physical import meant that there would be some kind of real impact on the Danish electricity market of the projects realised abroad but funded by Denmark. This was a mechanism applied in order to secure public acceptance. In general, in the course of the work on the cross-border pilot Denmark and Germany paid much attention to mechanisms that could be introduced in order to secure

---

[34] This is closely described in the preparatory work on the Act on a Pilot Tender for Price Premiums for Electricity Produced by Solar Photovoltaic Installations.

public acceptance of the cross-border project. Indeed, questions were raised as to the reason why an electricity consumer or taxpayer in Denmark should pay for supporting electricity produced on an installation located abroad; the same concern applied in Germany.

3.3.2. Germany

The German Renewable Energy Sources Act 2014 and the Ordinance for Cross-border Renewable Energy Auctions provide that there are three conditions for foreign participation in the tender process:

i) reciprocity;
ii) physical import of electricity; and
iii) the conclusion of a cooperation agreement.

The reciprocity requirement (i) entailed that Germany could only open its national pilot tender to Denmark if Denmark opened its pilot tender to Germany in return. However, this did not mean that the capacities of the openings had to be the same in absolute numbers, and indeed, in the pilot project, Germany opened 50 MW to installations in Denmark while Denmark opened 2.4 MW to installations in Germany. Reciprocity with its 'give and take' approach is also one of the tools implemented in the cooperation to serve public acceptance purposes of the cross-border project.

The German requirement of physical import (ii) of the German-funded electricity produced on installations located in Denmark was considered met for this one specific cross-border pilot project, given the high degree of direct interconnection between Denmark and Germany and the small volume of the pilot tenders.

4. THE COOPERATION AGREEMENT

4.1. INTERNATIONAL AGREEMENT (TREATY) AND NATIONAL LEGISLATION

An important starting point for any cooperation agreement is the need to regulate exhaustively circumstances surrounding the treatment of installations financed by one country but placed on the territory and having effect on the territory of the other country. Obviously, national legislation does not apply to the territory of the partner country. This entails that all relevant circumstances from national legislation that would have an impact on the territory of the partner country have to be agreed upon by the participating countries and included in the cooperation agreement. This is also the only way that a country participating in a cross-border project can actually control in which way the increase of renewable energy is carried out within its territory.

4.2. TENDER DESIGN: A LEVEL PLAYING FIELD FOR DANISH AND GERMAN PROJECTS?

The Danish–German pilot consisted of one national German tender of 50 MW,[35] carried out and designed by Germany, opened to installations located in Denmark,[36] and one national Danish tender, carried out and designed by Denmark, with a capacity of 20 MW of which 2.4 MW were opened to installations located in Germany.[37] In other words, the two national tenders were separate but mutually open.

At the beginning of the negotiations, Denmark and Germany did consider whether the pilot project could perhaps consist of one joint tender with a single design. But since the execution of both national tenders was subject to a firm deadline,[38] and since the set-up of a joint tender requires time,[39] the countries opted for the adoption of two national tenders with two separate tender designs. Naturally, in the course of the negotiations, Denmark and Germany discussed the two tender designs but the first basic principle of the cooperation was that each country decided how to design its own tender, except for elements of the tender design that would affect the territory of the other country.

Germany intends to implement further cross-border tenders in the years to come. Thus, the pilot project with Denmark was merely one of many future German tenders. On the other hand, in Denmark, the Danish pilot tender was – and is still today – the only cross-border tender in the pipeline. It was also the only tender in the pipeline at that time on support for electricity from solar PV.[40]

Some of the differences in the two tender designs were that in the Danish tender a fixed premium was applied while the German tender had a floating premium (guaranteed price).[41] In times of negative prices there would be

---

35 The 50 MW constitutes 50 MWp (panel effect) that in this case amounts to approximately 34 MW measured by the inverter. Thus the inverter capacity composes 34 MW.

36 Article 7(1), CA.

37 Article 8(1), CA.

38 Both pilot tenders had to be completed before 2017.

39 Since the participating countries have to reach an agreement on all of the many aspects of tender design.

40 Since then, in 2017 three national tenders were decided in Denmark to be carried out in 2018 and 2019. In two of these – in Denmark referred to as technology-neutral tenders – solar PV projects will be set to compete against onshore wind and coastal offshore wind projects while one tender is for solar PV only. These three tenders are not cross-border tenders (only projects planned on Danish territory are allowed to participate). For the first technology-neutral tender a call for tenders was made on 27 September 2018, while the second technology-neutral tender will be carried out in 2019. For the solar PV tender a call for tenders was made on 13 September 2018.

41 This entails that German bids include the market price, while the Danish bids do not.

no financial support paid in the Danish tender while in the German tender payments would only cease if there were more than six hours of negative prices (grace period). In the German tender, a maximum price was included, while there was no maximum price in the Danish tender.

A more political starting point when working on cross-border tenders is the effects the opening of the national scheme will have on the national policy for the deployment of renewables in the partner country. As an acknowledgement of this, Denmark and Germany established that in principle the location-specific conditions of the country where the installation is located shall apply.[42] Examples of such location-specific conditions are relevant applicable national legislation and other regulations such as rules on spatial planning and construction, licensing laws, grid connection and taxation. These location-specific conditions were thus not aligned in the pilot project. It was agreed that exceptions to the principle of location-specific conditions could only be accepted in case of incompatibility with existing national legislation of the financing country or if it contradicted the political context in the financing country. Any exception had to be agreed upon by the partner country where the installation was to be located, since it concerned that country's territory.

Relying on that possibility, Germany requested and Denmark accepted that PV installations located in Denmark but financed by Germany have to be mounted on the ground. Indeed, German legislation only allowed for financial support from the German national support scheme for electricity from ground-mounted PV installations,[43] regardless of the location of the installation. The Danish Government accepted that this requirement stemming from German legislation would apply to German-financed installations on Danish territory. The definition of what constitutes a ground-mounted installation was included in the CA.[44] When assessing what constitutes a ground-mounted installation supported by Germany on Danish territory, the reference definition is found in the CA and not in German legislation.[45]

The mutually-opened capacities in the two tenders were not reserved for installations located in the partner country. The aim of the pilot was to enable the cheapest bid to win irrespective of whether the winning installation was to be established in Germany or in Denmark. In this way, PV installations in Denmark and Germany could participate and compete in the two national tenders alongside one another.[46] However, concerns have been raised as to whether there was a

42 Preamble, CA.

43 Since then German national legislation has been revised: it now follows from the German Renewable Energy Sources Act 2017 that ground-mounted solar PV installations can also receive support from the German national support scheme.

44 Article 1, litra d), CA.

45 This is due to the obvious fact that German legislation does not apply on Danish territory. See section 4.1 above.

46 Articles 7(3) and 8(4), CA.

level playing field between German and Danish projects, due to the restriction on eligible sites in Germany. It follows from German legislation that only specific sites are available for German-funded installations: for instance a PV installation on German agricultural land cannot receive financial support from the German national support scheme. The reason for this is that Germany wishes to limit changes in the landscape, in particular in rural areas, and to ensure the availability of agricultural land. The establishment of solar PV installations on agricultural land in Germany was not prohibited by German legislation, but it was not favoured and thus not eligible for the national support scheme for renewables.[47] However, PV installations on German agricultural land could receive financial support from abroad, in this case from Denmark. Danish legislation did not include similar site restrictions, which would also not have been in accordance with the Danish political context. The result is that the site restrictions are only applicable to German territory, while being recognised and endorsed by Denmark in the CA.[48] As a consequence, projects planned to be established on German territory and participating in the Danish pilot tender would have to follow the German site restrictions as stated in German legislation on support for electricity from renewable energy sources. Denmark thus chose to respect the way in which Germany wishes to deploy renewables on German territory.

Further, if both the site restrictions and the condition that installations have to be ground-mounted were applied to Danish territory this would probably have meant that there would in fact be hardly any available sites in Denmark compared to available sites in Germany. Also, one of the aims of the Danish pilot tender was to include as few restrictions as possible in an attempt to foster competition between bidders.

The outcome of the negotiations thus led to the site restrictions applying only to German territory in both the Danish and German pilot tenders. Some stakeholders have raised concerns that these differences may have represented disadvantages for projects developed in Germany compared to projects in Denmark.[49]

4.3. EXCHANGE AND VERIFICATION OF INFORMATION ON INSTALLATIONS LOCATED ABROAD

The set-up of the system on the exchange of information between countries on installations receiving support but located abroad is tremendously important.

---

47 This meant that a PV installation could be established on agricultural land if it was in accordance with the local planning rules of the relevant German area, but the installation on agricultural land would not then be able to receive financial support from the German national support scheme.

48 Preamble, CA.

49 See section 5 below.

In order to calculate the amount of support that an installation located abroad has to receive, it is necessary to have production data on that specific installation, including the amount of electricity produced, and in this case for Germany the market price in the relevant zone of the electricity market. In the present context, the question is therefore to know how a country can collect the relevant data if the installation is not located on its own territory.

This was the most time-consuming part of the negotiating process since the deliberations involved many different actors such as, for instance, the relevant German Transmission System Operators (TSOs) and the Danish TSO. These are very technical discussions and sufficient time has to be allocated in order to identify the necessary and relevant information and how to transfer it to the partner country.[50] The information necessary for a country to have in order to pay support to an installation located in the partner country was identified and specified in the CA, since the financing country could not gather the necessary information itself on foreign territory.

The obligation was implemented in the CA for the country where the installation is located to transfer the specified information (relevant production data and confirmations with relevant information) to the financing country. The exchange of information also encompasses the transfer of so-called 'confirmations with relevant information'[51] to be sent from the country where the installation is located to the financing country. For instance, if a German-financed installation is located in Denmark as a result of the pilot, Denmark must confirm to Germany that the installation is actually ground-mounted and not, for instance, placed on a roof.

On the question of how incoming information from the partner country is verified, a simple approach was adopted which builds on trust and mutual recognition, namely: if the control system of the partner country is adequate for the installations that are nationally supported there, then it is also adequate for the installations that are supported from abroad. Thus an obligation was implemented in the CA for each country to ensure that the data control system applying to its own national support system would also apply to installations receiving support from the partner country.[52] This approach was based on Germany and Denmark having confidence in each other's control systems but also on the nature of the pilot. It was necessary to find pragmatic solutions and Denmark and Germany were able to test those solutions.

---

50 Data protection rules may also be of relevance in this regard.

51 Article 10(4), CA, to be read with Articles 11(2) and 12(2), CA.

52 Article 13(1), CA.

4.4. STATISTICAL TRANSFERS

The CA forms the legal basis for statistical transfers between Denmark and Germany as provided for in Article 6 of the RES Directive.[53] The RES Directive defines general accounting rules for using the cooperation mechanism of statistical transfers, but does not give any specification of their design. The detailed design and practical implementation of the mechanisms are left to the participating Member States.

In the case of the Danish–German cooperation, the countries agreed on the principle according to which the energy produced will be attributed to the country financing the PV installation.[54] Together with the reciprocity principle,[55] this principle aimed, among other things, to secure public acceptance of the cross-border projects. In the case of the accounting principle, it makes clear that the country that pays support for electricity from an installation located abroad receives the produced energy from that installation to be understood as that it can use it to comply with its national renewable energy target.

Looking ahead beyond 2020, Denmark and Germany have agreed that any statistical transfers shall be made in accordance with any European legislation succeeding the RES Directive.

Finally, as a safety net, Denmark and Germany have agreed to meet if necessary to discuss the implementation of the CA and to propose amendments if needed.[56]

4.5. RISK AND LIABILITY

When assessing risk and liability in the Danish–German cooperation agreement, one of the main concerns was to safeguard investment protection. In the absence of a CA, the system for the exchange of information established would cease and no payment could be made to installations located on the other side of the border.

As a consequence of this – and also due to the basic principle of trust in the cooperation and the acknowledgement of the pilot nature of the cross-border project – no definite exit provisions were included in the CA. By not including such provisions, Denmark and Germany aimed to send the signal to investors that investments could be made without the risk that one of the countries might, at some point in the future, terminate the CA or withdraw from

53 Part V, CA. On statistical transfers, see section 3.1 above.
54 Article 14(1) and (2), CA.
55 See section 3.3.2 above.
56 Article 25, CA.

it without considerable difficulties. It follows from the CA[57] that termination by Denmark or Germany is only possible when it is in accordance with the Vienna Convention from 1969,[58] therefore very difficult.

In case of dispute, the CA provides that the countries will attempt to resolve it through negotiation in good faith;[59] no further specific dispute settlement instruments were introduced. This is further proof of the high level of trust between the two countries. This approach was also based on the pilot/test nature of the cross-border project: since this is the first time that a cross-border project on the tendering of support for renewable energy has taken place, there is a good chance of encountering unforeseen situations during the course of the pilot project, in which case the commitment to negotiate and find solutions to such challenges would probably prove more advantageous to Denmark and Germany than solving such issues through arbitration or other dispute settlement instruments.

5. THE RESULTS OF THE TWO TENDERS

This was the first time Denmark had carried out a tender on financial support for electricity from solar PV, at a time with no other support scheme in place in Denmark for the support of electricity from solar PV installations with delivery to the grid.[60]

Under the Danish tender round, 36 bids were received for a total volume of 79.45 MW. Thus, the 20 MW were exceeded almost fourfold. All of the bids included installations with placements in Denmark, and there were thus no bid for projects with placements in Germany in the mix. The winning bids included a premium of only 12.89 Danish øre/kWh (1.81 euro cents/kWh) as a premium on the top of market price, which was surprising and constitutes a historic low price for solar PV in Denmark. Initially, Denmark expected to commit 8 million Danish kroner annually for 20 years for the subsidy but the estimate for the subsidy is now closer to 2.8 million Danish kroner, which is quite remarkable.

Under the German pilot tender round, 43 bids were received for a total volume of 297 MW. Of that total, 17 bids were for projects with placements in Denmark for a volume of 154 MW, and 26 bids were for projects with placements

57 Article 26(1), CA.

58 Vienna Convention on the Law of Treaties of 23 May 1969.

59 Article 19, CA.

60 It was a condition in the Danish pilot tender for receiving the price premium that the electricity from the winning installation(s) has to be delivered to the transmission grid or to a distribution grid in Denmark, or to an electricity grid in Germany which is electrically connected to the transmission grid in Denmark. See again the Conditions for the pilot tendering procedure for a price premium for electricity generated at solar photovoltaic installations.

in Germany for a volume of 143 MW. Thus, the 50 MW were exceeded almost sixfold.

Surprisingly, a Danish developer cleared the German pilot tender with five winning bids. These winning bids fell to 5.38 euro cents/kWh, which is a very low price by European standards and two cents below the previous national tender held in Germany of support for electricity from solar PV.[61] As the German tender was for a floating premium while the Danish tender was for a fixed premium, the results are difficult to compare. Bids in the Danish tender correspond to the future support costs, whereas in the German tender the future market price has to be deducted from the bids in order to determine the actual support level.

So why did projects located in Denmark clear both tenders in the cross-border pilot run? Could the explanation be that installations in Denmark can be established on agricultural land while installations in Germany cannot? In fact, this would be too simplistic. Even though all five winning bids in the German tender had installations planned to be located on Danish agricultural land, the winning installations in the Danish tender were not planned to be established on Danish agricultural land but on industrial land. In addition, some have indicated that what is being compared here are apples to oranges since the margin between the prices of agricultural land is not identical to the price for certain other types of land in areas fit for solar PV in the two countries. In some parts of Germany, agricultural land is a great deal cheaper than certain other types of land, while in some areas of Denmark the price of agricultural land is around the same level as certain other types of land.

Some commentators have noted that perhaps certain developers for German installations may have been reluctant to participate in the cross-border pilot project since German installations could also participate in a subsequent national German tender to be held later the same year. The assumption made here is that developers for Danish installations may have been more eager to participate since there were no subsequent solar PV tenders planned in Denmark.

Others have suggested that scale could have influenced the fact that no bids with placements in Germany were submitted in the Danish tender, since the opening constituted a rather small volume of only 2.4 MW. It is interesting to note that in order to attract foreign investors, Denmark doubled the effective share of tendered capacity for which the investors could bid from an indispensable 1.2 MW to a total capacity of 2.4 MW.[62]

Moreover, the fixed premium in the Danish pilot tender may perhaps have been unusual for developers of solar PV projects in Germany, where they are used to a floating premium when receiving support from the German support scheme. A sliding price premium assumes variable levels depending on the evolution of

61 This tender attracted winning bids with an average of 7.25 euro cents/kWh.

62 See section 2 above on the set-up of the Danish opening.

market prices and is calculated on a continuous basis as the difference between market prices (usually averaged over a certain period of time) and the awarded price premium. Contrary to the sliding premium, a fixed premium assumes a constant level independent of market price, which means that in the Danish tender – where a fixed premium is received – it is the project developer that assumes the full risk for the development of market prices.

Other observations are of a more technical nature, arguing that a PV installation functions more effectively in cold surroundings, so better in Denmark than in Germany. This is probably not as relevant for the business case as the expected amount of sun radiation for the chosen site. In general, sun radiation in total would be at a lower level in Denmark than in Germany, but this only applies on a general level.

A final hypothesis for explaining the results was that all good sites were already taken in Germany, while good sites were still available in Denmark.

At present, the Danish Energy Agency does not have a full picture and the exact reasons of why installations planned in Denmark won the full capacity of the pilot. Maybe there are no simple and exact answers on the outcome due to the complexity of investor decisions and factors influencing them.

6. CONCLUSION AND OUTLOOK

For Denmark, the pilot project eliminated the risks of potential incompatibility with EU law of the support for electricity from renewables in Denmark in the years 2015 and 2016. In 2016, the Danish Parliament passed the long-term solution concerning the legality of the Danish PSO charge. The long-term solution was approved by the European Commission.[63] Denmark will gradually phase out the PSO charge as a financing means for support for electricity from renewables by January 2022.[64] Support for electricity from renewables will hereinafter be financed directly and totally through the national budget. In the meantime, in order to alleviate any concern regarding compliance with Articles 30 and 110 TFEU, Denmark will invest in infrastructure that would increase cross-border electricity flows.[65] Since the PSO charge from 2022 will no longer be added to the

---

63 Commission decision of 14 December 2016 concerning state aid case no. SA.46882 (2016/N) – Denmark Amendment to the financing of renewable energy.

64 Point (19) of SA.46882 (2016/N).

65 Thereby increasing both the export and the import capacity towards Germany (East Coast connection), including the internal network reinforcement linked to the East Coast connection which is necessary to integrate the increased interconnection capacity. The infrastructure investments will also enhance the interconnection between Sweden and Denmark via the division of Hovegaard Station in two. The total estimated cost of these projects (DKK 889 million/ €118.6 million) exceeds the estimated amount of potential discrimination against imported RES electricity for the period 2017–22 (DKK 850.7 million/ €114 million), *cf.* point (17) of SA.46882 (2016/N).

electricity bill, there will be no direct link between the financing of support for electricity from renewables and the support granted under the Danish support scheme. Thus the risk of the potential discrimination is deemed eliminated[66] and no further cross-border projects are currently in the pipeline in Denmark.

In Germany, the national legal basis for cross-border RES projects was revised in the summer of 2017. Under the German Renewable Energy Sources Act 2017, it is now possible to carry out cross-border tenders of support for electricity from solar PV and from onshore wind for 300 MW each year starting from 2017.

Further, some of the other Member States have committed themselves to open their national support schemes to foreign producers of electricity from renewables, thereby alleviating any concern regarding compliance with Articles 30 and 110 TFEU (potential discrimination against foreign renewable energy producers).[67] The openings are subject to specific conditions and appear to be situations similar to the ones experienced by Denmark and Germany.[68]

Moreover, the RES Directive is currently under revision for the post-2020 regime. In its RES II proposal dated November 2016, the Commission proposed mandatory openings.[69] However, the Council and the European Parliament decided that the opening of renewable support towards neighbouring states will remain voluntary, at an aspirational pace of at least 5% between 2023 and 2026 and 10% between 2027 and 2030.[70]

---

66 Point (19) of SA.46882 (2016/N).

67 The following is a non-exhaustive list of all Member States that have opening commitments in relation to their national support schemes: Commission decision of 8 December 2016 concerning state aid case no. SA.45867 (2016/N) – Belgium, The Belgian federal regime governing renewable energy certificates and aid to the Rentel and Norther wind farm projects; Commission decision of 28 October 2014 concerning state aid case no. SA.36023 (2014/NN) – Estonia, Support scheme for electricity produced from renewable sources and efficient cogeneration; Commission decision of 16 November 2016 concerning state aid case no. SA.44666 – Greece, New operating aid scheme for the production of electricity from RES and HECHP; Commission decision of 11 July 2017 concerning state aid case no. SA.44076 – Hungary, RES support scheme – METÁR; Commission decision of 28 April 2016 concerning state aid case no. SA.43756 (2015/N) – Italy, Support to electricity from renewable sources in Italy; Commission decision of 4 May 2016 concerning state aid case no. SA. 41694 (2015/N) – Portugal, Support to renewable electricity in Portugal, and Commission decision of 4 May 2015 concerning state aid case no. SA.37177 (2015/NN) – Romania, Amendments to the green certificates support system for promoting electricity from renewable sources.

68 The cooperation between Denmark and Germany was born from the circumstance that both countries agreed to open their pilot tenders in order to secure State aid approval for their respective renewables support systems from the Commission.

69 Proposal for a Directive of the European Parliament and of the Council on the promotion of the use of energy from renewable sources (recast) – COM(2016) 767 final.

70 See press release 417/18 from the Council, of 27 June 2018, 'Renewable energy: Council confirms deal reached with the European Parliament', available at: http://www.consilium.europa.eu/en/press/press-releases/2018/06/27/renewable-energy-council-confirms-deal-reached-with-the-european-parliament/pdf.

However, the question can be raised as to the lessons learned from the Danish–German CA. In other words, could the Danish–German cooperation serve as a blueprint for future cross-border RES projects?

To answer this question, it must be noted that the Danish–German pilot is an important test case and that Denmark and Germany as first movers in this field are gathering valuable practical hands-on experience. Furthermore, many of the solutions to difficult problems in the set-up of the cooperation were only possible because Denmark and Germany based the cooperation on trust and mutual recognition, working with the aim of finding pragmatic and effective solutions and acknowledging that this is a test case.

What the Danish–German pilot project demonstrates is that sufficient time and resources have to be allocated for the set-up of these kinds of cross-border RES projects as they are complex, detailed and cover many elements to take into account. This is also the reason why these kinds of projects cannot be handled by a set of common rules, but rather on a case-by-case basis, taking in the specificities of each participating country.

Moreover, it is crucial to understand that the tender design, national legislation, State aid approvals and cooperation agreement (treaty) between the participating countries are all interdependent instruments. There is a close interaction between those different legal instruments and regulatory processes. For instance, national tender conditions have a direct influence on the shaping of the cooperation agreement. Similarly, the bidding process cannot start before the conclusion of the cooperation agreement. Caution is also urged around including detailed provisions when drafting national legislation that could affect the deployment of renewables in the partner country since the partner country would have to agree on all such elements when negotiating the cooperation agreement.

It is also important to note that the Danish–German pilot did not consist of one joint tender. A joint tender would have presented a wide range of new challenges since an agreement would have to be reached between the countries on all aspects of tender design.

The question of whether there is a need to align national conditions would also be relevant, especially in cases where the participating countries have very different legal, political and economic conditions (taxes, environmental standards, grid connection, etc). Sufficient time would have to be allocated for the screening of local conditions and perhaps also for the design of mechanisms to make up for any substantial circumstances that could distort competition due to different location-specific circumstances.

At the current stage of the Energy Union, countries should have as much flexibility as possible when negotiating a cooperation agreement on cross-border RES projects. There is obviously a risk that this approach could prove to be time-consuming since sufficient time would have to be allocated for the set-up of all of the relevant components in a cooperation agreement. However, there is a good chance that any additional time would be well-spent. A high degree of flexibility would ensure that the many different national concerns are taken into consideration, and that there is no unintended or undesirable interference by the financing country with the way that the partner country wishes to deploy renewables on its own territory.

Treaties between countries are in this case the best option. If any active support is to be made by the Commission the best way forward would be the drafting of a non-binding best practice document based on the Danish–German experience. When drafting provisions in the future RES Directive on the opening of national support schemes, it would be preferable not to include in a Directive detailed provisions that could be better addressed in a bilateral treaty between participating countries.

What the Danish–German pilot clearly shows is that there seems to be cost-cutting potential when cross-border RES tenders are introduced.[71] In general support schemes for electricity generated from renewable sources have proved to be an effective way of fostering deployment of renewable electricity. It also seems that competitive procedures are adding cost-efficiency to this mix so that electricity generation from renewable sources is to be deployed at the lowest possible cost for consumers and taxpayers. This is a trend in Europe, supported by the Commission, of switching funding for renewable energy from support levels fixed by the administration/government/parliament to support levels set by competitive tenders.

When preparing cross-border RES projects on the opening of national support schemes, attention should be given to the introduction of specific tools to secure public acceptance. In the Danish–German pilot, the chosen tools were physical import of electricity, statistical transfers and reciprocity.

The Danish–German project is a remarkable step forward, where difficulties were overcome and surprising positive outcomes reached. Other countries now have a basis to build on for future cross-border projects on the opening of national support schemes for the support of electricity from renewable energy sources. It will be interesting to see what significance and role the experiences from the Danish–German pilot will play for the design of the opening of national support schemes as the EU strives for closer cooperation and coordination of Member States' energy policies.

---

71 However, it is important to keep in mind that competitive bidding may not effectively reduce support costs if there is not sufficient competition: thus in some circumstances of very limited competition, competitive bidding may not lead to efficient price discovery.

PART III

ENERGY CONSUMERS AS RENEWABLE ENERGY PRODUCERS: THE CONCEPT OF PROSUMERS

CHAPTER VI
PROSUMER LEGISLATION IN GERMANY

Matthias Lang*

1. INTRODUCTION

Germany has plenty of energy legislation.[1] The reason is that German politicians like energy law, or rather the use of it to implement their political goals. For many decades the energy industry has been a key focus area of German policy. A great number of laws and their amendments cover the desired – or undesired – form of energy generation and supply. Since the 1990s a key theme has been the promotion of renewable energies to achieve the *Energiewende* (energy turnaround), ie the change from nuclear and conventional fuels to renewable energy sources.[2] Starting with the initial Energy Feed-in Act (*Stromeinspeisegesetz*) of 7 December 1990,[3] the German energy industry has undergone numerous changes. Further changes have been strongly influenced by different versions of the Renewable Energy Sources Act[4] (EEG), the successor of the Energy Feed-in Act.[5]

The concept of 'prosumers' has not been at the forefront of German renewable energy interest. However, recent interest in controlling the costs of the *Energiewende* has led to specific rules for prosumers. In recent years, the need to allocate costs and to integrate the ever growing quantities of renewable energy[6] into the energy market has become increasingly important. As renewable energy installations are often not owned by traditional energy supply companies, the number and range

* With thanks to Geraldine Laux, research assistant of Bird & Bird, for her assistance in preparing this chapter.

1 For an overview of legislation governing Germany's energy supply system, see the Federal Ministry for Economic Affairs and Energy map of key strategies, acts, directives, regulations and ordinances, available at: http://www.bmwi.de/Redaktion/EN/Publikationen/gesetzeskarte.pdf?__blob=publicationFile&v=9.

2 An overview of political aspects is available on the website of Federal Ministry for Economic Affairs and Energy at: http://www.bmwi.de/Redaktion/EN/Dossier/energy-transition.html.

3 Federal Law Gazette (*Bundesgesetzblatt*) 1990, part I, 2633.

4 Gesetz für den Vorrang Erneuerbarer Energien, Federal Law Gazette 2000, part I, 305.

5 Commonly referred to as EEG 2000, 2004, 2009, 2012, 2014 and EEG 2017.

6 For an overview of data concerning German electricity, see: http://www.smard.de, which is a special electricity market data platform of the Federal Network Agency.

of actors in the energy sector has increased.[7] In addition to the conventional larger energy generators more and more private households, farmers, energy cooperatives and other independent power producers have started to generate electricity from renewable energy sources.[8] Furthermore, several (often larger) power consumers have built their own (conventional and renewable) generating plants due to a commercially favourable regulatory framework, as prosuming leads to particular benefits. Consequently, prosuming, ie combining production and consumption, has attracted more interest. With decreasing costs of photovoltaic installations and possible battery storage, the potential for becoming prosumers, particularly in the private residential sector, is now further increasing in another area.

The term 'prosumer' does not as yet appear in German energy law. Despite the growing popularity of prosumption, the overarching concept is not recognised in German law, neither in the Renewable Energy Sources Act nor in any other of the various energy statutes.[9] In Germany issues relating to 'prosumption' are dealt with under the heading of 'self-supply' (*Eigenversorgung*), often also referred to as 'auto-supply', 'auto-generation' or 'self-consumption'.[10]

Before 2014, the EEG did not contain any definition of 'self-supply'. The term was subject to interpretation.[11] The first definition of 'self-supply' made its way into the 2014 edition of the Renewable Energy Sources Act[12] and remained in the current EEG 2017.[13] Self-supply is defined as 'consumption of electricity which a natural or legal person consumes himself in the immediate vicinity of the electricity-generating installation if the electricity is not fed through a grid system and this person operates the electricity generating installation himself'.[14] It should be noted that the definition is based on criteria developed through case law. This applies in particular to the decisive criterion involving the requirement that the person generating and the person consuming the electricity should be

7 See also H. J. Inderberg, K. Tews and B. Turner, 'Power from the people' FNI report 5/2016, p 19.

8 Ibid, p 15.

9 Some think tanks are starting to explore certain aspects of self-supply scenarios further, like the analysis commissioned by Agora Energiewende, and carried out by Prognos "Eigenversorgung aus Solaranlagen. Das Potenzial für Photovoltaik-Speicher-Systeme in Ein- und Zweifamilienhäusern, Landwirtschaft sowie im Lebensmittelhandel", 2016, available at: https://www.agora-energiewende.de/fileadmin/Projekte/2016/Dezentralitaet/Agora_Eigenversorgung_PV_web-02.pdf.

10 In the following, 'self-supply' is used as translation for the German term '*Eigenversorgung*'.

11 *Cf.* W. Danner, C. Theobald and F. Lietz, 'Energierecht', CH Beck, Munich June 2017, Sec. 60 EEG 2017.

12 An English translation of the EEG 2014 can be found on the website of the Federal Ministry for Economic Affairs and Energy: http://www.bmwi.de/Redaktion/EN/Downloads/renewable-energy-sources-act-eeg-2014.pdf?__blob=publicationFile&v=1.

13 See Sec. 3 No 19 EEG 2017. An English translation of the EEG 2017 can be found on the website of the Federal Ministry for Economic Affairs and Energy: https://www.bmwi.de/Redaktion/DE/Downloads/E/eeg-2017-gesetz-en.pdf?__blob=publicationFile&v=8. Please note that the EEG is frequently changed and the English translation may not reflect the applicable version of the EEG.

14 Sec. 5 No 12 EEG 2014.

one and the same (*Personenidentität*).[15] For this purpose it is decisive who has actual control (*tatsächliche Sachherrschaft*) over the generating facility and the consuming appliances (*Verbrauchsgeräte*), who determines their operation on one's own authority and who bears the economic risk.[16]

The following sections will first present the background and development of the German legislation governing self-supply. This will be followed by an analysis of the regimes that were introduced in 2014 and 2017 respectively. The final section will present a conclusion and outlook.

2. BACKGROUND AND INCENTIVES FOR SELF-SUPPLY REGULATION

2.1. THE EEG REALLOCATION SCHEME

It is necessary to get an impression of the German renewable energy surcharge (EEG surcharge) reallocation scheme to understand the economic incentives of large and small companies to invest in self-supply.

The following visualisation may help understand the money and energy flow in the EEG system:

Figure 1. EEG Money and Energy Flow

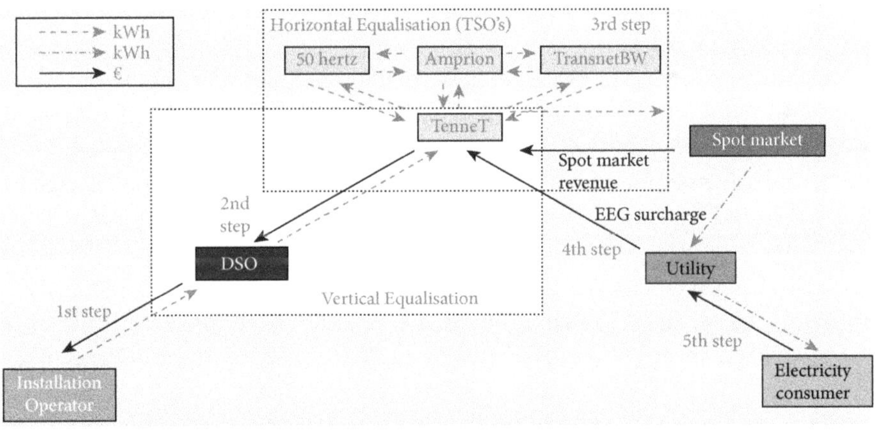

Source: Produced by the author.

15 W. Danner, C. Theobald and F. Lietz, 'Energierecht', Munich, June 2017, Sec. 60 EEG 2017; Federal Network Agency, Guidelines on self-supply, June 2016, p 29, available at: https://www.bundesnetzagentur.de/SharedDocs/Downloads/DE/Sachgebiete/Energie/Unternehmen_Institutionen/ErneuerbareEnergien/Eigenversorgung/Finaler_Leitfaden.pdf?__blob=publicationFile&v=2.

16 Characteristics marked by case law: Federal Supreme Court, 2008, NVwZ 1154; Federal Supreme Court, 2010, NVwZ-RR 315; Federal Network Agency, Guidelines on

Renewable energy producers typically feed electricity into the power grid, usually the distribution grid. The distribution system operators (DSOs) are required to buy the electricity or to pay the market premium.[17] The DSOs can pass these costs on to one of the four transmission system operators (TSOs). The TSO sells the electricity on the electricity exchange, typically getting paid substantially less than they previously had to pay to the DSO. The losses of the TSOs are put on a separate EEG account. Every year an EEG surcharge is determined in order to cover the expected deficit on the EEG account. Payments from the EEG surcharge thus cover the difference between the revenue and the expenditure of the transmission system operators. This surcharge is paid by the consumer for every kWh supplied, through higher power prices.

2.2. THE DEVELOPMENT AND IMPACT OF THE RENEWABLE ENERGY SUPPORT SCHEME

The increasing relevance of self-supply in Germany is closely linked to the development and composition of German electricity prices, rather than a political or individual desire to become energy independent.

For the final consumer, electricity prices – with the exception of a small digression from 2014 to 2015 – have been rising since 2000.[18] An average three-person household consuming on average 3,500 kWh per year, would pay 13.94 ct/kWh in 2000 and 29.23 ct/kWh in 2017.[19] This is a price increase of more than 100% in only 17 years.

Key drivers for this increase are in particular the renewable energy surcharge (and also rising grid fees). Both are closely related to the growth of renewable energy in Germany.

As already mentioned, the EEG surcharge is added to the price of electricity per kWh and aims to cover the extra costs of generating electricity from renewable energies in comparison to other fuels. This surcharge alone rose annually from 0.08 ct/kWh in 1998 to 3.53 ct/kWh in 2011 and 6.880 ct/kWh in 2017.[20] However, at the same time the wholesale power price dropped from 5.112 ct/kWh in 2011 to 2.898 ct/kWh in 2016. In 2018 the EEG surcharge

self-supply, June 2016, pp 30 *et seq*, available at: https://www.bundesnetzagentur.de/SharedDocs/Downloads/DE/Sachgebiete/Energie/Unternehmen_Institutionen/ErneuerbareEnergien/Eigenversorgung/Finaler_Leitfaden.pdf?__blob=publicationFile&v=2.

17 See Sec. 11 EEG 2017.

18 Federal Association of the Energy and Water Industry (BDEW), 2017, '"Strompreisanalyse 2017"', p 8. Available at: https://www.bdew.de/internet.nsf/res/ACB6766AE4CA66E0C1258132004BC873/$file/170531_BDEW_Strompreisanalyse_Mai2017.pdf.

19 Ibid.

20 Ibid, p 10. Available at: https://www.bdew.de/internet.nsf/res/ACB6766AE4CA66E0C1258132004BC873/$file/170531_BDEW_Strompreisanalyse_Mai2017.pdf.

marginally decreased to 6,792 ct/kWh as a result of higher wholesale power prices, which are expected to rise to 3.541 ct/kWh.[21] Higher wholesale prices would decrease the difference between the EEG-supported prices that the transmission system operators have to pay and the prices that the utilities achieve by selling that power to the consumer, thus reducing the loss which has to be balanced using the EEG surcharge.

The increase of the EEG surcharge has in fact contributed to the growth in self-supply. Self-supply has proven to be financially attractive as a result of the way in which the EEG surcharge was levied from electricity consumers.

The obligation to pay the EEG surcharge was originally attached to the 'supply' of power by an electricity supplier. Power that was not 'supplied' to the consumer by another party (but generated by the consumer) was up and until the EEG 2012 not subject to the EEG surcharge.[22] Hence, such an 'internal' supply by a prosumer was exempted from the EEG surcharge. As the EEG surcharge had constantly[23] and substantially been rising,[24] being exempted from paying the surcharge meant a substantial financial saving, creating an increasingly strong incentive for consumers to generate their own power. That incentive applied both to conventional and renewable energy generation. The fact that other (constantly increasing) costs and levies were also charged on the basis of kWh supplied, further contributed to an increasing interest by consumers to generate their own power.

As more and more large consumers (businesses) became interested in developing a system of self-supply, this concept became a problem for the EEG surcharge reallocation scheme. The EEG surcharge reallocation costs amounted to €24.2 billion in 2016.[25] The savings gained by the exempted prosumers on the one hand, led to higher costs for the remaining persons paying the EEG surcharge (and other costs and levies) on the other hand.[26] Increasing levels of

---

21 Federal Ministry for Economic Affairs and Energy, 2017, '"EEG Umlage 2018. Fakten & Hintergründe"'. Available at: http://www.bmwi.de/Redaktion/DE/Downloads/E/eeg-umlage-2018-fakten-hintergruende.pdf?__blob=publicationFile&v=12; and the calculation of the EEG surcharge for 2018 from the German transmission system operators 'Prognose der EEG-Umlage 2018 nach EEV', available at: https://www.netztransparenz.de/portals/1/Content/EEG-Umlage/EEG-Umlage%202017/20171016_Ver%c3%b6ffentlichung_EEG-Umlage_2018.pdf.

22 *Cf.* M Lang and A Lang, 'The 2014 German Renewable Energy Sources Act Revision – From Feed-in Tariffs to Direct Marketing to Competitive Bidding' (2015) JERL 141.

23 With the exception of year 2014/15 in which the EEG surcharge dropped slightly.

24 Federal Association of the Energy and Water Industry (BDEW) (2017), 'Strompreisanalyse 2017'. Available at: https://www.bdew.de/internet.nsf/res/ACB6766AE4CA66E0C1258132004BC873/$file/170531_BDEW_Strompreisanalyse_Mai2017.pdf.

25 Ibid.

26 German Federal Network Agency (2016), 'Guideline on self-supply'. Available at: https://www.bundesnetzagentur.de/SharedDocs/Downloads/DE/Sachgebiete/Energie/Unternehmen_Institutionen/ErneuerbareEnergien/Eigenversorgung/Finaler_Leitfaden.pdf?__blob=publicationFile&v=2.

renewable energy involves higher surcharge costs but these have to be borne by fewer consumers. To stop this development, a revision of the EEG in 2012 introduced the first provision containing certain conditions under which self-supply also could be subject to payment of the EEG surcharge. This concept was further refined with the introduction of the EEG 2014 and 2017.

2.3. THE IMPACT OF EU STATE AID LAW

The cost reallocation issue was not the only reason to change the EEG-surcharge scheme for self-supply. Another reason was that EEG surcharge exemptions came under the scrutiny of European State aid law.[27] The European Commission came to the conclusion that both the support scheme as well as the compensation scheme can qualify as State aid.[28] This assessment was confirmed in the first instance by the General Court.[29]

The Federal Republic of Germany argued that the contested decision of the European Commission infringes Article 107(1) of the Treaty on the Functioning of the European Union (TFEU) in that the Commission wrongly took the view that the operation of the EEG 2012 involves State resources whereas, and in line with the findings of the judgment in *PreussenElektra*,[30] it should be accepted that there is no State aid involved.[31] In line with *PreussenElektra*, the EEG 2012 was said to be legislation issued by a Member State which, first, requires private electricity supply undertakings to purchase electricity produced in their area of supply from renewable energy sources at minimum prices higher than the real economic value of that type of electricity and, secondly, allocates the financial burden resulting from that obligation amongst those electricity supply undertakings and upstream private electricity network operators (ie the DSOs and the TSOs).[32] The Federal Republic of Germany contended that the system under the EEG 2012 is not part of the budget of the State or of a public body, so that the involvement of State resources is precluded.[33]

---

27 *Cf.* C Kahle, 'Die beihilferechtliche Genehmigung des EEG 2014 durch die Europäische Kommission' (2014) NVwZ 1563; M-C Fuchs and F Peters, 'Die Europäische Kommission und die Förderung Erneuerbarer Energien in Deutschland – Die Bewertung des EEG Beihilfeverfahrens und der neuen Umwelt- und Energiebeihilfeleitlinie mit einem kritischen Blick auf die Leitlinienpolitik der Europäischen Kommission' (2014) RdE 409.

28 European Commission, decision of 25 November 2014, 015/1585, SA.33995 (2013/C).

29 General Court, judgment of 10 May 2016, *Germany v European Commission*, T-47/15, EU:T:2016:281.

30 Court of Justice, judgment of 13 March 2001, *PreussenElektra*, C-379/98, EU:C:2001:160.

31 General Court, judgment of 10 May 2016, *Germany v European Commission*, T-47/15, EU:T:2016:281, para 71.

32 Ibid.

33 Ibid, para 72.

However, the General Court decided otherwise. It stated that the system drawn up by the Federal Republic of Germany was substantially different from the system applied by *PreussenElektra*, in the light, in particular, of the detailed rules governing the administration, use, levying and allocation of the EEG surcharge funds.[34]

The Commission stated further that the EEG surcharge therefore must be qualified as a State fund, in particular because final consumers are required to pay a price supplement that can be assimilated to a levy for implementation of a policy set by the State. Also the German transmission system operators act within a framework clearly defined by the German legislature. They are, moreover, strictly monitored by the competent German administrative bodies. Funds financed through compulsory contributions imposed by the legislation of the Member State, administered and apportioned in accordance with that legislation, may be regarded as State resources within the meaning of Article 107(1) TFEU even if they are administered by entities separate from the public authorities.[35]

The General Court therefore concluded that the EEG surcharge of the EEG 2012 involves State resources within the meaning of Article 107(1) TFEU. While contesting this decision, the German Parliament at the same time made major revisions to the self-supply concept in the following EEG 2014 (and the EEG 2017), in order to bring it in line with the Commission's State aid law reasoning.

In fact, while aligning German energy law with the Commission's State aid law position, the German Government upheld its position that neither the EEG support scheme nor the EEG surcharge exceptions should be qualified as State aid. The appeal against the decision of the General Court is pending,[36] and it is hoped that the Court of Justice will soon provide legal certainty.

3. THE EEG 2014 SELF-SUPPLY CONCEPT

Mainly due to the impact of European State aid law, the EEG surcharge provisions for self-supply were modified in the EEG 2014.[37] Exemptions from the EEG surcharge for self-supply and other reasons were from then on severely restricted.[38] The main changes will be discussed below.

34 Ibid, para 104.

35 Ibid, para 125.

36 Court of Justice, *Germany v European Commission*, C-405/16 P.

37 For an overview of the revised EEG 2014 see M Lang and A Lang, 'The 2014 German Renewable Energy Sources Act Revision – From Feed-in Tariffs to Direct Marketing to Competitive Bidding' (2015) JERL 141.

38 *Cf.* Sec. 61 EEG 2014; on the consequences of the EEG 2014 see also M Ruttloff, 'Eigenversorgung durch Bestandsanlagen unter dem EEG 2.0 – wie weit reicht der Bestandsschutz?' (2014) NVwZ 1130.

3.1. EXISTING INSTALLATIONS

To protect justified interests of those consumers who have invested in generation facilities based on earlier versions of the EEG, some self-supply exemptions from the EEG surcharge were maintained.[39]

First, generators facilities constructed prior to 2014 are considered as 'existing plants' (*Bestandsanlagen*) and remained fully exempt from the EEG surcharge. For this to apply, the final consumer needs to:

- operate the electricity-generating installation as a self-producer;
- to the extent that the final consumer consumes the electricity itself;[40] and
- to the extent that the electricity is not conducted through a grid system unless the electricity is consumed in the spatial context of the electricity-generating installation.

Plants are considered 'existing plants' if an installation has been in operation before 1 August 2014 and has been used for self-supply, or if an installation that has been authorised before 23 January 2014 in accordance with the Federal Immission Control Act (*Bundes-Immissionsschutzgesetz*) or permitted pursuant to another provision of federal law and that has been in operation and used before 1 January 2015 for self-supply. Plants are also considered 'existing plants' if an existing installation is being modernised, expanded or replaced at the same site, unless the installed capacity is raised by more than 30% as a result of the modernisation, expansion or replacement.

For existing installations which were commissioned before 1 September 2011 the exemption from paying the EEG surcharge can also apply, but with the following provisos:

- the condition that the electricity is not conducted through a grid system does not apply; and
- the condition that plants are considered existing installations if an existing installation is being modernised, expanded or replaced at the same site, can only be applied if (i) the electricity is not conducted through a grid system

39 See also FJ Säcker, 'Eigenversorgung im EEG 2014. Die Neuregelung zur Belastung von Eigenversorgungsanlagen mit der EEG- Umlage' (2015) EnWZ 264 *et seq*; M Ruttloff and A Lippert, 'Neues und Altbekanntes zur Eigenversorgung' (2015) NVwZ 1719; S Herz and F Valentin, 'Direktvermarktung, Direktlieferung und Eigenversorgung nach dem EEG 2014' (2014) 363. For an overview of constitutional requirements for the protection of legitimate interests see J Panknin, 'EEG-umlagefreie Eigenerzeugung – Status quo und Ausblick' (2014) EnWZ 18 *et seq*.

40 There was some discussion on the relevant time frame for consumption, eg during the same 15-minute interval, for more details see G Sinning and R Ringwald, 'Zu den Voraussetzungen einer EEG-umlagefreien Energieerzeugung' (2014) IR 50 *et seq*.

unless the electricity is consumed in the spatial context of the electricity-generating installation or (ii) the entire electricity-generating installation was owned even before 1 January 2011 by the final consumer, who takes advantage of the privilege of being exempted and the electricity-generating installation was erected on the commercial property of the final consumer.

3.2. EXEMPTED NEW INSTALLATIONS

The exemption also applies to (i) certain new installations for self-suppliers to the extent that the electricity is consumed in the auxiliary and ancillary installations (*Neben- und Hilfsanlagen*) of an electricity-generating installation to generate electricity in the technical sense (electricity consumed by the power station itself)[41] and (ii) self-suppliers that are neither directly nor indirectly connected to a grid-system.[42] Installations are also exempt from the duty of paying if the self-supplier fully supplies itself with electricity from renewable energy sources and does not claim any financial support for the electricity from its installation which it does not consume itself.[43]

Small plants with a total maximum installed capacity of 10 kW are also exempted and the EEG surcharge does not have to be paid for the first maximum 10 MWh of self-consumed power electricity per calendar year. This provision applies from the commissioning of the electricity-generating installation for the duration of 20 calendar years plus the year of commissioning.[44]

3.3. OTHER NEW INSTALLATIONS

All other new installations intended for self-consumption are subject to the full EEG surcharge. Hence, self-supply became, in principle, no longer privileged. Self-supply for new installation has therefore become less attractive.[45]

In addition, a partial exception was introduced for highly efficient combined heat and power plants (CHP-plants or *KWK-Anlagen*). For those installations only a percentage of the EEG surcharge has to be paid. The share was set at 30% in 2015, 35% in 2016 and 40% of the otherwise applicable surcharge in 2017.

41 See Sec. 61 (2) No 1 EEG 2014.
42 See Sec. 61 (2) No 2 EEG 2014.
43 See Sec. 61 (2) No 3 EEG 2014.
44 See Sec. 61 (2) No 4 EEG 2014.
45 See also C Moench and A Lippert, 'Eigenversorgung im EEG 2014. Neue Hürden für die Privilegierung selbst erzeugten Stroms' (2014) EnWZ 397; S Herz and F Valentin, 'Direktvermarktung, Direktlieferung und Eigenversorgung nach dem EEG 2014' (2014) EnWZ 365.

3.4. COMPATIBILITY WITH EUROPEAN LAW

The European Commission accepted the above EEG 2014 exemptions, but only for a transitional period until 2017.[46] As a consequence, the EEG had to be revised in 2017 to meet the requirements of the European Commission.[47]

4. THE EEG 2017 SELF-SUPPLY CONCEPT

4.1. INFLUENCE OF THE EUROPEAN COMMISSION

The EEG 2017 was again amended in 2016 in close coordination with the European Commission. After the EEG 2014 discussions, the Commission published its Guidelines on State Aid for Environment and Energy (Environmental and Energy Aid Guidelines, EEAG).[48] Those Guidelines determine the legal framework under which the Commission would not qualify the EEG surcharge as State aid.

The Guidelines affect, inter alia, the exemption from the EEG surcharge for self-supply. Pursuant to the Guidelines, aid which has been granted before the date of application of the Guidelines can be declared compatible if the adjustment plan foresees a minimum own contribution of 20% of the additional costs of the surcharge without reduction.[49] A progression of the EEG surcharge exemption has to be established by 1 January 2019 at the latest.[50]

In its clearance decision, the European Commission issued some rules on how Germany should adjust the rules governing the EEG surcharge. Undertakings that benefitted from exemptions or reductions before the entry into force of the EEAG, but would no longer be eligible for reductions on renewable charges can see their renewable surcharge being capped at 20% of the full surcharge.[51] The increase of the surcharge must be progressive.[52] Existing installations may however benefit from a full exemption (only) until 2017.[53]

Due to differences between the former EEG 2012 and the EEG 2014 the Commission noted that the establishment of the EEG surcharge under the EEG 2012 followed a different logic to that followed under the EEG 2014.[54] While under the EEG 2012 the surcharge related to all electricity supplied by electricity

46 European Commission, decision of 23 July 2014, C(2014) 5081 final, SA.38632, para 327.
47 Ibid, para 324.
48 European Commission, Guidelines on State aid for environmental protection and energy 2014–2020 (2014/C 200/01). See also for these guidelines chapter 3 of this volume.
49 European Commission, Guidelines on State aid for environmental protection and energy 2014–2020, (2014/C 200/01), para 197.
50 Ibid.
51 European Commission, decision of 23 July 2014, C(2014) 5081 final, SA.38632, para 321.
52 Ibid, para 324.
53 Ibid, para 320.
54 Ibid, para 325.

suppliers (which logically excluded self-supply), the EEG 2014 rested on the principle that the costs of the support to renewables (ie the EEG surcharge) should be borne by and allocated between all electricity consumers. Under that logic, existing self-supply installations should also be subject to the EEG surcharge. However, the self-supply regime is not subject to the EEG surcharge in full since its inception, rather, it is intended to apply a gradual approach to amend the surcharge. Hence, the progression can start less intensely at the beginning of the adjustment period (1 August 2014 to possibly 31 December 2017) and increase towards the end.[55]

Germany committed to review the new exemptions by 2017 and that the revised provisions would be drafted in accordance with State aid rules.[56] In order to avoid legal uncertainties, the German legislature introduced a revised self-supply regime in the EEG 2017.

4.2. THE REVISED EEG 2017 SELF-SUPPLY REGIME

In principle, Germany's goal for the current EEG 2017 was to maintain the self-supply EEG surcharge exemptions for existing installations and to protect justified interests of those who have invested in self-supply installations based on earlier versions of the EEG.[57] This means that exemptions for existing plants will also apply in the future. The obligation to pay the EEG surcharge therefore only applies to existing installations that are fundamentally altered (replacement of the power generator[58]) or for installations that have been recently established. To achieve this, two important amendments were included to the new EEG 2017.

The first amendment contained a material overhaul of the EEG, mainly dealing with the introduction of auctioning to establish support levels.[59] Auctioning will result in a transparent, non-discriminatory and competitive procedure that enables the determination of the parties entitled to support and the level of support to be applied.[60] In this regard, stakeholder diversity and best possible cost effectiveness is to be maintained for electricity generation.[61]

The second amendment contained a major overhaul of the specific self-supply provisions.[62] It contains in fact a very detailed and sophisticated self-supply

55 Ibid, para 325.

56 Ibid, para 324.

57 BT-Drs. 18/10209, p 134; see also T Richter and M Schellberg, 'Schutzloser Bestandsschutz für die Energieerzeugung im Konzern nach dem EEG 2017?' (2017) EnWZ 348 *et seq*.

58 BT-Drs. 18/10209, p. 2.

59 Introduction of the auctioning system already in EEG 2014, see BT-Drs. 18/1304, p 2.

60 See Sec. 3 No 4 EEG 2017.

61 See Sec. 2 (3) EEG 2017.

62 A brief summary of the revised self-supply regime in the EEG 2017 can be found in M Boemke and M Uibeleisen, 'Update: Erste Änderungen des EEG 2017 und des WindSeeG' (2017) NVwZ 287.

regime,[63] whereas the earlier versions of the EEG only marginally overhauled the self-supply provisions. The wording concerning the self-supply rules of the EEG 2017 is longer and more detailed than all of the original precious provision of EEG 2000 put together.

As a general rule, under the 2017 EEG all final consumers, including self-suppliers, are required to pay the full EEG surcharge.[64] An exemption from the obligation to pay the EEG surcharge only applies in exceptional cases.[65] Self-supply is not subject to the EEG surcharge in the following four situations:

- for installation to the extent that the electricity is consumed in the auxiliary and ancillary installations of an electricity-generating installation to generate electricity in the technical sense (so-called generating plant self-consumption or *Kraftwerkseigenverbrauch*);[66]
- if the self-supplier (*Eigenversorger*) is neither directly nor indirectly connected to the grid system;[67]
- if the self-supplier fully supplies itself with electricity from renewable energy sources and does not claim any financial support for the electricity from its installation which it does not consume itself;[68] or
- if electricity is generated by electricity-generating installations with a total maximum installed capacity of 10 kW, for a maximum of 10 MWh of self-consumed electricity per calendar year. This applies from the commissioning of the electricity-generating installation for the duration of 20 calendar years plus the year of commissioning.[69]

The EEG 2017 also contains special grandfathering clauses for existing plants. Under specific conditions these plants are not subject to the EEG surcharge.[70] The EEG surcharge can be reduced to 0%, only if the final consumer operates the electricity-generating installation as a self-producer (*Eigenerzeuger*),[71] insofar as the final consumer consumes the electricity himself[72] and insofar as the electricity is not conducted through a grid system unless the electricity is consumed in the spatial context of the electricity-generating installation.[73]

63 The own-supply regime is being set up in Sec. 61 EEG 2017 *et seq.*
64 See Sec. 61 EEG 2017.
65 These exceptional cases are set up in Secs. 61a and 61b EEG 2017.
66 See Sec. 61a No 1 EEG 2017.
67 See Sec. 61a No 2 EEG 2017.
68 See Sec. 61a No 3 EEG 2017.
69 See Sec. 61a No 4 EEG 2017.
70 See Secs. 61c and 61d EEG 2017.
71 See Sec. 61c (1) No 1 EEG 2017.
72 See Sec. 61c (1) No 2 EEG 2017.
73 See Sec. 61c (1) No 3 EEG 2017.

According to the EEG 2017 an existing installation is defined as an electricity-generating installation which:

- the final consumer has operated before 1 August 2014 as a self-producer and in accordance with the requirements of section (1) EEG 2017;[74,75]
- was authorised before 23 January 2014 pursuant to the Federal Immission Control Act or permitted pursuant to another provision of federal law, generated electricity for the first time after 1 August 2014 and was used before 1 January 2015 in compliance with the requirements of sentence 1;[76] or
- modernises, expands or replaces an electricity-generating installation pursuant to numbers 1 or 2 at the same site unless the installed capacity is raised by more than 30% as a result of the modernisation, expansion or replacement;[77] and
- has not been modernized, expanded or replaced after the 31 December 2017.[78,79]

In addition to a full exemption from the obligation to pay the EEG surcharge, there are also rules providing for surcharge reductions. In case of self-supply the EEG surcharge can be reduced to a certain percentage. That is to say, such reductions apply to self-supply using CHP plants[80] and existing plants which have been replaced without increasing capacity.[81]

Additional rules apply in case of the transfer of ownership of existing installations,[82] withdrawal of surcharge exemptions if notification obligations are not complied with,[83] metering and invoicing for own-supply combined with other supply,[84] levying the EEG surcharge for certain self-supply installations and final consumers,[85] network operator obligations,[86] payment obligation

---

74 That means the consumer operates the electricity generating plant as an auto-producer, the final consumer consumes the electricity by himself and the electricity is not passed through a grid unless the electricity is consumed in a spatial connection with the electricity generating plant.

75 See Sec. 61c (2) No 1a EEG 2017.

76 See Sec. 61c (2) No 1b EEG 2017.

77 See Sec. 61c (2) No 1c EEG 2017

78 See Sec. 61c (2) No 2 EEG 2017.

79 Further reduction of the EEG surcharge to zero percent shall apply to so-called older existing plants (*ältere Bestandsanlagen*) under the requirements of Sec. 61d EEG 2017.

80 Sec. 61b EEG 2017.

81 Sec. 61e EEG 2017.

82 Sec. 61f EEG 2017. It should be noted that the self-supply privilege only applies to the legal person who supplies its own energy and cannot be transferred to a legal successor, *cf.* T Richter and M Schellberg, 'Schutzloser Bestandsschutz für die Eigenversorgung im Konzern nach dem EEG 2017' (2017) EnWZ 351 *et seq.*

83 Sec. 61g EEG 2017.

84 Sec. 61h EEG 2017.

85 Sec. 61i EEG 2017.

86 Sec. 61j EEG 2017.

exemptions,[87] transmission system operator obligations,[88] information obligations for final consumers and self-suppliers,[89] involvement of the Federal Network Agency[90] and EEG surcharge labelling.[91]

4.3. COMPATIBILITY WITH EUROPEAN LAW

Germany notified the EEG 2017 in July 2016 under the EU State aid rules and the European Commission decided on this in December 2016.[92] This decision of the European Commission referred only to the original version of the EEG 2017.[93] It considered the auction scheme to be in line with EU State aid rules.[94] The Commission reminded Germany that, in accordance with Article 108 (3) TFEU, any plans to refinance, alter or change the surcharge regime have to be notified to the Commission. In practice this means that all amendments to the EEG have to be drafted in cooperation with the Commission.

The new self-supply provisions were only part of the first amendment of the EEG 2017,[95] not its original version. The amendment was notified separately. For this reason, the European Commission addressed the rules on self-supply in a second decision.[96] In the second decision the European Commission endorsed German plans on the exemptions and reductions of the EEG surcharge for all existing self-suppliers (ie having entered into operation before August 2014), new suppliers (ie having entered into operation as of August 2014) using renewable energy sources and new small self-supply installations.[97]

---

87 Sec. 61k EEG 2017.

88 Sec. 74 EEG 2017.

89 Sec. 74a EEG 2017.

90 Sec. 76 EEG 2017.

91 Sec. 78 EEG 2017.

92 European Commission, decision of 20 December 2016, C(2016) 8789 final, SA 45461, para 307.

93 Law for the introduction of auctions for electricity produced from renewable energies and for other modifications of the legal framework applicable to renewable energies (*Gesetz zur Einführung von Ausschreibungen für Strom aus erneuerbaren Energien und zu weiteren Änderungen des Rechts der erneuerbaren Energien*), Federal Law Gazette 2016, part I 2258.

94 European Commission, decision of 20 December 2016, C(2016) 8789 final, SA 45461, para 307.

95 By the law for the amendment of provisions for electricity generation from CHP and for self-supply (*Gesetz zur Änderung der Bestimmungen zur Stromerzeugung aus Kraft-Wärme-Kopplung und zur Eigenversorgung*), Federal Law Gazette 2016, part I 3106.

96 European Commission, press release of 19 December 2016, IP/17/5366. The decision text is not yet available. The non-confidential version of the decision will be made available under the case number SA.46526.

97 European Commission, press release of 19 December 2016, IP/17/5366.

5. OUTLOOK

Germany has a sophisticated self-supply system allowing consumers to be active as energy producers, ie being prosumers.[98] The system has, however, undergone some important changes.

In contrast to the self-supply regime provided by earlier versions of the EEG, the current system does not intend to promote self-supply. Its key purpose is to address the cost allocation issue created by Germany's policy of increasing the use of renewable energy sources. This allocation cost regime has been strongly influenced by financial and State aid law reasons.

The financial reasons are largely related to the costs of renewables, in particular cost reallocation due to the rising EEG surcharge. The original German approach was to include these costs in every kWh supplied by someone else. This means that originally self-supplied power did not have to pay these costs. Not surprisingly, the possibility of being exempted from the requirement to pay these costs was the main commercial incentive to become a self-supplier and increased self-supply. This led to a situation where all other suppliers had to pay more to support RES, which increased due to the higher use of renewable energy sources. The view of the European Commission, that the support granted is to be considered State aid, constitutes an additional complication to the EEG regime.

Germany has tried to address the issues partly by changing the cost allocation scheme, so that self-suppliers too may have to bear certain additional costs as a result of which the regime no longer (or at least on a smaller scale) supports self-supply.

Despite the decreasing incentive for self-supply the use of self-supply is growing. Therefore it will be necessary to bear in mind how costs associated with renewables support schemes are allocated in the future. With a decreasing amount of non-renewably generated power, any cost allocation scheme to support certain types of power generation will have to find a solution for this challenge. We will need solutions that allocate costs and benefits fairly, taking account of physical requirements to maintain a secure and affordable supply of energy, in compliance also with European State aid law. Any prosumer support regime will have to take this into account.

---

98 The Federal Network Agency introduced a guideline for self-supply, in which it gives opinion on the interpretation of the complex regulations in the area of self-supply, see Federal Network Agency, Guidelines on self-supply, June 2016, p 29, available at: https://www.bundesnetzagentur.de/DE,/Sachgebiete/ElektrizitaetundGas/Unternehmen_Institutionen/ErneuerbareEnergien/Eigenversorgung/Eigenversorgung-node.html. It should be noted that the guidelines are only interpretation suggestions and are not binding. *Cf.* M Ruffloff and A Lippert, 'Neues und Altbekanntes zur Eigenversorgung. Der Leitentwurf der Bundesnetzagentur' (2015) NVwZ 1716 *et seq.*

CHAPTER VII
LEGAL FRAMEWORK FOR PROSUMERS IN THE NETHERLANDS

Lea DIESTELMEIER and Dirk KUIKEN*

1. INTRODUCTION

Driven by the EU Renewables Directive[1] obligation to achieve a 14% share of renewable sources in gross final energy consumption in 2020, the Netherlands has introduced various legal provisions aiming at incentivising the generation of electricity based on renewable energy sources (RES). Those provisions mainly entail financial support measures which led, for example, to the implementation of large-scale on- and offshore wind turbines, but also to small-scale generation such as photovoltaic (PV) installations on residential houses. While the latter can be integrated by individual small consumers on their own premises (referred to as 'behind the meter', or in law 'transfer point'),[2] larger facilities (wind turbines or PV parks) can also be deployed in a collective effort of small consumers beyond their own premises.[3] In this way, small consumers can engage in electricity generation and gain subsequent financial benefits. However, engaging in electricity generation does not necessarily enable small consumers

---

* Lea Diestelmeier, LL.M. and Dirk Kuiken, LL.M. are Ph.D. researchers at the Groningen Centre of Energy Law, University of Groningen. The authors wish to express their gratitude to Prof Dr Martha M Roggenkamp and Prof Dr Hans Vedder for their valuable support in the writing of this chapter and to the Netherlands Organisation for Scientific Research (NWO) for enabling this research under the projects SmaRds (No 408-13-005) and DISPATCH (No 408-13-056), both part of the 'Uncertainty Reduction in Smart Energy Systems' call.

1 Article 3(2) in conjunction with Annex I, A. Directive 2009/28/EC (OJ L140/16). The total share of renewable energy consumption in 2014 was 5.5%; European Commission, 'Renewable Energy Progress Report', Brussels, 1 February 2017, COM(2017) 57 final. The share of renewable electricity consumption in 2014 was 9.98%, see: http://statline.cbs.nl/statweb/publication/?dm=slnl&pa=82610ned.

2 The transfer point is the physical point which separates the electricity network and the installation, see Begrippencode elektriciteit, *Stcr.* 2016, 21418 (Definition Code). For the latest version see: http://wetten.overheid.nl/BWBR0037938/.

3 Small consumers are consumers having a connection of 3*80A or less. See Article 95a Elektriciteitswet 1998, *Stb.* 1998, 427 (Electricity Act). For the latest version, see: http://wetten.overheid.nl/BWBR0009755/.

to be self-sufficient. Even though they might generate the same amount they consume, usually the intermittent character of RES does not coincide with the main consumption periods. Storage facilities (eg batteries or electric vehicles) could capture excess electricity for later consumption, but so far storage is not deployed on a wide scale. Therefore, small consumers who start generating electricity (individually or collectively) remain dependent on electricity supply by a supply company. These small consumers who also produce electricity are often referred to as 'prosumers'. While this term is not legally defined in the Netherlands, several legal provisions exist which incentivise consumers to engage in electricity generation (in the following, 'prosumer legislation'). This chapter outlines the main legal provisions and reflects on whether these provisions are suitable for a future electricity sector with increasing numbers of 'prosumers'.

In order to provide guidance and structure to the analysis of the legal framework of prosumers in the Netherlands, the chapter first analyses how prosumers are defined in the Netherlands (section 2). Legal provisions on prosumers in the Netherlands can be categorised as those which either incentivise individual consumers, mostly small consumers, or groups of consumers (communities) to produce RES. This chapter discusses in more detail the categorisation of 'individual' and 'collective' prosumers (sections 3 and 4 respectively) by discussing and assessing the main regulatory provisions. Subsequently the chapter reflects briefly on the development of prosumers in the Netherlands, the recent legal developments on EU level and how these developments interact with the legal framework of the Netherlands (section 5). Section 6 concludes.

2. DEFINITION

The term 'prosumer' is not defined in law. Nonetheless, the term 'prosumer' is often used in practice and refers to a composition of the words 'producer' and 'consumer', which suggests that a prosumer is a consumer that also produces electricity. Both terms 'producer' and 'consumer' are defined in the Dutch Electricity Act (E-Act). According to the E-Act, a producer is an organisational unit that produces electricity, whilst a consumer is in principle any person with a grid connection.[4] The definition of a consumer further unfolds in two sub-categories: small and large consumers. Small consumers include both households and small undertakings having a grid connection with a capacity below 3*80A. Large consumers have a grid connection of more than 3*80A.[5] The remainder of this chapter concentrates on prosumer regulation applicable

4 Article 1(1)(c) and 1(1)(g) Electricity Act.

5 See Definition Code.

to small consumers. From a legal perspective, prosumers are considered to be consumers, as it is very unlikely that they can be considered as an 'organisational unit' (which is a requirement for falling within the legal definition of a producer). Therefore, most requirements in the electricity codes applicable to producers do not apply to prosumers. Focusing on small consumers as prosumers, a further distinction can be made between individual prosumers and collective prosumers. For both types specific rules apply, defining their legal position in the electricity sector. This chapter analyses both types of 'prosumers', starting with the individual prosumers.

3. INDIVIDUAL PROSUMERS

3.1. INTRODUCTION

Individual prosumers consume and produce electricity. The produced electricity can of course be consumed within the installation of the consumer itself (self-consumption). Yet, surplus electricity could also be provided and sold to other consumers. However, in the Netherlands, selling electricity to other (small) consumers is limited to those suppliers holding a licence for supplying small consumers.[6] Although in theory small consumers could apply for such a licence, the administrative burden and the requirements connected to it render it unlikely that prosumers would be interested or fulfil the conditions for being awarded a supply licence. This leaves individual prosumers with two options: a) sell the electricity they have produced to a supplier, or b) consume all electricity they have produced. In selling their (excess, not self-consumed) electricity to a supplier, prosumers in the Netherlands have a right to a reasonable compensation for the excess production.[7] Apart from the discussion on what constitutes reasonable compensation, this option seems fairly straightforward. The option of self-consumption is more complicated.

Self-consumption can be understood in two different ways. One is from a technical–economic perspective, in which self-consumption is defined on the basis of the actual amount of electricity which is consumed within the installation of a consumer. The other is from a legal perspective, in which law defines what counts as self-consumption. Whilst the first perspective describes the physical process of electricity flows, the second perspective defines how much prosumers have to pay for their electricity supply. The remainder of this section explains how self-consumption is regulated in the Netherlands. More specifically, the first subsection explains how the 'net-metering scheme' (which defines how self-consumed electricity is settled) in the Netherlands works. Given that the goal

6 Article 95a Electricity Act.

7 Articles 95c(2) and 31c(3) Electricity Act.

of this scheme is to incentivise small consumers to invest in RES and, in doing so, promoting the use of RES, this subsection also briefly assesses the extent to which the net-metering scheme is succeeding in terms of RES promotion. Based on the conclusion of this assessment, the section analyses how a more recent regulatory development, the roll-out of smart meters, enables a different regulatory approach, which seems to better correspond to the technical–economical perspective.

3.2. NET-METERING

In the Netherlands, a net-metering (in Dutch, *saldering*) scheme is applicable.[8] This is a tax-exemption scheme, aimed at incentivising prosumers (consumers) to invest in RES. Under this scheme, small consumers can offset their total production with their total consumption annually, with a cap of 5,000 kWh.[9] More generally, net-metering is a system in which the total consumption and production is 'netted' and settled for a pre-defined period of time. This can be illustrated by the following example: over the period of one year, person A has consumed 2,500 kWh and produced 2,100 kWh. When settling the amount of consumption and production, an amount of 400 kWh net consumption remains. This amount is charged by person A's electricity supplier. However, in reality person A did not self-consume all of his produced electricity. Assuming person A used a PV installation for producing his electricity, peak production took place at the sunniest hours of the day. Those hours do not necessarily coincide with (peak) consumption periods. Person A simply consumes electricity produced elsewhere during peak-consumption hours, whilst the surplus of produced electricity is fed back into the electricity system during RES peak-production hours. If a prosumer produced more than he consumed, as mentioned above, the prosumer's supplier is required to provide a reasonable compensation for the excess (amount that cannot be netted) production.[10]

Regardless of whether person A actually self-consumed all electricity produced, the net-metering scheme enables person A to have his electricity supply costs calculated as if he self-consumed all of his own produced electricity up to the amount of consumption (not exceeding 5,000 kWh on a yearly basis). In the end, person A is only required to pay his supplier for any kWh he consumed more than he produced, whilst the price of person A's self-consumed (net-metered) electricity is based on the investment costs of his production installation.

---

8 Article 31c Electricity Act.
9 Article 31c(2) Electricity Act.
10 Article 31c(3) Electricity Act.

In the end, the net benefit to person A is mainly tax savings, as taxes only have to be paid for supplied electricity. For all self-consumed kWhs of electricity, no taxes are due. In the Netherlands, consumers have to pay VAT, energy taxes[11] and a charge for renewable energy (in Dutch *opslag duurzame energie*, ODA).[12] Although the costs for producing 1 kWh of solar power usually exceed the costs of electricity consumed from a supplier, the amount of taxes (around €0.14 gross)[13] is considerably higher than the actual costs of the kWh (between €0.06–0.07/kWh in 2017).[14,15] As mentioned above, these taxes are not due under the net-metering scheme. Depending on the investment costs and the investment period, the costs per kWh can be determined. For example, in order to produce 5,000 kWh/year whilst using a PV installation, around €11,000 should be invested. In this scenario, the payback period would be around 10–11 years.[16] After this period, every net-metered kWh is in principle free of charge. This makes the net-metering scheme economically very attractive for small consumers.

Although the rationale behind the net-metering scheme is largely considered to be financially incentivising RES production, net-metering also has a more practical component. The traditional electricity meters, that were designed to measure the amount of electricity consumed annually, are unsuitable to apply shorter netting periods. Having shorter netting periods (eg hourly, in order to measure production and consumption in peak and off-peak periods) would require prosumers to collect and send their meter-values more frequently to their supplier. A net-metering scheme that nets the amount of consumed and produced electricity annually reduces the required human resources for both

---

11 The energy taxes are regulated at EU level by Directive 2003/96/EC (OJ L283/51). This Directive fixes minimum energy tax levels. For electricity the levels are set at a minimum of €0.50/MWh for commercial use and €1.00/MWh for non-commercial use (Annex I, C). RES can however be exempted from this minimum (Article 15(1)(b)).

12 The renewable energy charge is aimed at funding the support scheme for (non-household) renewable production (*Stimulering Duurzame Energieproductie* – SDE). See Explanatory Memorandum Regels voor de opslag duurzame energie (Wet opslag duurzame energie), *Kamerstukken* 2011–12, 33 115, 3.

13 VAT is 21%, see Article 9(1) Wet op Omzetbelasting 1968, *Stb.* 1968, 329, for the latest version see: http://wetten.overheid.nl/BWBR0002629/2017-03-10. Energy taxes for a small consumer are €0.1013/kWh (2017), see Article 59(1)(c) Wet belastingen op milieugrondslag, *Stb.* 1994, 923, for the latest version see: http://wetten.overheid.nl/BWBR0007168/2017-01-01. The renewables charge is set at €0.0074, see Article I Wijziging van de Wet opslag duurzame energie in verband met de vaststelling van tarieven voor 2017, *Kamerstukken* 2015–16, 34 497, 3.

14 See: http://statline.cbs.nl/Statweb/publication/?DM=SLNL&PA=81309NED&D1=7-8&D2=1&D3=l&D4=0-3,5-8,10-13,15-18,20-23,25-28,30-33,35-38,40-43,45-50&HDR=G1,G2,T&STB=G3&VW=T.

15 It should however be noted that all small consumers receive a yearly reduction of their energy taxes of around €308.54, see Article 63(1) Wet belastingen op milieugrondslag. Assuming a yearly consumption of 3,500 kWh would give an average tax reduction of €0.09/kWh, leaving around €0.05/kWh of taxes.

16 Based on a supply tariff of €0.21/kWh: (11000/0.21)/5000 = 10.47 per year.

prosumers and suppliers to register the required measurements for settling the amount of consumed and produced electricity. Therefore, the annual net-metering scheme provides not only an economic advantage to small consumers, but also a highly practical solution for settling RES production by prosumers in their electricity bills.

However, the annual net-metering scheme is not without flaws. During peak-consumption hours, the electricity price is higher than during off-peak consumption hours. Likewise, during RES peak production-periods, the price of electricity is lower. An annual net-metering scheme is incapable of capturing those price differences. As such, a major downside of net-metering is its inability to consider the actual price of electricity. Consequently, consumers are not incentivised to respond to market signals.[17] Another downside of the net-metering scheme is its inefficiency in promoting RES.[18] According to a recent study, the net-metering scheme is a relatively inefficient method for promoting RES compared to other incentive schemes. As a consequence, it is anticipated that the Dutch Government will replace the annual net-metering scheme by 2023.[19]

Yet, replacing the net-metering scheme with a different scheme would be impossible in combination with a traditional electricity meter. The introduction of smart meters promises to bring about new opportunities.[20] Smart meters are able to measure and communicate frequent measurements, up to milliseconds, without requiring large capacities of human resources. Therefore, the above mentioned practical barrier for prosumers to correspond to market signals, going beyond the net-metering scheme, disappears.

3.3. SMART-METERING

Smart meters[21] are digital meters which can communicate meter readings between consumers and, for example, system operators or suppliers up to real

17 For further background on consumer participation in the electricity market, see, eg, L Diestelmeier and D Kuiken, 'Smart Electricity Systems: Access Conditions for Household Customers under EU Law' (2017) *European Competition and Regulatory Law Review* 1(1), 36–46.

18 ECN, 'De Salderingsregeling: Effecten van een aantal hervormingsopties' 5 May 2017.

19 Brief van de Minister van Economische Zaken, 12 juli 2017, Stimulering duurzame energieproductie, Kamerstukken 2016–17, 31 239, 263. The following four alternative schemes are considered: 1) Netting of taxes only, having different tariffs for electricity consumed and electricity delivered (back) to the supplier; 2) Netting of taxes only with a pre-specified cap (maximum percentage that can be netted); 3) Subsidy from the Government for every kWh fed back into the electricity system, additional to the tariff paid by the supplier; 4) One-time subsidy from the government, available to prosumers when purchasing a PV installation.

20 Brief van de Minister van Economische Zaken, 12 juli 2017, Stimulering duurzame energieproductie, Kamerstukken 2016–17, 31 239, 263.

21 *Slimme meters* or *op afstand uitleesbare meetapparaten* in Dutch.

time. The biggest advantage of smart meters is that they enable frequent and accurate data flows on electricity consumption and network power flows. This enables system operators to gain more information on the (expected) loads (power flows) in their systems, suppliers to use smart meter data to optimise their energy trades and consumers to gain more control over their own energy consumption, to react on real time market prices or take into account the system state to provide supporting services to the system operator.[22] In other words, smart meters are able to generate information necessary for the system user, service suppliers and system operators to become more flexible and increase the overall efficiency of the electricity system.[23]

In the EU, all Member States are required to implement smart meters. Directive 2009/72/EC states that, subject to a cost-benefit analysis, 'at least 80% of consumers shall be equipped with [smart meters] by 2020'.[24] Following this obligation, the Netherlands carried out a cost-benefit analysis, which was assessed positively.[25] In this analysis, the smart meter was expected to contribute to the following goals: integrating RES and facilitating smart grids; increasing energy efficiency; increasing energy savings; enabling more efficient connection management by the system operator; more accurate and frequent billing; network monitoring; involving consumers in the electricity system; and facilitating market players in offering services to, for example, consumers or system operators.[26] Following the cost-benefit analysis, the Netherlands adopted a smart meter decree.[27] Based on this decree, all small consumers should be equipped with a smart meter by the end of 2020.[28] Consumers are not, however, obliged to accept a smart meter being installed in their installation: they have the right to refuse a smart meter.[29]

---

22 See, eg, D Kuiken, HF Más, M. Haji Ghasemi, N Blaauwbroek, TH Vo, T van der Klauw and PH Nguyen, 'Energy Flexibility from Large Prosumers to Support Distribution System Operation–A Technical and Legal Case Study on the Amsterdam Arena Stadium' (2018) Energies 11(1), 120.

23 See, eg, N Blaauwbroek, D Kuiken, PH Nguyen, H Vedder, MM Roggenkamp and H Slootweg, 'Distribution Network Monitoring: Interaction between EU Legal Conditions and State Estimation Accuracy' (2018) Energy Policy 115, 78–87.

24 Annex I(2) Directive 2009/72/EC (OJ L211/55).

25 R van Gerwen, F Koenis, M Schrijner and G Widderschoven, *Intelligente Meters in Nederland, Herziene financiële analyse en adviezen voor beleid*, DNV KEMA 13 July 2010.

26 Ibid.

27 Besluit van 16 oktober 2014, houdende wijziging van het Besluit op afstand uitleesbare meetinrichtingen ten behoeve van de grootschalige uitrol van de slimme meter, *Stb.* 2014, 392.

28 Article I Besluit op afstand uitleesbare meetinrichtingen ten behoeve van de grootschalige uitrol van de slimme meter.

29 Article 26ae(11) Electricity Act. It should be noted here that the implementation of smart meters in the Netherlands led to much public debate on privacy and security concerns, see eg C Cuijpers and B Koops, 'Smart Metering and Privacy in Europe: Lessons from the Dutch Case' in S Gutwirth, R Leenes, P de Hert and Y Poullet (eds), *European Data Protection: Coming of Age*, Springer, Dordrecht 2012.

Once installed, based on the E-Act, the smart meter can be configured in three different reading modes.[30] The first is the 'default' mode. In this mode, smart meters are read bimonthly for supply purposes and at any rate required for, for example, contractual or legal obligations for, for example, system operators or energy service providers.[31] The second is the 'administratively-off' mode. In this mode, the smart meter is set to 'switched off', forcing the meter to function as a traditional meter.[32] The third is the 'consent' mode. In this mode, the consumer has given its consent for more frequent readings (beyond the readings of the default mode) for pre-specified purposes.[33] Unfortunately, the pursued goals are not secured by the first two modes. Only the 'consent' mode could enable the functions required for ensuring the goals used for the cost-benefit analysis (hence, grounds for the smart meter implementation).

In any case, in order for the prosumer to become more active and to allow for more benefits than mere net-metering, detailed and accurate data flows are required. These data flows allow prosumers and, for example, system operators or suppliers to lower their costs or increase their revenues. As such, smart meters are considered as an important tool for the further integration of prosumers in the Netherlands. Nevertheless, it remains to be seen to which extent the smart meter will realise its potential in practice.

4. COLLECTIVE PROSUMERS

4.1. INTRODUCTION

The preceding sections outlined the provisions on net-metering, which is tailored for consumers generating on their own premises. This limits the potential benefit of investing in small-scale renewable generation to consumers possessing the necessary space for installations and sufficient financial means for such investment. To also enable persons who do not possess those necessary means, legislation in the Netherlands allows for collective organisations to engage in electricity generation. The following sections explain and discuss two options provided by Dutch legislation for consumers to collectively engage in RES-based generation. Both result from the so-called 'Energy Agreement for Sustainable Growth' (in Dutch *Energieakkoord voor duurzame groei*), which was agreed between public and private parties in 2013 in order to promote the use

---

30 Article 4 Besluit op afstand uitleesbare meetinrichtingen, *Stb.* 2011, 511.

31 Article 26ab(1), art. 7(1) Besluit factuur, verbruiks- en indicatief kostenoverzicht energie, *Stb.* 2015, 190.

32 Article 26ac(2) Electricity Act.

33 Article 26ab(3)–(4) Electricity Act, and Article 8(a) Wet bescherming persoonsgegevens, *Stb.* 2000, 302.

of RES.[34] In this agreement the goal of enabling and incentivising decentralised generation of RES by new organisational forms was reiterated. The first resulting regulatory option is the so-called 'Postal Code Area Arrangement', which incentivises joint investments in RES-based generation. The second option is somewhat more intricate as it is not simply a stimulus for joint generation, but provides legal space for small-scale pilot projects. These pilot projects are meant for experimenting with new actors and roles, but also deliver insights on how to adjust electricity sector legislation. This option is therefore called the 'Decree for Experiments with Decentralised Renewable Electricity Generation'.[35]

4.2. POSTAL CODE AREA ARRANGEMENT

The 'Postal Code Area Arrangement' (PCA)[36] incentivises collective generation by providing tax reductions for the members of the collective. The amount of tax reduction depends on the member's share. The collective makes an investment in RES generation and is the owner of that installation which allows them a similar tax reduction as in the net-metering scheme outlined above. This arrangement is also sometimes referred to as 'distant net-metering'.[37] The name, 'Postal Code Area Arrangement', stems from the condition that the members and the generation installation have to be located in the same or bordering postal code areas. The idea behind this geographical delineation is to encourage local engagement by incentivising people living close to each other to invest in local renewable generation. The legal basis of the PCA arrangement is the option to grant tax exemptions to electricity generated from RES, which is a similar approach as for the net-metering scheme.[38] This section outlines the functioning and conditions of the PCA arrangement, mentioning first obstacles and adjustments, and finally evaluating its implementation to date.

The PCA arrangement has been in force since 1 January 2014. People who want to invest in renewable energy generation must first engage in or establish a legal entity in the form of a cooperative or an owners' association for the purpose of collective generation. Membership of these entities is restricted to small consumers.[39] This may include small businesses as long as they do not

---

34 Sociaal-Economische Raad, 'Energieakkoord voor duurzame groei', September 2013.

35 Besluit van 28 februari 2015, houdende het bij wege van experiment afwijken van de Elektriciteitswet 1998 voor decentrale opwekking van duurzame elektriciteit (Experimental Decree), *Stb* 2015, 99.

36 PCA arrangement or in Dutch, *de postcoderoos regeling*. The official title of the Regulation is 'reduced tariff for collective generation' (in Dutch, *verlaagd tarief voor collectieve opwek*). For the original publication see Wet van 18 december 2013 tot wijziging van enkele belastingwetten en enige andere wetten (Belastingplan 2014), *Stb*. 2013, 565.

37 In Dutch, *salderen op afstand*.

38 Article 64(1) Wet belastingen op milieugrondslag. Also see section 3.2 above on net-metering.

39 Article 59a(1) Wet belastingen op milieugrondslag.

possess more than 20% of the share.[40] Once the collective has established a legal entity (hereafter 'the entity'), it has to apply to be recognised as a legal entity which is eligible to receive the tax reduction under the PCA arrangement from the tax authority[41] by stating that it fulfils the following conditions. First, the entity holds the legal and the economic ownership of the generation installation. This condition ensures that the entity is indeed the legal person making the investment and is not controlled by a third party. Second, the generation must be solely based on RES and must not receive any other financial compensation from the State for the generated electricity or the installation.[42] If the exemption of the general tax regime is granted, the entity can sell the generated electricity to a contracted supplier. Individual members are not required to have a contract with the same supplier with whom the collective entity concluded the agreement. The entity has to provide a statement to each of its members' suppliers, stating the amount of electricity produced that can be ascribed to each supplier's contracted customer(s).[43] As this entails an additional administrative burden for suppliers, they may request an extra administrative charge. The tax can be reduced to zero for the delivered electricity for volumes not exceeding 10,000 kWh on annual basis, which is twice the amount that can be 'net-metered'.[44] In contrast to the net-metering regime (see section 3.2 above), collective generation developed on the basis of the PCA arrangement does not take place 'behind the transfer point',[45] meaning not on the consumers' premises. All electricity is thus sold to the supplier and is not 'self-consumed' behind the meter. This also means that the generated electricity needs to be transported (distributed) by the responsible distribution system operator (DSO) via the public system to the members of the collective entity.

Following its implementation in 2014, the PCA arrangement has been amended several times to make it more flexible and to broaden the scope of its application.[46] Whereas the arrangement initially prescribed that the generation installation had to be located in the geographical centre of the postal code area and only the members of the collective entity could be located in the surrounding postal code areas, the subsequent amendments allow the generation installation to be placed anywhere within the postal code areas. Another important change in the arrangement was the increase of the tax reduction. Initially, the tax reduction was €0.075/kWh for a maximum of 10,000 kWh on annual basis. Since 2016, the PCA arrangement allows for a full tax reduction for 10,000 kWh on annual

---

40 Article 59a(3) Wet belastingen op milieugrondslag.
41 Article 59b and 59a(3) Wet belastingen op milieugrondslag.
42 Article 59a(2a–e) Wet belastingen op milieugrondslag.
43 Article 19b(6) Uitvoeringsregeling belastingen op milieugrondslag, *Stcr.* 2013, 36216.
44 Article 59a(1) Wet belastingen op milieugrondslag. Also see section 3.2 Net-Metering.
45 See n 2 above.
46 Wet van 23 december 2015 tot wijziging van enkele belastingwetten en enige andere wetten (Belastingplan 2016), *Stb.* 2015, 538.

basis, which enhanced the financial aspects of such projects and thus possibly the willingness of individuals to invest in a collective entity. The number of PCA projects has gradually been increasing. While by the end of 2015 only 17 projects were implemented, by the end of 2016 in total 55 were implemented.[47] However, because the arrangement has only been in force since the beginning of 2014, it remains to be seen how the projects will develop in the future and subsequently, what legal changes will be necessary for the viability of the PCA arrangement in the longer term.

4.3. DECREE GOVERNING EXPERIMENTS WITH DECENTRALISED RENEWABLE ELECTRICITY GENERATION

Subsequent to the abovementioned 'Energy Agreement for Sustainable Growth', the Dutch Government wishes to investigate the potential of new organisational forms that can accelerate the decentralisation of renewable electricity generation.[48] For this purpose, the so-called Experimental Decree was adopted. The main goal of the Experimental Decree is to investigate whether the rules of the Decree could stimulate the development of decentralised renewable electricity generation and a more efficient use of the electricity system. If evaluations show that this is indeed the case, the legislator might respond by adjusting the legal framework accordingly. Essentially, the Experimental Decree allows small customers via collective entities not only to engage in collective generation of renewable electricity, but also to become suppliers and, under certain conditions, even system operators. This of course constitutes a remarkable option as it sets aside the incumbent unbundling rules. This section first outlines the legal basis and the key provisions of the Experimental Decree. Second, it briefly describes the initiated projects, and third, it evaluates the extent to which the Experimental Decree can achieve its goals.

The legal basis for experimental spaces that allow for derogations from the current legal framework is provided in the E-Act. The derogations are exclusively applicable to experiments intended to stimulate generation, distribution or supply of decentralised renewable electricity.[49] The Experimental Decree specifies this aim and also includes the involvement of consumers through collective entities (cooperatives or owners' associations) as a requirement.[50] In that sense, the Experimental Decree furthers the idea of collective prosumers.

47 Hier Opgewekt, 'Lokale energie monitor 2016', p 4, see: https://www.hieropgewekt.nl/sites/default/files/hier_opgewekt_monitor_2016.pdf.
48 Explanatory Memorandum Experimental Decree, para 1.2.
49 Article 7a Elektriciteitswet 1998.
50 Explanatory Memorandum Experimental Decree, para 1.3.

The collective entities can apply for approval under the Experimental Decree which allows them to implement projects which can be exempted from conditions of the E-Act regarding grid operation and supply. The entities need to be either a cooperative or an owners' association which is entirely controlled by its members, of which not less than 80% have to be consumers.[51] The control through members is core to the Decree, which is explained in the explanatory memorandum as changing role from 'protected to empowered consumers'.[52] This might even trigger the question whether members are consumers at all. Furthermore, DSOs and electricity suppliers are not allowed to be a member of the collective entity, which again relates to the main aim to enable and empower consumers in novel organisational forms to engage in system operation and supply.[53] The applicants have to prove that they can ensure the reliability, safety, consumer and environmental protection of system operation and supply, and can comply with the technical standards applicable to DSOs.[54] The collective entity has to finance the entire project.[55]

The Experimental Decree provides three main exemptions from the E-Act. First, an exemption can be granted from Article 16(3) of the E-Act, which prohibits any party other than a designated system operator to operate an electricity system.[56] This is the main exemption of the Decree and it provides the option for novel organisational forms, which might stimulate decentralised RES generation as envisaged by the overall aim of the Decree. Second, collective entities which have been granted an exemption automatically obtain the necessary licence for electricity supply for the purpose of supplying the members of the cooperative or owners' association of the project.[57] This essentially allows the members to supply electricity to each other via the collective entity, which acts as the supply undertaking. Third, the collective entity can determine their network tariffs, which are not subject to approval of the Dutch National Regulatory Authority (NRA); instead the NRA only has to approve the method of calculation and not the tariff itself.[58] The collective entities can thus act as an integrated electricity undertaking by taking over the role of generator, supplier and, under certain conditions, also as system operator.[59]

The Experimental Decree distinguishes between two types of projects which are determined by their size in terms of connected customers. So-called

51 Article 7(1q) Experimental Decree.
52 Explanatory Memorandum Experimental Decree, para 1.5.1.
53 Article 7(1j) Experimental Decree.
54 Articles 4 and 7(1d,e) Experimental Decree.
55 Article 7(1l) Experimental Decree.
56 Article 2 Experimental Decree. This exemption contains some specific conditions regarding the size of the project, these are outlined further below.
57 Article 13 Experimental Decree.
58 Article 12 Experimental Decree.
59 I Lammers and L Diestelmeier, 'Experimenting with Law and Governance for Decentralized Electricity Systems: Adjusting Regulation to Reality?' (2017) Sustainability 9(2)212, 10.

'project networks'[60] have one connection to the public distribution system, are located within a geographically delineated area and have a maximum of 500 connected customers.[61] The other projects are called 'large experiment projects'.[62] 'Large experimental projects' take place within the existing service area of DSOs with a maximum of 10,000 customers connected to the system. The most important difference in the applicable rules concerns the asset management and system operation of the grid. In contrast to the project networks, 'large project networks' require that the asset management of the system remains an unbundled activity for the incumbent DSO. Asset management includes the development and maintenance of the technical components.[63] Yet, the collective entity may decide to designate a third party as system operator with the task of system operation including the management of electricity flows, demand-response and peak-shifting by means of IT systems.[64] Collective entities can apply to the Ministry of Economic Affairs and Climate (MEA) once per year for an exemption. The MEA can grant 10 exemptions per year for 'project networks' and 10 exemptions for 'large experimental projects' in the period from 2015–19. The exemption is valid for a maximum of 10 years, but evaluations have to take place during the course of the project.[65]

The Experimental Decree entered into force on 1 April 2015. In the same year, four projects were already designated under the Experimental Decree, all of which were 'project networks'. In 2016 five new projects were designated, of which two projects were 'large experimental projects'.[66] All projects implement decentralised renewable electricity generation, but may vary as regards other activities the projects intend to develop. The majority (seven projects) deploy energy management through ICT (smart grid technology), six projects engage with peer-to-peer supply, meaning that the members can deliver electricity to each other via the collective entity, and three projects establish dynamic electricity tariffs in their projects which can vary in shorter time-frames than the current tariffs and thereby incentivise flexible use of the energy and the system. The setting of the Experimental Decree provides a very strong position for the collective entity (cooperative or owners' association) that is running the project. The collective entities have to be effectively controlled by their members. However, first insights in practice provide reason to doubt whether this is indeed the case. Five of the nine projects are led by professional project developers,

---

60 In Dutch, *project net*.

61 Article 1 Experimental Decree.

62 In Dutch, *groot experiment*.

63 Explanatory Memorandum, para 2.3.3.

64 Ibid.

65 Articles 15 and 16 Experimental Decree.

66 For a more detailed description of the individual projects see I Lammers and L Diestelmeier, 'Experimenting with Law and Governance for Decentralized Electricity Systems: Adjusting Regulation to Reality?' (2017) Sustainability 9(2) 212, 8.

a PV panel installation business and a real estate company as members of the collective entity.[67] Considering the central role ascribed to the collective entity, it appears that there is no space for innovation of new actors who could play a central role in future electricity systems (such as aggregators who provide energy services on basis of pooled flexibilities of system users). Instead, the collective entity acts as vertically integrated electricity undertaking (most obvious in the 'project grids'). This construction even includes the consumers as part of that undertaking as they are the members of the collective entity. This also leads to ambiguities regarding third party access (TPA).[68] The collective entity still needs to ensure TPA, which means that consumers still possess the right to freely choose a supplier other than the collective entity. However, as the consumers are themselves part of the supplying entity, it is unlikely that they will choose another supplier, which potentially restricts competition for electricity supply. Moreover, it remains unclear which procedure applies if a consumer (a member) decides to leave the project for whatever reason. The whole nature of the collective entity is based on the contribution of the member and the members as consumers. The arguments for collectively generating, distributing and supplying electricity can be strong, but for the same reasons, may also be considered a weak construction. Considering the overall goal of the Experimental Decree, investigating new organisational forms which accelerate decentralised generation and efficient usage of the grid, the scope of the Decree seems to be too restricted. The bundling of supply chain activities provides no space for other innovative approaches to reach that goal. Therefore, it is likely that the outcomes will result in incremental knowledge instead of the anticipated new insights. It remains to be seen whether the first official evaluation (anticipated in 2019) will reveal similar conclusions.

5. REFLECTIONS AND RECENT DEVELOPMENTS

The above sections suggest an evolution of the legal understanding of who the prosumer could or should be, and how prosumers can contribute to a more sustainable and efficient electricity system. While the net-metering regulation is a rather blunt way of settling consumption and production by small consumers, the idea behind the Experimental Decree shows that consumers might take completely new roles in the future electricity sector. Within the Netherlands, the concept of prosumers is thus slowly moving towards a broader concept in law. Technical options may facilitate this development by enabling prosumers to

---

67 Ibid, 9.

68 JF Koenders and SL Pipping, 'Het Besluit experimenten decentrale duurzame elektriciteitsopwekking doorgelicht' (2016) Nederlands Tijdschrift voor Energierecht 4/2016, 152 (only available in Dutch).

carry out more functions in the electricity system. By means of new technologies such as smart meters and storage (eg home batteries or electric vehicle batteries), prosumers can take control of their consumption and their production. This flexibility in generation and consumption will become increasingly important in electricity systems based on intermittent RES. While harnessing this flexibility is technically feasible, legislation needs to ensure that prosumers can develop an independent role in the electricity market to benefit from their flexible, cost-reflective behaviour. The current legal framework does not, however, enable or incentivise the value of flexibility of prosumers.

The need for legal adjustments has also been recently noted on the EU level. In November 2016, the EU Commission acknowledged the need for legislative change with a proposal for reforming legislation on the internal market of electricity (most commonly known as the 'Winter package').[69] This led to the introduction of a new concept, 'the active customer'. In the proposed amendments of the Directive the Commission suggests the definition of 'active consumer', which reads as follows:

> '[A]ctive customer' means a customer or a group of jointly acting customers who consume, store or sell electricity generated on their premises, including through aggregators, or participate in demand response or energy efficiency schemes provided that these activities do not constitute their primary commercial or professional activity.[70]

This definition goes beyond the current common understanding of prosumers; a consumer who also produces. Instead, the definition also entails the participation of active consumers in demand-response mechanisms, which includes the deployment of flexibility in generation and loads. This connects to the need for a legal framework which stimulates flexibility rather than merely the generation of RES. The proposal also introduces a new definition which allows for collective generation. The proposal defines 'local energy community' (LEC) as:

> an association, a cooperative, a partnership, a non-profit organisation or other legal entity which is effectively controlled by local shareholders or members, generally value rather than profit-driven, involved in distributed generation and in performing activities of a distribution system operator, supplier or aggregator at local level, including across borders.[71]

---

69 European Commission, 'Clean Energy for All Europeans' 30 November 2016.

70 Article 2(6) Proposal for a Directive of the European Parliament and of the Council on common rules for the internal market in electricity (Electricity Directive Proposal), Brussels, 30 November 2016, COM(2016) 864 final.

71 Article 2(7) Electricity Directive Proposal.

This definition comes close to the collective entities defined in the Experimental Decree, as they may also take over tasks of distribution grid operation. However, the definition proposed by the EU Commission includes a wider range of legal organisational forms compared to the Experimental Decree. The wide range of options may be a reasonable approach considering that many organisational forms are still in development. And yet the current proposal remains extremely vague and does not clarify the role of LECs in the market, as they are envisaged to be 'generally value rather than profit driven'. The proposal is currently in the legislative process and the extent to which the first proposals will be included in a final version (the Fourth Electricity Directive) remains to be seen. Certainly, the proposal suggests a more central role for prosumers/active consumers (individually and collectively organised). Whether and to what extent they will be enabled to take an independent role in the electricity market and expand their activities to offering flexible services, depends not only on the exact definition of 'prosumer' or 'active consumer', but also on other changes in the regulatory framework.

While the current legal framework in the Netherlands for prosumers aims mainly at incentivising consumers to engage in RES-based generation, future regulation should also focus on flexibility offered by consumers. In that context, the term 'prosumer' is not fitting anymore, as the value is not only in additional RES-based production but also in producing and consuming on the basis of market signals. Every system user (regardless of whether they are a producer or consumer) puts more stress on the system, and this is becoming more severe by the uncontrollable character of intermittent RES. This 'stress' can be relieved by system-user flexibility, providing for a more efficient use of the system. This setting would ideally move away from the current roles of 'producers' and 'consumers' and instead focus on the functioning of the system, which is determined by timing, capacity and reaction speed of system users. The current legal framework is far away from this ideal setting as it is exclusively based on the strict definition of actors and delineation of their tasks.

6. CONCLUSION

This chapter has outlined the legal framework applicable to small consumers engaging in RES-based generation in the Netherlands. While the different sections have explained that the main aim of the legislation is incentivising RES-based production, the final section reflects that this aim alone is insufficient, given that flexibility is becoming crucial in a RES-based electricity sector. Without legal changes, the intermittent RES-based production peaks in periods of low consumption, and high demand peaks in periods of low generation, will only reinforce the need for conventional generation sources (fossil or nuclear). The legal framework for prosumers is not a goal in itself but strives to increase the overall amount of RES-based production. To this end, the legal framework needs to keep up with technical developments in the sector, for example the quest to harness flexibility to use RES efficiently. The current legal framework in the Netherlands does not enable or incentivise the flexibility of small consumers. Simply amending definitions (eg from 'consumer' to 'prosumer' to 'active consumer') will not suffice to regulate for an efficient RES-based electricity sector. Instead, the legal framework needs to focus on the functioning of the system and the contribution of the system users thereto.

CHAPTER VIII
PROSUMER LEGISLATION IN NORWAY
A First Step for Empowering Small Energy Consumers

Catherine BANET*

1. INTRODUCTION

Electricity generation in Norway is almost totally based on renewable energy sources, mostly hydropower (96.3% in 2016), followed by thermal power (2.3%) and wind power (1.4%).[1] The price of electricity for end-users is also relatively low compared to the rest of Europe. The absence of an immediate need to 'green' the energy generation mix any further[2] or to generate cheaper electricity explains the absence, for the majority of energy consumers, of a strong need to start producing electricity themselves and to turn into prosumers. This can be illustrated by the fact that in early 2018 only 1,000 Norwegian consumers have become prosumers.[3]

---

* The chapter builds on the presentation held by Erlend Sandnes, Legal Advisor, Norwegian Water Resources and Energy Directorate (NVE), at the 28th European Energy Law Seminar in January 2017. The chapter has also benefited from discussions with Bjørnar Araberg Fladen, Senior Advisor, NVE, and Trond Svartsund, Industrial Policy Advisor, Energy Norway (Energi Norge). The author would like to thank them all for their feedback while taking the sole responsibility for the conclusions drawn. The author is affiliated to CREE – Oslo Centre for Research on Environmentally friendly Energy.

1 Source: Statistics Norway, SSB, https://www.ssb.no/en/energi-og-industri/statistikker/elektrisitet.

2 This comes also from interviews conducted by researchers in the report by 'Power from the People? Prosuming Conditions for Germany, the UK and Norway', Fridtjof Nansens Institutt, FNI Report 5/2016. Note that this report does not include the latest legislative developments in Norway.

3 There are no direct reporting requirements for prosumers, beside the fact that they may need to contact their network company before installing any generation appliances. This makes it difficult to know exactly how many prosumers there are in Norway. The figure indicated here is based on the data reported by the major DSOs, the Transmission System Operator (TSO) Statnett and the suppliers, under their reporting obligations (transport volumes, trade

Meanwhile, households and other small energy consumers are becoming increasingly aware of the existing opportunities and may find new financial motivations in higher electricity prices. As elsewhere, the costs of solar panels are continuously decreasing, and both attractive and innovative market offers are focusing on prosumers as a market segment.[4] As such, the increase in electricity prices may motivate energy consumers to develop a hedging strategy by producing more electricity themselves. In the first half of 2018, electricity prices have risen significantly compared to previous years because of higher consumption due to a cold winter and because of higher and more expensive imports than usual due to a dry spring.[5] This situation worried consumers, but is expected to return to normal shortly; however, a certain fact is that grid tariffs will increase in the near future due to the need for grid investments. Finally, many Norwegian consumers find the idea of consuming self-produced electricity attractive, in particular when this electricity is based on renewable energy sources. In fact, the vast majority of registered prosumers make use of solar panels, followed by a small number using hydropower, which is traditionally very common in Norway. The topology of the country is such that many landowners develop mini- and micro hydropower plants, primarily for their own consumption, making small-scale hydropower an established practice in the countryside, based on enabling legislation.[6] The prospect of developing smart houses and buildings that are not only achieving zero-emissions, but which are also energy positive, is a growing trend.[7] Still, prosumers are a minority.

---

volume, etc), pursuant to Chapter 4 of the Regulations governing financial and technical reporting, income caps for network operations and transmission tariffs (the Regulations on network tariffs).

4 Some innovative Norwegian companies in the solar power market have distinguished themselves, such as Otovo.

5 The average price of electricity for households, excluding taxes and grid rent, was 42.5 øre per kWh in the first quarter of 2018, which is a 24% increase compared to the first quarter in 2017. For the same period, the overall price was 106.4 øre per kWh including grid rent and tax. The majority of Norwegian households have an electricity contract tied to spot price (almost 70%), which explains the increase in electricity price experienced in 2018. Source: SSB, Electricity prices, https://www.ssb.no/en/energi-og-industri/artikler-og-publikasjoner/higher-electricity-prices-for-households--351026.

6 In Norway, small-scale hydroelectric power plants are classified into three categories, namely, 'small power plants', with an installed effect between 1 and 10 MW; 'mini power plants' with an installed effect between 100 kW and 1 MW; and 'micro power plants' with an installed effect of less than 100 kW. Micro power plants are the most fitted for the purpose of prosumption under the current legal framework, due to the threshold defined in the legislation. See section 2.1.2.

7 The Directorate for Building Quality is running a specific programme, *Lavenergiprogrammet*, aimed at developing knowledge and good practices for building energy efficient, zero-emissions and energy positive buildings. See: http://lavenergiprogrammet.no.

Likewise, the Norwegian authorities have not shown great ambition in the area of prosumption. The 2012 National Renewable Energy Action Plan[8] does not include any specific quantitative objectives for prosumers. This changed slightly in 2016 when the Government adopted a White Paper on Energy Policy.[9] The document refers to prosumers but only in relation to the deployment of smart-metering.[10] Other parts of the White Paper related to Distribution System Operators' (DSOs) regulation[11] and grid tariff regulation are meanwhile relevant for the future of prosumers policy in Norway and can affect their increase, either positively or negatively.[12]

Together with the direct grants provided by the state enterprise Enova SF for the installation of renewable energy solutions,[13] one of the strongest signals given by the Government in favour of prosumption comes from a recent amendment to the network tariffs legislation. As of 1 January 2017, Norway has revised its legislation in order to provide a clear legal basis for the regime applicable to prosumers, with a focus on residential prosumers, small businesses and buildings. The new provisions are contained in the Regulations governing financial and technical reporting, income caps for network operations and transmission tariffs (the Regulations on network tariffs),[14] which have been amended by the Norwegian water resources and energy directorate (NVE), which is the energy regulatory authority.[15] Prior to this, a first regime facilitating prosumers was already in place. From March 2010 to 1 January 2017, an exemption regime applied, based on a derogation from the general tariffs legislation.[16]

---

8 Ministry of Petroleum and Energy, National Renewable Energy Action Plan, 2012. The plan has been made for the purpose of complying with Directive 2009/28/EC on the promotion of the use of energy from renewable sources after its incorporation into the EEA Agreement. The Plan is available at: https://ec.europa.eu/energy/sites/ener/files/documents/dir_2009_0028_action_plan_norway__nreap.pdf.

9 *Energimelding* (Meld. St. 25 (2015–16)).

10 Ibid, p 144.

11 The Norwegian Government has notably expressed its desire to limit the number of DSOs, which is extremely high in Norway (approximately 145 DSOs). This goes against the trend which consists of increasing the number of actors at the end of the grid and promoting decentralised generation.

12 There are numerous distribution operators (around 150) and most of them are publicly owned. A recent committee report ordered by the Government (Reiten-*utvalget*, 'A Better Organised Electricity Network', 2013) has advised the consolidation of the sector through the creation of larger companies instead of those numerous grid operators. The effect of any consolidation of the grid operation sector on the development of prosumption has not been assessed by public authorities.

13 See section 4.2 below.

14 Regulations No 302 of 11 March 1999 governing financial and technical reporting, income caps for network operations and transmission tariffs (the Regulations on network tariffs) (*Forskrift om kontroll av nettvirksomheten – kontrollforskriften*).

15 NVE has delegated competence in the matter.

16 NVE, Decision on exemption from the Regulations on reporting, income and tariffs in connection with grid activity, of 16.03.2010 (*Håndtering av plusskunder og vedtak om dispensasjon fra forskrift 302 om økonomisk og teknisk rapportering m.v.*).

This exemption from certain network tariffs, initially given through a decision made by NVE, and which already focused on residential and small-scale prosumers, is now codified into the legislation and adjusted to recent government policy on prosumption. Consequently, the current legal framework for prosumption in Norway is composed of a few specific provisions based on a production threshold approach, while the general rules governing energy production, transport and consumption continue to apply as soon as the threshold is met.

This chapter discusses the changes that have been made to the Norwegian legal regime to accommodate the development of prosumers. Section 2 examines how the law defines the concept of prosumers. Section 3 discusses permitting requirements and the prosumers' rights and duties as to grid and market access. Section 4 gives an overview of the existing financial incentives in favour of prosumption. Section 5 concludes with an assessment of the current legal regime.

2. THE DEFINITION OF PROSUMERS IN NORWEGIAN LEGISLATION

Recent legislative amendments have ressulted in the adoption of a legal definition for prosumers, which was not the case previously. This is to be considered a major improvement, although the regulatory approach remains relatively simple. In the Norwegian context, prosumers are defined as energy consumers who are generating their own electricity and, within a certain threshold, feed-in and sell the surplus of production that they are not using themselves. Prosumers are defined as a separate category of customer.

2.1. DEFINITION OF PROSUMERS AND THRESHOLDS

The definition of prosumers is included in section 1-3 of the Regulations on network tariffs, as amended.[17] Section 1-3 defines prosumers – called 'plus-customers' (*plusskunder*) – as any end-user with consumption and production behind the connection point, where fed input power at the connection point at no time exceeds 100 kW. Where the consumer owns an installation located on their side behind the connection point which requires a licence (eg for purpose of generation or distribution), or where they are required to hold a power trading licence, they will no longer qualify as a prosumer.

[17] *Forskrift om økonomisk og teknisk rapportering, innteksramme for nettvirksomheten og tariffer* – FOR-1999-03-11-302.

In terms of interpretation, the definition of section 1-3 establishes three main criteria which are reviewed below.

2.1.1. *'End-User with Consumption and Production Behind the Point of Connection'*

The prosumer must be an end-user as a starting point. An end-user is defined in Norwegian legislation as 'someone who buys electric energy but does not re-sell it afterwards.'[18] Since the prosumer will be able to sell the surplus electricity generated that they do not consume, there is a distinction to be made between a regular end-user and a prosumer.[19]

The connection point is the physical point of connection to the grid operator's grid. This is defined in the Regulations on network tariffs as 'the point in the electric transport network where electricity is fed in or fed-out, or where there is electricity exchange between grid companies.'[20] To ensure common practices, the sector has also developed guidelines containing technical definitions, including one for 'connection point'.[21] The connection point is there defined as the point in the distribution grid where a decentralised generation unit is connected to the grid operator's grid. It is also commonly referred to as the point of change of ownership between the grid operator and the consumer. In practice, the connection point is usually the meter, ie as of 1 January 2019 the smart meter which enables the measurement of the electricity flow in both directions.[22]

2.1.2. *'Where the Electricity Fed into the Grid (Input Power) at the Connection Point at No Time Exceeds 100 kW'*

When the new prosumer definition was being discussed, a main discussion point was whether the threshold should be set in terms of input generation capacity (*innmatet produksjon* or *installert effekt*) or input power (power fed into the grid, *innmatet effekt*). After discussions with stakeholders, NVE has opted for 'input power' as the key criterion. First, it was felt that the wording was more accurate as a prosumer will not feed production capacity, but power into the

[18] Section 1-3, Regulation on the measurement, calculation, billing of grid services and electric energy, grid operators' neutrality, etc. (*Forskrift om måling, avregning, fakturering av nettjenester og elektrisk energi, nettselskapets nøytralitet mv.*).

[19] On sale of surplus electricity from prosumers, see section 4.1 below.

[20] Section 1-3, Regulations on network tariffs.

[21] See, eg, the definition and technical requirements applied to houses, apartments and holiday homes in the standard NEK 399 (*Tilknytningspunkt for el- og ekomnett*), where the cabinet containing the smart meter is defined as the connection point. The configuration may however differ according to the building type, eg individual house or apartment block.

[22] The roll-out of smart meters is due to be completed by 1 January 2019 for all metering points, including for households. See section 4-5, Regulations on metering and settlement no 301 of 11 March 1999, as amended.

grid. Second, it was decided not to set a generation cap as other countries may have done.[23] Setting a generation cap would entail measuring and limiting power capacity at each prosumer's premises, which was neither deemed appropriate for the purpose of prosumption nor practical to implement. There is therefore no requirement as to the measurement and reporting of the total amount of electricity generated at the prosumers' premises (and thus no requirement to install a meter for production), but a requirement based on the reading of metering data at the connection point, where both electricity consumed and fed into the grid is measured.

Setting the limit at 100 kW for the input power was another core issue discussed with stakeholders during the public consultation phase. Some actors (notably DSOs) were of the opinion that the threshold was set too high, and would be too generous towards large consumers that should not be subject to the same preferential regime than prosumers.[24] Other actors (eg small producers' associations, environmental organisations) claimed that the threshold was set too low and would result in artificial limitations of the potential for prosumption. For example, it could entail the splitting of buildings into smaller units for the purpose of avoiding reaching the limit with the negative consequence of not building the most energy-efficient buildings with the biggest possible surfaces (in particular for apartment blocks, public or commercial buildings and farms). Another consequence pointed out by stakeholders was that not all parts of the grid can stand an input power of 100 kW. Some stakeholders also raised concerns as to the consequences the threshold would have on grid dimension and the manner in which DSOs may try to minimise investment costs by dimensioning otherwise, whether that was by under-dimensioning to exclude prosumption or over-dimensioning to anticipate the inclusion of prosumers' input. NVE deems this risk to be non-existent as any miscalculation of grid dimensioning will negatively impact the efficiency component integrated into the tariffs calculation applied to DSOs, which will negatively affect their income.[25] The objective pursued by the Norwegian authorities in setting a 100 kW limit is to enable households, but also small public or commercial consumers and apartment buildings, to be included within the prosumer regime. Therefore, they decided in favour of flexibility, waiting for the market to mature. Compared to other European countries, 100 kW input power is a relatively high threshold, but not uncommon (eg Spain, Iceland, France).[26]

---

23 For an overview of the criteria applied in other European countries, see the Annex to the Third Report on the State of the Energy Union presented on 23 November 2017 (COM(2017) 688 final): Study on 'Residential Prosumers in the European Energy Union,' GfK Belgium consortium, 2 May 2017.

24 See the description of the tariffs exemption regime in section 3.2.1 below.

25 NVE, Report 47-2016.

26 The study undertaken in the context of the Third Report on the State of the Energy Union presented on 23 November 2017 (COM(2017) 688 final) reveals that a group of European

It is the responsibility of each prosumer to stay within the threshold limit of 100 kW fed into the grid. If the DSO discovers that the prosumer has gone over that threshold, the prosumer will lose its status and be obliged to pay more of the tariffs (eg the generation charge).[27] Meanwhile, anyone who loses their prosumer status can regain it if the necessary measures are taken to bring it back under the 100 kW-threshold.[28] In case of disagreement, grid operators and prosumers can bring the case before NVE, which will reach an administrative decision.

2.1.3. *'A Prosumer Cannot Possess an Installation Which Requires a License Behind the Connection Point or Any License for Sale of Electricity Behind the Connection Point'*

This entails that the status of prosumer is restricted to persons or legal entities who are not subject to licensing obligations or balancing agreement, as requested for normal production, transmission/distribution installations or entities involved in power trading. This means that no licence is required for prosumers under the Energy Act (generation, transport, trade)[29] as long as the installation is below the indicated threshold, which will be the case for most residential and small-scale commercial prosumers. At the same time, this also means that prosumers cannot carry out activities otherwise requiring a licence, such as the sale of electricity. No electricity distribution or trade is allowed behind the connection point if they want to keep the status of prosumers.[30]

Prosumers remain subject to other regulatory obligations in relation to building permit and construction works requirements.

First, prospective prosumers will need to assess whether they need to apply for a building permit under the Plan and Building Act (PBA) for the installation of the generation appliances at their premises.[31] As said, prosumers will mostly be interested in installing solar panels on the roof or the facade of their house/building. This type of installation or construction work may be encompassed by the permitting obligation under the PBA, where the house/building owner will need to apply for a permit from the responsible municipality, unless they fall

countries uses a 10 kW generation capacity cap to define residential prosumers, following the recommendation of the International Energy Agency (IEA). Study on 'Residential Prosumers in the European Energy Union,' GfK Belgium consortium, 2 May 2017.

27 On tariffs structure and the exemption regime for prosumers, see section 3.2.1 below.

28 *Endringer i kontrollforskriften vedrørende plusskundeordningen, Oppsummering av høringsuttalelser og endelig forskriftekst*, Rapport 47-2016, NVE (hereafter NVE, Report 47-2016). Available at: http://publikasjoner.nve.no/rapport/2016/rapport2016_47.pdf.

29 Prosumers are, in principle, exempted from the licensing obligation according to section 3-1 of the Energy Act.

30 For example, a prosumer cannot supply or sell electricity to their neighbours.

31 Section 20-1 (list of operations) and section 20-2 (application obligation), Plan- and Building Act (*Lov om planlegging og byggesaksbehandling, plan- og bygningsloven*).

under one of the exemptions defined in the Act.[32] Where the installation of the appliances results in minor alterations to the building or where it is consistent with the local town plan, there is no need to apply for a permit. This means that the requirement for a building permit will be assessed on a case-by-case basis, depending on the type of housing/building, the size of the installation, the surroundings and the content of the local town plan. In practice, the installation of solar panels on the roof of residential consumers' house rarely requires a building permit.

Second, prospective prosumers will remain subject to the Regulations on technical requirements for construction works (TEK 17 Regulation), notably the part defining requirements for energy supply solutions.[33] Fulfilling the requirements of the TEK 17 Regulation has practical implications as to the manner in which the generation appliances are integrated into the building. The use of renewable energy as a supply solution may also help to meet the general requirement relating to energy efficiency in buildings.

2.1.4. Assessment

The Norwegian prosumers legislative framework currently applicable is an enabling framework, focusing on small-scale energy consumers. The legislation does not distinguish between the different sources of energy for the purpose of electricity generation. The Norwegian definition of prosumers is to be deemed technology neutral.[34] All sources of energy and technologies used for generating electricity are covered, although the use of non-renewable sources for the production of electricity is very unlikely to happen. This is in line with the official view of the Government as to prosumption. In the summary of the public hearing,[35] the energy regulator NVE explained that the new prosumer regime is not meant as a support scheme for renewable energy.

2.2. THE PARTICULAR CASE OF HOUSING COOPERATIVES

A criticism expressed by stakeholders during the public consultation phase is that the new definition does not fit very well with the situation for apartment

32 Section 20-5 f, Plan- and Building Act (*Plan- og Bygningsloven*).

33 *Forskrift om tekniske krav til byggverk* (*Byggteknisk forskrift* – TEK17), Chapter 14 (Energy), Section 14-4 (Requirements for energy supply solutions) and Section 14-5 (Exceptions and requirements for special projects).

34 While the legal definition of prosumers and the tariffs regime are technology neutral, the available financial incentives vary according to the type of installation. See section 4.2 below.

35 Endringer i kontrollforskriften vedrørende plusskundeordningen, Oppsummering av høringsuttalelser og endelig forskriftekst, Rapport 47-2016, Norwegian Water Resources and Energy Directorate, NVE. Available at: http://publikasjoner.nve.no/rapport/2016/rapport2016_47.pdf.

buildings, housing cooperatives or joint properties, which could represent a large number of prosumers.[36] Those often possess large areas on the roof, which suits the purpose of electricity generation well, notably through solar PV panels. The reason for this shortcoming is that residential consumers in, for example, an apartment building could generate electricity jointly but the meters are normally individual ones for each apartment, meaning for each consumption unit.[37]

The solution advocated by NVE is to wait until the introduction of the Elhub, which is the national point of data management (data hub).[38] NVE has assigned the Norwegian Transmission System Operator (TSO), Statnett, the task of establishing a data hub that will encompass all metering data for electricity in Norway.[39] The Elhub will aggregate the data of several consumers from different metering points and enable the exchange of the collected data. The purpose of the Elhub, therefore, is to establish an economically efficient IT-infrastructure for an improved retail electricity market in Norway, as well as to encourage demand response by enabling the development of related services. Delayed several times, the new introduction of the Elhub is now fixed at 18 February 2019.[40] As mentioned above, the parallel roll-out of smart meters is supposed to be completed by 1 January 2019.

When the Elhub starts functioning, it is expected that housing cooperatives in apartment buildings, as well as joint properties, will find it easier to claim the status of prosumers.[41] The solution envisaged by NVE[42] is to maintain the system of individual metering of each consumption unit (like apartments) adopted in 2010, but to split ex post the generated electricity and the surplus between the different units. By maintaining a system of individual metering, the objective of the Norwegian authorities is also to promote energy efficiency measures by making each consumer aware of its exact consumption. Each consumer will also get full access to the new services which can develop and which are associated with the use of individual smart meters. This will also ensure that each consumer gets information from the grid company about, for example, power outage, and the customers' rights associated with such events. NVE finally argued that if the individual metering of each unit was not allowed, this would result in an unfair allocation of network costs between end-consumers.

---

36 'Endringer i kontrollforskriften vedrørende plusskundeordningen, Oppsummering av høringsuttalelser og endelig forskriftstekst', Rapport 47-2016, NVE. Available at: http://publikasjoner.nve.no/rapport/2016/rapport2016_47.pdf, p 11.

37 See NVE, Report 47-2016, p 11.

38 See NVE, Report 47-2016, p 11. See also the article on NVE website: 'Mulig å bli plusskunde i boligselskap', latest updated 10.01.2018, available at: https://www.nve.no/nytt-fra-nve/nyheter-reguleringsmyndigheten-for-energi/mulig-a-bli-plusskunde-i-boligselskap/.

39 The Elhub will be operated by a subsidiary owned by Statnett.

40 Further information on the Elhub is available at: http://elhub.no/.

41 Discussions on the treatment of joint properties (*sameie*) are less advanced and still ongoing.

42 This solution was already described by NVE in the supplementary public hearing related to prosumers which took place in 2015.

3. THE TREATMENT OF PROSUMERS IN GRID REGULATION

While most prosumers will already be connected to the grid, the installation of additional energy generation appliances will impact the functioning of the local grid to varying extents. DSOs will need to accommodate this new form for flexibility in the use of the grid. The relationship between the end-users and the grid company is also slightly different, as the status of 'prosumer' generates new rights and obligations for both the prosumer and the grid company. The perspective of not only generating electricity for self-consumption (reduced use of the network) but also feeding electricity into the grid can create needs for grid reinforcement. In the case of new smart buildings, or already self-sufficient buildings in more remote areas (like holiday houses or farms), there may be a need to build new grid connections, which involves higher infrastructure investments since there is no pre-existing connection. It is indeed expected that a significant number of prosumers will consist of new buildings without a connection yet, whether this be for residential purposes (like zero-emissions or energy positive houses), or for non-public/commercial purposes (like offices, supermarkets or schools).[43] The following sections analyse the requirements related to grid connection and access to the grid, and how the regime applies to prosumers.

3.1. CONNECTION OF PROSUMERS TO THE GRID

3.1.1. General Rules for Connection to and Reinforcement of the Grid

A particular feature of the Norwegian grid is that it is split into three grid levels: the national, regional and distribution grids. The national grid corresponds to the transmission grid and is under the responsibility of the TSO, Statnett. The regional and distribution grids are both encompassed by the concept of distribution grid under the EU Electricity Directive.[44] The regional grid makes the link between the transmission and distribution grids, and consists mainly of power grids between 66kV and 132kV.[45] The Norwegian distribution grid corresponds to local power grids. It normally delivers electricity to end-users at a voltage of up to 22 kV.[46] This means that prosumers, as defined under

43 The owners of those commercial buildings will often aim to reach the Breeam-certification standard. Breeam stands for Building Research Establishment Environment Assessment Method and is used to help measure the sustainability of buildings.

44 Article 2(5), Directive 2009/72/EC of the European Parliament and of the Council of 13 July 2009 concerning common rules for the internal market in electricity.

45 The regional grid encompasses network infrastructures over 22 kV which are not qualified as transmission infrastructure. Section 1-3, Regulations on network tariffs.

46 Ibid.

Norwegian law, may be connected to regional or distribution grids, the latter being most likely.

Chapter 3 of the Energy Act defines the regime for access to the grid.[47] Pursuant to section 3-3 of the Act, a distribution company shall provide physical delivery of electricity to all consumers within the geographic area covered by its local area license. Pursuant to section 3-4 of the Act, all entities holding a licence according to sections 3-1 and 3-2 (network and production facilities) shall connect new electricity generation installations, as well as new installations, for electricity consumption. The grid connection obligation covers all necessary network installations from the point of connection to the point of supply to consumers and includes the need to make new investments. The licence defines detailed duties and conditions, including the rules for providing access to the grid at non-discriminatory and objective terms and conditions. The Ministry of Petroleum and Energy (MPE) (when it comes to consumption) and NVE (when it comes to production) may, under exceptional circumstances, provide for an exemption to the physical delivery and connection obligations (including needs to invest).[48] The further relationship between the grid operator and the consumer is governed by a contractual agreement.

Although those provisions are not specific to prosumers, sections 3-3 and 3-4 on the grid connection obligation are both equally important for them. Prosumers, because they also are consumers, will rely on the physical delivery of electricity (section 3-3) when they are not able to produce sufficiently themselves. Then, electricity generation units and consumers, including prosumers, are given a right to access the grid, which includes grid connection and access (section 3-4). Equally important is that the connection obligation is associated with a duty to invest in infrastructure development when necessary. The background for section 3-4 (which entered in force on 1 January 2010) was the implementation of EU requirements on access to the grid in the Renewable Energy Directive, the purpose of which was to support the increase of new renewable energy generation, and in particular small-scale generation.[49] This provision also fits the purpose of prosumers. In sum, prosumers will be entitled to the rights of both consumers and producers for the purpose of physical delivery and connection to the grid.

The Implementing Regulations No 959 pursuant to the Energy Act define further the conditions of application of the grid connection requirement. Section 3-4 of the Regulations requires that:

- The connection obligation applies where it is the most rational to connect the generation facility;

---

47 See in particular section 3-3 to section 3-5, Energy Act.

48 Section 3-3, para 2, and section 3-4, paras 2 and 3, Energy Act.

49 Article 16, Directive 2009/28/EC on the promotion of the use of energy from renewable sources; incorporated into the EEA Agreement by Decision of the EEA Joint Committee No 162/2011 of 19 December 2011 amending Annex IV (Energy) to the EEA Agreement.

- If the connection requires further investments in the main part of the licensee's grid, this must, in principle, be covered by the licensee;
- The licensee must put forward a schedule for the connection;
- Access shall be provided on non-discriminatory and objective terms and conditions;
- Any request for exemption must be handed over to NVE.

The questions would therefore be: (i) whether a DSO can refuse to connect a prosumer, and in which capacity – consumer or producer – when there is no pre-existing connection; and (ii) whether a DSO can refuse to upgrade the grid and make the necessary investments in order to accommodate the additional power fed in by the prosumers, in case of pre-existing connection.

Finally, the connection/reinforcement obligation only applies if the connected installations of the prosumers fulfil the technical requirements outlined in the legislation and the technical standards for electricity supply quality as defined in their contract with the grid operator, as noted in section 3.2.2 below.

3.1.2. Connection Procedures for Prosumers' Generation Installation

The procedure for assessing the need for connection or reinforcement of the grid as a consequence of prosumption is managed directly by the grid operator. In the absence of a legally defined procedure, grid operators have had to develop their own procedures. Although these can vary, some common patterns and practices can be identified. The procedure is subject to private arrangement with the distribution company.

When a consumer envisages installing a small generation facility on their premises and also feeding the surplus of electricity generated to the grid, they will first make contact with an electrical installation contractor. Together, they will assess the prosumer's facility and submit an application to the grid operator. The application will contain several documents, including: a notification on installation work (*Melding om installasjonsarbeid*, MOI); and a declaration of connection (*erklæring om tilkobling*).[50] If the application is approved by the DSO, and following the various connection requirements defined by law, the DSO will either: approve the connection, reinforce the connection, or proceed to a new connection, including making new investments if necessary. The connection will be subject to a private contractual arrangement between the prosumer and the DSO, replacing the existing agreement in case of pre-existing installations. Prosumers must contact their electricity supplier in parallel with the above procedure.

[50] See, as an example, the process describe on the website of one of the main DSOs: https://www.eidsivanett.no/plusskunder/.

The DSO can itself require the payment of a grid investment fee (*anleggsbidrag*) for the investments that it would need in order to connect the prosumer (new production facility) or to reinforce the grid connecting existing customers (reinforced or increased connection).[51] The methodology for calculating how much a system operator can ask for that purpose is regulated by law[52] and controlled by NVE. The purpose of the investment contribution is to make customers aware of the costs of expanding and upgrading the grid. Customers can weigh the need for grid access or reinforcement against the costs involved. In addition, the investment contribution is intended to separate the investment costs between the customer who triggers the investment and the other grid customers. As a general rule, grid investments triggered by a particular customer's needs are to be paid by that customer. Similarly, the connection of new customers to the grid should not negatively impact other customers connected to the same local grid, whether that be due to new inputs from generation or outputs from consumption. However, as long as the prosumer's activities do not involve changes in its overcharge profile, the DSO cannot require the payment of the grid investment fee.

As mentioned above, the grid operator will also set technical requirements for connection of any new generation facility, including generation installation at prosumers' premises. Respecting the technical requirements is meant to avoid disruption (reduced supply quality) on the network for other customers. The grid operator also usually requires that the prosumers' installation is able to be disconnected automatically in case of power outage on the network.[53] The prosumer is responsible for making sure their installation complies with the technical requirements.

3.2. USE OF THE GRID, NETWORK TARIFFS AND THE TREATMENT OF PROSUMERS

The main rule is that all producers must pay the tariff for feeding into the grid. In the case of prosumers, the central provision in the regime is an exemption from certain network charges for the consumers who would like to feed their surplus electricity. The following describes both the exemption regime for prosumers and the conditions under which they can feed electricity into the grid.

3.2.1. Network Costs: The Exemption Regime for Prosumers

Grid transport tariffs are fixed by the network operator in accordance with the criteria and the methodology defined by law and supplemented by guidance

51 Section 17-5, Regulations on network tariffs.

52 Chapter 8, Regulations on network tariffs.

53 It is predicted that smart-metering will assist in that task.

from NVE. The tariffs must be set in a non-discriminatory manner, but can be differentiated based on network-related criteria that are objective and verifiable. Another fundamental principle of optimal tariffs design is that all grid users should pay a price that is equal to the short-term marginal cost incurred through their use of the grid. The marginal loss can be positive or negative depending on whether changes in electricity fed into or tapped from the grid increase or decrease the energy loss.

For small energy customers (households, holiday homes and small commercial customers), the legislation defines two main components of the network tariffs that also apply to producers, ie the energy component (NOK/kWh) and the fixed component (NOK/year).[54] The energy component, or usage-dependent energy component, corresponds to compensation for the energy losses in the network system. The energy component for producers who feed into the distribution is set based on marginal losses in the network system as a whole. The energy component from the distribution grid may therefore be used to cover a share of the other fixed costs of grid operation. The energy component is not sufficient to cover all grid operation costs and must therefore be supplemented by a fixed component. Grid operators use other tariff components to cover the remaining costs and to provide a fair return on grid investments in the form of a fixed charge. For the purpose of calculating the fixed charge, the grid companies can divide customers into different categories (residential, holiday homes, public/commercial buildings) who are offered different tariffs on the basis of relevant grid conditions. The fixed component is paid by metering point, and therefore the metering data is used to adjust this fixed component.[55] The fixed charge constitutes about 30% of the network tariff.[56]

Under the new regime, which came into force in January 2017, prosumers are exempted from the payment of other tariff elements for feeding electricity into the grid, ie the fixed component. The legal basis for the exemption is section 16-2, paragraph 3 of the Regulations on network tariffs. This exemption regime is *de facto* the main financial incentive for energy consumers to become prosumers, although it will not save them enormous sums compared to their initial investment.[57] Furthermore, prosumers who reduce the costs of power

---

54 Customers with an installed capacity exceeding a set limit, eg over 80 or 125 amperes, or customers with an expected annual consumption exceeding 100 000 kWh, usually have a capacity charge (NOK/kW) in addition to the fixed and energy charges. The capacity charge is based on used capacity within defined periods of time.

55 The requirements applicable to metering are defined in the Regulations on metering and settlement.

56 Source: SSB. For a comparison with other Nordic countries, see Nordic Energy Regulators (NorREG), 'Tariffs in Nordic countries – survey of load tariffs in DSO grids,' Report 3/2015, Annex 4.

57 In the public summary of the submissions to the public consultation (NVE, Report 47-2016), NVE calculated that, for a producer with 100 kW installed power, the fixed component will amount to NOK 1800/year (in 2016).

losses on the grid may receive payment from the energy component. As explained above, the marginal loss can be positive or negative. This is justified by the fact that prosumers pay a price for the energy-component which reflects the short-term marginal cost incurred.[58]

According to NVE, exemption from the fixed component must be understood as a 'tariff-provision' and is not meant as a financial support scheme. This argument can be debated, as the exemption provision does confer an advantage to a separate category of producers. Meanwhile, prosumers are not allowed to trade electricity on the market and will not be licensed for it. Therefore, it can also be argued that this will not directly distort competition on the relevant product and geographic market, as long as the surplus electricity is offered to suppliers for the purpose of re-sale on the open market. The situation would be different if the prosumer were obliged to sell its surplus electricity to only one actor on the market, which could then distort competition. Questions of compatibility with internal market rules could have been raised as to the practice followed until the new provisions came into force, and which may still apply until the Elhub becomes operative, consisting in selling the surplus electricity directly to the grid operator.

3.2.2. Contractual Conditions for Feeding into the Grid and Billing Prosumers

The legislation does not determine contractual conditions for feeding electricity into the grid. Prosumers will need to conclude a specific 'prosumer agreement' with the grid company for the purpose of feeding electricity into the grid, referred to as a 'plus-customer agreement' in the Norwegian context (*plusskundeavtale*). The prosumer agreement between the prosumer and the grid company is subject to contractual freedom and each company has designed its own agreement. However, conditions for setting tariffs in general are covered by the Regulations on network tariffs, as explained above.[59]

---

58 In order to bring even more flexibility to the interpretation of the threshold and to facilitate feeding into the grid more electricity from small energy consumers interested in prosumption (especially from buildings), NVE has recently proposed revisions to the Regulations on network tariffs. The new rules will entail that the fixed component of the tariffs will be based on the actual volume of electricity fed in by all producers, including those under 1 MW, a component which was before based on installed capacity but not the precise use of the grid. Therefore, hydropower generation could be treated preferentially to, eg solar power (with shorter time of use). The calculation of the tariffs will therefore better reflect the actual use of the network, without discriminating between types of generation facilities. Prosumers who exceed the 100 kW threshold and that will need to pay the fixed component, will consequently pay a 'fairer' contribution than previously. The new rules will enter into force on 1 January 2019. See the hearing document: NVE, *Forslag til endring i forskrift om kontroll av nettvirksomhet*, Høringsdokument, 6-2018.

59 See section 3.2.1 above.

General conditions on billing apply and there are no special billing conditions for prosumers.[60] The sale of electricity or other related services will fall under the provisions of the Marketing Act. The Consumer Ombudsman and the energy industry have also developed joint guidelines for the marketing of electricity which will apply to the relationship between prosumers and their grid operator/supplier.

A general requirement of quality of electricity supply applies, pursuant to the Regulations No 1557 on the quality of supply in the electricity market. The Regulations define the technical criteria for supplying electricity into the grid. Those criteria will be applied by the grid operator when electricity is fed into the grid. Those conditions will apply to prosumers. If the electricity supplied to the grid by prosumers does not comply with those technical standards, the grid operator may refuse access to the grid as it will threaten electricity system management. Until general technical standards are adopted by the sector, several DSOs have indicated that they will apply the existing technical standard 'VDE-AR-N 4105:2011-08'.[61]

4. FINANCIAL INCENTIVES IN FAVOUR OF PROSUMPTION

Empirical research has found that the main motivation for becoming a prosumer may not necessarily be related to economic considerations based on the savings or additional incomes for the energy consumers, but often relates to a personal choice of lifestyle (eg greater autonomy, environmental protection, desire to follow technological trends, stylish aspect of solar panels).[62] This assessment may be slightly different for public or commercial entities for which the earnings may be higher. Nevertheless, there is a series of financial rewards from not only producing and consuming one's own electricity, but also selling the surplus electricity.

The primary financial incentive in favour of prosumption consists in the revenues from the sale of the surplus electricity that prosumers will produce. This economic gain is combined with the money saved from not paying the full grid fees (the fixed component), which normal producers must pay and, in the

60 Requirements related to the billing of end-customers are defined in Chapter 7, Regulations on metering and settlement.

61 https://www.vde-verlag.de/normen/0102017/vde-ar-n-4102-anwendungsregel-2012-04.html.

62 H Westskog, TH Jackson Inderberg, H Sæle and T Winther, 'Strøm fra folket? Drivkrefter og barrierer', CICERO Report 2018:04, April 2018. As to international research, see 'Residential prosumers – drivers and policy options (re-prosumers)', International Energy Agency's Renewable Energy Technology Deployment (IEA-RETD), 2014.

case of prosumers, can be equal to zero or even negative, as explained above. In addition, prosumers may benefit from direct grants and local support schemes for the capital investment in the generation installation.

4.1. REVENUES FROM SELLING THE SURPLUS ELECTRICITY

When it comes to the surplus of electricity generated by the prosumer, the latter will need to re-negotiate its agreement with the electricity supplier. After the Elhub becomes operative, the prosumer will need to sell the surplus electricity to an electricity supplier. Prosumers will be required to contact the electricity supplier and negotiate the selling terms. As there cannot be more than one electricity supplier per connection point, the prosumer will offer the surplus electricity to the supplier it already has a supply agreement with. Where the prosumer wishes to offer the surplus to another supplier, they will need to change supplier. So far, suppliers have offered to buy the prosumer's surplus electricity at spot price in the relevant pricing area (in average 1 øre/kWh). To keep it simple, the price offered by the supplier for the surplus electricity will be deducted from the electricity bill of the energy customer turned prosumer.

It is submitted that the approach followed in Norway appears to be more market-friendly than, for example, in countries where the surplus electricity fed into the grid is reimbursed by the State through a fixed direct compensation (eg Austria, Germany). In most cases, the latter practice will qualify as State aid under the definition of Article 107(1) TFEU, but is exempted from the use of a bidding process for allocation of the aid under the Guidelines on State Aid for environmental protection and energy (2014–20) (EEAG).[63] Most residential prosumers will be well below the limits set out in the EEAG, but Member States can choose to set lower limits. Norway has not taken that opportunity, choosing, once again, a more market-oriented approach.

However, until the Elhub becomes operative, a temporary exemption regime approved by authorities applies, under which the prosumer can sell the surplus electricity to its grid company.[64] If, during that transition phase, the prosumer insists on selling the surplus electricity to its supplier, the DSO cannot refuse it. Compared with other European countries, selling the surplus electricity back to the grid operator appears to be a common practice (eg Denmark, Germany). In some circumstances, this results in an equivalent reduction from grid costs. However, letting the DSO buy electricity raises questions of possible distortions

---

63 Guidelines on State Aid for environmental protection and energy (2014–2020) (EEAG), para 127. See chapter VI of this volume, discussing the case of Germany.

64 NVE, Decision on exemption from the Regulations on reporting, income and tariffs in connection with grid activity, of 16.03.2010 (*Håndtering av plusskunder og vedtak om dispensasjon fra forskrift 302 om økonomisk og teknisk rapportering m.v.*).

of competition. The volume purchased from prosumers is very limited at the moment, but with a large number of local DSOs and an increasing number of prosumers, the risks of market distortion could increase in some parts of the Norwegian grid. This accepted practice also raises question of compatibility with unbundling requirements applicable to DSOs.

A final incentive linked to the sale of electricity could originate from the non-payment of the value added tax (VAT) for the surplus electricity sold by the prosumer. In some European countries, the surplus electricity sold is exempted from VAT up to a certain threshold.[65] It is worth noting that the European Court of Justice (ECJ) ruling in the *Fuchs* case (C-219/12) has established that the operation of a photovoltaic installation (ie solar panel) on or adjacent to a private house, which results in the supply of electricity to the network in exchange for income on a continuing basis, does constitute an 'economic activity.' Such activities are normally liable to tax. In Norway, in principle, the electricity sold by the prosumers to the DSO or supplier, is not exempted from VAT. However, prosumers will not pay the electricity tax (*elavgift*) for the electricity they produce and use themselves.[66] The budget line refers to 'the producer', which raises questions of interpretation when the owner of the solar panels and the consumers are not the same (eg in apartment buildings), a matter which still needs to be clarified. It is notable that this exemption applies differently to solar PV installations and other sources of energy. The tax exemption on self-consumed electricity is consequently not technology neutral. The fiscal treatment of the electricity which can be stored in the buildings (eg in electric cars or batteries) and re-used or injected into the grid, has not yet been investigated.

Finally, another financial incentive from electricity generation could originate from the sale of guarantees of origin. Because residential prosumers will barely reach the production threshold (1 MWh over a set period), there is no measurement requirement for their production and prosumers are not able to engage in electricity trading, thus they are not expected to receive guarantees of origin for the electricity they produce.[67]

4.2. SUPPORT SCHEMES

The most relevant financial scheme measures in favour of self-consumption and prosumption are under the competence of Enova SF, a public enterprise owned

[65] For example, in Austria, up to an annual household income of €30,000. Source: see n 23 above.

[66] This exemption regime developed as a practice, without legal basis until the state budget for 2018. The exemption has been recognised for the first time in the State Budget for 2018 and will be codified in the legislation. See Chapter 5541 post 70 'Om avgift på elektrisk kraft' in Prop. 1 LS (2017–2018), Skatter, avgifter og toll 2018, p 336.

[67] *Forskrift om opprinnelsesgarantier for produksjon av elektrisk energi.*

by the MPE.[68] Enova manages the Energy Fund[69] and provides for a system of direct grant for the installation of appliances at home, such as solar panels.[70] The grant is increased if the installation works in combination with other energy solutions, such as energy efficiency measures. In practice, the majority of the current prosumers have received a grant from Enova.[71]

Municipalities can adopt local support schemes in favour of electricity generation from specific sources. This has been the case for example in Oslo, where the municipalities provided financial support in the form of direct grant to households in the phase of prospection before the installation of solar PV or for the installation costs themselves. Most of those local schemes have been repealed on the grounds that the market is mature enough for prospective prosumers to find the information by themselves.

As stated by NVE, the prosumers regime currently in place in Norway is not meant as a support scheme for renewable energy sources. Meanwhile, certain prosumers could be interested in applying to the existing support scheme, which in Norway is a tradeable green certificates scheme (called el-certificates).[72] The first question will be to determine whether the consumer interested in becoming a prosumer is qualified to receive the green certificates for their surplus production. If they do qualify, the prosumers will get green certificates in proportion to the electricity they produce, and will then be able to sell them on the market. In practice, it is not expected that residential prosumers would be interested in applying for these because the application fee is too high to make it economically interesting for them. However, commercial consumers that fall under the definition of prosumers could be interested in applying to the green certificates scheme. Recently released data shows that the announcement in 2015, that it would be possible to obtain green certificates and become a prosumer, encouraged the installation of more solar panels in 2016, mostly for the benefit of more commercial actors.[73] Where the prosumers' facility qualifies

---

68 Enova SF was established in 2001. Enova's action focuses on the promotion of measures in favour of energy efficiency and renewable energy sources, with various financial support programmes in place, including for households.

69 The Energy Fund has been approved by the EFTA Surveillance Authority, ESA. The Energy Fund is financed via a small additional charge to electricity bills. In addition, the Energy Fund has been also allocated the proceeds from 'The Green Fund for Climate, Renewable Energy and Energy Efficiency Measures'.

70 For an overview of the different grants provided by Enova to households, see: https://www.enova.no/privat/.

71 Enova: Enovatilskuddet fordelt på tiltak og fylker, April 2018.

72 For a description of the green certificates scheme in Norway, see: O Boge, 'The Norwegian-Swedish Electricity Certificates Market' in MM Roggenkamp and H Bjørnebye (eds), *European Energy Law Report X*, Intersentia, Cambridge, Antwerp, Portland 2014, Chapter IX.

73 'Det er flere tak å ta av, vi har så vidt bare skrapt litt i overflaten', Teknisk Ukeblad, 27 February 2017, at: https://www.tu.no/artikler/norsk-solkraftutbygging-naer-firedoblet-i-2016-vi-har-savidt-skrapt-i-overflaten/377031.

under the green certificates scheme, receiving green certificates and financial support from Enova at the same time is not possible as that would amount to overcompensation.[74]

5. ASSESSMENT

As in many other energy matters, Norway distinguishes itself from other European countries on the question of prosumption. This is mainly explained by the absence of a clear need for greening the generation mix or ensuring additional generation flexibility, and by a lack of serious requests from energy consumers. Meanwhile, prosumers are a small but growing community among energy consumers. Norwegian authorities have also provided a regulatory incentive by clarifying the legal basis for the prosumption regime. The latest legislative changes represent both a codification of previous practices (based on an exemption regime) and a slight tightening-up of the rights and duties of prosumers and DSOs as to tariffs regulation.

The regulatory approach followed is relatively simple, based on one single law provision and focusing on the need to ensure that the excess electricity generated by prosumers is fed effectively into the grid. The prosumer regime consists almost exclusively in an exemption to part of the grid tariffs. Financial incentives are to be found primarily in the cumulated effects of the savings from grid costs, the sale of surplus electricity and the support for the purchase of generation appliances such as solar panels.

As the market grows and the financial attractiveness of self-generation technologies such as solar PV increases, there will be a need for amendments to the regime. The treatment of groups of prosumers such as a cooperative or apartment blocks could be improved and prosumption made more attractive for those consumers. Adjusting the threshold of 100 kW input power is also a political decision concerning the type of prosumption policy the Norwegian authorities want to pursue, not least the share of prosumption in the retail market. The interaction between self-consumption, prosumption and demand response is not promoted to a great extent. The legislation also prevents prosumers from engaging in electricity sales activities, which is the prospect of peer-to-peer energy trading and one of the possible applications of blockchain technologies.[75] Meanwhile, allowing prosumers to enter the retail

---

74 Rules on cumulation of aid are defined in both the EEAG and bilateral Treaty between Norway and Sweden on a joint green certificates market (*Avtale mellom Norge og Sverige om et felles marked for elsertifikater*, 29 June 2011, as amended).

75 See for such prospects and the need for regulatory reforms: S Lavrijssen and A Carrillo Parra, 'Radical Prosumer Innovations in the Electricity Sector and the Impact on Prosumer Regulation' (2017) Sustainability 9(7) 1–21.

power market would raise practical issues, not least in terms of grid balancing, which are not precisely assessed in Norway. Another source of forthcoming regulatory amendments will be the need to align Norwegian legislation with the forthcoming revision of the Electricity Directive and Renewable Energy Directive as part of the Clean Energy for All Europeans legislative package put forward by the European Commission on 30 November 2016, which relates mostly to legal acts already incorporated into the EEA Agreement. Therefore, the adoption of the recent amendments to national legislation should be seen as a first step towards a more elaborate regime for prosumption in Norway and greater empowerment for energy consumers.

PART IV

BALANCING RENEWABLE ELECTRICITY PRODUCTION WITH SUPPLY SECURITY: NATIONAL EXPERIENCES WITH CAPACITY MECHANISMS

CHAPTER IX
THE CAPACITY MARKET IN GREAT BRITAIN

Julian ROBERTS

1. INTRODUCTION

This chapter outlines the Capacity Market (CM) which exists in Great Britain (GB). It covers some of the context and history of the mechanism including how the CM was designed, the process required for State aid approval and the legislation that underpins it. It then briefly refers to the economic theory behind capacity mechanisms and reviews how the CM in GB works in practice. Finally, it analyses the results seen so far in GB and some of the future challenges as the energy market continues to evolve.

2. CONTEXT AND HISTORY

2.1. CHANGES TO THE ENERGY SYSTEM

Great Britain, like many countries in Europe, is facing significant changes in its electricity system. Many traditional generators, such as large coal and nuclear plants, are coming to the natural end of their lives. This is not only a recent phenomenon: 11.5 GW of coal and oil capacity closed before 2015 due to the implementation of the EU Large Combustion Plant Directive.[1] At least a further 8 GW of capacity is expected to close by 2030[2] as they become uneconomic, leading to a greater need for investment in replacement capacity. In addition, the power sector must make significant reductions in its carbon intensity in order to meet legally binding emissions targets. The Government's most recent Carbon

1 Royal Academy of Engineering, 'GB Electricity Capacity Margin: A Report by the Royal Academy of Engineering for the Council for Science and Technology', 2013.

2 National Grid Electricity Transmission, 'Future Energy Scenarios', 2017.

Budget set a target for 2030 for reducing carbon emissions by 57% compared to 1990 levels.[3]

Intermittent generating technologies such as solar and wind are an increasingly significant part of the electricity system with almost 30GW installed by the end of 2017. Renewable sources provided almost a quarter of total UK electricity generation in 2016 compared to only 5% in 2006.[4] This creates an increasing need for flexibility and for backup generation to cover periods where intermittent technologies are not delivering.

The way the system is being used is also changing. New technologies such as electricity storage are being deployed on a commercial scale as costs reduce. And more generators are now locating closer to customers and connecting directly to the distribution system. All of these changes are creating new challenges for the market, system operators, regulators and government.

2.2. THE POLICY CHALLENGES

The Project Discovery report by the Office of Gas and Electricity Markets (Ofgem),[5] the first version of which was published in 2009, outlined some of the policy challenges facing the energy system as it changes, which are often described as being a 'trilemma' between security of supply, affordability and decarbonisation.

One of the obstacles to meeting these challenges is the scale of investment needed in new capacity, both to replace the old plants that are closing and to build low carbon generation to meet emissions targets. At the time of Project Discovery, Ofgem estimated that up to £200 billion of investment might be required by 2020, of which at least £110 billion would be needed in new generation and transmission assets in electricity.

The scale of investment needed meant that a 'capacity crunch' was expected, with new generation not able to replace the closing power plants fast enough and leading to falling capacity margins in the middle of the decade. This led to widespread media attention[6] and energy security being brought to the forefront of public minds.

3 Climate Change Act 2008 and the Carbon Budget Order 2016.

4 Department for Business, Energy and Industrial Strategy (BEIS), 'Digest of UK Energy Statistics 2017'.

5 Office of Gas and Electricity Markets (Ofgem), 'Project Discovery – Options for Delivering Secure and Sustainable Energy Supplies', 2010.

6 Daily Mail, 'Blackout Britain warning as Government predicts severe power shortages within year', 2009.

2.3. THE INTRODUCTION OF A CAPACITY MARKET

The reflection around a capacity mechanism of some form started in 2010, following a change in government in the UK. A plan to 'cut carbon emissions and rebuild our energy security' was part of the Conservative Party's manifesto[7] (who formed a coalition government with the Liberal Democrats following the 2010 General Election).

The choice to introduce a capacity mechanism was not a one-off decision, but a policy position that was developed over a number of years. In his annual energy statement to Parliament in July 2010,[8] the Secretary of State for Energy and Climate Change announced that the Government would publish a consultation to examine the reforms necessary to achieve its objectives on decarbonisation, renewable energy, security of supply and affordability. The consultation was published in December of the same year,[9] alongside an impact assessment,[10] which identified 'a number of existing market failures and imperfections whose effect becomes exacerbated as levels of low marginal cost, low-carbon generation increase'. Together those documents concluded that some form of policy intervention was likely to be necessary.

The Government then published a paper in 2011 entitled 'Planning our Electric Future: A White Paper for Secure, Affordable and Low-Carbon Electricity'.[11] This paper determined that a capacity mechanism should be introduced, as part of a wider set of measures, collectively called Electricity Market Reform.[12] The reform consisted of four main policies: (1) an emissions performance standard which effectively ruled out new coal; (2) a carbon price floor which topped up the European Union Emissions Trading System (EU ETS) price; (3) a new policy for funding low carbon generation through contracts for difference (CFD), which aimed to reduce the costs of building renewables by reducing price risk; and (4) a capacity mechanism to ensure security of electricity supply.

Following further development, a policy overview of the Capacity Market was published in 2012,[13] which set out among other clarifications, that the mechanism should be market-wide and would be similar to capacity markets

---

7 The Conservative Party, 'The Conservative Manifesto 2010'.

8 Department of Energy and Climate Change (DECC), 'Annual Energy Statement 2010', 2010.

9 Department of Energy and Climate Change (DECC), 'Electricity Market Reform, Consultation Document', 2010.

10 Department of Energy and Climate Change (DECC), 'Electricity Market Reform – Options for Ensuring Electricity Security of Supply and Promoting Investment in Low-Carbon Generation', 2010.

11 Department of Energy and Climate Change (DECC), 'Planning our Electric Future: A White Paper for Secure, Affordable and Low-Carbon Electricity', 2011.

12 Department of Energy and Climate Change (DECC), 'Implementing Electricity Market Reform (EMR)', 2014.

13 Department of Energy and Climate Change (DECC), 'Electricity Market Reform: Policy Overview', 2012.

in the United States. It also suggested the first auction could be run in 2014 for delivery in 2018. At the time this was considered an important publication to ensure there was no investment hiatus while the policy was developed, although the Government had still not confirmed that it would run the auctions, as this would be based on a needs assessment carried out in 2013.

Legislation was brought into force in the form of the Energy Act 2013 and subsequently, in 2014, secondary legislation which implemented the new CFDs and Capacity Market. The main legislative instruments are:

- The *Energy Act 2013* sets out the powers and duties of government, Ofgem, and the Delivery Body in running the Capacity Market;
- The *Electricity Capacity Regulations 2014* (the 'Regulations') set out the high-level design of the Capacity Market, for example, the technologies that can participate;
- The *Electricity Capacity (Supplier Payment etc.) Regulations 2014* make provisions about the payments to be made by and to electricity suppliers in relation to the Capacity Market; and
- The *Capacity Market Rules 2014* (the 'Rules') contain the detailed policy and procedures, for example, the eligibility requirements and the mechanism of the auction, which is governed by Ofgem.

At the same time the primary legislation was published, the Government committed to running the first Capacity Market Auction.[14]

2.4. DESIGNING A CAPACITY MARKET

The design of the Capacity Market took place over the period 2010–14. A Capacity Market was not the leading option at the start of this period. Originally, the Government had thought to introduce a strategic reserve, whereby the transmission system operator would hold a small amount of capacity outside the market. However, there was a generally negative response to this proposal from stakeholders. It was thought that a strategic reserve could reduce prices in the market and cause plant to become unprofitable, which could create a 'slippery slope' with increasingly more plant needed in the strategic reserve to remain operational.

As noted above, the Government eventually settled on a market-wide mechanism, which would allow participation from all generators and demand-side response, provided they were not receiving support in favour of renewable energy production.

[14] Department of Energy and Climate Change (DECC), 'Electricity Market Reform: Delivering UK Investment', 2013.

It is useful to understand the market context while the mechanism was being designed. Demand for electricity was expected to rise significantly as transport and other sectors were being electrified. The price of electricity was also expected to rise, as subsidies for low carbon generators increased, which bolstered concerns over affordability. Spark spreads, which measure the profitability of gas plants, had fallen, leading to fears of plants closing earlier than expected and consequently capacity margins over winter were forecast to fall to dangerously low levels.[15]

These factors helped lead to a focus on long-term certainty for investors, which resulted in policy choices including multi-year capacity agreements and caps on the penalties a capacity provider can receive; and the focus on a delivery assurance model, where participants are required to go through a rigorous prequalification process before they can participate.

2.5. STATE AID APPROVAL

In order to introduce a capacity mechanism, the Government sought State aid approval towards the European Commission. The measure was considered to constitute State aid within the meaning of Article 101 of the Treaty on the Functioning of the European Union (TFEU), as the capacity payments are a resource that is under the control of the State; the payments confer an economic advantage to those that receive them; and the payments risks distorting competition and affecting trade within the internal market. Great Britain's mechanism was the first to be assessed against the Commission's Environmental and Energy State Aid Guidelines (EEAG) (2014–20), which were developed at the same time as the Capacity Market was being designed.

A number of other changes to the electricity market were being made at that time, and these were helpful to the case for State aid as they demonstrated that the UK had considered alternative options to address the problem, which was a requirement of the State aid guidelines. In particular, Ofgem was making reforms to the electricity balancing market and taking measures to improve the liquidity in the wholesale electricity market. These aimed to improve the underlying signals to invest in appropriate capacity and therefore complemented the Electricity Market Reform programme.

In order to gain authorisation of State aid for the Capacity Market, the GB Government made a commitment that interconnectors would be able to participate from 2015. Whilst the Government had always intended for the mechanism to be technologically neutral, the original design did not include the participation of interconnectors or non-GB capacity, and the Commission was

15 Office of Gas and Electricity Markets (Ofgem), 'Electricity Capacity Assessment', 5 December 2012.

worried about the impact this could have on market coupling. Changes to the legislation were required to implement their inclusion and given the timing of the legislative process these could only be made in 2015.

The Government also committed to reviewing the mechanism after five years and the first report is expected in 2019.

Approval for the State aid was given in July 2014[16] for a period of 10 years. Shortly after, in December 2014, the State aid decision for the Capacity Market was challenged before the Court of Justice of the EU on a procedural basis.[17] Tempus Energy, who brought the challenge, have argued that the decision is anti-competitive as demand-side response providers are not able to access 15-year agreements, unlike generation. The applicants also argued that the Commission failed to properly assess the potential role of Demand-Side Response in the UK Capacity Market and seek the annulment of the Commission's Decision C(2014) 5083 final of 23 July 2014 in the State aid case SA.35980 (2014/N-2) – United Kingdom, Electricity Market Reform – Capacity Market. At the time of writing, the appeal has not yet concluded.

In 2016, the first full delivery year of the Capacity Market was brought forward, with a supplementary auction being run in January 2017 for delivery the following winter. This was regarded as a notifiable change within the meaning of Article 108(3) TFEU as the aid would begin before the time period for approval previously given. A new request was made in early 2016 and approved in December the same year, with the Commission concluding the supplementary auction was also in line with EU State aid rules.[18]

3. THE ECONOMIC THEORY

Prices in the wholesale electricity market act as an investment signal to provide capacity. During periods of relative scarcity, prices rise and plant may be able to receive scarcity revenues, which represent the difference between the market price and the most expensive generator. These rents are paid infrequently but allow those generators to cover their capital costs and make a return on their investment.

However, on its own the electricity market cannot always set a price. Supply is fixed in the short term and demand is not sufficiently flexible to reduce when

---

16 European Commission, State Aid SA.35980 – United Kingdom – Electricity market reform – Capacity mechanism', decision of 23 July 2014.

17 Case T-793/14, *Tempus Energy and Tempus Energy Technology v Commission*, application lodged on 4 December 2014.

18 European Commission, State Aid SA.44475 – United Kingdom – Supplementary Capacity Auction, decision of 5 December 2016.

prices are high so there may be periods where electricity is demanded but not satisfied. At these times, the market has not cleared and no price has been set.

Figure 1. In the Short Run, the Market Fails to Set a Price

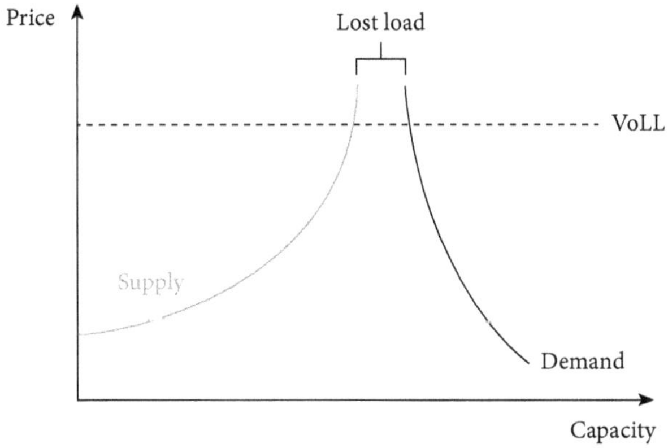

Source: Produced by the author.

Intervention of some kind is required to price the market when demand exceeds supply. The most basic solution is for the system operator to determine the price. Economic theory suggests that if the price is set exactly at the value consumers place on secure electricity, it will be sufficient to ensure adequate investment in capacity.[19] This is called 'value of lost load' (VoLL) pricing. This does not mean that there will never be lost load – at some point the marginal benefit of having additional capacity will not outweigh the marginal costs of building it – but it should ensure that capacity is built if it is beneficial to do so.

It should be noted that this is still not a completely optimal outcome, as we will have assumed all consumers have the same value for their lost load. In reality, different customers will have different values. In GB, a study conducted by London Economics determined that the average VoLL for domestic customers was £10,000/MWh and the average VoLL for small and medium enterprises was £35,000/MWh.[20]

There are a number of problems with this VoLL pricing approach which means adequate capacity may still not be delivered. Collectively, these issues are sometimes called 'missing money' to reflect the missing investment case for additional capacity.

The first and most obvious issue is that VoLL pricing may be set too low. Price caps still exist in some markets which would prevent prices rising to

[19] P Joskow and J Tirole, 'Reliability and Competitive Electricity Markets' (2007) RAND Journal of Economics 38(1), 60–84.

[20] London Economics, 'The Value of Lost Load (VoLL) for Electricity in Great Britain', Final report for Ofgem and DECC, July 2013.

sufficient levels to attract adequate investment. The Commission, in its Clean Energy for All Europeans package has suggested that all wholesale price caps should be removed.[21] In GB, there is no price cap but the price set by the system operator for periods of lost load is £3,000/MWh (rising to £6,000 in November 2018). This is lower than the £17,000/MWh estimate of VoLL determined by the London Economics study noted above.

Another issue is the uncertainty that prices will be allowed to rise to VoLL levels by regulators and government. In 2015, there were high prices seen in the balancing market in GB, including periods where the system operator needed to pay up to £2,500/MWh, over 30 times the average price. These caused a number of media headlines and prompted one parliamentary committee to ask National Grid and Ofgem to investigate the prices in order to satisfy themselves that market power had not been abused.[22] This uncertainty may deter investors from the market resulting in suboptimal amounts of capacity.

Another problem is that investors may be reluctant to finance large infrastructure projects with the assumption of few and infrequent price spikes. Periods of scarcity may happen only every 10 or 20 years and some plants may only be in merit, and therefore earning revenue, during these times. Although the scarcity revenue earned in these periods would be very high, the returns would carry a much greater risk.

Allowing prices to spike near to the VoLL may also cause market power concerns, as generators become pivotal to the market and may be able to restrict output to increase prices.

Capacity mechanisms can help to avoid some of these problems by spreading scarcity revenues over a greater number of periods, reducing the number of price spikes in the market and guaranteeing a revenue that can help to cover fixed costs. This can reduce some of the public attention and uncertainty from price spikes, helping to reduce the uncertainty faced by investors. It can also help to reduce opportunities for generators to exploit positions of market power.

4. THE DESIGN OF THE GB MECHANISM

The operation of the Capacity Market can be roughly split into the following six stages: analysis, prequalification, auction, payments and penalties, delivery and trading. These stages will be discussed in more detail below.

---

21 European Commission, Proposal for a Regulation of the European Parliament and the Council on the internal market for electricity (recast), COM (2016) 861 final, 30 November 2016, as corrected.

22 Utility Week, 'MPs question National Grid on Calon Energy's £2.5k/MWh windfall', 24 November 2015.

4.1. DETERMINING THE VOLUME OF CAPACITY NEEDED

In GB, the Government has set an enduring reliability standard. This reflects the trade-off between the value consumers put on secure electricity supplies and the costs of securing additional capacity. The reliability standard is defined in the Electricity Capacity Regulations 2014 as 'the cumulative duration of periods in a capacity year in which it is to be presumed … that, on average over the long term, loss of load should occur.' The standard is set at three hours per year. This does not necessarily equate to actual lost load (ie blackouts), but times where the system operator would be required to take action outside of the market, for example by reducing voltage.

Each year, from around April to June, the system operator carries out analysis to determine the amount of capacity required to meet the reliability standard. After assessing a number of national scenarios it recommends to the Government a volume of capacity to target in the auction. The system operator's analysis is scrutinised by an independent panel of technical experts, comprised of academics appointed by the Government. The final decision on the target capacity to be auctioned and other parameters such as a price cap is made by the Secretary of State for Business, Energy and Industrial Strategy.

4.2. ELIGIBILITY AND PREQUALIFICATION

Prospective capacity providers must meet certain eligibility requirements, as defined in the Capacity Market Rules, before they can participate in the CM auctions. Generators, demand-side response, storage, and interconnection are all eligible as the mechanism is technology-neutral. This includes existing capacity as well as prospective units which will be built if they win a Capacity Market agreement. Generators receiving other forms of subsidy, such as support in favour of renewable energy production, cannot participate.

To determine the eligibility of entrants, the Delivery Body, which is part of the system operator, runs a prequalification process, which normally takes 22 weeks. Potential providers submit information including the size and location of their capacity, their connection arrangements and their technology and fuel type. The primary purpose is to provide some assurance that the capacity will be able to deliver. Applicants who fail the prequalification process can appeal against this decision to Ofgem. The Delivery Body publishes the results of this process on a public register.[23]

[23] EMR Delivery Body, 'Capacity Market Register', available at: https://www.emrdeliverybody.com/CM/cm-register.aspx.

When applying, each generator or demand-side response provider creates a number of Capacity Market Units (CMUs), each of which acts as one quantum of capacity in the auction. A CMU could be comprised of several individual units, for example, a typical generating CMU may include multiple turbines from the same power plant. A demand-side CMU might contain hundreds of small components, each one a customer which provides demand response.

New generators can prequalify for agreement lengths up to 15 years. This is to provide sufficient certainty to allow new projects to become financeable. Similarly, projects that are undergoing significant refurbishment, as defined by an expenditure threshold, are able to gain three-year agreements. Existing generators and demand-side response providers can only access one-year agreements.

4.3. AUCTION

The price of the capacity agreements, which reflects the amount paid to each provider, is determined via competitive auctions, held four years (T-4 Auction) and one year (T-1 Auction) before each delivery period. Each auction has a single clearing price measured in £/kW/year. The Delivery Body runs the auctions via an online system in line with the requirements set out in the Capacity Market Rules.

The auction takes place over several days using a descending clock format. This means that the price starts at a high level and then drops each round. Participants will exit the auction when the price drops below the point at which they are willing to take on an agreement. The auction clears at the lowest price at which there is still sufficient capacity to meet demand. All providers who have not exited the auction at this point are offered an agreement at the clearing price.

Only price is used to determine which bidders receive agreements. Other parameters, such as the technology, location or length of the agreement are ignored. It is expected that participants will have factored all relevant parameters into their bids.

In addition to the T-4 and T-1 auctions, transitional auctions were run in 2015 and 2016 for delivery in 2016/17 and 2017/18 respectively. Only demand-side response providers were able to participate in these auctions as the auctions were aimed as a nursery for this technology. These were much smaller auctions with only a limited amount of capacity being targeted.

4.4. THE SECONDARY MARKET AND OBLIGATIONS BEFORE THE DELIVERY YEAR

Between the auction and the delivery year, certain providers have additional obligations which help to ensure delivery of the capacity.

New generators must meet a financial commitment milestone, requiring their projects to have the final investment decision made and have committed 10% of the total spend for the project. Failure to complete this 18 months before the delivery year will result in termination of the agreement. New generators will need to provide regular construction reports. Demand-side response providers have to complete a DSR test to prove they have signed up customers able to reduce demand to the level of capacity promised. All providers must complete a metering assessment and some may have to complete metering tests, depending on their setup.

The one-year-ahead auction takes into account whether any capacity agreements have been terminated and changes in the forecast demand and supply for electricity. This auction can be used to 'top up' any capacity that is still needed.

After the one-year-ahead auction has taken place capacity providers may use the secondary market to trade their agreements. This allows participants to trade some or all of their capacity agreements with other prequalified applicants, for example, they made trade out of their obligation for periods where the plant is undergoing maintenance. The Delivery Body is responsible for registering all trades on the Capacity Market register.

4.5. DELIVERY OF CAPACITY

The capacity agreement is not a contract and confers no contractual rights on the holder. Instead, a capacity agreement simply comprises the rights and obligations accruing to a capacity provider by virtue of the Regulations and the Rules. It does not need to be signed, as a capacity agreement will automatically be awarded to any successful bidder in the auction. The notice which providers receive following an auction contains the basic information about their agreement, such as the year it was issued, the size in MW and the price.

During the period of their agreement, which runs from 1 October to 30 September, capacity providers are required to be generating electricity, reducing demand or importing electricity whenever the system enters a period of stress. A stress period is defined as a half hour where the system operator needs to take demand control actions, such as disconnections or voltage reduction due to system adequacy. Actions taken because of constraints on the network are not counted as stress periods.

The obligation to be providing capacity will only take effect if the system operator has given a warning four hours before the period of stress. This warning is not an instruction to capacity providers and it is expected that the market price will still provide the primary signal for generators to be running.

The exact obligation of each provider is determined by a load-following formula. This means that when demand is high the obligation will be at or close to the full level of capacity agreement. During summer, when the demand on the system is lower, the obligation will also be lower, becoming only a percentage of the full agreement. This is designed to prevent inefficiently keeping a lot of plant warm over summer.

During the delivery year there may not be any periods of stress. However, all providers will still be required to demonstrate that they are able to meet their full obligation three times over winter. Providers are able to self-nominate periods where they have done this. Providers failing to meet this requirement will not receive capacity payments for that year.

4.6. PAYMENTS AND PENALTIES

Payments and penalties are defined in the Electricity Capacity Regulations 2014 and the Electricity Capacity (Supplier Payment etc.) Regulations 2014. Capacity providers are paid monthly for holding a capacity agreement. The agreement obligates them to be providing electricity or reducing demand when the system enters a period of stress. Failing to provide during these periods results in a penalty equal to 1/24th of the auction clearing price, expressed in MWh.

The rules of the balancing market, as set out in the Balancing and Settlement Code,[24] mean that during stress periods the imbalance price should be equal to the administrative value of lost load, which is currently £3000/MWh, rising to £6000/MWh in 2018. The penalties do not try to incentivise providers to deliver during stress periods as the wholesale electricity price already sets an adequate incentive.

There are caps on the total penalties payable. There is a monthly cap of 200% of the total monthly income and an annual cap of 100% of the annual income. That means that a capacity provider cannot lose more in non-delivery penalties than it is given in capacity payments.

There are also penalties for providers whose agreements are terminated before the delivery year. The penalties differ based on the timing and reason for termination but range from £5/kW to £35/kW.

5. RESULTS SO FAR

There have been eight capacity auctions to date: the early auction for delivery in 2017/18, four auctions for the full delivery years 2018/19, 2019/20, 2020/21 and 2021/22; a year-ahead auction for delivery in 2018/19; and two Demand-Side Response (DSR) transitional auctions for delivery in 2016/17 and 2017/18.

---

24 Elexon, 'Balancing and Settlement Code', available at: https://www.elexon.co.uk/bsc-and-codes/balancing-settlement-code/bsc-sections/.

The clearing prices for these auctions have generally been below market expectations. In the first auction, for delivery in 2018/19, the clearing price was £19.40/kW, below investor forecasts of £25–50/kW, and below the Government's estimated cost of new entry of £49/kW. One reason for this is the type of new capacity that came forward in the auction: a significant number of small gas and diesel reciprocating engines won agreements. These plants tend to have low capital costs and high marginal costs, relying on stable capacity market revenue rather than electricity market revenue. This helps them bid at a lower capacity price. They also tend to be connected directly to the distribution network, which can allow them to collect 'embedded benefits' for their ability to help suppliers avoid transmission network charges.

The auction results highlighted a number of advantages that certain generators, such as small gas plant, can receive. Since the auction, a number of steps have been taken to ensure different technologies are competing on a level playing field. First, Ofgem approved a change to the transmission charging methodology which aimed to remove distortive elements of the embedded benefits, taking effect from 1 April 2018. Secondly, the Department for Environment Food and Rural Affairs (DEFRA) implemented the Medium Combustion Plant Directive,[25] which formed part of the European Union's Clean Air Policy Package.[26] The changes introduced emissions standards for small new generators from December 2018, which effectively limited the number of hours diesel generators could run, reducing their economic viability. Finally, the Government made changes through the Finance (No 2) Act 2015,[27] which excluded reserve electricity generation from being able to collect tax exemptions as part of the Enterprise Investment Scheme, Seed Enterprise Investment Scheme and Venture Capital Trusts.

Another reason for the lower price in the first year could have been the level of termination fees for plants failing to deliver on their agreements. One larger Combined Cycle Gas Turbine (CCGT) project did win an agreement in the first auction but later had its agreement terminated as it failed to get financing at this price. Some observers have suggested plant were willing to take this risk because the penalties for failing to build were not high enough. Since then, the Government has increased the termination rate to discourage projects that do not have a realistic prospect of being built.

In the second auction, for delivery in 2019/20, the price remained low at £18/kW. Interconnectors participated for the first time in this auction and all of the existing interconnectors won an agreement. The third auction, for delivery in 2020/21 cleared at £22.50/kW. Part of the reason for the slightly

---

25 The Environmental Permitting (England and Wales) Regulations 2016.

26 Directive (EU) 2015/2193 of the European Parliament and of the Council of 25 November 2015 on the limitation of emissions of certain pollutants into the air from medium combustion plants.

27 Finance (No 2) Act 2015.

higher price is likely to be the increased target for capacity, with less capacity being held back for the one-year-ahead auction.

The early auction, for delivery in 2017/18 was held in January 2017. It cleared far below expectations, with a clearing price of £6.95/kW. It is likely that many plants were able to bid much lower in this auction because they were already obligated to be providing capacity in future delivery years. There was also competition from a number of smaller new generators who had won agreements for later years and were able to accelerate their development.

The one-year-ahead auction for delivery in 2018/19 cleared at £6.00/kW, the lowest price yet seen. The auction was characterised by a high level of competition. In the same year, the four-year-ahead auction for delivery in 2021/22 cleared at £8.40/kW, which was again below market expectations. New interconnector projects won agreements for the first time in this auction.

The Capacity Market is still new. The first full delivery year for capacity is still in progress and therefore it is too early to judge the success of the mechanism. The auction results so far have shown it is difficult to predict market outcomes, and they have highlighted areas of the market where reform would be beneficial.

6. FUTURE CHALLENGES

In the past, the energy industry has been characterised by supply-side flexibility, with large power plants able to ramp up and down generation to satisfy demand. As intermittent renewables enter the system and older plants close down, the requirements for flexibility have changed, and technological developments have changed the way in which it can be provided.

In the future we are likely to see more demand-side flexibility, with energy consumers able to curtail or shift their demand to reduce peak load. Smaller distributed generators are likely to become more economically viable, as they can generate during the periods where renewables are not providing and provide flexibility services to the system operator. Battery storage is also likely to play a larger role in the system, using fast response times to provide flexibility. New interconnectors also have the potential to reduce the need for new generation, helping to meet the investment challenge at a lower cost. The GB energy market currently has 4GW of interconnectors to other electricity markets.[28] This is set to increase significantly in the future, with 8GW of additional interconnection planned.

Changes in the energy system are likely to drive a need for changes to the Capacity Market. We have already seen a number of examples of this.

[28] The 500MW HVDC Moyle to Northern Ireland, the 2GW Interconnexion France-Angleterre (IFA) to Ireland, the 500MW East–West Interconnector to the Republic of Ireland, and the 1GW BritNed to the Netherlands.

Demand-side response providers have highlighted a number of challenges in the current design for their participation. Changes to the policy to allow better options for portfolio management are already under consideration. Battery storage is able to participate in the Capacity Market and was successful for the first time in the 2016 auction. However, batteries are limited in their duration and many may only be able to deliver for 30 minutes, whereas the system operator believes stress events could last up to two hours. Changes to the assumption of the level of capacity that batteries can provide, given their limited duration, have recently been made by the Government.

The changes to the energy system are also driving changes in other markets, including the wholesale electricity market and the ancillary services market, which contains the products used by the system operator to balance the system. For example, the system operator has recently launched a System Needs and Product Strategy, which contains a product roadmap for frequency response.[29] With less traditional generation on the system there is less inertia and the requirements of the system operator have changed, with faster response times needed to deal with larger swings in frequency. A future challenge for the Capacity Market will be to ensure interactions with these markets are taken into account.

In recent years GB has faced significantly lower capacity margins – the excess of installed generation over demand – than in the past. This has led to a focus on security of supply. Now that the Capacity Market is in place, some of that focus is likely to move away from security of supply and to affordability. The costs of the Capacity Market are passed through to consumers via suppliers. Although these costs do not appear separately on consumers' bills, it will still be a crucial area to ensure the right amount of capacity agreements are given out. Small changes in the demand for capacity can have large impacts on the cost of capacity.

As the cost of building renewable technologies has fallen, some technologies, such as onshore wind, are no longer eligible to participate in subsidy schemes and are now looking to compete in the Capacity Market instead. Ofgem are currently considering how to expand the technologies that can participate, including hybrid sites, which could contain several interlinked technologies, such as wind and storage.

With the number of changes to the energy system, it is likely the Capacity Market will need to stay flexible enough to deal with new challenges. Improvements to the governance framework may be required to ensure changes can happen quickly enough to keep up. There will be a review of the capacity market legislation by both the Department for Business, Energy and Industrial Strategy (BEIS) and Ofgem after five years and this is likely to be one catalyst for change.

---

[29] National Grid Electricity Transmission, 'Product Roadmap for Frequency Response and Reserve', December 2017.

CHAPTER X
CAPACITY MECHANISMS IN GERMANY

Kai PRITZSCHE and Christina HEBER

1. INTRODUCTION

This chapter presents the introduction and use of capacity mechanisms in Germany. The background for establishing this regime is the energy transition process, generally referred to as *Energiewende*, which was adopted in 2010. The chapter starts by exploring the background and rationale for introducing a system of capacity mechanisms in Germany, before presenting the way in which the first capacity reserve mechanisms were developed and shaped in 2012 and how this early regime was impacted by the European Commission's Sector Inquiry on Capacity Mechanisms in 2015. This is followed by an analysis of the four capacity reserve mechanisms that currently apply. The chapter concludes by looking at the functioning of the German electricity sector in the future and the role of these capacity mechanisms in the German electricity market.

2. RATIONALE FOR THE ADOPTION OF CAPACITY MECHANISMS IN GERMANY

Capacity mechanisms in Germany currently consist of four capacity reserve facilities. They are established and described in detail in the German Energy Industry Act (*Energiewirtschaftsgesetz*, EnWG).[1] The reserve facilities are intended to ensure temporarily the security of supply in the electricity market against various consequences resulting from the transition process called the Energy Transition (*Energiewende*) in the German energy-only-market. The German Energy Transition was officially adopted by the German Government

---

1 Sec 13 ff EnWG, German Energy Industry Act (*Energiewirtschaftsgesetz*), dated 7 July 2005 (BGBl. I p. 1970, 3621), as amended most recently by Art 2 para 6 of the Act dated 20 July 2017 (BGBl. I p. 2808).

in September 2010 in a strategic policy document called the Energy Concept.[2] The Energy Concept provides a vision for the energy market until the year 2050. The defined objective is to achieve a transition from electricity generation based on fossil fuels to generation from renewable energy sources, an exit from nuclear power and the reduction of greenhouse gas emissions.[3] These different components of the Energy Concept are reviewed below.

2.1. RENEWABLE ENERGY

The first main objective of the Energy Transition is the switch towards more electricity generation from renewable energy sources.[4] In Germany, this switch relies primarily on wind power (both onshore and offshore) and solar energy, with biomass, hydropower and geothermal playing a lesser role.[5] In 2016, renewable energies already represented 32.2% of gross electricity generation in Germany.[6] The Energy Concept's ambitious targets have been set even higher by the Renewable Energies Act (*Erneuerbare Energien Gesetz*, EEG).[7] In the latest version of the Act, the national targeted share of renewable energies in gross final electricity consumption is 40–45% by 2025, 55–60% by 2035 and at least 80% by 2050.[8] In order to reach those targets, the EEG defines different measures aimed at promoting the use and integration of renewable energy sources, notably through priority grid access, a fixed remuneration and a market premium. With the last change of the EEG in 2017, the support system has moved to a system of a predefined extension path and an auction system for the additional capacities to be newly built.[9]

---

2 German Government publication, Energy Concept for an environmentally friendly, reliable and affordable energy supply, 28 September 2010, available at: http://www.bmwi.de/English/Redaktion/Pdf/energy-concept,property=pdf,bereich=bmwi,sprache=en,rwb=true.pdf.

3 Ibid, p 1.

4 Ibid, p 7.

5 Sec 3 para 21 EEG.

6 Eurostat, Share of electricity from renewable sources in gross electricity consumption 2004–2016, Germany (http://ec.europa.eu/eurostat/statistics-explained/index.php/Renewable_energy_statistics); see also Federal Ministry of Economic Affairs and Energy (*Bundesministerium für Wirtschaft und Energie*, BMWi), Renewable Energies, https://www.bmwi.de/DE/Themen/Energie/Erneuerbare-Energien/erneuerbare-energien-auf-einen-blick.html.

7 German Renewable Energies Act (*Erneuerbare Energien Gesetz*), dated 21 July 2014 (BGBl. I p. 1066), as amended most recently by Art 1 of the Act dated 17 July 2017 (BGBl. I p. 2532).

8 Sec 1 para 2 EEG.

9 Sec 28 ff EEG.

2.2. NUCLEAR PHASE-OUT

The second main element of the German Energy Transition is the decision to phase out nuclear energy. This historic decision was only taken after highly controversial discussions resulting in a repeated back and forth.[10] After the nuclear accident in Fukushima, Japan, in March 2011, the public view on nuclear power was drastically changed. As a consequence, the German Government decided that instead of extending the running times of the operating plants, nuclear energy would be phased out by 2022. In July 2011, the 13th Amendment to the Atomic Energy Law (*Atomgesetz*) was enacted,[11] which led to an immediate shut-down of eight nuclear power plants.[12] For the remaining nuclear power plants, the reform of the Atomic Energy Law set down fixed end dates for their operation.[13]

2.3. CLIMATE CHANGE

The third main element of the Energy Transition is the reduction of greenhouse gas emissions in the fight against climate change. The Energy Concept sets out targets for the reduction of greenhouse gas emissions of 40% reduction by 2020 and 80–95% by 2050, using 1990 as the base year for the calculation.[14] To reflect this, in 2016, the Federal Ministry of Economic Affairs and Energy (*Bundesministerium für Wirtschaft und Energie*, BMWi) amended its climate targets and adopted the Climate Action Plan 2050.[15]

2.4. RESULTING DIFFICULTIES AND NEED FOR CAPACITY MECHANISMS

In an energy-only-market, where power plant operators only receive remuneration for energy delivered and not for the available generation capacity, the process of the German Energy Transition has encountered a number of challenges. One of the main ones is that power from wind and photovoltaics is volatile. This means that the generation of electricity is dependent on the weather and varies according to the daytime and the season of the year.

---

10 J-C Pielow and H-M Koopmann, 'Energy Law in Germany' in MM Roggenkamp, C Redgwell, A Rønne and I del Guayo (eds), *Energy Law in Europe – National, EU and International Regulation*, OUP, Oxford 2016.

11 Thirteenth Amendment to the Atomic Energy Act (*Dreizehntes Gesetz zur Änderung des Atomgesetzes*) dated 31 July 2011, BGBl. 2011 part I no 43.

12 BT-Drs. 17/6070.

13 Sec 7 para 1a Atomic Energy Act.

14 See Energy Concept 2010 (n 2) p 4.

15 BMWI, Climate Action Plan 2050.

Short-term variations are solved by relying on the mechanism of 'control energy'.[16] Control energy is a concept used by the four German transmission system operators (TSOs) to secure the stability of the electricity grid if demand and supply are not balanced. However, if more and more energy is generated from renewable energy sources, it becomes increasingly uncertain how to deliver sufficient capacity in times of little or no wind or sun. For long-term variation, capacity mechanisms appear necessary in order to secure capacity reserve and an uninterrupted availability of energy.

The increased generation of electricity from renewable energy resources also leads to a North–South imbalance. Most of the German population lives in the West and in the South, whilst energy generation from renewables is most cost-efficient in the East of Germany and on the northern coast where the offshore and most onshore wind farms are located. Some conventional power plants, which are also located in the West and in the South, have been or will be phased out, such as the nuclear power plants Biblis A, Neckarwestheim 1, Biblis B, Brunsbüttel, Isar 1, Unterweser, Philippsburg 1, Krümmel (on 6 August 2011), Grafenrheinfeld (on 31 December 2015), Gundremmingen B (on 31 December 2017), Philippsburg 2 (by 31 December 2019), Grohnde, Gundremmingen C, Brokdorf (by 31 December 2019) and Isar 2, Emsland, Neckarwestheim 2 (by 31 December 2022).

Other conventional power plants in Germany's economic and population centres, including gas-fired power plants, cannot be operated economically, because, under the merit order system, these power plants are not operating during a sufficient number of hours per year. As a consequence of the limited number of hours of operating time during the year, the operators need very high peak prices to cover their fixed costs. In the past, these price peaks did not occur often enough, first because solar power fills the peak demand at noon time and then because, during peak price periods, prices at the energy exchange EPEX Spot were capped at 3,000 EUR/MWh, which was insufficient. In the meantime, the price caps for the day-ahead market in the German/Austrian TSO zones have been abolished and in the intraday market the price range has been extended to -€9,999 to €9,999.[17] It remains to be seen whether this will be sufficient to encourage investments in new conventional generating capacity once the market is no longer of the opinion that there is overcapacity.

3. SHAPING APPROPRIATE RESPONSES

Those difficulties and risks resulting from the unexpectedly fast development of the German Energy Transition led to the adoption of the first reserve

16 Sec 13 para 1 lit b EnWG.

17 See: http://www.epexspot.com/products.

mechanisms in 2012 and prompted broader discussions on how to ensure the continued security of supply. The concept of security of supply is defined in Section 1 EnWG and is one of the central targets of German energy law. It is usually understood to mean that sufficient generation and transmission capacities exist to satisfy short- and long-term demand.[18]

3.1. THE FIRST ATTEMPTS: NETWORK RESERVE MECHANISM

After Germany experienced seasonal shortage in the winter of 2011/12, the Government implemented in 2012 the network reserves which consisted of two elements. The network reserve was incorporated in the EnWG to protect against regional and seasonal shortages:

- the 'winter reserve' (*Winterreserve*);[19] and
- the 'strategic network reserve' (*strategische Netzreserve*).[20]

The winter reserve required power plants which were to be permanently or temporarily decommissioned to stay available in reserve in order to manage network congestion and to ensure voltage stability in times of high demand and low renewable production.[21] The main objective of the strategic network reserve was to ensure the system's stability and to help with the North–South imbalance.[22] The responsible TSO was required to determine whether certain gas-fired power plants with more than 50 MW, which were to be decommissioned, were 'system relevant'. If they were considered to be 'system relevant', this lasted for up to 24 months and the power plants could be required to stay available against compensation. Such assessment needed to be approved by the Federal Network Agency (*Bundesnetzagentur*, BNetzA). If BNetzA decided accordingly, the gas suppliers could not cut the supply of gas to such 'system relevant' power plants.

However, against the background of the ongoing Energy Transition, the electricity market faced challenges which could not be solved solely by the network reserve. Therefore, in Germany, a political debate on the future electricity market design started.

---

18 FJ Säcker and A Timmermann, 'Section 1 EnWG' in FJ SÄCKER, *Berliner Kommentar Energierecht*, Deutscher Fachverlag GmbH, Frankfurt am Main 2014, 3rd edn, side note 8 ss.

19 Sec 13a EnWG 2012.

20 Sec 13c EnWG 2012.

21 BT-Drs. 17/11705, p 52.

22 Federal Government, Reserve Power Plant Ordinance (*Reservekraftwerksverordnung*), recital A.

3.2. NATIONAL DISCUSSIONS: THE 2014 GREEN PAPER AND THE 2015 WHITE PAPER

In October 2014, the BMWi released a so-called 'Green Paper' (*Grünbuch*) which started a broad consultation about the future market design of the German electricity market.[23] The considerations started with the current German electricity market being an energy-only-market. Because of the merit order resulting from the day-ahead auctions at the spot exchange EPEX SPOT SE in Paris, France, the increase of renewable energy with marginal costs of almost zero replaces conventional power plants with higher marginal costs. As a consequence, conventional plants such as gas-fired power plants, with high gas prices, can often not be operated economically because they are only 'in the money' when no sufficient renewable energy is available.

Against this background, the BMWi started discussing the future design of the electricity market in its 2014 Green Paper. The Green Paper was followed by a broad consultation initiated by the BMWi. Government authorities, associations, trade unions, companies, research institutions and citizens participated in the public consultation which lasted until March 2015. The results and analysis were published by the BMWi in a 'White Paper' (*Weißbuch*) published in July 2015. The 2015 White Paper was the basis for extending the network reserve and the introduction of additional capacity mechanisms in Germany.[24]

A key question raised in the Green Paper was whether there was a need for developing a new Capacity Market in addition to the energy-only-market or if an optimised electricity market would be sufficient.[25] In any case, the objective should be to create a sufficient, cost-efficient and sustainable electricity market to ensure power supply at all times.[26] Another question which was raised in the Green Paper was whether to extend the network reserve. Meanwhile, the BMWi already categorised the network reserve in its Green Paper as a measure that would be needed in any event.

The first option discussed in the Green Paper was an optimisation of the electricity market, the so-called 'Electricity Market 2.0'. The concept underlying the model of an 'Electricity Market 2.0' was that if market powers are not unduly restrained, a working electricity market creates sufficient price signals so that sufficient capacity is built. To set incentives for the investment in conventional generation capacities, price caps at the energy exchange are prohibited. Resulting price peaks are accepted because they do not affect the average price very much.

---

23 BMWi, Discussion Paper of the Federal Ministry for Economic Affairs and Energy (Green Paper), October 2014.

24 BMWi, White Paper, An Electricity Market for Germany's Energy Transition, July 2015.

25 BMWi, Green Paper, p 39.

26 Ibid, p 4.

As an additional safeguard, additional capacities would be procured in a capacity reserve as a strategic reserve.[27]

The 'Electricity Market 2.0' option was set against the alternative of the creation of a Capacity Market as it was being created in other European countries, in particular in the UK and in France. The assumption underlying the concept of the Capacity Market is that not only work (*Arbeit*) but also the availability of capacity (*Leistung*) should be purchased by the customer based on a market-based system. In case of the separate Capacity Market, price peaks are not expected to appear at the spot markets because in times of energy shortage, the availability of capacity has been secured by the Capacity Market.[28]

The conclusion reached by the Government in its 2015 White Paper was to not implement a Capacity Market but to further develop the current electricity market into the 'Electricity Market 2.0' with additional capacity mechanisms.[29]

According to the German Government, the overall objectives of security of supply, cost efficiency, innovation and sustainability will be better achieved through an improved electricity market design rather than an additional Capacity Market.[30] The Government placed a strong emphasis on the expected costs and risks related to capacity markets. It was assumed that capacity markets often generate over-capacities which, in the end, must be paid by the electricity consumer. Capacity markets were also considered to be complex and tending to lead to regulatory failures.[31]

This conclusion was by no means unanimous. Despite the Government's position in the White Paper, the Federal Association of the Energy and Water Industry (*Bundesverband der Energie- und Wasserwirtschaft e.V.*, BDEW) and the Association of Municipal Enterprises (*Verband kommunaler Unternehmen e.V.*, VKU) are of the opinion that a strategic reserve implemented in the energy-only-market could only be an intermediate step for implementing a decentralised Capacity Market in Germany.[32] With the example of France implementing a decentralised Capacity Market, BDEW and VKU proposed to implement a decentralised Capacity Market in Germany as well and coordinate these two markets.[33] In the meantime, until the German legislation on the decentralised Capacity Market is finalised, capacity mechanisms could be implemented.[34] This approach was not favoured by the Government.

---

27 Ibid, p 40.

28 Ibid, p 42.

29 BMWi, White Paper, p 4.

30 Ibid, p 20.

31 Ibid, p 40.

32 BUNDESVERBAND DER ENERGIEWIRTSCHAFT E.V., Comment on the Discussion Paper of the Federal Ministry for Economic Affairs and Energy (Green Paper), 11 December 2014, p 3; VERBAND KOMMUNALER UNTERNEHMEN E.V., Comment on the Green Paper of the Federal Ministry for Economic Affairs and Energy, 27 January 2015, p 18.

33 Ibid.

34 Ibid.

3.3. EUROPEAN COMMISSION'S SECTOR INQUIRY ON CAPACITY MECHANISMS

With several European Union (EU) Member States now implementing capacity mechanisms, the European Commission started to review the manner the European electricity market developed and the different national capacity mechanisms put in place. In April 2015, the European Commission launched a State aid sector inquiry, which reviewed the mechanisms in place in 11 Member States.[35] The Member States under assessment have opted for the introduction of one or more capacity mechanisms. Those mechanisms vary widely but all have in common the underlying principle of enabling revenues for capacity providers and addressing perceived residual market failures.[36]

Most of these mechanisms will be qualified as State aids, which, if not justified, would fall under the prohibition of Article 107 paragraph 1 of the Treaty on the Functioning of the European Union (TFEU). In its sector inquiry, the European Commission aimed to assess the national capacity mechanisms based on the Guidelines on State aid for environment protection and energy (the Guidelines, EEAG).[37] The Guidelines had been adopted two years before, in 2014, and did contain a section on generation adequacy. Meanwhile, the European Commission felt the need to develop additional guidance for capacity mechanisms. In its final Sector Inquiry of November 2016, the Commission developed criteria for the European Commission's assessment of capacity mechanisms under which the means would be deemed to be compatible with the internal market, Article 107 paragraph 3 TFEU.[38]

In the view of the European Commission, capacity mechanisms can be an adequate measure to ensure the security of supply.[39] In order to establish a capacity mechanism, the Member States have to make a detailed assessment of its need.[40]

The European Commission grouped the different types of capacity mechanisms in categories and allocated which of four concerns they are expected to solve. Accordingly, it judged the legality of national capacity mechanisms from a State aid perspective.

---

35 European Commission, Final Report of the Sector Inquiry on Capacity Mechanisms, 20 November 2016, COM (2016) 752 final; European Commission, Accompanying the document to the Final Report of the Sector Inquiry on Capacity Mechanisms, 30 November 2016, SWD (2016) 385 final.

36 Ibid, p 2.

37 European Commission, Guidelines on State aid for environment protection and energy (2014–2020), 2014/C 200/01.

38 European Commission (n 35) p 2.

39 Ibid, p 7.

40 Ibid, p 8.

4. THE CURRENT GERMAN CAPACITY MECHANISMS

4.1. INTRODUCTION

Currently, four capacity mechanisms are implemented in Germany:

- the network reserve (*Netzreserve*),
- the capacity reserve (*Kapazitätsreserve*),
- the security stand-by mode (*Sicherheitsbereitschaft*) and
- the network stability plants (*Netzstabilisierungsanlage*).

The establishment of these four mechanisms followed the conclusions reached in the 2015 White Paper. The initial versions of those mechanisms were implemented in July 2016 by the Energy Market Act (*Strommarktgesetz*),[41] which modified the network reserve and introduced three additional measures: the capacity reserve, the security stand-by mode and the network stability plants. Since its adoption, the provision on network stability plants has already been revised with the Modernisation on Grid Fees Act (*Netzentgeltmodernisierungsgesetz*), which was finally adopted in June 2017.[42] As will be described below, the European Commission has thoroughly reviewed the four German capacity mechanisms for the purpose of State aid approval.

A common pre-requirement for all four reserve mechanisms is that the capacity under the German reserve mechanisms can only be used by the TSOs if security of supply cannot be achieved by other regular measures. Such other measures are grid-related measures (*netzbezogene Maßnahmen*, Section 13 paragraph 1 no 1 EnWG) and market-related measures (*marktbezogene Maßnahmen*, Section 13 paragraph 1 no 2 EnWG) such as, for example, control energy.

4.2. THE NETWORK RESERVE (*NETZRESERVE*)

As mentioned above, the first version of the network reserve was already introduced under the EnWG 2012 and has been modified by the Energy Market Act in 2016. The objective remains the same, which is to keep the electricity grid stable even in times of high demand and low renewables production. The improvements of the 2016 reform consisted in making the provisions more uniform and providing further clarification on how the mechanism works.

41 *Gesetz zur Weiterentwicklung des Strommarktes* (*Strommarktgesetz*), 29 July 2016, BGBl. 2016 Teil I Nr 34.

42 Modernisation on Grid Fees Act (*Netzentgeltmodernisierungsgesetz*), 17 July 2017, BGBl. 2017 part I no 17.

4.2.1. Description

The network reserve is based on power plants which are

- either not currently operable but system relevant, or
- to be permanently or temporarily decommissioned, or
- located in other EU Member States.

The latest amendments to the network reserve have been implemented in Section 13d paragraph 1 EnWG by the 2016 reform. The Grid Reserve Ordinance (*Netzreserveverordnung*, NetzResV) has now replaced the old Reserve Power Plant Ordinance (*Reservekraftwerksverordnung*) based on Section 13i EnWG. The NetzResV is valid until 2023.[43]

The 2016 reform also introduced several legal definitions, inter alia, allowing for a better differentiation between permanently and temporarily decommissioned power plants. A power plant is now regarded as temporarily decommissioned if the power plant is no longer operable but can be made operable within a year after the TSO's request.[44] A power plant is permanently decommissioned when the generation of electricity from this plant is technically impossible or if the plant cannot be made available within one year.[45]

Power plant operators who plan to temporarily or permanently decommission their power plants are obliged to notify the planned decommissioning to the system responsible TSO 12 months in advance. During this 12-month period the decommissioning of the power plants is prohibited (Section 13b paragraphs 1, 5 EnWG).

Section 13b paragraph 2 EnWG sets out the procedure on how to determine whether power plants with more than 10 MW are 'system relevant' if they are to be permanently or temporarily decommissioned. Section 13d paragraph 5 EnWG sets out the procedure for power plants with more than 50 MW and Section 13f EnWG contains a specific provision for gas-fired power plants with more than 50 MW. The term 'system relevant' is now defined in Section 13b paragraph 2 EnWG for all types of power plants which are to be decommissioned. A power plant is considered as being 'system relevant' if: (i) its decommissioning would, with sufficient probability, lead to a not insignificant danger or disturbance of the security and reliability of the electricity supply system; and (ii) if this danger or disturbance cannot be eliminated with other security measures. The term 'danger or disturbance of the security and reliability of the electricity supply system' is defined in Section 13 paragraph 4 EnWG. It refers to the risk of regional outages in the transmission grid or short-term grid bottlenecks and

---

43 Sec 63 para 2a EnWG.

44 Sec 13b para 3 s. 1 EnWG.

45 Sec 13b para 3 s. 2 EnWG.

the situation when the maintenance of frequency, voltage or stability cannot be secured by the TSOs to the necessary extent.

The capacities which are needed for the network reserve are analysed by the four TSOs every year.[46] The BNetzA reviews this analysis and publishes the required capacities until 30 April of each year.[47] Power plant operators can show their interest in participating in the network reserve until 15 May of each year.[48] Power plant operators which take part in the network reserve enter into contractual agreement with the system responsible TSO.[49] During the period, in which the power plants are part of the network reserve, the power plant cannot participate in the regular electricity market.

If the analysis by the system responsible TSO of the individual power plant shows that the power plant is 'system relevant', the temporary decommissioning of the power plant with more than 10 MW is prohibited. For the power plants with more than 50 MW, which are to be permanently decommissioned, the decision by the TSO must be approved by BNetzA because of the especially high restriction the decisions create for the power plant operator.[50] The prohibition period can last for up to 24 months and can be extended. During this time, the power plant operator is obliged to keep the power plants to be temporarily decommissioned operable so that the responsible TSO can request the generation of energy from them.[51] Power plants which are to be permanently decommissioned are to be kept in a condition which enables the TSO to ask that the power plant is made operable.[52]

During the consultations, the idea of prohibiting the shutdown of the 'system relevant' power plants was harshly criticised. It was perceived as an undue restriction to the constitutional right of ownership.[53]

The power plant operators receive a remuneration for the time that the power plant is part of the network reserve. The EnWG and the NetzResV establish a detailed system on the reimbursement of expenses the power plant operators receive. The main distinction to the energy-only-market lies in the fact that the power plants which are part of the network reserve also receive a remuneration for the available generation capacity and not only for the electricity actually delivered.

---

46 Sec 13 para 10 EnWG, Sec 3 para 2 NetzResV.
47 Sec 3 para 1, Sec 4 para 1 NetzResV.
48 Sec 4 para 2 NetzResV.
49 Sec 13d para 3 EnWG, Sec 4–6 NetzResV.
50 Sec 13b para 5 sentence 4, Sec 13f para 1 sentence 3 EnWG; J SÖTEBIER, 'Section 13a EnWG' in G BRITZ, J HELLERMANN and G HERMES, *Energiewirtschaftsgesetz*, C H Beck, Munich 2015, 3rd edn, side note 30.
51 Sec 13b para 4 EnWG.
52 Sec 13b para 5 sentence 10 EnWG.
53 See in particular M SCHMIDT-PREUß, 'Das Stilllegungsverbot gem. §13a EnWG' in JF BAUR, P SALJE and M SCHMIDT-PREUß (eds), *Regulierung der Energiewirtschaft*, Carl Heymanns, Cologne 2016, ch 107, p 1628.

4.2.2. *State Aid Procedure*

In its decision of 20 December 2016, the European Commission declared the German network reserve compatible with the European Single Market and approved it as a temporary measure until 30 June 2020.[54] The network reserve is a strategic reserve within the meaning of the 2016 Sector Inquiry of the European Commission. It is considered to be a generation adequacy mechanism as referred to in the EEAG Guidelines, Section 3.9 on regulations regarding State aid for generation adequacy.

The seven prerequisites defined in the Guidelines and which must be met in order to declare the measure compatible were considered fulfilled, that is:

- an objective of common interest: the network reserve serves the objective of security of supply in southern Germany and so until a solution is provided to the severe bottleneck in the electricity grid which currently hinders the transport of electricity from the North to the South;
- the need for State intervention: the objective cannot be achieved by market mechanisms alone, as the construction of new transmission capacity would take too long and the necessary analysis for the network reserve is properly done by the responsible German TSO and BNetzA;[55]
- appropriateness: the existing installed capacity is used to ensure the security of supply for the transitional period until the grid infrastructure is sufficient;[56]
- an incentive effect: the network reserve is built from power plants which are not operable or which are to be permanently or temporarily decommissioned and which therefore would not supply electricity without being part of the network reserve;[57]
- proportionality: there is no lesser means available and the power plant operators receive cost reimbursement and not high returns;[58]
- the avoidance of undue negative effects on competition and trade: the network reserve does not negatively affect competition and trade because it is excluded from the energy-only-market and is only utilised if the electricity available on the energy-only-market cannot satisfy the demand of electricity; and
- transparency: the transparency obligations required by the Guidelines are met.[59].

---

54 European Commission, State aid No SA.42955 (2016/N-2) – Germany Network Reserve, 20 December 2016, C (2016) 8742 final; European Commission, Press Release, 27 May 2016, IP 16/1911.

55 European Commission, C (2016) 8742 final, p 12.

56 Ibid, p 17.

57 Ibid, p 25.

58 Ibid, p 25.

59 Ibid, p 27.

4.3. CAPACITY RESERVE (*KAPAZITÄTSRESERVE*)

The centrepiece of the capacity mechanisms introduced by the 2016 Electricity Market Act is the capacity reserve. The legislator opted for a capacity mechanism in the form of a strategic buffer rather than for a separate Capacity Market.

4.3.1. Description

The regulation regarding the capacity reserve is implemented by Section 13e EnWG. In application of the power to issue statutory instruments (*Verordnungsermächtigung*) in Section 13h EnWG, the BMWi proposed a Draft Capacity Reserve Ordinance (*Kapazitätsreserveverordnung*, KapResV) on 30 April 2018.

The capacity reserve forms a capacity buffer outside of the regular electricity market. It is envisaged that the TSOs tender 2 GW of capacity for the first period, starting in winter 2019/2020. This capacity buffer is only to be used in extraordinary cases when the electricity market has not been cleared and there is not enough supply to cover the demand. The capacity buffer aims to ensure the security of supply for the time until there will be no more overcapacities in the electricity market. The situation of overcapacity is expected to be solved in mid-2020s, after the nuclear phase-out and the shutdown of lignite-fired power plants.

The capacity reserve is acquired in a competitive bidding process. The first bidding procedure, with a total amount of 2 MW, should have been started in 2017 for winter 2018/19 (Section 13e paragraph 2 EnWG). However, due to the State aid procedure, the first bidding procedure was postponed to start in 2018 for the winter 2019/2020. It is expected that power plants which participate are power plants that are threatened by closure (*stilllegungsbedroht*).[60] The legislator's idea was that these power plants, due to their small amount of profit, will offer their capacities for a relatively minor remuneration under the scheme. The Draft Capacity Reserve Ordinance sets out that power plants which can participate in the auction need to have a minimum of 5 MW and must be able to be operable within 12 hours (Section 14 paragraph 6, Section 9 paragraph 1 no 2 KapResV).

Power plants taking part in the capacity reserve may not participate in the electricity market and need to be decommissioned afterwards (*Vermarktungs- und Rückkehrverbot*). However, power plant operators may participate in the auction repeatedly. The responsible TSO and the power plant operator enter into a contractual agreement. The feed-in of electricity only happens at the TSO's request (Section 13e paragraph 1 EnWG). Remuneration is generally paid to the plant owner in the amount determined in the competitive bidding procedure. Section 13e paragraph 3 EnWG sets out matters relating to expenses, which are

60 BT-Drs. 542/15, S. 112.

remunerated separately. The TSOs may recover the remuneration through their grid tariffs levied on electricity consumers.

The participating power plants can also participate in the capacity reserve, because the network reserve has a different approach than the capacity reserve. Because the network reserve aims to ensure security of supply in case of grid shortages, its regulation is of a technical nature. The capacity reserve, on the other hand, aims to compensate when supply and demand on the electricity market are unbalanced. Power plants that participate in both reserves are most likely to be reserves which are strategically well located in the South of Germany. Power plants of the network reserve which are part of the capacity reserve are remunerated from the capacity reserve although they are obliged to generate electricity on the TSO's request for the network reserve (Section 13d paragraph 2 EnWG).

4.3.2. State Aid Procedure

The new regulation regarding the capacity reserve has been approved by the European Commission on 7 February 2018.

On 7 April 2017, the European Commission opened an in-depth investigation pursuant to Article 108 paragraph 2 TFEU to assess whether the German capacity reserve complies with EU State aid rules.[61] In its decision to open the in-depth investigation, the European Commission stated that the capacity reserve is State aid within the meaning of Article 107 paragraph 1 TFEU. The European Commission argued that although the remuneration for the capacity reserve is paid by the electricity consumer, state resources are involved because those financial transactions are determined by the State. The State controls and therefore finances the measure through state resources.[62] The European Commission further argued that the capacity reserve provides an advantage on a selective basis.[63] It pointed out that the capacity reserve may grant a benefit according to the exemption for the 'service of general economic interest'[64] (*Daseinsvorsorge*) as interpreted in the *Altmark Trans* case.[65]

---

61 European Commission, State aid No SA.45852 (2017/N) – Germany Capacity Reserve, 7 April 2017, C (2017) 2224 final; European Commission, Press Release, IP/17/903.

62 Ibid, recital 37.

63 Ibid, recital 61.

64 The General Court decided that the term 'common interest' has the same meaning as the 'service of general interest' in Art 106 para 2 TFEU. General Court, Judgement dated 12 February 2008, C-289/03, recital 162; European Commission, Communication from the Commission on the application of the European Union State aid rules to compensation granted for the provision of services of general economic interest, OJEU 2012, C 8/02, recital 47. The Commission defines the 'service of general economic interest' as economic activities which deliver outcomes in the overall public good that would not be supplied, or would be supplied under different conditions in terms of quality, safety, affordability, equal treatment or universal access, by the market without public intervention. EUROPEAN COMMISSION, 20 December 2011, C (2011) 900, p 4.

65 ECJ, Judgement, 24 July 2003, C-280/00, recital 88 ff; European Commission, 2017/C 159/03, recital 55.

The European Commission expressed doubts as to whether the capacity reserve is necessary in accordance with Article 107 paragraph 3 TFEU and Section 3.9 EEAG Guidelines. It also doubted whether Germany had sufficiently analysed the electricity market in order to determine the measure's necessity.[66] In addition, the Commission had concerns on the temporary measure of the capacity reserve due to its design in the EnWG.[67] The Commission also had concerns about the appropriateness of the capacity reserve, especially as interruptible loads and capacities located in other EU Member States are not allowed to participate in the capacity reserve.[68] In order to determine the proportionality, the Commission invited Germany to give more detailed information on the duration of the completion of the Energy Transition and the need for the capacity reserve.[69] Finally, the Commission had doubts about the separation between the energy-only-market and the capacity reserve.[70]

The German Government, by letter dated 17 May 2017, addressed the concerns of the European Commission.[71] In order to remove the grounds for the concerns of the Commission on the necessity of the capacity reserve, the German Government provided a detailed analysis of a 'reasonable worst case'. On the appropriateness of the capacity reserve, the German Government argued that against the background of the objective and the concept of the capacity reserve, interruptible loads should not participate in the capacity reserve. This is mainly because interruptible loads should participate in the normal energy-only-market in which the capacity reserve is not allowed to participate. Finally, regarding the participation of capacities located in other EU Member States, the German Government pointed out the lack of interconnector capacities.

In the Commission's decision of 7 February 2018, it appears that Germany has succeeded in demonstrating the need for the measure and that it has adapted the capacity reserve's design to comply with EU State aid rules.[72] The capacity reserve is provided to address a clearly identified and quantified security of supply risk. During the European Commission's in-depth investigation, Germany committed to modify the capacity reserve's calculation of the necessity and the scope to better reflect market realities. The capacity reserve mechanism is open to different potential capacity providers to ensure competition. The costs to the electricity consumers are kept low by regular, competitive tenders and potential distortions to competition are limited.

---

66 European Commission, C (2017) 2224 final, recital 101.

67 Ibid, recital 99.

68 Ibid, recitals 136, 145.

69 Ibid, recital 160.

70 Ibid, recital 172.

71 German Government, Mitteilung der Bundesregierung an die Europäische Kommission, SA.45852 – Deutschland – Kapazitätsreserve, 17 May 2017.

72 European Commission, State aid No SA.45852 – 2017/C (ex 2017/N) which Germany is planning to implement for Capacity Reserve, 7 February 2018, C(2018) 612 final; European Commission, Press Release, 07/02/2018, IP/18/682.

4.4. SECURITY STAND-BY MODE (*SICHERHEITSBEREITSCHAFT*)

The third capacity mechanism which exists in Germany is the security stand-by mode of lignite-fired power plants. It is not a capacity mechanism in the usual sense of the concept as its main objective is to achieve the climate targets of Germany and the EU through the reduction of greenhouse gases.

Nevertheless, as the decommissioned lignite-fired capacities remain in stand-by and thus theoretically available to the market and it was notified to the European Commission as such, it has to be considered as a capacity mechanism. Interestingly, it shows that capacity mechanisms can be used for a wide variety of purposes. This also means that it is necessary to keep them under close monitoring and control.

4.4.1. Description

Under the security stand-by mode (*Sicherheitsbereitschaft*), eight lignite-fired power plants, with a total capacity of 2.7 GW, equalling 13% of the lignite-fired German capacity, will finally be decommissioned by 2023.[73] The German Government aims to reduce CO_2 emissions by 11–12.5 million tons per year as of the year 2020, when all eight plants will have stopped operating.[74] For the interim period, these eight lignite-fired power plants are transferred into the security stand-by mode (pursuant to Section 13g EnWG) in exchange for cost reimbursement, each for a period of four years. The power plant Buschhaus is the first lignite-fired power plant which was transferred into the security stand-by mode as per 1 October 2016. The lignite-fired power plant operators receive remuneration in the total amount of €1.61 billion which are levied on the electricity consumers.[75]

The utilisation of the reserves in the security stand-by mode is to be used as a last resort in case of extraordinary shortages. The power plants need to be operable within 240 hours after the TSO's request. The security stand-by mode is therefore only suitable for foreseeable and long-term shortages. When the lignite-fired power plants are in an operable mode, the power plants need to be ready with minimum power within 11 hours and within another 13 hours they need to be able to reach their full performance.

---

73 European Commission, State aid No SA.42536 – Germany, 27 May 2016, C (2016) 3124 final, p 2.

74 European Commission, Press Release, 27 May 2016, IP 16/1911.

75 Ibid.

4.4.2. *State Aid Procedure*

The European Commission approved the security stand-by mode in its decision of 27 May 2016.[76] In its notification letter, the German Government argued that the measure is not a State aid because remuneration of the lignite-fired power plants during the security stand-by mode does not involve state resources. Furthermore, Germany argued that there is no advantage for the companies because the remuneration constitutes only compensation for damages.[77]

The European Commission is of the opinion that along the lines of the decision of the European Court on the German 2012 Renewable Energy Act,[78] state resources are involved even though the remuneration is not paid directly by the State. The remuneration for the security stand-by mode is paid by the electricity consumer to the TSO via a higher electricity rate. These costs, even if between private persons, are determined and controlled by the State. Therefore, the European Commission considers the compensation for the plant beneficiaries to be controlled by the State.[79]

Concerning the second argument, the European Commission is of the opinion that where a measure solely grants the compensation for damages incurred, this compensation does not provide an advantage and hence does not constitute State aid within the meaning of Article 107 paragraph 1 TFEU. However, whether all power plant operators only receive an amount of compensation corresponding to their damages is a factual question the answer to which is not certain. The European Commission does not see the need to clarify this factual circumstance because it is of the opinion that the security stand-by mode, as State aid, is compatible with the European Single Market.[80] The reason is that the positive impact of the aid towards an objective of common interest exceeds its potential negative effects on trade and competition. The common interest of the security stand-by mode of the lignite-fired power plants is the reduction of CO_2 emissions and the reduction of air pollution.[81]

4.5. NETWORK STABILITY PLANTS (*NETZSTABILISIERUNGSANLAGEN*) AND SPECIAL GRID OPERATING EQUIPMENT (*BESONDERE NETZTECHNISCHE BETRIEBSMITTEL*)

The fourth capacity mechanism in Germany relates to the 'network stability plants'. This measure was also introduced by the Electricity Market Act, but it has

---

76 European Commission, State aid No SA.42536 – Germany, 27 May 2016, C (2016) 3124 final.
77 Ibid, p 6.
78 ECJ, Judgement, 10 May 2016, T-45/15.
79 European Commission, C (2016) 3124 final, p 7.
80 Ibid, p 8.
81 Ibid, p 13.

already been revised by the Act on the Modernisation of the Grid Fee Structure (*Netzentgeltmodernisierungsgesetz*) on 30 June 2017.

4.5.1. Description

Against the background of the Energy Transition and the missing or delayed creation of the necessary North–South grid infrastructure, the German Government introduced the mechanism of 'network stability plants' as a measure to maintain the security and reliability of electricity supply in case of regional outages. The provision, which was introduced in 2016, allowed the TSOs to construct and own themselves up to 2 MW new generation capacities. The former Section 13k EnWG provided for a first necessity assessment of the network stability plants to be performed by the TSOs by 31 January 2017. The four German TSOs analysed the necessity and concluded that this additional capacity mechanism might become necessary in the course of the development of the Energy Transition. The BNetzA approved this assessment on 31 May 2017.[82] The implementation measures were adopted in the subsequent legislation.

However, due to concerns about the compatibility of the measure with EU law,[83] the German Government abolished Section 13k EnWG with the network stability plants in June 2017 with the Act on the Modernisation of the Grid Fee Structure. Instead, it created by the same law a new Section 11 paragraph 3 EnWG. Instead of the network stability plants, it introduced the 'special grid-technical operating equipment' (*besondere netztechnische Betriebsmittel*). The mechanism is described in detail in the law, but it is assumed that – with a few exceptions – they are basically to build on the same requirements than for the former network stability plants. The most significant difference is that the TSOs are not allowed to build and operate the 'special grid-technical operating equipment' themselves, but that they 'may' keep them available.[84] The capacity can be made available by the construction of new power plants or interruptible schemes.[85] Under the new regulation, third parties are responsible for the operation and the construction of the new power plants, as well as for the interruptible schemes. The third parties will be selected by the TSOs according to a transparent and non-discriminatory procedure.[86] As with most other capacity mechanisms in Germany, the 'special grid-technical operating equipment'

82 BNETZA, Bericht zur Ermittlung des Bedarfs an Netzstabilitätsanlagen, 31 May 2017.

83 BNETZA, Annual Report, p 18; VERBAND KOMMUNAKER UNTERNEHMEN E.V., '*Wie aus Netzstabilitätsanlagen besondere netztechnische Betriebsmittel werden*', 10 July 2017, available at: https://www.vku.de/themen/energiewende/netzstabilitaetsanlagen-besondere-netztechnische-betriebsmittel/.

84 Sec 11 para 3 s. 2, 3 EnWG.

85 BT-Drs. 18/1299, p 16.

86 Sec 11 para 3 s. 4-6 EnWG.

is excluded from the participation in the regular electricity market.[87] For the acquisition of the capacity of 'special grid-technical operating equipment', the TSOs are obliged to present analyses on the necessity and the concept on the competitive tendering procedure to the BNetzA. On 31 May 2017, the BNetzA announced that it had determined the need for 1.2 MW 'special grid-technical operating equipment' in the form of gas-fired power plants in southern Germany.[88]

4.5.2. *State Aid Procedure*

The European Commission had not yet approved the regulation regarding the network stability plants in the form of the old Section 13k EnWG when the law was changed in 2017. According to the BNetzA, under the former concept the European Commission had reservations against the compatibility of the network stability plants with the internal market.[89] Because of the adoption of the new legislation, the European Commission has not decided about the permissibility of the new instrument. However, it can be expected that the European Commission will start an assessment of the measure under normal State aid procedure.

5. OUTLOOK

The German Energy Transition involves a fundamental restructuring of the country's energy supply away from nuclear energy and fossil fuels and towards renewable energy. It is an ongoing and gradual process, with complex implications. The success of the 'Electricity Market 2.0' depends to a large extent on whether the energy industry and/or other investors will rely on the promise of free market prices despite the capacity reserves. If power market actors do not manage this, it is unlikely that they will invest in new conventional generating facilities, even if those are deemed necessary to secure electricity supply against the volatility of renewable energy.

Electricity generation based on renewable energy sources depends on natural circumstances of the geography, such as more wind in northern Germany and not in southern Germany. However, geographic generation and consumption patterns do not necessarily fit, since more electricity is consumed in the South in relation to industrial activities. This means that electricity needs to be transported over long distances to strike the grid balance. At least this is the case until the energy generation and consumption structures change to a mostly

87 Sec 11 para 3 s. 7 EnWG.

88 BNETZA, Press Release, Bundesnetzagentur veröffentlicht Bedarf an Netzstabilitätsanlagen nach §13k EnWG, 31 May 2017, https://www.bundesnetzagentur.de/SharedDocs/Pressemitteilungen/DE/2017/31052017_Netzreserve.html.

89 See n 84.

decentralised supply. Thus, a key task lies in the expansion of the supra-regional transmission grids and a strengthening of the local distribution grids, where a lot of the renewable energy is fed into the system. Of the 1,800 km planned for in the German grid expansion plans under the Power Grid Expansion Act (*Gesetz zum Ausbau von Energieleitungen*) roughly 35%, about 650 km, have so far been constructed and 900 km have been authorised. The German TSOs plan to build a further 10% by 2017.[90] But there is still a gap to fill.

Until the strong long-distance DC-transmission lines are operational, interim measures, like the capacity reserves, will increasingly be necessary. Such capacity mechanisms will probably be considered State aids and therefore permitted under certain circumstances and on a temporary basis. This leads to the following question: will investors invest billions of euros into new conventional generation facilities required for capacity reserves once nuclear, and possibly all lignite or even all coal fired, power plants are shut down in Germany, if it is foreseeable that those new generation facilities will only be permitted to run for a relatively short time? There is scepticism in the market whether the current regime will provide sufficient incentive for investments into new conventional power plants in Germany. Until now, it has not triggered new investments. One thing to take into account is the current situation of overcapacity in conventional generation on the German and European markets, which means that no new investments are required. In addition, the proponents of the German Energy Transition argue that if new capacities are to be created, they should be based on renewables combined with storage capacity and other modern technologies, instead of conventional sources.

In the current German version of the energy-only-market, the Electricity Market 2.0., the TSOs play a central coordinating role. Under the network reserve, the TSOs assess the need for generation capacity every year and enter into contractual agreements with the power plants. Regarding the capacity reserve, under the current Draft Capacity Reserve Ordinance, the TSOs are responsible for the competitive bidding procedure. Under the new provision on special grid-technical operating material, the TSOs are responsible for keeping this reserve operational. Besides the determination of the power plant for these reserves, the four German TSOs are responsible for the feed-in of the electricity generated in the different capacity mechanisms. As the four capacity mechanisms aim to ensure in different ways the security of supply, the TSOs need to monitor the market and calculate which mechanism is needed at which point. In addition, they have all the traditional responsibilities of a TSO, including the purchase and use of reserve power and the construction of new power lines necessary to accommodate the new system. Thus, their role in the market is becoming

90 BNETZA and FEDERAL CARTEL OFFICE, Monitoring Report 2016, p 21.

increasingly important, but they are also under tight regulatory control by the *Bundesnetzagentur*, the German regulator.

Finally, this chapter has demonstrated how quickly the features of national capacity mechanisms can develop and change. Those changes are closely followed by the European Commission, and further EU guidance may develop, in order to keep a level playing field between Member States. On 30 November 2016, the European Commission published its 'Clean Energy for All Europeans Package' which consists of numerous legislative proposals.[91] The proposal for the recast of the existing Regulation (EC) 714/2009 on conditions for access to the network for cross-border exchanges in electricity sets out requirements for capacity mechanisms. It provides that in the future, capacity mechanisms can only be introduced where the European resource adequacy assessment by the ENTSO-E has identified a resource adequacy concern (Section 23 paragraph 5, Recital 27). Prior to introducing capacity mechanisms, EU Member States should eliminate distortions (Recital 28) and should establish reliability standards indicating their desired level of security of supply (Article 18, Recital 29). The specific obligations arising from the Regulation will be dependent on the exact design of the Regulation arising out of the ordinary legislative procedure.

91 See the proposals at: http://ec.europa.eu/energy/en/news/commission-proposes-new-rules-consumer-centred-clean-energy-transition.

CHAPTER XI
THE FRENCH CAPACITY MECHANISM

Thomas HERMAN and Emma FRANCE*

1. INTRODUCTION

The need for the adoption of a capacity mechanism in France has primarily been justified by reasons of security of electricity supply. Following a market-based and country-wide approach, the French authorities have made the choice of a Capacity Market as the main capacity remuneration mechanism. The rules for the Capacity Market have been progressively developed since 2010 until the adoption of a detailed regime in 2015. Despite delays related to legal proceedings and the need to rapidly adjust the capacity mechanism design in order to secure State aid approval, the first capacity auction took place in December 2016.

This chapter analyses the Capacity Market introduced in France by examining: the evolution of its legislative and regulatory framework and related litigation; its current regime; the modifications induced by the European Commission's decisions on State aid control; and finally an overview of the market practices and some perspectives.

2. BACKGROUND FOR THE INTRODUCTION OF A CAPACITY MECHANISM IN FRANCE

2.1. SECURITY OF SUPPLY AS A PRIMARY CONCERN

The security of the supply of electricity to consumers, which can be defined as: 'the ability of energy systems to satisfy continuously and at a reasonable cost, the expected market demand',[1] has been the focus of the French energy transition.

---

* The authors wish to acknowledge the assistance of their colleagues, Mathias Dantin and Artem Soloshchenkov, in the writing of this chapter.

1 Programmation Pluriannuelle de l'Energie (PPE), Synthesis report, 2016, p 17, available at: https://www.ecologique-solidaire.gouv.fr/sites/default/files/Synth%C3%A8se.pdf. The PPE was adopted by Decree of 28 October 2016 and covers Metropolitan France, the oversea

The latter has recently been reaffirmed as part of the 'Multiannual Energy Programme' (*programmation pluriannuelle de l'énergie*, PPE)[2] of 2016 which sets out the Government's energy policy for the next five years, in accordance with the objectives defined in the 2015 Energy Transition Law for Green Growth.[3] The PPE is subject to a revision process in 2018.

Security of supply is a complex issue as a constant balance must be maintained in the network between the production and the consumption of electricity. Additional complicating factors are related to the fact that, on the one hand, electricity cannot be stored in sufficient quantities, and, on the other hand, electricity consumption is variable depending on the time of day and the season.[4]

In France, the main challenge facing security of supply is caused by the winter consumption peak due to consumption that is 'highly heat sensitive', given the predominance of electric heating.[5]

2.2. CHOICE OF MODEL

The previous market model is challenged by recent developments in the energy sector and calls for new solutions. Indeed, the economic model theory that prevailed in France and Europe during the liberalisation of the electricity markets, which theory economists call the 'Energy Only'-model,[6] has shown its limits. It has become difficult to ensure, in a sustainable manner, a sufficient security of supply in a context where: (i) growth of peak consumption has advanced faster than levels of overall electricity consumption;[7] (ii) development of renewable energy, the intermittency of which reinforces balancing constraints on the network; (iii) interconnection of the network with other countries; (iv) the cost of existing high-end equipment and their low flexibility; and (v) the lack of incentive for electricity players to invest in new high-end

territories being subject to separate PPEs. The adoption of the PPE is a requirement introduced by the 2015 Energy Transition Law for Green Growth, now codified in the Energy Code.

2 Decree No 2016-1442 of 27 October 2016 relating to the Multiannual Energy Programme. It replaces, in a broader and more integrated way, the three pre-existing programmes related to power generation, heat generation and gas investments.

3 Energy Transition Law for Green Growth No 2015-992 of 17 August 2015, JOFR No 0189 of 18 August 2015, p 14263, as codified in the Energy Code; see Arts L. 141-3 and L. 141-4 I, Energy Code.

4 Note: '*horosaisonnalité*' has no translation.

5 Programmation Pluriannuelle de l'Energie (PPE) (n 1).

6 On the analysis of the 'Energy only' model, see the RTE Report, Capacity Mechanism, 2014.

7 Ibid, p 27.

equipment, given uncertainties in the frequency and volume of consumption peaks.[8]

In accordance with the proposals of the 'Poignant-Sido' Parliamentary Report, published on 1 April 2010, Law No 2010-1488 of 7 December 2010 on the new organisation of the electricity market (the Nome Law) introduced two complementary mechanisms with the aim of enhancing the security of supply: demand-side response and a capacity mechanism. Whilst demand-side response focuses on reducing electricity consumption during peak consumption times in order to optimise electricity consumption, the capacity mechanism values the availability of a unit of production rather than the volume of electricity actually produced and injected into the network.

The capacity mechanism implemented in France (hereafter, the Capacity Mechanism), which is the focus of this chapter, is similar to an 'insurance for the security of supply'[9] and is based on three principles:

- *an obligation for suppliers* to ensure the supply of electricity to its consumers during peak periods of consumption;
- *the grant of capacity guarantees* by RTE (the French Transmission System Operator, TSO) based on the ability of operators to produce electricity or reduce consumption during peak periods; and
- the possibility offered to suppliers to cover their obligation via *a capacity guarantee exchange.*

The purpose of the Capacity Mechanism is therefore to ensure the adequacy of capacities of production and reduction during peak consumption periods. In this respect, the French mechanism forms part of a broader context of the implementation of different capacity mechanisms by different countries of the European Union.[10]

3. EVOLUTION OF THE LEGISLATIVE AND REGULATORY FRAMEWORK AND RELATED LITIGATION

In 2010, Mr Jean-Louis Borloo, Minister in charge of energy (Minister of Energy), commissioned a report outlining the necessity to control the electric peak periods by Mr Serge Poignant, Member of Parliament, and Mr Bruno

8 Report of Mr Serge Poignant, Member of Parliament for Loire-Atlantique and Mr Bruno Sido, Senator of Haute-Marne, Working Group on the Control of the Electric Peak, April 2010, p 20.

9 RTE Report, A Revised Capacity Mechanism, 2016, p 12.

10 Agency for the Cooperation of Energy Regulators Report, Capacity remuneration mechanisms and the internal market for electricity, 2013, p 8.

Sido, Senator. The explanatory statement of the Nome Law draft bill, filed by the Government on 14 December 2010, explicitly refers to the conclusions of this report regarding the creation of a capacity mechanism in France.

Whilst the 2010 Nome Law establishes the Capacity Mechanism,[11] the task of specifying the methods of its application was left to a decree, an infra-legislative instrument.[12] By Decree No 2012-1405 of 14 December 2012[13] (2012 Capacity Decree), the Government sets out the general organisational framework of the new scheme, in particular:

- the nature of the obligations imposed on the capacity operators;[14]
- the nature of the obligations on the suppliers;[15]
- the procedures for the exchange of capacity guarantees;[16]
- the introduction of a loopback device allowing the Minister of Energy, in exceptional circumstances, to organise a call for tenders in order to ensure the security of supply;[17]
- the set-up of a transitional tendering process,[18] that has ended on 31 December 2016.[19]

The draft 2012 Capacity Decree has been submitted for opinion to the Competition Authority and to the Energy Regulatory Commission (Commission de Régulation de l'Energie, CRE).

The Competition Authority,[20] gently admonishing the lack of an impact study, notes in particular that the draft 2012 Capacity Decree does not sufficiently regulate the way in which Electricité de France (EDF) exercises its dominant position under the Capacity Mechanism, both in its production activity[21] (supply of capacity guarantees) and in its supply activity[22] (demand for capacity

11 Art 6, Nome Law.

12 Art L. 335-6, Energy Code.

13 Decree No 2012-1405 of 14 December 2012 relating to the contribution of suppliers to the security of electricity supply and creating a capacity obligation mechanism in the electricity sector, now codified under Arts R. 335-1 *et seq*, Energy Code.

14 Art 3, 2012 Capacity Decree.

15 Art 8, 2012 Capacity Decree.

16 Arts 15 *et seq*, 2012 Capacity Decree.

17 Art 23, 2012 Capacity Decree.

18 Art 26, 2012 Capacity Decree.

19 Art 7, Nome Law as amended by Law No 2015-992 dated 17 August 2015 regarding the energy transition for the sustainable growth.

20 Competition Authority, Opinion No 12-A-09 of 12 April 2012 concerning a draft decree on the establishment of a capacity mechanism in the electricity sector.

21 In 2011, EDF was in charge of 79.4% of France's electricity generation capacity: Competition Authority, Opinion No 12-A-09 of 12 April 2012 on a draft decree on the establishment of a capacity mechanism in the electricity sector, point 101, p 13.

22 In 2011, the CRE Market Observatory evaluated the market share of EDF and local public distributors at 94% of the consumption of residential customers and at 78% of the

guarantees). In addition, it notes that the regime proposed in the draft Decree could cause numerous distortions of competition (capacity retention risks induced by the introduction of the feedback loop, incorporation of the price of capacity into regulated sales tariffs, deadweight effects for facilities under a purchase obligation or operators buying on the wholesale market, etc).

On its side, CRE issued a favourable opinion, but subject to proposed changes being taken into account to ensure the proper functioning of the system.[23]

These competing criticisms have been compounded by other grievances, in particular concerning the incompatibility of the Capacity Mechanism with European Union (EU) law.

By an application dated 17 June 2013, the National Association of Energy Retail Operators (ANODE) filed a cancellation claim (*recours pour excès de pouvoir*) before the State Council (*Conseil d'Etat*, France's highest administrative court) regarding the 2012 Capacity Decree. ANODE founded its claim on four main legal grounds. First, it argued that the Capacity Mechanism involves State aid within the meaning of Article 107(1) of the Treaty on the Functioning of the European Union (TFEU) which should, as such, have been notified to the European Commission under the terms of Article 108(3) TFEU. Second, it argued that the Decree disregards the proportionality and non-discrimination requirements deriving from sectoral directives applicable to measures taken by States to ensure security of electricity supply.[24] Third, ANODE argued that the Capacity Mechanism necessarily and automatically places EDF – being a dominant electricity producer – in a position to abuse its dominant position on the future market for capacity certificates, and to extend its reach for the generation and supply markets. Fourth, ANODE argued that the regime put in place constitutes an obstacle to the free movement of goods in breach of Articles 34 and 36 TFEU.

By a decision dated 9 October 2015,[25] the State Council rejected the first three lines of argument. However, it decided, in accordance with Article 267 TFEU, to refer a preliminary question to the Court of Justice of the European Union (CJEU) on the fourth plea due to its lack of expertise regarding the free movement of goods.[26] By a decision dated 16 March 2016,[27] the State Council acknowledged the discontinuance of the ANODE proceeding and removed the preliminary question accordingly.

consumption of non-residential sites: Competition Authority, Opinion No 12-A-09 of 12 April 2012 concerning a draft decree on the establishment of a capacity mechanism in the electricity sector, point 102, p 13.

23 CRE, deliberation of 29 March 2012 giving an opinion on the draft decree adopted for the application of Art L. 335-6, Energy Code relating to the system of contribution of suppliers to the security of electricity supply and setting up a mechanism for capacity.

24 Directives 2005/89/EC of 18 January 2006 and 2009/72/EC of 13 July 2009.

25 State Council, 9 October 2015, *ANODE*, No 369417.

26 For an analysis of the ANODE case before the CJEU, see chapter II of this volume.

27 State Council, 16 March 2016, *ANODE*, No 369417.

In parallel, by a request dated 3 February 2014, the company Voltalis asked the State Council to annul the implied decision rejecting the silence maintained by the Prime Minister on his appeal for the repeal of Articles 8 and 9 of the 2012 Capacity Decree. It also asked the State Council to order the Prime Minister to repeal these articles of the 2012 Capacity Decree. Articles 8 and 9 of the 2012 Capacity Decree provide in part that:

- the certification application file is presented to the TSO or the distribution system operator (DSO), depending on the network to which the capacity is connected;
- when a DSO receives such a file, it concludes a contract with the operator and transmits it (and a copy thereof) to the transmission system operator, accompanied by a proposal for a certification contract;
- the certification contract includes the billing arrangements, by the network operator to which the capacity is connected, of the costs incurred by the latter for certification and capacity control; and
- the operators of public electricity distribution networks are responsible for the control of the capacities connected to their networks and informing the manager of the public electricity transmission network of the result of this control.

By a decision dated 13 May 2016,[28] the State Council found that sections 8 and 9 of the 2012 Capacity Decree create obligations with respect to public electricity system operators, which may apply on local authorities.[29] It considered, therefore, that these provisions should be subject to prior consultation of the Standards Assessment Advisory Commission, which is competent to decide on regulatory measures having a financial impact on local and regional authorities.[30] As a consequence, the State Council urged the Prime Minister to repeal, within three months from the notification of the decision, sections 8 and 9 of the Decree Capacity 2012.

4. CURRENT FRENCH CAPACITY MECHANISM REGIME

Notwithstanding the various challenges and claims brought against some of the underlying provisions of the Capacity Mechanism in France, the implementation of the first technical rules started on 1 April 2015 and the first year of the Capacity Mechanism in France started on 1 January 2017.

---

28 State Council, 13 May 2016, *Voltalis*, No 375120.

29 Arts L. 511-2 and L. 511-4, Energy Code.

30 Art L. 1211-4–2, general code of local authorities.

The general framework of the capacity mechanism is now based on the following legal texts:

- Articles L. 335-1 to L. 335-7 and Articles L. 321-16 to L. 321-17 of the Energy Code (codifying the provisions of the 2010 Nome Law);[31]
- Articles R. 335-1 to D. 335-54 of the Energy Code (codifying the 2012 Capacity Decree);[32] and
- a ministerial order dated 22 January 2015 defining the rules for the Capacity Mechanism.

The mechanism as a whole is based on the creation of a country-wide market of the capacity guarantees that can be traded between market operators (see section 4.1) and the thorough regulation of this market by the regulatory authorities (see section 4.2).

4.1. DESIGN OF THE FRENCH CAPACITY MARKET

The Nome Law, codified today in the Energy Code, requires each electricity supplier to contribute to the secure supply of electricity in mainland France. This obligation is quantified according to the level and patterns of consumption of their customers.[33] In addition to electricity suppliers, this obligation also applies to the DSOs – for their electricity losses – who do not purchase power from a supplier and some customers for consumption outside a supply contract with an electricity supplier.[34] These different entities can, however, transfer their obligation to another entity via a contractual arrangement. For example, a supplier can transfer its obligation regarding the consumption of one customer to another customer.[35]

The compliance with this obligation is ensured through *a market for capacity guarantees*. On the one hand, to meet their obligations, each electricity supplier (as well as relevant network operators and final consumers) (together, referred to as suppliers) shall secure capacity guarantees, either by certifying the electricity production or demand-side (*effacement*) capacities it operates or by purchasing capacity guarantees from players that hold them, consequently

31 Art 13, Law No 2013-312 of 15 April 2013, aiming to prepare for the transition towards a sober energy system and containing various provisions on the pricing of the water and wind turbines, has notably modified Art L. 335-2, Energy Code in order to specify that the Capacity Mechanism gives, at equal cost, priority to consumption reduction with regard to production capacities.

32 Decree No 2015-1823 dated 30 December 2015 regarding the codification of the regulatory part of the Energy Code.

33 Art L. 335-1 I, Energy Code.

34 Art L. 335-1 II, Energy Code.

35 Art L. 335-5, Energy Code.

creating a demand for capacity guarantees (see section 4.1.1). On the other hand, electricity producers or operators of demand-side capacities (together, referred to as operators) are obliged to have certified their capacities by the national TSO (RTE) and are allocated capacity guarantees according to the contribution of their capacities to reducing the risk of shortfall at times of peak demand, creating a supply of capacity guarantees (section 4.1.2). The capacity guarantees can therefore be traded between the suppliers and the operators on a decentralised market (section 4.1.3).

4.1.1. Demand for Capacity Guarantees

Under the Nome Law, suppliers are required to hold capacity guaranties corresponding to the effective consumption of their customers in order to meet the balance between the supply and demand for electricity in mainland France at times of peak demand.[36] The capacity guarantee can be obtained by investing in new production facilities or demand-side capacities or from the operators.

The exact scope of their capacity obligation is calculated based on the supplier's reference power. Its calculation is made by RTE and takes into account the consumption patterns of each supplier's client and the French electricity interconnection capacities.[37]

The reference power is calculated by RTE as follows:[38]

- it takes into account peak-period consumption (PP1) of each final customer during a delivery year (ie period of 12 months) based on the figures reported by the local distribution grid operators (the Grid Operators) to RTE,[39] and
- various other parameters, including security factors reflecting the margins required to cover residual risks, that is, adjustments for temperature sensitivity of consumption (thermosensitivity) and the demand-side response capacities for the relevant customer.

The peak consumption period PP1 is defined to take into account the highest shortfall risk during the delivery year. As such, PP1 consists of 10 to 15 days per delivery year and the hours used to calculate the capacity obligation are the normal time-slots for 10 hours (7.00–15.00 and 18.00–20.00) of the relevant days. A day is announced to be a part of PP1 the day before (D-1) by RTE based on a demand forecast taking into account statistical distributions of historical load and the weather forecast. The number of PP1 peak hours is between

36 Art L. 335-2 I, Energy Code.
37 Arts L. 335-2 and R. 335-3, Energy Code.
38 Art R. 335-4, Energy Code.
39 Art R. 335-5, Energy Code.

100 and 150 hours per year and the PP1 days are notified to suppliers one day in advance (D-1).[40]

It follows from the above that the exact scope of the capacity obligation is not fixed in advance but is adjusted on a day-to-day basis. The parameters used to determine the actual need for capacity guarantees in the delivery year are published four years in advance.[41]

4.1.2. *Supply of Capacity Guarantees*

Capacity guarantees are issued by RTE to operators. Their delivery is based on the projected contribution of their capacities to reduce the shortfall risk during peak periods[42] and the technical characteristics of each capacity, on a transparent and non-discriminatory basis.[43] A request for certification must be made by each operator to RTE and is based on an estimate made by the operator of the capacity availability level during peak consumption periods (PP2) in a given delivery year. PP2 period is calculated as comprising PP1 period and including from 10 to 25 days. PP2 days that are not PP1 days are selected in advance by RTE and the time-slots concerned are the same as those for PP1 days. There are between 100 and 250 PP2 peak hours per year.[44]

The issuance of the capacity guarantee is based on a contract between RTE and the relevant operator.[45] The request to enter into this contract is made by the operator and comprises a number of commitments, including a commitment to sign the contract as such, as well as availability levels of the capacity and the modalities under which the capacity can be triggered.[46] The contract is based on the elements transmitted by the operator and includes, among other things, the operator's commitment to maintain the availability of the certified capacity, the control of such availability by RTE and the rebalancing conditions.[47]

Therefore, upon issuing of the capacity guarantees, operators commit to a certain level of capacity (certified capacity level). Operators are affiliated with portfolio managers (*responsable du périmètre de certification*), with the latter being financially liable for the imbalances of capacity operators within the relevant electricity perimeter.[48] Operators may act as their own portfolio managers or enter into a contract with a portfolio manager.

The capacity guarantee issued by RTE is valid for a period of one year.[49]

---

40 RTE Report, Capacity Mechanism, 2014, pp 81–117.
41 Ibid, p 117.
42 Art L. 335-3, Energy Code.
43 Art L. 335-4, Energy Code.
44 RTE Report, Capacity Mechanism, 2014, pp 120–44.
45 Art L. 335-3 II, Energy Code.
46 Art R. 335-13, Energy Code.
47 Art R. 335-16, Energy Code.
48 Art L. 335-3 II, Energy Code.
49 Art R. 335-1, Energy Code.

4.1.3. *Trading of the Capacity Guarantees*

The Energy Code expressly provides that the capacity guarantees can be traded.[50] The exchange of the capacity guarantees is conducted through a decentralised market. This is to be distinguished from a centralised market, whereby one central buyer acquires the guarantees granted to the generation units. A decentralised Capacity Market enables both the demand side (ie suppliers) and the supply side (ie operators) to be involved. The logic behind this decentralised set-up is that 'the demand side is respected to be adaptive and demand-side reactions, which can lower the shortfall risk to the same amount as additional generation capacities, are triggered as well by the mechanism.'[51] A decentralised mechanism is also deemed to be more cost-efficient than a centralised mechanism.[52]

The exchange of capacity guarantees is performed through a trade register which reflects available guarantees (section 4.1.3.1) and trade conditions laid down by the texts (section 4.1.3.2).

4.1.3.1. Capacity Guarantees Trade Register

The capacity guarantees are recorded in a public trade register held by RTE. Each supplier and operator is obliged to open an account with RTE.[53] The trade register contains the following information for each capacity guarantee: date of certification, the detailed level of the certified capacity, technical characteristics of the capacity, its availability during the PP2 period and its portfolio manager.[54]

The ownership of a capacity guarantee is granted after RTE has registered the guarantee on the holder's account.[55] Each capacity guarantee has an identification number.[56]

4.1.3.2. Trade Conditions

Transfers of capacity guarantees are recorded in the capacity guarantees trade register, at the request of both parties. This operation is conditional upon the relevant capacity guarantee being already entered into the trade register.[57]

---

50 Art L. 335-3 III, Energy Code.

51 E KRAFT, *Analysis and Modelling of the French Capacity Mechanism. Impact Assessment of Energy Policy Measures on the Security of Supply*, Springers, Karlsruhe 2017, p 18.

52 Ibid.

53 Art R. 335-35, Energy Code.

54 Art R. 335-34, Energy Code.

55 Art R. 335-36, Energy Code.

56 Art R. 335-36, Energy Code.

57 Art R. 335-36, Energy Code.

Such transfer may result either from a guarantee transaction (the parties agree upon a sale price) or a mere transfer (no payment involved).[58]

Capacity guarantees may be traded directly or on organised markets. On the one hand, the supplier and the operator may agree on the object of the trade and its price and finalise the transaction by submitting a request to RTE for changes in each actor's account in the capacity guarantees trade register.[59] On the other hand, the trade may be carried on through a specific platform which will centralise the sale and purchase offers. The implementation of such platform is outlined by the rules of capacity mechanism.[60]

4.2. REGULATION OF THE FRENCH CAPACITY MARKET

The design of the Capacity Market in France is completed by the thorough regulation framework involving various regulatory authorities (section 4.2.1) and regulatory proceedings (section 4.2.2).

4.2.1. Regulation Authorities

The main regulatory authorities in the French Capacity Market are the Minister of Energy (see section 4.2.1.1) and the national independent energy regulator, CRE (section 4.2.1.2). RTE, as the national TSO, plays a key operating role in regulating the market (section 4.2.1.3).

4.2.1.1. Ministry of Energy

The Minister of Energy remains the ultimate regulatory authority. In fact, the regulatory framework allows the Minister a large measure of discretion for various technical rules to be implemented and approved. For instance, pursuant to the Energy Code the Minister of Energy approves the following rules applicable to the capacity mechanism:[61]

- rules determining delivery years and peak periods PP1 and PP2;
- the methodology for calculating the reference power levels and suppliers' commitments, as well as the power factor of the capacity guarantees; and
- the methods for certifying capacities and their control.

58 RTE Report, Capacity Mechanism, 2014, p 164.
59 Art R. 335-37, Energy Code.
60 RTE Report, Capacity Mechanism, 2014, p 167.
61 Art R. 335-2, Energy Code.

4.2.1.2. The French Energy Regulator (CRE)

CRE monitors the functioning of the Capacity Market to ensure that the signals sent to market stakeholders are meaningful and contribute to safeguarding the security of supply.[62] In addition, CRE collects data, analyses the state of the market and communicates the results of those analyses.[63]

CRE is also closely involved in the definition of various technical rules which, prior to their approval by the Minister of Energy, are submitted to CRE for its opinion.[64]

CRE is also in charge of approving some of the technical rules relating to the capacity mechanism. For instance, CRE approves the following documents:

- exchange agreements between RTE and grid operators for transmission of information required for the calculation of the suppliers' reference power;[65]
- procedures and amount of incurred expenses for calculating and sending obligation-related data;[66]
- rules underlying the management of the capacity guarantees trade register.[67]

Finally, as a part of its monitoring function, CRE is also in charge of monitoring the settlement of imbalances[68] and applying relevant sanctions (see section 4.2.2.2 below).[69]

4.2.1.3. National Transition System Operator (RTE)

Finally, RTE plays a key role in the regulation of the French Capacity Market. Technical rules are defined by RTE, prior to their submission for opinion to CRE and for approval to the Minister of Energy. It is in charge of global management of the Capacity Market, by determining the scope of capacity obligations for the suppliers,[70] issuing capacity guarantees for the operators,[71] controlling the effectiveness of the production capacities and controlling the calculation of capacity gaps. It is also in charge of keeping records of the capacity guarantees through three different registers:[72]

---

62 Art L. 131-2, Energy Code. *cf.* also RTE Report, Capacity Mechanism, 2014, p 65.
63 Art L. 135-1, Energy Code.
64 Art R. 335-2, Energy Code.
65 Art R. 335-4, Energy Code.
66 Art R. 335-19, Energy Code.
67 Art R. 335-34, Energy Code.
68 Art R. 335-12, Energy Code.
69 Art L. 335-7, Energy Code.
70 Art R. 335-3, Energy Code.
71 Art R. 335-13, Energy Code.
72 RTE Report, Capacity Mechanism, 2014, p 66.

- the capacity guarantees trade register, a public document, listing all the capacity guarantees connected to the transmission or distribution systems;
- the capacity guarantees register, not public, which records in a secure manner all transactions involving the issuance, transfer or destruction of the capacity guarantees; and
- the peak demand-side management register.

In general, RTE identifies capacity needs and energy consumption forecasts during consumption peak periods and provide the market players with the relevant information.

4.2.2. Regulation Proceedings

The regulation of the French Capacity Market is based on two types of public authorities' intervention. On the one hand, imbalances between forecasts and actual results are managed through specific instruments (section 4.2.2.1). On the other hand, specific sanctions are also provided for infringements of capacity mechanism rules (section 4.2.2.2).

4.2.2.1. Settlement of the Imbalances

The imbalances settlement mechanism is designed to ensure the accountability of the suppliers and portfolio managers. It also allocates responsibility between each for the imbalances between the forecast energy consumption during peak period and real results. It is designed to encourage suppliers to cover their obligations as accurately as possible and to incentivise the operators to submit their best power availability estimates for their facilities.[73]

The imbalance settlement mechanism is therefore based on a bonus/malus scheme, where suppliers and portfolio managers have to pay a financial settlement in the event of a negative imbalance and receive a financial settlement for a positive one.

A financial fee is paid as follows. The difference between a supplier's obligation and the amount of capacity guarantees held in its account is calculated, and the supplier shall pay any resulting imbalance settlement.[74] At the end of the delivery year, RTE calculates, for each portfolio manager, the difference between the sum of certified capacity levels within its portfolio, reflecting the self-assessment-based commitments of the operators, and effective capacity levels. The capacity

73 Ibid, p 152.
74 Art R. 335-11, Energy Code.

portfolio manager is financially liable for the amount of the settlement imbalance thus calculated[75] and pays the relevant fee.[76]

All the payments are made on separate accounts for suppliers' imbalances ('fund for the settlement of suppliers' capacity rebalancing')[77] and portfolio managers' imbalances ('fund for the settlement of portfolio managers' imbalances').[78] These accounts are managed by RTE.[79] RTE is also responsible for invoicing and recovering amounts owed by each market player and for recording any defaults on payment.[80]

4.2.2.2. Sanctions

A supplier who does not comply with its obligation to hold capacity guarantees is subject to a financial penalty imposed by CRE, after formal notice to provide justifications has not been successful.[81] The decision imposing a financial penalty shall include the reasons for such decision[82] and may be challenged before the Council of State.[83]

The scope of this penalty is based on the following principles.[84] First, the penalty is determined in such a way as to ensure, in the medium term, an economic incentive for suppliers to fulfil their obligations. Then, the amount of the penalty shall be proportionate to the seriousness of the breach, the particular circumstances of the individual concerned, the extent of the damage and the benefits derived from it, and it cannot exceed, for one year, €120,000 per megawatt of missing certified capacity. Finally, if a supplier fails to pay this financial penalty, the Minister of Energy[85] may also suspend the authorisation required to perform purchase for resale activities issued pursuant to Article L. 333-1 of the Energy Code.

Following the publication of various documents, certification of the capacities for the first delivery years commenced on 1 April 2015, in respect of the first implementation of the capacity mechanism during winter 2016/17, that is, starting from 1 January 2017.

However, the schedule for adoption of the French Capacity Mechanism has been set back by the European Commission's investigations into whether or not

---

75 RTE Report, Capacity Mechanism, 2014, p 65.
76 Art R. 335-30, Energy Code.
77 Art R. 335-8, Energy Code.
78 Art R. 335-29, Energy Code.
79 Arts R. 335-8 and R. 335-29, Energy Code.
80 Arts R. 335-12 and R. 335-32, Energy Code.
81 Art L. 335-7, Energy Code.
82 Art L. 134-34, Energy Code.
83 Art L. 134-34, Energy Code.
84 Art L. 335-7, Energy Code.
85 Art D. 335-54, Energy Code.

the French Capacity Market scheme complies with EU State aid rules. Other State aids investigations have been conducted by the European Commission in relation to specific capacity mechanisms in France, but with a more limited scope of application[86] or requiring only an adjustment to the main Capacity Market mechanism described above.[87]

5. THE CHANGES REQUIRED AS A RESULT OF THE EUROPEAN COMMISSION'S DECISION

5.1. THE EUROPEAN COMMISSION'S APPROVAL PROCESS

After a phase of informal exchange of views in October/November 2014, and after the formal notification of the scheme by the French authorities on 27 April 2015, the European Commission initiated a formal investigation procedure into the French Capacity Market on 13 November 2015 (Opening Decision).[88] The procedure was motivated by two main concerns related, on the one hand, to the risk that the Capacity Market, as envisaged, could favour certain companies over their competitors, and that, on the other hand, it could hinder the entry of new players on the market. Both circumstances would have effect on competition and trade between Member States. Following a series of exchanges with the French authorities and after receiving comments from interested parties, the Commission reached its final decision on 8 November 2016 where it approved the scheme (Final Decision).[89]

In its Opening Decision, the Commission came to the conclusion that the proposed French Capacity Market constituted State aid within the meaning of Article 107(1) TFEU[90] and reiterated this conclusion in the Final Decision, even taking into account the proposed amendments. Thereafter, the Commission assessed whether the measure could nevertheless be deemed compatible with the internal market pursuant to the Guidelines on State aid for environmental protection and energy (2014–20). Based on the amendments proposed by the

---

86 European Commission's Decision in case SA.40454, France – Tender for additional capacity in Brittany, 15 May 2017.

87 European Commission's Decision in case SA.48490, France – Specific demand response tender – 7 February 2018.

88 European Commission, Letter to Member State, State Aid SA.39621 (2015/C) (ex 2015/NN), French country-wide capacity mechanism – C(2015) 7805 final, 13 November 2015; Press release, IP/15/6077.

89 European Commission Decision of 8 November 2016 on State Aid Scheme SA.39621 2015/C (ex 2015/NN), C(2016) 7086 final; Press release IP/16/3620.

90 Ibid, paras 100–43.

French authorities, the scheme was approved for a limited period of 10 years, consistent with the duration of the UK Capacity Market mechanism.[91]

It is notable that the Commission stressed the fact that France started implementing the measure before the Commission reached its final decision, which is in breach of Article 108(3) TFEU and thus unlawful.[92] Nevertheless, based on the different remedies proposed by the national authorities, it decided to approve the scheme under State aid rules.

5.2. EVOLUTION OF THE CAPACITY MECHANISM RULES FOLLOWING THE DECISION

Following the Commission's decision, RTE has elaborated a new set of technical rules designed to address the issues raised by the Commission. The revised rules focused on three key elements, which are:

- the creation of a specific mechanism for new capacities enabling them to benefit from revenues over seven years, in order to increase the visibility for new investments and to facilitate the entry of new players into the market;
- the opening of the scheme to new capacity providers, including foreign capacities and in demand response; and
- the introduction of a series of measures to prevent market manipulations. Three main sets of measures have been discussed. First, rules for the supervision of certification procedures (ie certification range and rebalancing conditions) have been developed in order to ensure that the supply of capacity guarantees reflects as closely as possible the forecast state of availability of the French generation and demand-side capacities, thus enabling the setting of a robust capacity market price. Second, financial incentives have been strengthened in order to limit the possibility for the major players (such as EDF, France's historical electricity operator) to disrupt the price-setting of the capacity guarantees, and in order to improve the liquidity of the Capacity Market. Third, rules have been adopted in order to enhance transparency in market operations.

Following the proposal submitted by RTE, CRE issued a favourable opinion on 24 November 2016.[93] In its opinion, the revised rules effectively prevent anti-competitive practices both in the wholesale market for capacity guarantees and in the retail market. CRE deems that several provisions are particularly aimed at

---

91 European Commission Decision of 3 October 2001, SA.35980 – GB capacity mechanism, para 162.

92 Final Decision in State aid case SA.39621, para 215.

93 CRE deliberation dated 24 November 2016.

controlling the behaviour of the dominant player(s), without impacting smaller players. Combined with the additional efforts for transparency in the Capacity Market, CRE concludes that the revised draft rules provide a better competitive framework for the overall capacity mechanism.

Following CRE's favourable opinion, the new rules were approved by the Minister of Energy on 29 November 2016.[94] The revised rules take the form of amendments to the previous technical rules on the capacity mechanism, as well as additional provisions submitted to CRE for approval.

On 1 December 2016, CRE also approved some of the new technical provisions, relating to: the market reference price (MRP); the calculation of the observed consumption and the observed consumption for losses; the calculation of the settlement price related to the rebalancing; the management conditions of various capacity guarantee registers; and the methods of publication of the forecasts for a delivery year and the calendar of publication of the parameters relating to this delivery year.

Consequently, notwithstanding legal uncertainties resulting from the EU's inquiry into the French mechanism, all the relevant regulatory and technical provisions were approved at the end of 2016 and the first delivery year commenced on 1 January 2017, as forecast.

During 2017, CRE issued a number of decisions designed to complete the existing rules. Those decisions relate to the recovery methods and level of costs incurred by transport and distribution system operators in calculating and transmitting power reference data.[95] They also set the conditions under which capacity guarantees are taken into account in the price of capacity guarantees transfers.[96] Finally, they lay down the methodology for determining costs related to the capacity guarantees register.[97]

6. MARKET PRACTICES AND PERSPECTIVES

A market reference price (MRP) is regularly published by CRE following auctions organised by EpexSpot.[98] As a public reference of the market price, the MRP represents as far as possible the price of capacity established by the market. In order to do so, it must incorporate a sufficiently large volume of transactions and cover a sufficiently wide period to take into account all the dynamics of the economic signals revealed by the capacity mechanism in the years preceding the delivery year.

94 Order dated 29 November 2016 *définissant les règles du mécanisme de capacité et pris en application de l'article R. 335-2 du code de l'énergie.*
95 CRE deliberation dated 5 January 2017.
96 CRE deliberation dated 13 April 2017.
97 CRE deliberation dated 24 May 2017.
98 Art R. 335-51, Energy Code.

For each delivery year, at least 15 auctions are held over the four-year period preceding the delivery year. Following the first auction dated 15 December 2016, the MRP for the delivery year 2017 was fixed at €9,999.8/MW. It should be noted that the transfer of capacity guarantees over-the-counter performed before this first auction were made at the same price.[99] Therefore, the final price is capped at:

- 2017: €20,000/MW;
- 2018 and 2019: €40,000/MW;
- 2020: €60,000/MW.[100]

For the delivery year 2018, auctions were held on 9 November 2017 and 14 December 2017. For the delivery year 2019, the first auction took place on 14 December 2017.

The example of energy markets shows that liquidity on long-term products traded over-the-counter is fairly low. This can be a significant obstacle to the formation of a credible price signal. An organised market is therefore necessary to concentrate the liquidity of the Capacity Market in auctions and to improve the quality of the price signal to guide the expectations of market players. In addition, an organised market price has other advantages such as transparency, payment and delivery security, anonymity, market rules and surveillances.

---

99 For further information on trading activities and auction calendar, see the EpexSpot website on capacity auctions in France: https://www.epexspot.com/en/product-info/capacity_auction.

100 Order dated 29 November 2016 *définissant les règles du mécanisme de capacité et pris en application de l'article R. 335-2 du code de l'énergie.*

PART V

PROMOTING THE USE OF SUSTAINABLE GAS AND SECURITY OF GAS SUPPLY

CHAPTER XII

THE USE OF POWER-TO-GAS IN REFINERIES

Regulatory Challenges from an EU and German Perspective

Martha M ROGGENKAMP*

1. INTRODUCTION

The impact of climate change concerns on the energy sector is undisputed and has led to various governmental initiatives to limit greenhouse gas emissions. Since the 1990s a wide range of measures and instruments have been developed on EU and national level to combat climate change. In the EU these measures vary from the introduction of a CO_2 emissions trading regime to the promotion of renewable energy sources and energy efficiency measures. These measures have a direct impact on the fossil fuels sector and the electricity generation sector. One of the sectors that will be affected by these changes is the refinery sector. Oil refineries transform crude oil into a range of usable products such as liquefied petroleum gas (LPG), petrol, kerosene, jet fuel, diesel oil and fuel oils. It is an energy intensive process[1] and refineries consequently also emit large quantities of greenhouse gasses, in particular CO_2. In order to reduce greenhouse gas emissions, the EU has put in place a range of instruments varying from an EU emissions trading system (EU ETS) to measures focusing on energy savings and energy efficiency (including the use of waste heat), as well as the possibility

* This chapter is based on the presentation, 'Regulating the Production and Use of Hydrogen' presented by Ruprecht Brandis at the 28th European Energy Law Seminar on 23 January 2017 in The Hague. Use has also been made of the article 'Potenzial und Regelungsbedarf für Power-to-Gas in Raffinerien' by Timo Eickelkamp and Ruprecht Brandis, published in *Energiewirtschaftliche Tagesfragen* (2017) 1(2), 2–5. The author wishes to thank Ruven Fleming and Gijs Kreeft for their valuable input.

1 See, eg, the statistical overview presented each year by the US Energy Information Administration, available at: https://www.eia.gov/dnav/pet/pet_pnp_capfuel_dcu_nus_a.htm

for carbon capture and storage. Apart from reducing greenhouse gas emissions, there are also other attempts to make the refinery sector more sustainable by using 'green' hydrogen instead of natural gas in the refinery process.

So far little has been written about the impact of these climate goals on the refinery sector: this chapter tries to fill this lacuna by presenting a brief overview of some of the challenges the refinery sector faces and how law can play a role in addressing these issues. It will focus in particular on the need to make the refinery sector and its end product – the transport fuel – more sustainable by using 'green' hydrogen instead of natural gas in the refining process. By doing so, the focus will be on the EU and Germany. The reason for choosing Germany is this country's strong focus on energy transition and the large number of pilot projects involving 'green' hydrogen.

The chapter will therefore begin with the current EU and German climate policy. This will be followed by a brief description of the refinery sector and refinery process. Then the chapter will discuss the concept of 'green' hydrogen. As well as introducing the concept, it will look at how it can play a role in the refinery process and how this technique has been applied in some German pilot projects. Last but not least, the chapter will examine the legal challenges these projects face and how these may create an obstacle to a large scale introduction of this technique in the refinery sector, and thus to making the refinery sector more sustainable.

2. CLIMATE GOALS AND ENERGY TRANSITION POLICIES IN THE EU AND GERMANY

2.1. POLICY GOALS

Since the 1992 UN Framework Convention on Climate Change (UNFCCC) and the subsequent Kyoto Protocol of 1997,[2] the need to address climate change has become more and more apparent. The 2015 Paris Agreement presents a climate change regime after the end of the second commitment period of the Kyoto Protocol in 2020 and aims at strengthening the global response to climate change by keeping a global temperature rise below 2 degrees Celsius above pre-industrial levels and to pursue efforts to limit the temperature increase even further to 1.5 degrees Celsius.[3] Additionally, the agreement aims to strengthen the ability of countries to deal with the impacts of climate change.[4]

2 These documents can be found at: http://www.unfccc.int.

3 Art 2.1 (a) Paris Agreement.

4 See also C Banet, 'The Paris Agreement to the UNFCCC: Underlying Dynamics and Expected Consequences for the Energy Sector', *European Energy Law Report XI*, Intersentia, Cambridge 2017, pp 71–91.

The EU and its Member States are party to the UNFCCC and the Paris Agreement. In order to meet the climate change goals, the EU has issued since the 1990s a wide range of policy goals and several implementing measures aiming at CO_2 emissions reduction, including EU directives establishing an EU emissions trading system (EU ETS) and promoting the use of renewable energy sources.[5] These directives will be further amended and/or replaced as a result of the Clean Energy Package presented in November 2016.[6] The 20-20-20 goals presented in the 2007 Energy and Climate Package have been replaced by new climate targets and a more restricted use of fossil fuels for 2030 and 2050.[7] In addition, energy efficiency now also features more prominently as a policy goal and an important means to achieve energy savings. These changes and climate goals are basically creating a process of energy transition, ie a process of gradually replacing the use of fossil fuels by renewable energy sources. This also entails a gradual increase of electricity consumption and possibly 'green' hydrogen for, inter alia, heating and transport purposes.

In Germany, the process of energy transition started in 1998 when the red-green government announced its intention to phase out nuclear energy and to focus instead on renewable energies, energy efficiency and climate protection. The 2011 Fukushima nuclear catastrophe intensified the nuclear phase-out and led to the enactment of a number of new energy laws, which are commonly known under the heading *Energiewende* (Energy Transition). As a result, the German climate goals have become increasingly ambitious. Whereas in 2010 the German Government included in its 'National Energy Concept'[8] a climate goal of 40% greenhouse gas emissions reduction by 2020 and 80–95% by 2050 (base year 1990), this changed as a result of the Paris Agreement. In the National Climate Protection Plan (*Nationaler Klimaschutzplan*) of November 2016,[9] the German Government increased the overall greenhouse gas emissions reduction target to 55% by 2030 and presented individual emissions reduction targets for the energy, industry, transport and agricultural sectors. For the transport sector a 40–42% greenhouse gas (mainly CO_2) emissions reduction goal has been set

---

5 See also MM Roggenkamp et al, *Energy Law in Europe, National, EU and International Regulation*, OUP, Oxford 2017, 3rd edn, p 191.

6 The Clean Energy Package was published on 30 November 2016 and aims at amending most directives and regulations governing the electricity sector and introduces a new legislative proposal on EU governance. See also: https://ec.europa.eu/energy/en/topics/energy-strategy-and-energy-union/clean-energy-all-europeans.

7 In 2014 the European Council agreed on new targets for 2030, which include a cut in greenhouse gas emissions by at least 40% by 2030 compared to 1990 levels and an EU-wide binding target for renewable energy of at least 27%. See also: http://ec.europa.eu/energy/en/topics/energy-strategy-and-energy-union.

8 *Energiekonzept der Bundesregierung für eine umweltschonende, zuverlässige und bezahlbare Energieversorgung* of 28 September 2010. See: http://www.bundesregierung.de.

9 This plan can be found at: https://www.bmub.bund.de/en/publication/klimaschutzplan-2050-klimaschutzpolitische-grundsaetze-und-ziele-der-bundesregierung/.

for 2030. So far the German transport sector has not been able to achieve the set emissions reduction goals. Hence, the current goal to achieve at least 40% greenhouse gas emissions reduction by 2030 is very ambitious, especially as it has to be achieved within 12 years.

2.2. THE GERMAN NATIONAL CLIMATE PROTECTION PLAN

The National Climate Protection Plan is broader in scope than merely reducing existing greenhouse gas emissions. It aims at a complete 'decarbonisation' of the energy sector before 2050 but extends to other economic sectors as well, including the transport sector.[10] To illustrate, in 2016 some 98.4% of the 45 million private cars made use of either petrol (66.2%) or diesel fuel (32.2%); the remaining 1.6% of the cars used alternative fuels like LPG, natural gas or are operated as hybrid or electric vehicles.[11] In addition, there were some 5.3 million commercial vehicles and 4.2 million motorcycles using diesel or petrol fuel. In order to decarbonise the transport sector, most German vehicles will need to opt for other fuel options.

The National Climate Protection Plan essentially aims at the full electrification of the German energy and transport sectors by 2050 based on the use of renewable energy sources. This aim is closely connected to another key principle of the National Climate Protection Plan and that is the need for 'sector-coupling'. The principle of 'sector-coupling' refers to the need to use electricity from renewables for other economic sectors than merely the power sector. There are various possibilities to convert 'green' electricity into another energy source, power-to-X. The X could involve heat as well as gas. One of the key arguments for developing such a conversion (power-to-X) relates to the issue of grid expansion, which would otherwise be required. The rapid increase of 'green' power is hampered by current grid design and the fact that the required largescale grid expansion is taking longer than the time to develop renewable energy projects. These processes are not running in parallel. This is a challenge in Northern Germany in particular where most of Germany's wind energy is generated and which needs to be transmitted to the industrial centres in the West and South of Germany.[12] This process is generally hampered by insufficient network capacity.[13] One other option to deal with any excess of renewable

---

10 See above footnotes 9 and 10.

11 These figures can be found at the website of the German Transport Authority (*Kraftfahrtbundesamt*), https://www.kba.de/EN/Statistik_en/Fahrzeuge_en/fahrzeuge_node_en.html.

12 See: http://www.bbsr.bund.de/BBSR/DE/Raumentwicklung/EnergieKlimaschutzpolitik/Projekte/Archiv/Erneuerbare/EE_im_Raum.html?nn=1037294.

13 See also G Kühne, 'Regulating the Extension of the Electricity Networks – A German Perspective' in MM Roggenkamp et al (eds), *Energy Networks and the Law – Innovative Solutions in Changing Markets*, OUP, Oxford 2012, pp 371–93.

electricity and a key technological idea involving sector-coupling would be the possibility for electricity storage and the option to turn power into 'green' hydrogen.

Finally it should be noted that Germany is not only aiming at a complete energy transition but has also gained some experience in doing so by phasing out important parts of the domestic coal and nuclear energy sectors. These experiences have shown that replacing an important energy source for another will require a transition period of some 20 to 25 years.[14] A complete transformation of the entire energy system will take a significantly longer period of time. It seems that the German National Climate Protection Plan has taken this presumption into account when it set the timescale for energy transition to 2050.

3. THE REFINERY SECTOR

3.1. THE REFINERY PROCESS

The energy transition process clearly affects the refinery sector, as this is a very energy intensive sector, but also produces a range of fuels emitting greenhouse gasses like LPG, petrol, kerosene, jet fuel, diesel oil and fuel oils.[15] The specifics of the refinery operations differ from location to location, but virtually all refinery processes can be classified into three stages: separation, treatment and conversion.[16]

The first stage is known as distillation. In this process, crude oil is heated and fed into a distillation plant. As the temperature of the crude oil in the distillation column rises to circa 360°C, the crude oil separates itself into different components, called 'fractions'. The fractions are then captured separately. Each fraction corresponds to a different type of petroleum product, depending on the temperature at which that fraction boils off the crude oil mixture. Lighter fractions such as LPG, naphtha and kerosene have lower boiling points, lower carbon content and higher hydrogen content than heavier factions such as

14 T Eickelkamp and R Brandis, 'Potenzial und Regelungsbedarf für Power-to-Gas in Raffinerien' *Energiewirtschaftliche Tagesfragen* (2017) 1(2) 2.

15 In addition, refineries also produce a range of specialty products necessary for the production of petrochemicals such as plastics and fibres. This chapter will not discuss legal issues relating to these products.

16 The information in this section is largely based on Commission Staff Working Document, *On Refining and the Supply of Petroleum Products in the EU*, of 17 November 2010, SEC (2010) 1398 final. This working document accompanies the document to the Communication to the European Parliament, the Council, the European Economic and Social Committee and the Committee of the Regions, 'Energy Infrastructure Priorities for 2020 and Beyond – A Blueprint for an Integrated European Energy Network', COM (2010).

vacuum gas oil and vacuum residues. Generally the heaviest fractions are lower in value than the lighter fractions. This process is known as simple distillation, also referred to as topping or hydro skimming when done in the presence of hydrogen.

Treatment is the next step in the process and necessary to improve the quality of petroleum fractions distilled in order to meet the specifications of finished products. Hydro treating processes[17] use hydrogen and catalysts to remove sulphur and other contaminants such as salts, nickel and nitrogen oxides.

The conversion process is also known as cracking. It is applied to the various fractions produced through distillation. As the heaviest fractions are lower in value than some of the lighter fractions, refineries apply the process called 'cracking' in order to break apart the molecules in the fractions to produce some higher-value products. Cracking is most often utilised to produce gasoline and jet fuel from heavy gas oils.[18] The most common crackers are fluid catalytic crackers (FCCs) and hydrocrackers. These traditional conversion refineries would typically require more energy per unit of crude intake compared to hydro skimming refineries and would therefore also generate more greenhouse gasses per unit of crude oil intake. With the increasing demand for lighter, cleaner products and the rapidly declining use of heavy residual fuels, more and more use is made of 'deep conversion units', which are the most sophisticated types of refineries as they convert vacuum residue into lighter products. These refineries are, however, more energy intensive than traditional conversion units and emit more greenhouse gasses per unit of crude oil intake.

It follows from the above that depending on the processes applied, refineries can produce a variety of light to heavy distillates. Most distillates are used in the transport sector, but, whereas light distillates like gasoline and LPG are mainly used for motor vehicles, middle distillates are used as jet fuel in the aviation sector and heavy distillates are used as bunker oil for large ships or as heavy fuel oil for industrial installations.

3.2. REFINERIES IN THE EU

The above shows that petroleum refineries are very large industrial installations that involve many different processing units and auxiliary facilities such as utility units and storage tanks. In practice each refinery has its own unique arrangement

17 Examples of hydro treating processes include hydrogenating, hydrofining and hydrodesulphurisation.

18 Another conversion method is the reforming process, which also aims at producing more gasoline but is typically utilised on lower-value light fractions. The reforming process involves inducing chemical reactions under pressure to change the composition of the hydrocarbon chain.

and combination of refining processes which are primarily determined by the refinery location, desired products and economic considerations. Refineries in the EU are generally smaller in scale than elsewhere and only one refinery in North-Western Europe has a capacity of more than 400,000 barrels per day.[19]

The EU is the second largest producer of petroleum products in the world after the United States. It has a crude refining capacity of about 15 million barrels per day, which represents 16% of total global refining capacity. There are refineries in 21 Member States with the exceptions of Cyprus, Estonia, Latvia, Luxembourg, Malta and Slovenia. Over half of the refining capacity in the EU is situated in North Western Europe (NWE), slightly more than a quarter in the Mediterranean region and the rest in Central and Eastern Europe. In the EU, Germany has the largest refinery capacity (14 refineries and a total capacity of 102,155 kt/year).[20]

In Europe use is made of several sources of crude oil supply. Whereas the Mediterranean is largely dependent on supply from the Arabian Gulf, Central Europe mainly makes use of crude oil from Russia. Crude oil from these areas has a relatively high sulphur content. North-Western Europe is able to make use of crude oil production from the North Sea, which is a lighter crude oil and thus has lower sulphur content. Crude oil production from the North Sea, however, is declining and more expensive than heavier crude oils. The additional costs of these lighter crude oils may be outweighed by the fact that these need less desulphurisation. Falling crude oil production in the North Sea may also be a concern as there is a higher demand for lighter distillates. The latter, however, will depend on policies affecting the transport sector and sustainability requirements applying to motor fuels.[21]

3.3. CHALLENGES

The energy transition challenges affect the entire refinery chain, ie the refineries' energy use, the refinery process and the refineries output, ie fuels.

The processes of distillation, treatment and conversion are energy intensive. Fossil fuels are the main sources used by the refineries and the refining process leads to considerable greenhouse gas emissions. The costs involved in the refinery process thus depend not only on the costs of the fossil fuels used but also on the costs of the greenhouse gas emissions allowances refineries need to

19 R van den Bergh, M Nivard and M Kreijkers, 'Long-term Prospects for Northwest European Refining', Clingendael International Energy Programme, CIEP paper 2016/1.

20 SEC(2010) 1398 final. See also for the most recent figures on German refinery capacity: https://www.mwv.de/statistiken/raffineriekapazitaeten/.

21 SEC(2010) 1398 final.

submit annually according to the EU Emissions Trading System (EU ETS).[22] Replacing fossil fuels with renewable energy sources could be an alternative. Although few renewable alternatives are available, one of them could be the use of power-to-gas, which enables the conversion of renewable energy sources like (offshore) wind energy to be converted into gas. The use of such an alternative will enable the refinery process itself to become more 'green', for example when petroleum fractions are treated. During this treating process hydrogen is used to remove sulphur and other contaminants. Currently, natural gas is usually used as a feedstock for hydrogen but by replacing natural gas for a 'green' gas on the basis of the above mentioned power-to-gas technique, this part of the refinery process can also play an important role in achieving the climate change goals.

The energy transition process will also have an important impact on the refineries output: the transport fuels. As mentioned before, the aim is to drastically transform the transport sector by, for example, promoting the use of electric driving rather than using petrol in combination with biofuels. Another alternative for the transport sector is the use of green hydrogen as fuel for fuel cell electric vehicles (FCEV). Currently it is unclear to what extent, when and in what form electrical mobility or another alternative automotive power source will have its break-through. In the meantime petrol and diesel will need to be available to supply the existing fleet of petrol and diesel vehicles, and thus to make these fossil fuels more sustainable as well.

4. GREENING THE REFINERY PROCESS

It appears from the above that one of the options to make the refinery process more sustainable is to make use of 'green' gas instead of natural gas. Green gas can, for example, be the result of a process called power-to-gas. The sections below present first, the concept of power-to-gas and how this can become a green energy source, before going on to discuss how this concept is applied in Germany and the refinery sector.

4.1. POWER-TO-GAS

Power-to-gas is a process where electricity is used as input for the production of hydrogen (H_2) and oxygen (O_2) through the decomposition of a water molecule by electrolysis ($2H_2O \rightarrow 2H_2 + O_2$). The oxygen can be released into the atmosphere and the hydrogen can be used as a separate product or be

22 *cf.* Directive 2003/87/EC as amended by Directive 2009/29/EC.

synthesised with carbon dioxide (CO_2) into methane (CH_4). Commercially, there are two electrolysis technologies: the alkaline electrolysis and the polymer electrolyte membrane (PEM) electrolysis.[23] Whereas the alkaline electrolysis can be categorised as an available and industrially proven technology, one of the advantages of PEM electrolysis is its ability to operate at high current densities, which can result in reduced operational costs, especially for systems coupled with very dynamic energy sources such as wind and solar.[24]

The power-to-gas concept becomes a 'green' option if use is made of electricity from renewable energy sources such as onshore and offshore wind energy. Using this technique has several advantages. From the perspective of the electricity sector, this technique will enable the use of intermittent renewable energy sources 'locally' when the electricity prices are very low and thus reduce the need for electricity grid extensions and extra transport costs. It will thus provide a flexibility option for electricity networks and enable the integration of additional renewable energy into the system, as well as being an innovative step towards large-volume electricity storage. From the gas perspective, the conversion of power-to-gas can play a role in securing gas supply if it is converted into methane and injected into the natural gas system. In addition, the hydrogen can be used for other purposes such as those discussed in this chapter. When converting renewable power-to-gas, one of the main advantages is that the hydrogen will result in almost 100% greenhouse gas emissions reduction compared to conventionally produced hydrogen.[25]

4.2. POWER-TO-GAS DEVELOPMENTS IN GERMANY

The German Government is supporting the use of power-to-gas. Following a position paper on power-to-gas by the Environmental Protection Agency (*Umweltbundesamt*) issued in March 2016,[26] the Ministry of Economic Affairs published a green paper on energy efficiency in September 2016, which also

---

23 There is a third option, high-temperature electrolysis, which is still in a process of technical development and not yet commercially available. The high-temperature electrolysis process uses a solid oxide electrolyte. An advantage of this technology is that a share of the energy used for splitting the water molecule is provided thermally using super-heated steam at approximately 800° C. This can reduce the specific electrical energy use and increase the electrical efficiency.

24 See for more details of these processes T Eickelkamp and R Brandis, 'Potenzial und Regelungsbedarf für Power-to-Gas in Raffinerien' *Energiewirtschaftliche Tagesfragen* (2017) 1(2), 4.

25 M Götz et al, 'Renewable Power-to-Gas: A Technological and Economic Review' Renewable Energy (2016) 85, 1371–90.

26 K Purr, D Osiek, M Lange, K Adlunger et al, *Integration von Power-to-Gas/Power-to-Liquid in den laufenden Transformationsprocess. Umweltbundesamt*, Federal Environment Agency, Berlin 2016.

explicitly referred to power-to-gas as a solution for making use of any excess of electricity from renewables.[27] According to the Environmental Protection Agency, power-to-gas (and power-to-liquids) constitute a long-term solution to achieve a complete transition to renewable energy supply, even without using biomass and can also play an important role in the transport sector.[28] The long-term availability of the power-to-gas/liquids technology will thus be vital in the energy transition process and achieving the abovementioned goals of the National Climate Protection Plan. However, in order to apply power-to-gas commercially there is the need to further examine and develop the techniques via pilot and demonstration projects.[29]

In Germany, mention can be made of two demonstration plants, each of them using a different electrolyser technique. In the state of Brandenburg, the world's first demonstration power-to-gas plant was constructed by Uniper in Falkenhagen in 2013. The plant makes use of electricity generated by wind turbines. Around 360 Nm^3/h of hydrogen, which corresponds to a total electrical power of approximately 2 MW, is produced by means of alkaline electrolysis and is fed into a 1.6 km hydrogen pipeline of 55 bar, which is connected to the gas transmission grid operated by ONTRAS Gastransport GmbH.[30] The second demonstration plan was established by Uniper in Hamburg-Reitbrook in 2015. As in the case of the Falkenhagen plant it converts electricity from wind energy into hydrogen. However, this plant makes use of PEM electrolysis and has led to a maximum hydrogen production of 290 Nm^3/h (with a total electrical power consumption >1 MW). The hydrogen is fed into the natural gas distribution network of Hamburg.[31]

These pilot projects were designed as a means of gaining technical, economic and administrative experience. As each of these pilot plants make use of a different technology – the alkaline and the PEM electrolysis – it has also been possible to compare these technologies as regards their efficiency and flexibility. Whereas the Falkenhagen plant was assessed in relation to its role in the control reserve market (secondary capacity reserve and minute reserve), the assessment of the Hamburg plant focused on the entire process chain and the purity of the hydrogen produced. Since the hydrogen produced by both pilots was injected into the natural gas grid, the pilots also enabled the companies to assess the impact of admixing quantities of hydrogen with natural gas (starting with

---

27 Federal Ministry for Economic Affairs and Energy, *Green Paper on Energy Efficiency*, Berlin, September 2016.

28 See K Purr, D Osiek, M Lange, K Adlunger et al (n 26) pp 5, 10.

29 See ibid, pp 10, 19.

30 In the first year of operation (until July 2014) more than 2 million kWh of hydrogen was fed into the natural gas grid.

31 See T Eickelkamp and R Brandis, 'Potenzial und Regelungsbedarf für Power-to-Gas in Raffinerien' *Energiewirtschaftliche Tagesfragen* (2017) 1(2), 4.

a mixture of 10% and increasing to 15%).[32] As regards the planning and construction stage, the pilots assessed some safety issues such as the minimum distance between electrolysers and nearby buildings, as well as the steel used for constructing hydrogen pipelines. Experiences with the Falkenhagen plant showed that it was best to use conventional steel pipes with a slightly increased wall thickness than normally used for natural gas pipelines. Finally, practical insight in the contractual and legal framework was achieved as a result of the various contracts that were concluded, varying from network access agreements to electricity purchase and hydrogen sales contracts.

The main conclusion following both pilot projects is that the power-to-gas technology (both electrolysis technologies) is market-ready and can be used. In order to make the technique economically viable it will be necessary to achieve cost reductions. The latter will depend on the number of plants installed and the time needed for technical improvements. One of the possibilities to develop power-to-gas plants commercially is to integrate them in the refinery process. This will be discussed below.

4.3. INTEGRATING POWER-TO-GAS IN REFINERIES

Refineries are large consumers of hydrogen in Germany. The use of 'green' hydrogen could make the refinery sector more sustainable. It should be noted that chemically the refinery process will not be affected by the use of green hydrogen as it does not make any difference whether the refinery products have been produced whilst using 'green' hydrogen or conventional hydrogen. The use of 'green' hydrogen (instead of hydrogen produced from natural gas) for desulphurisation in the refinery process nevertheless has several environmental, economic and technical advantages. A conversion to 'green' hydrogen will not affect the refinery's installations as the existing infrastructure and engines can be used without any changes. Be that as it may, initially 'green' hydrogen will not be able to completely substitute all conventionally produced hydrogen as the interaction between 'green' and conventional hydrogen production must be tested in order to gradually increase the proportion of 'green' hydrogen. Given the uncertainty in the availability of 'green' hydrogen as a result of the increasing amount of fluctuating renewable electricity production, it will also be necessary to develop possibilities to store 'green' hydrogen as the refinery's requirement for hydrogen remains constant.

In order to further investigate the use of 'green' hydrogen in the refinery sector, Uniper and BP signed a cooperation agreement in 2016, which aims at investigating the possibilities of using Uniper's power-to-gas technology in

32 See ibid, 5.

BP's refinery at Lingen.[33] Both companies have agreed to jointly examine the technical and economic feasibility of power-to-gas for the Lingen plant whilst taking into account the technical conditions, the dimensions of the site, the choice of electrolysis technology and the optimal technical and operational concept for the system. Apart from the technical and economic feasibility of a power-to-gas plant at BP's Lingen refinery, this project will also assess the applicable legal framework.

5. LEGAL FRAMEWORK AND CHALLENGES

5.1. INTRODUCTION

'Green' hydrogen can play an important role in realising the intended energy transition. In refineries the use of green hydrogen has numerous advantages as it enables the integration of renewable energy sources in this fossil fuel dominated sector, as well as a reduction of CO_2 emissions. The power-to-gas technology, however, is a new and innovative technology and is therefore currently more costly than using traditional hydrogen. As the power-to-gas process and the production of 'green' hydrogen is not yet regulated, we will discuss below how this development fits within the regulatory framework and how its use can be incentivised. For this purpose we need to take into account that the refinery sector is both a large energy consumer and an energy producer. We will therefore consider the impact that 'green' hydrogen may have on refinery process itself and the impact it has on the end product: the fuel. Finally we will discuss possible new legislative developments.

5.2. THE IMPACT ON THE REFINERIES' ENERGY CONSUMPTION

Refineries are large energy consumers principally using fossil fuels. As a result, the industry is subject to, amongst others, the Industrial Emissions Directive, the Air Quality Directive and the EU Emissions Trading System (EU ETS). Whereas the Industrial Emissions Directive[34] aims at reducing harmful industrial emissions (other than CO_2 emissions), in particular through the application

33 See: https://www.bp.com/de_de/germany/presse/pressemeldungen/2016-pm-kooperation-bp-uniper.html.

34 Directive 2010/75/EU and replaces several directives, including the Large Combustion Plant Directive (2001/80/EC) and the Integrated Pollution Prevention and Control Directive (2008/1/EC).

of Best Available Techniques (BAT), the Air Quality Directive[35] provides new air quality objectives for fine particles ($PM_{2.5}$) and rules concerning reference methods, data validation and location of sampling points for the assessment of ambient air quality.[36] Both directives apply to the refinery sector and have a considerable impact as they have led to a 44% decrease in sulphur emissions in the EU already in the period 2004–12.[37]

One of the challenges identified in section 3.3 above is the impact on the refinery sector of the EU ETS. This regime has applied since 2003[38] and aims at reducing by 20% CO_2 emissions by 2020. It involves all industrial installations, including refineries. Each emitter is entitled to a specific number of allowances, which were initially awarded free of charge but increasingly need to be bought on the market. The EU ETS requires each CO_2 emitter to surrender annually as many allowances as necessary to cover its actual emissions. Any surplus of allowances or any shortage can be sold and bought on the market. The system is based on the key assumption that as emissions allowances become more expensive, the emitters will turn to other, less polluting techniques. This, however, requires a scarcity in allowances and so far over-allocation of allowances has created the opposite effect.[39] As long as the price of these allowances is too low to cover additional costs of developing new techniques and/or producing innovative products like 'green' hydrogen, there is no real incentive to do so. In 2017, for example, the price of a CO_2 allowance fluctuated from €4.5 to €8.[40] In 2018 the price increased to €14 and it will probably rise even more because less allowances will be available following new rules for the EU ETS that will apply to the period 2021–30 and to which the European Parliament and Council agreed in November 2017.[41] Depending on the price of CO_2 emissions allowances, the switch from fossil-based hydrogen to 'green' hydrogen is a means of limiting CO_2 emissions and could result in a situation where refineries could sell their surplus of allowances on the market.

Implementing legislation in Germany is included in the Federal Immission Control Act and the Greenhouse Gas Emissions Trading Act (GGETA).[42]

---

35 Directive 2008/50/EC merges four directives and one Council decision into a single directive on air quality.

36 See Directive 2015/1480/ec amending several annexes of directive 2004/107/EC and directive 2008/107/EC.

37 JRC Science for Policy Report – EU Petroleum Refining Fitness Check: Impact of EU Legislation on Sectoral Economic Performance, 2015, p 243.

38 Directive 2003/87/EC as most recently amended by Directive 2009/29/EC.

39 E Woerdman, 'The EU Greenhouse Gas Emissions Trading Scheme' in E Woerdman, MM Roggenkamp and M Holwerdan, *Essential EU Climate Law*, Edward Elgar, Cheltenham 2015, p 65.

40 See: http://markets.businessinsider.com/commodities/co2-emissionsrechte.

41 See: https://ec.europa.eu/clima/policies/ets/revision_en.

42 *Bundesimmissionsschutzgesetz*, 15 March 1974, revised version published on 26 September 2002 (BGBl I, 3830), as amended and *Gesetz über den Handel mit Berechtigungen zur Emission von Treibhausgasen*, 21 July 2011 (BGBl I, 1475), as amended.

Both acts provide for a licensing regime for installations emitting hazardous substances. Initially these emission permits were granted under the Federal Pollution Control Act.[43] Since 1 January 2013 GGETTA has provided for a new type of permit, although this is still issued under the Federal Pollution Control Act as before.

5.3. THE IMPACT ON THE REFINERIES END-PRODUCT: TRANSPORT FUELS

One of the main refinery products is transport fuel like LPG, petrol, kerosene, jet fuel, diesel oil and fuel oils. Using these fuels leads to considerable greenhouse gas emissions and reducing these emissions in the transport sector has proven to be a real challenge. In 2017 the EU published its Clean Mobility Package, which amongst other things aims at making the transport sector more sustainable by developing cleaner vehicles and alternative fuels infrastructure.[44] This package does not specifically focus on the need to make the transport fuels more sustainable. For this purpose the EU has developed legislation since 1998 regulating the quality of transport fuel, ie more specifically, it provided for specifications of fuel types like petrol/gasoline, diesel and fuel oil. The next section will discuss the EU law governing fuel quality and the attempts to make transport fuels more sustainable by blending them with biofuels. Thereafter it discusses the option to make use of the power-to-gas technique to improve sustainability.

5.3.1. Regulating Fuel Quality

Currently, fuel quality is governed by the Fuel Quality Directive (FQD), which specifically governs the quality of gasoline, diesel and gasoil fuels.[45] The FQD requires a reduction of the greenhouse gas intensity of the fuels used in vehicles by 6% by 2020. The greenhouse gas intensity of fuels is calculated on a life-cycle basis, meaning that the emissions from the extraction, as well as the processing and the distribution of fuels, are taken into account. Direct life-cycle greenhouse gas emission reductions are calculated from a 2010 baseline of fossil fuel greenhouse gas intensity. The 6% reduction target can be achieved in several ways such as the use of biofuels and electricity, as well as the use of less carbon

---

43 *Bundesimmissionsschutzgesetz*, 15 March 1974, revised version published on 26 September 2002 (BGBl I, 3830), as amended.

44 See: https://ec.europa.eu/transport/modes/road/news/2017-11-08-driving-clean-mobility_en.

45 Directive 2009/30/EC of 23 April 2009 amending Directive 98/70/EC as regards the specification of petrol, diesel and gas-oil and introducing a mechanism to monitor and reduce greenhouse gas emissions and amending Council Directive 1999/32/EC as regards the specification of fuel used by inland waterway vessels and repealing Directive 93/12/EEC.

intense, often gaseous, fossil fuels.[46] As before, the directive aims at setting technical specifications for transport fuels. In order to be able to assess these performance standards, the FQD has also introduced a regime of monitoring, reporting and verification of the greenhouse gas intensity of the fuel.[47]

For this purpose it obliges Member States to designate the supplier or suppliers responsible for monitoring and reporting life-cycle greenhouse gas emissions per unit of energy from fuel and energy supplied. These suppliers shall report annually to a designated authority on the greenhouse gas intensity of fuel and energy supplied within each Member State and Member States must ensure that these reports are subject to verification. These reports should at least provide information with regard to: (i) the total volume of each type of fuel or energy supplied, indicating where purchased and its origin; and (ii) life-cycle greenhouse gas emissions per unit of energy. Moreover, if necessary, the European Commission may add supplementary measures with regards to, inter alia, the methodology for the calculation of life-cycle greenhouse gas emissions from fuels other than biofuels and from energy.[48]

The use of biofuels is regulated by Directive 2009/28/EC (RES directive), which governs the promotion of the use of energy from renewable sources. It also requires that Member States achieve by 2020, in a cost-effective way, a mandatory 10% target for the share of biofuels in transport petrol and diesel consumption. The biofuels need to meet some specific sustainability criteria and are subject to a reporting and verification process.[49] These sustainability criteria relate to the greenhouse gas emission reduction targets[50] as well as the raw materials for biofuels.[51] As the RES directive and the FQD are both part of the EU's energy and climate package (presenting the 20-20-20 goals), the directives have been aligned and the provisions regarding biofuels are identical in both directives. Last but not least, the FQD also allows for adequate levels of blending. However, there are some technical limitations to a further increase of the share of biofuel. Limits to the level of blending may arise in terms of compliance with the fuel parameters, as well as with compatibility with the installations and the engines.

---

46 In addition, it is important to reduce the fuel's sulphur content. Although generally the refinery sector has been able to meet the desulphurisation targets, it has also become clear that further measures for desulphurisation will require more energy and higher investments, ie higher total operating costs.

47 Art 7a FQD. See for such additional measures Directive 2015/652/EC, which defines the calculation methods and the details for reporting the greenhouse intensity of the fuels.

48 Art 7a para 5 sub a FQD. Such additional measures shall be adopted in accordance with the regulatory procedure referred to in Art 11(4) FQD.

49 Arts 17–19 RES Directive.

50 The greenhouse gas emissions must be at least 35% lower than from the fossil fuel they replace. From 2017, this will increase to 50%, and from 2018, the saving must be at least 60% for new installations.

51 These raw materials cannot be sourced from land with high biodiversity or high carbon stock.

In Germany, the Federal Immission Control Act (*Bundesimmissionsschutzgesetz* or BImSchG) of 1 January 2015[52] provides for a regime aiming at the reduction of greenhouse gas emissions in the fuel sector and replaces the earlier biofuels blending obligation of the 2007 Biofuel Quota Act. Consequently, suppliers of petrol and diesel fuel no longer need to blend a specified amount of biofuels measured by their energy content but need to add so much biofuel that a specifically defined reduction of the fuels' greenhouse gas emissions is achieved. Article 37d of the Federal Immission Control Act (BImSchG) also provides for the possibility that the Federal Ministry for the Environment (*Umweltministerium*) can support innovations in the field of alternative fuels and their production by counting these innovations against the greenhouse gas emissions reduction target. By Ordinance of 15 May 2017, use is made of this provision.[53] It explicitly states that greenhouse gas emissions reductions could be achieved by including fuels in the supply mix which have electricity as their feedstock.[54] In order to further decrease the greenhouse gas intensity of transport fuels and given some of the constraints of using biofuels, the refinery sector considers this Ordinance as a basis to consider green hydrogen in the refinery process as a means to make transport fuels more sustainable.[55]

5.3.2. Power-to-Gas as a Means to Reduce the Greenhouse Gas Intensity of Transport Fuels

In order to incentivise further greenhouse gas emission reductions, the FQD explicitly states that savings claimed from upstream emission reductions should be included in the calculation of suppliers' life-cycle greenhouse gas emissions.[56] Upstream emissions are defined as 'all greenhouse gas emissions occurring prior to the raw material entering a refinery or a processing plant where the fuel, as referred to in Annex I, was produced'.[57] For hydrogen sourced from electrolysis powered by non-biological renewable energy sources ('green' hydrogen), a life-cycle greenhouse gas intensity value is only provided for (i) hydrogen used in fuel cells and (ii) hydrogen processed in a 'Sabatier process' (reaction of hydrogen with carbon dioxide).[58]

---

52 See: https://www.gesetze-im-internet.de/bimschg.

53 Ordinance on the allocation of electricity-based fuels and co-processed biogenic oils to the greenhouse gas quota (*Verordnung zur Anrechnung von strombasierten Kraftstoffen und mitverarbeiteten biogenen Ölen auf die Treibhausgasquote*).

54 Art 3(1), Regulation on the allocation of electricity-based fuels and co-processed biogenic oils to the greenhouse gas quota of 15 May 2017.

55 See T Eickelkamp and R Brandis, 'Potenzial und Regelungsbedarf für Power-to-Gas in Raffinerien' *Energiewirtschaftliche Tagesfragen* (2017) 1(2), pp. 1–5.

56 Recital (3) Directive 2015/652/EC. Directive 2015/652/EC provides further rules with regard to the calculation methods and reporting requirements as required by Art 7 FQD.

57 Art 2 Directive 2015/652.

58 Annex I part 2 para 5 Directive 2015/652, p 5. See: https://ec.europa.eu/clima/sites/clima/files/guidance_note_on_uer_en.pdf.

Hence, the use of 'green' hydrogen for the transport sector seems to be limited to vehicles using hydrogen as a fuel source. The possibility to use 'green' hydrogen in the refinery process is not included and thus cannot be taken into account when calculating the transport fuels greenhouse gas emissions reductions. This assumption is confirmed in the 'Guidance Note' issued in 2016, which states explicitly that 'reductions in greenhouse gas emissions in the production of hydrogen to be used in the production of fuel in refineries cannot be considered as upstream emissions reductions for the purpose of Council Directive 2015/652/EC irrespective of where the hydrogen is physically produced'.[59] Although Directive 2015/652/EC provides for the possibility to amend Annex I in order to include the power-to-gas technology by refineries to the list of 'accepted' alternative technologies,[60] the European Commission has not made use of this possibility and concluded in May 2017 that there is no need for legislative amendments to the FQD as it aims at regulating the uptake of low-emission and renewable fuels for the period 2021–30 under the (recast) Renewable Energy Directive.[61] Apart from this it can be questioned whether the use of green hydrogen within a life-cycle approach can be considered an 'upstream activity'. However, even if 'green' hydrogen could be considered an upstream activity, in a life-cycle approach this could result in a situation of double counting of greenhouse gas emissions reduction as such reduction is also key to the EU ETS.

5.4. FUTURE DEVELOPMENTS

The decarbonisation of the transport sector is high on the political agenda as greenhouse gas emission reductions in this sector have proven difficult to achieve. It is therefore not surprising that the EU Commission addresses this issue in the proposal to amend the RES Directive, which is part of the earlier-mentioned 'Winter Package' or 'Clean Energy Package' presented by the EU Commission in November 2016.[62] This proposal provides more stringent rules with regard to the use of biofuels as it provides for new targets for the blending of biofuels and for sustainability criteria to be applied to biofuels.[63] In addition, it also recognises

---

59 Guidance note on approaches to quantify, verify, validate, monitor and report upstream emission reductions.

60 The European Commission had to issue such a proposal before 31 December 2017 and after consulting all EU Member States.

61 'Report from the Commission to the European Parliament and the Council in accordance with Article 9 of Directive 98/70/EC relating to the quality of petrol and diesel fuels' of 31 May 2017, COM(2017) 284 final.

62 See above footnote 7.

63 See Art 25 of the proposed Recast Directive. This provision states, inter alia, that the minimum share of biofuels in 2021 should be 1.5% and 6.8% in 2030 according to a trajectory set out in part B of Annex X.

the use of power-to-gas technologies as a means to developing more sustainable transport fuels.[64] Apart from this, the Commission also – indirectly – supports the development of power-to-gas as far as this technique is used as a potential option for electricity storage,[65] or as a means to be used in the gas supply sector.

6. CONCLUSION

Power-to-gas is a new technology which looks set to play a significant role in the energy transition process in the EU and Germany. It enables an efficient use of excess volumes of electricity from renewable energy sources. Instead of 'dumping' electricity on the market, this technique enables a conversion to a gaseous source such as 'hydrogen'. This hydrogen can be used for a variety of reasons but it can also serve as a means to store electricity. Most power-to-gas projects can be found in Germany. The reason for this may be the high volumes of electricity from renewable energy sources that need to be accommodated and the very early and strong interest in a process of energy transition (*Energiewende*).

This chapter discussed the role of power-to-gas in the refinery sector, which relies heavily on the use of hydrogen. Instead of using hydrogen from fossil fuels, power-to-gas may provide for a green alternative if use is made of renewable energy sources. Therefore, 'green' hydrogen could lead to almost 100% lower greenhouse gas emissions compared to hydrogen produced from fossil fuels. Also in the refinery sector, the technique could serve as a (short-term) storage option. When using 'green' hydrogen directly in the industrial process, it will also reduce some of the efficiency losses that would otherwise arise from any re-electrification of the hydrogen. Finally, this technique is relevant as it links several economic sectors. Apart from linking the electricity and gas sectors, it may also link the electricity and the transport sectors as it may assist in producing a more environmentally friendly fuel by incorporating hydrogen from renewable energy sources.

The environmental impact of using 'green' hydrogen is undisputed. Replacing hydrogen from fossil fuels with 'green' hydrogen will result in considerable greenhouse gas emissions reduction in the overall refining process. As a result, the refineries will be able to sell the 'unused' emission allowances on the market. In addition, this chapter also discussed whether power-to-gas could potentially be an end-of-pipe technology. Since the transport sector is one

64 Art 25 of the proposed Recast Directive explicitly refers to the use of 'gaseous transport fuels of non-biological origin'.

65 See also R Fleming and JP Fershee, 'The "Hydrogen Economy" in the United States and the European Union: Regulating Innovation to Combat Climate Change' in D Zillman, MM Roggenkamp, L Paddock and L Godden (eds), *Innovation in Energy Law and Technology: Dynamic Solutions for Energy Transitions*, OUP, Oxford 2018, pp 137–53.

of the major greenhouse gas emitters, some innovations are needed to reduce such emissions. Whereas EU policy is focusing on the introduction of electric cars (potentially by using hydrogen fuel cells) and the possibility of blending biofuels with 'traditional' transport fuels, it has been assessed whether the use of power-to-gas in the refining processes could be considered as a means to create more sustainable transport fuels. For this purpose it will be necessary to rely on the life-cycle approach as indicated in the FQD. However, the use of green hydrogen in the desulphurisation process does not change the carbon intensity of the transport fuel and thus also does not change the emissions in the transport sector. It is therefore not surprising that the European Commission has not classified this technology as an upstream emissions reduction. If it had done so, this would have led to double counting as the use of green hydrogen also leads to less CO_2 emissions reductions. Given the long term advantages of power-to-gas with regard to the process of energy transition, there is nevertheless a need for a more elaborate legal framework governing power-to-gas, including its role in the refinery sector.

CHAPTER XIII
SECURITY OF GAS SUPPLY
The New European Approach

Ruven FLEMING

1. INTRODUCTION

The EU introduced a new security of gas supply regulation in November 2017,[1] which replaces the security of gas supply regulation of 2010.[2] It is only the second regulation on gas security of supply that the EU has ever issued. Before that, gas security of supply was mainly governed by the light-touch rules of Directive 2004/67[3] and was considered to be largely provided for by the principles governing the internal European energy market.[4]

This notion changed considerably with the 2006 and 2009 Russia–Ukraine gas crises, which had a detrimental effect on the amount of gas that was received in Europe, causing, inter alia, Italian and German gas-fired power plants to shut

1 Regulation (EU) 2017/1938 of the European Parliament and of the Council of 25 October 2017 concerning measures to safeguard the security of gas supply and repealing Regulation (EU) No 994/2010 [2017] OJ L280/1 (hereinafter: Regulation (EU) 2017/1938).

2 Regulation (EU) 994/2010 of 20 October 2010 concerning measures to safeguard security of gas supply and repealing Council Directive 2004/67/EC [2010] OJ L 295/1 (hereinafter: Regulation (EU) 994/2010).

3 Directive 2004/67/EC of 26 April 2004 concerning measures to safeguard security of natural gas supply [2004] OJ L127/92. Directive 2004/67 was the first attempt to deal with the issue of security of gas supply, but did not succeed, partly due to its nature as a Directive (and thus not immediately applicable and enforceable in the Member States' national law).

4 See, eg, preamble 22 and Arts 1(32), 3(5) and (7) or Art 5 Directive 2009/73/EC of 13 July 2009 concerning common rules for the internal market in natural gas and repealing Directive 2003/55/EC.

down.[5] Subsequently, Regulation 994/2010 was put into place as an explicit response to the crises.[6]

The new Regulation (EU) 2017/1938 is the successor to Regulation 994/2010 and is supposed to deal with the latter's perceived shortcomings. Many instruments of the predecessor Regulation (EU) 994/2010 will stay in place unchanged and those have been discussed elsewhere.[7] This contribution will therefore focus on the innovations and changes being brought in by Regulation (EU) 2017/1938.

After providing a background on the development of Regulation (EU) 2017/1938, the chapter will make some remarks on its structure and aims. The chapter then focusses on the main innovation of Regulation (EU) 2017/1938, the imposition of obligatory solidarity between Member States in a gas crisis. This is to be achieved by two means: first, directly connected Member States are being clustered into so-called risk groups, and second, the new Article 13 of Regulation (EU) 2017/1938, which spells out concrete solidarity measures that Member States have to take in case of an emergency.

2. BACKGROUND

The EU deemed it necessary to introduce a new security of gas supply regulation after the Commission investigated the implementation of Regulation (EU) 994/2010 in October 2014. Although the EU insists that the old Regulation (EU) 994/2010 had a 'significant positive impact' on the security of gas supply in the Union,[8] the October 2014 report[9] identified areas in which improvements could further bolster the security of gas supplies to the Union.

---

5 J Stern, 'The Russian-Ukraine Gas Crisis of January 2006', Oxford Institute for Energy Studies, 2006, pp 9, 14; S Pirani, J Stern and K Yafimava. 'The Russo-Ukrainian Gas Dispute of January 2009: A Comprehensive Assessment', Oxford Institute for Energy Studies, 2008, pp 8, 19–25, 55; M Neumann, H Pleines and H Schröder, 'Russland Analysen Erdgaskonflikt mit der Ukraine' [2009] 176 Forschungsstelle Osteuropa an der Universität Bremen available at: http://www.laender-analysen.de/russland/pdf/Russlandanalysen176.pdf, pp 4–5.

6 European Commission, Commission Staff Working Document accompanying to the Proposal for a Regulation of the European Parliament and of the Council concerning measures to safeguard security of gas supply and repealing Directive 2004/67/EC 'The January 2009 Gas Supply Disruption to the EU: An Assessment' COM (2009) 977 final p 7.

7 SM Goldberg, 'Chapter IV Regulation 994/2010: A Measure to Improve The Security of Gas Supply in The EU?' in MM Roggenkamp and U Hammer, *European Energy Law Report VIII*, Intersentia, Cambridge 2011, pp 61–92 (hereinafter: Goldberg); SM Goldberg, 'Security of Supply in the Context of European Energy Market Liberalisation – a Brief Overview' (2011) International Business Law Journal 4, 433-62 in particular 438 *et seq*.

8 Preamble 4 of the new Regulation (EU) 2017/1938. The preamble is referencing the E-Directive (Directive 2009/72/EC of the European Parliament and of the Council of 13 July 2009 concerning common rules for the internal market in electricity and repealing

At the same time the European Network of Transmission Network Operators for Gas (ENTSO-G)[10] conducted a gas 'stress test' on the functioning of the gas infrastructure in Europe and the results were published in the same document on the same day in October 2014.[11] The results highlighted that purely national approaches are not very effective in the event of severe disruption.[12] In particular, a reiteration of the Russian–Ukrainian gas crises of 2006 and 2009, or a technical failure of equipment that causes gas supply via Ukraine to stop, would have severe impacts on East and South-East European Member States.[13]

But ENTSO-G did not stop at making this and other assessments. They also demonstrated how a more cooperative approach among Member States could significantly reduce the impact of very severe gas disruptions in the most vulnerable Member States, according to their geographic location and gas sourcing options.[14] The Commission is explicitly referring to this when justifying the introduction of Regulation (EU) 2017/1938 in its preamble.[15]

The Commission further underpins its decision to introduce a new security of gas supply regulation by reference to the Energy Union Strategy of 25 February 2015, which highlighted that an Energy Union, initially set up to give the EU

Directive 2003/54/EC (OJ L 211, 14 August 2009, p 55)), the G-Directive (Directive 2009/73/EC of the European Parliament and of the Council of 13 July 2009 concerning common rules for the internal market in natural gas and repealing Directive 2003/55/EC (OJ L 211, 14 August 2009, p 94)), the ACER-Regulation (Regulation (EC) No 713/2009 of the European Parliament and of the Council of 13 July 2009 establishing an Agency for the Cooperation of Energy Regulators (OJ L 211, 14 August 2009, p 1)), the E-Regulation (Regulation (EC) No 714/2009 of the European Parliament and of the Council of 13 July 2009 on conditions for access to the network for cross-border exchanges in electricity and repealing Regulation (EC) No 1228/2003 (OJ L 211, 14 August 2009, p 15)), the G-Regulation (Regulation (EC) No 715/2009 of the European Parliament and of the Council of 13 July 2009 on conditions for access to the natural gas transmission networks and repealing Regulation (EC) No 1775/2005 (OJ L 211, 14 August 2009, p 36)) and Regulation 994/2010 (Regulation (EU) No 994/2010 of the European Parliament and of the Council of 20 October 2010 concerning measures to safeguard security of gas supply and repealing Council Directive 2004/67/EC (OJ L 295, 12 November 2010, p 1)).

9 Commission Staff Working Document, 'Report on the implementation of Regulation (EU) 994/2010 and its contribution to solidarity and preparedness for gas disruptions in the EU' SWD(2014) 325 final (hereinafter: SWD Gas Security 2014).

10 ENTSO-G is the European Network of Transmission Network Operators for Gas, which aims to enhance cooperation between national gas transmission system operators (TSOs) across Europe in order to ensure the development of a pan-European transmission system in line with European Union energy goals. For details see http://www.entsog.eu.

11 Commission and Council 'Communication on the short term resilience of the European gas system Preparedness for a possible disruption of supplies from the East during the fall and winter of 2014/2015' SWD(2014) 322–26 final (hereinafter: Stress Test 2014).

12 Stress Test 2014 at 17–18; SWD Gas Security 2014 at 15 and 17.

13 Stress Test 2014 at 7–9.

14 Ibid.

15 Preamble 5 Regulation (EU) 2017/1938.

one common voice towards Russia, depends on solidarity and trust as necessary features of energy security.[16] Indeed, this 2015 document explicitly states that

> Solidarity among Member States, in particular in times of supply crisis, has to be strengthened. These issues and the experience gained in the implementation of the Regulation will be taken into account when proposing a revision of the Security of Gas Supply Regulation.[17]

This is what the European Commission subsequently did by launching a first draft proposal in February 2016,[18] which focused very much on solidarity and which went on to eventually become Regulation (EU) 2017/1938 roughly one and a half years later.

3. STRUCTURE AND AIMS OF REGULATION 2017/1938

The structure of Regulation (EU) 2017/1938 follows from the fact that the main instruments of its predecessor Regulation (EU) 994/2010 have been preserved and transferred to the new Regulation.[19] However, the structure of the new document has been streamlined and now flows more logically than that of its predecessor.

Article 1 Regulation (EU) 2017/1938 provides the overall aims of the Regulation, which have not changed much when compared to the predecessor Regulation. Security of gas supply, in the view of the European Union, is primarily linked to the proper functioning of the internal gas market.[20] However, the Regulation allows for exceptional measures if the market can no longer deliver the amount of gas that is required. The Regulation provides a clear definition and attribution of responsibilities and provides for

16 Preamble 6 Regulation (EU) 2017/1938; Commission Communication, 'A Framework Strategy for a Resilient Energy Union with a Forward-Looking Climate Change Policy' COM(2015) 80 final at 4 (hereinafter: Energy Union).

17 Energy Union para 2.1.

18 Commission. 'Proposal for a Regulation of the European Parliament and of the Council concerning measures to safeguard the security of gas supply and repealing Regulation (EU) No 994/2010' COM (2016) 52 final (hereinafter: first draft and explanatory memorandum).

19 For example, Art 3 (responsibility for the security of gas supply) is now followed by Art 4 on the Gas Coordination Group (which was discussed only at the end of the old Regulation in Art 12). Furthermore, infrastructure and the gas supply standard have been brought more to the fore in this Regulation and directly follow each other (they were Arts 6 and 8 and are now Arts 5 and 6 in the new regulation). The risk assessments, which function as a central tool for mitigating security of gas supply risks, have been moved closer to the start of the Regulation (was Art 9, now Art 7) and finally, emergency plans and the declaration of a crisis level, two distinct things that used to be part of the same Article have now been split over two Articles (was Art 10, now Arts 10 and 11).

20 Art 1 Regulation (EU) 2017/1938.

coordination of planning and responses to emergencies at national, regional and Union levels.[21]

The new Article 3 is key to understanding Regulation (EU) 2017/1938, as it establishes responsibilities for the security of gas supply. In general the three-level approach of Regulation (EU) 994/2010 is retained, which allocates responsibility for the security of gas supplies first to the relevant natural gas undertakings (and electricity undertakings where appropriate); second, to the Member States; and third, to the Union.[22] An interesting detail here is the inclusion of electricity undertakings in the chain of responsible actors, as they were not included in the old Regulation (EU) 994/2010.

This is part of a bigger mission of the Commission to bring electricity undertakings and industry more within the scope of the new security of gas supplies Regulation (EU) 2017/1938.[23] With these measures the Commission is trying to pre-empt a future where more gas-fired power plants are built/running in Europe so that large amounts of gas would be needed for electricity production, which in turn would need to be secured on the markets. These additional amounts of gas could make any gas crisis worse.

Alongside the three main actors, the three different levels of crisis have also been maintained (early warning, alert and emergency level) and are now established as a separate Article, new Article 11 Regulation (EU) 2017/1938. However, there is an interesting change in the question of who is eligible to declare a crisis level. Under the old Article 10(5) Regulation (EU) 994/2010 only Competent Authorities were allowed to do this. Under the new Regulation (EU) 2017/1938, the Competent Authorities can delegate certain important tasks, including the declaration of a crisis level, to TSOs, DSOs or other public authorities.[24,25] In case of delegation, the Competent Authorities then have

21 Ibid.

22 Compare Art 3(1) and (4) Regulation (EU) 994/2010 to Art 3(1) and (4) Regulation (EU) 2017/1938.

23 There are a number of examples for the inclusion of electricity into the gas security of supply Regulation (EU) 2017/1938. Art 5(8) Regulation (EU) 2017/1938 for instance prescribes that the integration between electricity and gas systems shall be taken into consideration when searching for bottlenecks and assessing the impacts of the failure of the single largest gas infrastructure. A further example is the fact that electricity producers have to be consulted to draw up preventive gas action and gas emergency plans, see Art 8(2) Regulation (EU) 2017/1938. Moreover, the preventive gas action plans under Art 9 Regulation (EU) 2017/1938 must include a definition of protected customer and, again, electricity undertakings are now included in the list of entities on which an obligation can be imposed in case of a crisis, see Art 9(1)(b) Regulation (EU) 2017/1938. The provisions on emergency plans include similar alterations: electricity (TSO for electricity where relevant) has been included in the preparation phase of the plan, an integrated view of the operation of energy systems across electricity and gas has to be adopted and electricity undertakings can have reporting obligations, see Art 10(1)(b), (l), (k) Regulation (EU) 2017/1938.

24 Art 3(2) Regulation (EU) 2017/1938.

25 Art 11(2) Regulation (EU) 2017/1938.

to supervise, for example, the TSO and the delegation must be made explicit in the preventive action and the emergency plan.[26] However, the Competent Authorities remain in charge of declaring the end of a crisis level and must inform the Commission and Competent Authorities and directly connected Member States of their decision.[27]

4. RISK GROUPS AND THE SOLIDARITY MECHANISM: THE TWO NEW MAIN FEATURES OF REGULATION (EU) 2017/1938

At the heart of the new Regulation (EU) 2017/1938 lie two main features. On the one hand the Regulation is introducing the concept of risk groups for gas supply threats, on the other hand a new solidarity mechanism for gas crises is being introduced. Section 4.1 below discusses the risk groups, whilst the new solidarity mechanism is assessed in section 4.2.

4.1. RISK GROUPS

4.1.1. The Creation of Risk Groups

The first major innovation of Regulation (EU) 2017/1938 is the creation of risk groups for gas supply. The risk groups have been established on the basis of gas supply routes, supply country risks and the cohesion of capabilities to exchange gas.[28] The main criterion for grouping countries together was, hence, whether or not they have a common supplier of gas and a common gas supply route.[29] As a consequence, only directly interconnected Member States have been clustered into gas supply risk groups.[30] These risk groups are to serve as the basis for enhanced regional cooperation and agreement on effective cross-border measures.[31]

Annex I of Regulation (EU) 2017/1938 establishes 13 risk groups, clustered into four categories (Eastern Gas, North Sea Gas, North African Gas and South-East Gas). Countries can be part of several risk groups across different

26 Art 3(1) and (2) Regulation (EU) 2017/1938.

27 Art 11(8) Regulation (EU) 2017/1938.

28 European Parliament, 'Briefing EU Legislation in Progress New rules on security of gas supply November 2017', p 7, available at: http://www.europarl.europa.eu/RegData/etudes/BRIE/2017/608810/EPRS_BRI(2017)608810_EN.pdf.

29 Preamble 12 Regulation 2017/1938.

30 Art 3(7) Regulation (EU) 2017/1938.

31 Ibid.

categories.[32] To give an example: the Netherlands is included, on the one hand, in the category 'Eastern Gas' in the risk groups concerning deliveries via

- Belarus and
- the Baltic Sea

But at the same time it is also included in the category 'North Sea gas' concerning

- Norway
- low-calorific gas and
- Denmark

This reflects the reality of gas supplies to and in Europe, which will often come from very different sources. For North-West Europe, there is an interesting feature in Annex I 2 (b) Regulation (EU) 2017/1938: a low-calorific gas risk group has been created, consisting of Belgium, Germany, France and the Netherlands. Given the Dutch Government's recent decision to completely shut down Europe's only significant source of low-calorific gas, the Groningen gas field, by 2030, this seems sensible.[33] If deliveries of low-calorific gas from the Groningen gas field to other countries comes to an end, it is due diligence to create a particular risk group around this energy carrier, although it is not concerned with gas imports into the Union.

The starting point for the idea of having obligatory gas supply risk groups was ENTSO-G's 2014 gas 'stress test',[34] discussed earlier. In the resulting 2014 report on the implementation of Regulation (EU) 994/2010, the Commission painted a gloomy picture of the functioning of regional cooperation mechanisms in a gas crisis, stating that 'the main weakness so far, however, has been that Risk Assessments and Plans have remained nationally focussed only and that the co-ordination between Member States has overall been poor'.[35]

---

32 European Parliament, 'Briefing EU Legislation in Progress New rules on security of gas supply November 2017', p 7 available at: http://www.europarl.europa.eu/RegData/etudes/BRIE/2017/608810/EPRS_BRI(2017)608810_EN.pdf.

33 For the Government's decision see Kamerstukken II 2017/2018, 33529, no. 457, pp 1 and 7; for the history of the Groningen gas field see MM Roggenkamp, 'Reducing Gas Production from the Groningen Field: The Need to Balance Safe Production with Supply Security' in MM Roggenkamp and C Banet (eds), *European Energy Law Report Volume XI* Intersentia, Cambridge 2017, pp 301–16.

34 Communication from the Commission to the European Parliament and the Council on the short term resilience of the European gas system, Preparedness for a possible disruption of supplies from the East during the fall and winter of 2014/2015, COM (2014) 654 final (hereinafter: Stress Test 2014).

35 SWD Gas Security 2014 at 16.

This part of the report ended with a bleak assessment of the Commission's current powers and a pledge for action by the European Union:

> The Commission's tools to co-ordinate actions are under the existing Regulation limited and the absence of Risk Assessments and Plans co-ordinated between Member States at regional level further complicate its overall co-ordination task at EU level significantly. In the context of a review of the Security of Supply Regulation, the Commission services intend to explore how the regional cooperation between Member States can be fostered, for example by replacing national Risk Assessments and Plans by regional ones. The lack of exchange on the Plans so far suggests that mandatory consultations between Member States may not be sufficient in this regard.[36]

In the first draft of the new security of gas supplies Regulation, dated February 2016, the Commission initially proposed nine risk groups,[37] but the Member States immediately began to oppose this. Five Member States (Austria, Belgium, France, Germany and Italy) were particularly critical.[38] They argued that the risk groups and the underlying regional approach to gas security of supply were not suitable to addressing gas emergencies efficiently, due to the great variety of roles, some more important than others, that gas plays in the different energy mixes of Member States.[39]

One can gain a clear impression of the tensions by the debate of the proposal in the two chambers of the Italian parliament. For instance, the Italian parliament was critical of preamble 12 of Regulation 2017/1938, which proposes the creation of risk groups on the basis of major transnational risks to security of gas supply. That is to say, it is clustering Member States into risk groups on the basis of main gas supply sources and along main gas supply routes. Italian politicians, however, highlighted how the region in which Italy was initially included did not respect these criteria in view of existing interconnections and the possibility of pooling resources and balancing risks for security of gas supply across the region.[40] Among the four other States included in the proposed South-East Region, one – Slovenia – was exempted from the infrastructure standard,[41] which

---

36 Ibid at 17.

37 First Draft and explanatory memorandum.

38 Bloomberg.com, 'Five Western EU Countries Seek to Soften Gas Security Proposal' (8 April 2016) available at: https://www.bloomberg.com/news/articles/2016-04-08/five-western-eu-countries-seek-to-soften-gas-security-proposal.

39 NaturalgasEurope.com, 'Belgium Wary of EU Gas Security Proposal' (18 April 2016) available at: https://www.naturalgasworld.com/belgium-wary-of-eu-gas-security-proposal-29085.

40 Senato della Repubblica Italiana 'Legislatura 17ª 14ª Commissione permanente, Resoconto sommario n. 186 del 27/04/2016, Proposta di Regolamento del Parlamento europeo e del Consiglio concernente misure volte a garantire la sicurezza dell'approvvigionamento di gas e che abroga il Regolamento (UE) n. 994/2010 del Consiglio, COM (2016) 52 final' available at: https://www.senato.it/japp/bgt/showdoc/frame.jsp?tipodoc=SommComm&leg=17&id=00971308&part=doc_dc-sedetit_isc-genbl_sadg&parse=no (hereinafter: Italian Senate).

41 Art 5(9) Regulation (EU) 2017/1938.

means that they had to provide less assurance of the robustness of the measures they had taken to withstand a severe gas crisis. The Italians doubted that, in case of gas disruptions, there would be equal burden sharing, as one Member State that is directly connected might be exempted from certain duties.[42] As a result they considered their risk-group to be ill-suited to addressing security of gas supply risks, arguing that not all countries included in it have to demonstrate the robustness and efficacy of their systems.[43]

Furthermore, there was a North-West risk group contemplated, made up of Ireland and the UK.[44] Following the Brexit referendum of 23 June 2016 and the huge difficulties in determining the future border between the UK and the EU on the Irish side, this risk group became obsolete.[45] Following these and other debates, the Commission amended the composition of the risk groups and their format in the final version of Regulation (EU) 2017/1938.

However, this is not a decision that is set in stone. Article 3(8) Regulation (EU) 2017/1938 entitles the Commission to update the composition of the risk groups to reflect the evolution of major transnational risks to the security of gas supplies for Member States.[46] In terms of decision-making on the composition of the risk groups the key body is the Gas Coordination Group (GCG), which is made up of the Competent Authorities of Member States, ACER, ENTSO-G, the industry, customers and representatives of the Energy Community. A particular feature of the GCG is the so-called 'restricted setting' mode, which did not feature in Regulation (EU) 994/2010. According to Article 4(4) Regulation (EU) 2017/1938 the GCG can be convened, upon request by one or more Member States/Competent Authorities, in a setting that features only the Member States and not the other parties. The GCG has to be convened in the 'restricted setting' if the European Commission wishes to update the composition of the risk groups.[47]

Possible amendments to the composition of the risk groups shall explicitly take into account the results of a Union-wide 'stress test' that had to be completed on the same day the new Regulation came into force (1 November 2017)[48] and that will be discussed below in the next section. The fact that the Commission finally established risk groups, but simultaneously allows itself to alter their composition, indicates that the current set-up of the risk groups is unlikely to be the last word.

---

42 Italian Senate.
43 Ibid.
44 A picture of the originally proposed risk groups is available at: http://europa.eu/rapid/press-release_MEMO-16-308_en.htm.
45 BBC.co.uk, 'EU "worried" by UK's Irish border proposals' available at: http://www.bbc.co.uk/news/uk-politics-41183041. For more information see chapter I of this volume.
46 Art 3(8) Regulation (EU) 2017/1938.
47 Art 3(8) Regulation (EU) 2017/1938.
48 Art 6(2) Regulation (EU) 2017/1938.

4.1.2. *Tasks of Risk Groups*

The main task of risk groups is the implementation of solidarity measures under the new Article 13 Regulation (EU) 2017/1938, which will be discussed in the next section. Besides this primary obligation, however, there is also the task for Competent Authorities of each risk group to create a 'common risk assessment' at risk group level, alongside their (remaining) obligation to make national risk assessments, which was already included in Regulation (EU) 994/2010.[49] In order to make that happen, Article 7 on Risk Assessment has been considerably amended compared to its old form in Regulation (EU) 994/2010. The national risk assessments have to be fully consistent with assumptions and results of the 'common risk assessment'.[50]

Article 7(4)(a) Regulation (EU) 2017/1938 further obliges the Competent Authorities to detail the N-1 formula[51] at national and regional levels, by taking into account the interrelation of risks of different risk groups.[52] Annexes IV and V Regulation (EU) 2017/1938 entail detailed templates for the common and national risk assessments, which the Commission can alter in the wake of the 'stress tests' and in coordination with the GCG.[53] By 1 October 2018, the Member States have to notify their first common risk assessments to the Commission, alongside the national risk assessments, and these are both subject to a four-year update cycle (in contrast to the two years in Regulation (EU) 994/2010).[54]

4.1.3. *Membership in Several Risk Groups*

If a country is a member of several risk groups, plans must include several regional chapters, which shall be developed jointly in the risk group and shall also implement the results of the 2017 'stress test'. Under the old Article 4(3) Regulation (EU) 994/2010, such regional cooperation was encouraged but not yet mandatory.

The Commission has a 'facilitating' role in putting these regional chapters together.[55] If the Competent Authorities cannot agree on a coordination mechanism in the regional plans, the Commission proposes one for the risk

---

49 Art 7(1) and (2) Regulation (EU) 2017/1938.

50 Ibid.

51 More on the N1 formula can be found at Goldberg 87–88. It remains unchanged, but attached to its definition is now the following statement in Annex II of Regulation (EU) 2017/1938: 'The parameters used for the calculation shall be clearly described and justified. For the calculation of the EPm, a detailed list of the entry points and their individual capacity shall be provided'. This can be read as a warning to Member States to pick realistic data for input into the N-1 formula.

52 Art 7(4)(d) Regulation (EU) 2017/1938.

53 Art 7(5) Regulation (EU) 2017/1938.

54 Art 7(7) Regulation (EU) 2017/1938.

55 Art 8(3)(4) Regulation (EU) 2017/1938.

group, which the Competent Authorities then have to take into account for a regional plan.[56]

According to Article 8(5) Regulation (EU) 2017/1938, there are templates for these plans in Annexes VI and VII. The Competent Authorities of neighbouring countries shall consult with each other on their plans to ensure consistency.[57] The plans must then be notified to the Commission and made public by 1 March 2019 at the latest.[58] The Commission then assesses the plans and can issue an opinion to the Competent Authorities[59] if it thinks that the plans do not comply with the obligation to not distort markets or if they hinder the effective functioning of the internal market.[60]

Where any disagreement between Competent Authorities and the Commission on one of these plans cannot be resolved, the Competent Authorities of the Member States concerned can diverge from the Commission's detailed reasons, but they need to make public the justification underlying their position after receipt of the detailed reasons of the Commission.[61]

The final word on the outline of preventive action plans and emergency plans[62] in the regional chapters therefore lies with the Competent Authorities of the Member States and not with the Commission. This might be viewed as somewhat contradictory to the overall purpose of Regulation (EU) 2017/1938 to increase solidarity and the oversight of the Commission on coordination and planning in a crisis.[63] Against this, however, it can be argued that it makes sense to give Member States the final say on preventive action plans and emergency plans as they have to be designed and ultimately implemented by the Member States. Leaving the 'last word' to the Competent Authorities of Member States is justified by the principle of subsidiarity of Article 5(3) TFEU, which states that the EU shall act in areas of shared competence only if and insofar as objectives of the regulatory action cannot be sufficiently achieved by Member States.[64]

---

56 Ibid.

57 Art 8(6) Regulation (EU) 2017/1938.

58 Art 8(7) Regulation (EU) 2017/1938.

59 Art 8(8) Regulation (EU) 2017/1938.

60 Art 8(8)(c) Regulation (EU) 2017/1938.

61 Art 8(9) Regulation (EU) 2017/1938.

62 Arts 8–10 concern the establishment of preventive action plans and emergency plans, which are now discussed in three consecutive Articles. However, the concepts as such remain the same as in Regulation (EU) 994/2010. Article 8(1) Regulation (EU) 2017/1938 features a new clarification to the extent that measures to ensure the security of gas supply shall be clearly defined in a preventive action plan and an emergency plan and they must be transparent, proportionate, non-discriminatory and verifiable. Moreover, they shall not unduly distort competition or the effective functioning of the internal market in gas and shall not endanger the security of gas supply of other Member States or of the Union, see Art 8(1) Regulation (EU) 2017/1938.

63 Art 1 Regulation (EU) 2017/1938.

64 Art 5(3) TFEU; P CRAIG and G DE BURCA '*EU Law Texts Cases and Materials*' 5th edition (OUP, Oxford 2011) 94–95.

The Member States will probably be very aware of the particularities of their countries and their risk groups given the high importance and sensitivity that the topic of gas supplies has for every EU country and may have more knowledge than the Commission.

4.2. SOLIDARITY MEASURES OF THE NEW ARTICLE 13

The second major innovation of Regulation (EU) 2017/1938 is the solidarity clause of Article 13. Member States are obliged to take certain pre-defined solidarity measures in a gas crisis. In order to fully understand those measures, their implications and their rationale, it is necessary to first take a step back and reflect upon solidarity and its emergence in energy law, before assessing the measures of Article 13 Regulation (EU) 2017/1938 in detail.

4.2.1. The History of Solidarity in European Gas Security of Supply Legislation

Solidarity is not a new concept in the history of EU energy security laws. The 'spirit of solidarity' has in fact been called upon many times: examples include Article 194 TFEU, preamble 13 and Article 9(4) Directive 2004/67,[65] Preambles 5, 22, 25, 36 and Articles 1 and 8(2) Regulation (EU) 994/2010, as well as the new Article 13 Regulation (EU) 2017/1938. Article 194 TFEU in particular, which functions as the primary law basis (the competence) for the introduction of Regulation (EU) 2017/1938,[66] notes:

> In the context of the establishment and functioning of the internal market and with regard for the need to preserve and improve the environment, Union policy on energy shall aim, *in a spirit of solidarity between Member States*, to:
>
> … (b) ensure security of energy supply in the Union;
>
> …[67]

However, this 'spirit of solidarity' is more of a programmatic statement that does not give a concrete definition.

Outside of the energy context a concrete solidarity clause features in Article 222 TFEU, which reads:

> 1. The Union and its Member States shall act jointly in a spirit of solidarity if a Member State is the object of a terrorist attack or the victim of a natural or

[65] Directive 2004/67/EC of 26 April 2004 concerning measures to safeguard security of natural gas supply [2004] OJ L127/92.

[66] Opening statement and preamble 6 of Regulation (EU) 2017/1938.

[67] Art 194(1) TFEU, emphasis added.

man-made disaster. The Union shall mobilise all the instruments at its disposal, including the military resources made available by the Member States, to:

(a) – prevent the terrorist threat in the territory of the Member States;
  – protect democratic institutions and the civilian population from any terrorist attack;
  – assist a Member State in its territory, at the request of its political authorities, in the event of a terrorist attack;
(b) assist a Member State in its territory, at the request of its political authorities, in the event of a natural or man-made disaster.

2. Should a Member State be the object of a terrorist attack or the victim of a natural or manmade disaster, the other Member States shall assist it at the request of its political authorities. To that end, the Member States shall coordinate between themselves in the Council. …

Article 222 TFEU thus provides Member States and EU institutions with the possibility to act jointly in the prevention and the management of terrorism, natural and manmade disasters. Its predecessor has been implemented in secondary legislation by the Critical Infrastructure Directive 2008/114/EC,[68] which applies to natural or manmade disasters.[69] Here an analogy to gas supply crises can be drawn, since gas disruptions can be the result of natural or manmade disasters.

4.2.2. Solidarity in Regulation (EU) 994/2010 and Lack of Reverse Flow Capacity

Silke Goldberg, assessing Regulation (EU) 994/2010 back in 2011, noted that 'the principle of solidarity underpins many of the obligations in the EU Regulation'.[70] However, she identified 'fundamental issues' with the approach of the EU to solidarity, both at the concrete and the conceptual level.[71]

At the concrete level, the need to install bi-directional interconnection capacity (or reverse flow) was the only concrete solidarity measure featuring in the old Regulation (EU) 994/2010.[72] Despite Goldberg's positive assessment back in 2011, stating that 'it may prove to be this provision that gives the Regulation its bite', developments were slow.[73] The share of bi-directional interconnections increased from 24 per cent in 2009 to 40 per cent of total interconnections

68 Council Directive 2008/114/EC on the identification and designation of European critical infrastructures and the assessment of the need to improve their protection [2008] OJ L 345/75 (hereinafter: Directive 2008/114/EC).

69 Preamble 3 Directive 2008/114/EC.

70 Goldberg 83.

71 Goldberg 84.

72 Goldberg 87.

73 Ibid.

in 2014.[74] But the large number of exemptions granted under Article 7 Regulation (EU) 994/2010 from the obligation to install reverse flow capacity has led to a situation where over 50 per cent of interconnectors still cannot have their gas flows reversed.

This poses a real threat that was recently highlighted, once again, in a new gas 'stress test' that ENTSO-G had to conduct by November 2017.[75] In the event of a new major gas disruption South-Eastern Member States, namely Romania and Bulgaria, would need to source gas from Western Europe.[76] ENTSO-G found that in case of a two-month disruption of all gas imports to the EU via Ukraine, Member States in South-Eastern Europe would need to curtail their gas demand significantly.[77] In case of a crisis, gas from Western markets (where diversification of gas supplies is traditionally more developed and LNG imports are starting to kick in) could not be transported to the Eastern European market (where Russia is the big supplier) due to the inability of gas interconnectors to have their gas flows reversed from West to East.[78] In Romania demand would have to be curtailed by 9 per cent, in Greece by around 2 per cent, but in Bulgaria 71 per cent of gas demand would have to be curtailed.[79] These numbers look even worse when modelled for a disruption via the same route during a peak day of exceptionally high gas demand, arising with a statistical probability of once in 20 years.[80] Numbers for Bulgaria look similarly bleak in case of disruption of the largest infrastructure to the Balkan region.[81] The exemptions from the bi-directional capacity obligation are therefore proving to be problematic for neuralgic points, although they are not necessarily restricted to the East-West gas flow, as a number of other shortcomings concerning Finland, Denmark and Sweden highlight.[82]

---

74 SWD Gas Security at 10.

75 ENTSO-G, 'Union-wide Security of Supply Simulation Report 2017' available at: https://www.entsog.eu/public/uploads/files/publications/sos/ENTSOG%20Union%20wide%20SoS%20simulation%20report_INV0262-171121.pdf (hereinafter: 2017 Stress Test).

76 2017 Stress Test at 28.

77 Ibid.

78 2017 Stress Test at 25. However, first signs that the issue is being tackled do exist. See for instance the following project: Net4gas, 'Reverse Flow in Direction West-East' available at: https://www.net4gas.cz/en/projects/eepr-projects/reverse-flow-direction-west-east/.

79 Ibid.

80 2017 Stress Test at 28.

81 2017 Stress Test at 37–38.

82 The report highlights two further, more 'traditional' gas infrastructure issues in Europe:

1) Finland – in case of a disruption of all imports to the Baltic States and Finland a 100 per cent disruption in Finland would occur, due to infrastructure limitations (no connection to another country), see 2017 Stress Test at 35;
2) Denmark and Sweden – in case of the disruption of the largest infrastructure to Denmark (technical disruption of Ellund) both Member States might have to implement up to 40 per cent demand curtailment, again due to limited infrastructure availabilities, see 2017 Stress Test at 48.

In order to limit the number of exemptions, a new procedure is included in Article 5(4) Regulation (EU) 2017/1938. To obtain an exemption from the obligation to have reverse flow capacity fitted to a gas interconnector between Member States, a particular template has to be followed, which is included in Annex III to the Regulation. The idea is to give Member States clearer guidance on the interpretation of conditions that have to be met to grant an exemption. The overall aim of the Commission is to limit the amount of exemptions granted and to narrow the leeway of discretion for Member States.[83]

However, the question why there is such a huge number of exemptions from the obligation to (retro-)fit interconnectors with reverse flow capacity goes deeper and touches upon the more conceptual criticism of Goldberg and others.[84] Solidarity can encourage free-riding.[85] A country might be inclined to be more lax in its introduction of obligatory measures to prevent a shortage in gas supplies if it knows that there are 27 other countries that 'might help out' in case of a real crisis.

4.2.3. The New Solidarity Mechanism of Article 13 Regulation (EU) 2017/1938

The new Article 13 Regulation (EU) 2017/1938 is an attempt to counter this issue. The main stipulation on solidarity in the new security of gas supply regulation in Article 13(1) reads:

> If a Member State has requested the application of the solidarity measure pursuant to this Article, a Member State which is directly connected to the requesting Member State or, where the Member State so provides, its competent authority or transmission system operator or distribution system operator shall as far as possible without creating unsafe situations, take the necessary measures to ensure that the gas supply to customers other than solidarity protected customers in its territory is reduced or does not continue to the extent necessary and for as long as the gas supply to solidarity protected customers in the requesting Member State is not satisfied. The requesting Member State shall ensure that the relevant volume of gas is effectively delivered to solidarity protected customers in its territory.[86]

According to this Article, the directly connected Member State must therefore reduce gas flows to customers other than 'solidarity protected customers' in case of a crisis, and instead needs to pump the volumes of gas that have been freed up to a Member State requesting solidarity. This must be continued for as long

[83] SWD Gas Security 2014 at 11–12.

[84] Goldberg 84; G Luciani, 'Working Paper 2: Security of Supply for Natural Gas Markets – What is it and what is it not?' (2004) OGEL 2, 9–10.

[85] Ibid.

[86] Art 13(1) Regulation (EU) 2017/1938.

as supply to 'solidarity protected customers' in the requesting Member States cannot be satisfied. This new mechanism then requires Member States in such situations to directly interfere with the markets and the contractual obligations of market players, the consequences of which will be discussed further below.

4.2.4. *The New Category of 'Solidarity Protected Customers'*

But what is a 'solidarity protected customer'? And how is it related to the concept of a 'protected customer'? Article 2 Regulation (EU) 2017/1938 sets out the definitions used in the Regulations, many of which already featured in Regulation (EU) 994/2010 and are linked to the Gas Directive (Directive 2009/73/EC).[87] A 'solidarity protected customer, in terms of Article 2(6) Regulation (EU) 2017/1938, is:

> a household customer who is connected to a gas distribution network, and, in addition, may include one or both of the following:
>
> (a) a district heating installation if it is a protected customer in the relevant Member State and only in so far as it delivers heating to households or essential social services other than educational and public administration services;
>
> (b) an essential social service if it is a protected customer in the relevant Member State, other than educational and public administration services;[88]

The definition of 'solidarity protected customer' is thus narrower than the definition of 'protected customer', which features in Article 2(5) Regulation (EU) 2017/1938 and has been maintained from Regulation (EU) 994/2010.[89] The difference is that the category of 'protected customer' can include 'small/medium size enterprises', whereas such enterprises cannot feature as 'solidarity protected customer'.[90]

Moreover, the 'solidarity protected customer' definition places further restrictions and qualifications on the extent to which district heating installations and essential social services can be qualified by Member States as 'solidarity protected customers'.[91]

---

87 Council Directive (EC) 2009/73 of 13 July 2009 concerning common rules for the internal market in natural gas and repealing Directive 2003/55/EC [2009] OJ L 211/94.

88 Art 2(6) Regulation (EU) 2017/1938.

89 Now in Art 2(5) Regulation (EU) 2017/1938.

90 Compare Art 2(5) and (6) Regulation (EU) 2017/1938.

91 Under Art 2(6)(a) Regulation (EU) 2017/1938 'a district heating installation if it is a protected customer in the relevant Member State and only in so far as it delivers heating to households or essential social services other than educational and public administration services'. Under Art 2(6)(b) 'an essential social service if it is a protected customer in the relevant Member State, other than educational and public administration services'.

The Member State providing solidarity can also resort to further non-market-based measures to achieve the aim of providing solidarity.[92] The requesting Member State is obliged to inform the providing Member State immediately when it is able to resume supply to its solidarity protected customers.[93]

However, under Article 13(7) Regulation (EU) 2017/1938, the obligation to provide solidarity in gas is subject to the safe and reliable operation of the gas system of the Member State that is asked to provide solidarity and the limit of maximum interconnection export capacity of the relevant Member State infrastructure towards the requesting Member State.

This provision might end up being used as a first 'exit-gateway', a way for Member States that are unwilling to provide solidarity to circumvent their obligations. Member States have very different provisions on the composition of natural gas streams and the possibility to admix other gases to those streams.[94] Member States that are unwilling to deliver gas to other Member States in a gas crisis might want to use these different configurations of the gas stream and other technical prescriptions as reasons for abstaining from the solidarity mechanism, based on the argument that there are limitations to the safe and reliable operation of the gas system.

4.2.5. Compensation Mechanism for Market Interference under Article 13

A crucial factor in limiting such tendencies and encouraging Member States to interfere with their energy markets and contractual arrangements of market players is the money that has to be paid as compensation for the emergency solidarity gas deliveries. Article 13(8) Regulation (EU) 2017/1938 foresees a strict and comprehensive compensation mechanism. The Member State requesting solidarity must promptly pay fair compensation to the Member State providing solidarity. Such fair compensation is to cover at least the following items:

(a) gas delivered into the territory of the requesting Member State;
(b) all other relevant and reasonable costs incurred when providing solidarity, including, where appropriate, costs of such measures that may have been established in advance;
(c) reimbursement for any compensation resulting from judicial proceedings, arbitration proceedings or similar proceedings and settlements and related

92 Art 13(5) Regulation (EU) 2017/1938.
93 Art 13(6) Regulation (EU) 2017/1938.
94 See R Fleming and J Fershee. 'The "Hydrogen Economy" in the US and the EU – Regulating Innovation to Combat Climate Change' in D Zillmann, L Godden, L Paddock and MM Roggenkamp (eds), *Innovation in Energy Law and Technology: Dynamic Solutions for Energy Transitions* OUP, Oxford 2018) chapter 8, pp 190–207.

> costs of such proceedings involving the Member State providing solidarity vis-a-vis entities involved in the provision of such solidarity.[95]

This shall also include all reasonable costs that the Member State which is providing solidarity incurs from an obligation to pay compensation by virtue of fundamental rights guaranteed by Union law, and by virtue of the applicable international obligations when implementing this Article.[96] This is referring to the right of all gas customers to be supplied and the possibility that this might have to be infringed in a crisis on the basis of Regulation (EU) 2017/1938.

Also, further reasonable costs incurred from payment of compensation pursuant to national compensation rules have to be reimbursed.[97] This situation might occur when a Member State orders its gas supply companies in a crisis to restrict supplies to 'solidarity protected customers'. This would mean, as mentioned above, that small- and medium-sized enterprises, for example, could suffer supply interruptions. However, they have a contract with their gas supplier for gas deliveries, which the gas supply companies are then violating. This can lead to compensation claims, which the companies can then pass on to the Member State.

Finally, the requesting Member State also has to compensate all costs that the Union incurs by virtue of any liability in respect of measures that Member States are required to take.[98] In other words, the request of solidarity comes with a heavy price-tag attached to it, which can make the strategy of relying on other Member States to 'help out' in a crisis a costly one.

The Member States must adopt the necessary measures by 1 December 2018, in particular deciding on the technical, legal and financial arrangements necessary to be able to pay compensation, as described above. The technical, legal and financial arrangements shall be agreed among the Member States which are directly connected or connected via a non-Member States and shall be described in their respective emergency plans.[99] Such arrangements may cover:

a) the operational safety of networks;
b) gas prices to be applied and/or the methodology for their setting, taking into account the impact on the functioning of the market;
c) the use of interconnections, including bi-directional capacity and underground gas storage;
d) gas volumes or the methodology for their setting;
e) categories of costs that will have to be covered by a fair and prompt compensation, that may include damages for curtailed industry;

---

95 Art 13(8) Regulation (EU) 2017/1938.
96 Ibid.
97 Ibid.
98 Art 13(16) Regulation (EU) 2017/1938.
99 Art 13(10) Regulation (EU) 2017/1938, more on the emergency plans below.

f) an indication of the method by which fair compensation could be calculated.[100]

Any compensation mechanism shall provide incentives to participate in market-based solutions such as auctions and demand–response mechanisms.[101] It shall not create incentives for market players to postpone their action until non-market-based measures are applied. All compensation mechanisms, or at least a summary thereof, shall be included in the emergency plans.[102]

There is a second 'exit-gateway' for Member States, this time for those that are unwilling to negotiate the comprehensive arrangements just described. Article 13(11) Regulation (EU) 2017/1938 states that a Member State shall be exempted from the obligation to conclude technical, legal and financial arrangements with directly connected Member States (or via non-Member States), as long as it can cover the gas consumption for its 'solidarity protected customers' from its own production. Such an exemption, however, shall not affect the obligation of the relevant Member State to provide solidarity to other Member States.[103]

A similar exemption has been drawn up specifically for Denmark and Sweden (rather unsystematically placed in Article 20(3) Regulation (EU) 2017/1938). Denmark and Sweden shall be exempted from the obligation to conclude technical, legal and financial arrangements for the purpose of Sweden providing solidarity to Denmark. This does not, however, affect Denmark's obligation to provide solidarity and to conclude the necessary technical, legal and financial arrangements to that effect.[104]

The Commission had a deadline of 1 December 2017 to provide guidance for the key elements of the technical, legal and financial arrangements.[105] However, at the time of writing, this guidance document had not yet been issued.

4.2.6. Resolutions for Ambiguities in Article 13

There are at least two questions that might be raised in relation to the mechanisms proposed by the new Article 13:

1) What if more than one Member State is directly connected to the requesting Member State – who has to provide the gas?
2) What if Member States that are directly connected cannot agree on the technical, legal and financial arrangements of compensation?

---

100 Ibid.
101 Art 13(10) Regulation (EU) 2017/1938.
102 Ibid.
103 Ibid.
104 Art 20(3) Regulation (EU) 2017/1938.
105 Art 13(12) Regulation (EU) 2017/1938.

Question one is answered by Article 13(4) Regulation (EU) 2017/1938:

> If there is more than one Member State that could provide solidarity to a requesting Member State, the requesting Member State shall, after consulting all Member States required to provide solidarity, seek the most advantageous offer on the basis of cost, speed of delivery, reliability and diversification of supplies of gas.

The Regulation, however, does not provide a precise mechanism by which these individual components are to be interpreted, which means that the interpretation of terms like reliability and diversification of supplies is left to the discretion of Member States. This could constitute a possible third 'exit-gateway', which could help a Member State to decline offers that it does not like.[106]

The second question is answered in Article 13(13) and (14) Regulation (EU) 2017/1938. If Member States do not agree on a compensation mechanism by 1 October 2018, the Commission will propose one, based on its (still to be issued) guidance document. Member States will then finalise their arrangements by 1 December 2018, taking 'utmost account' of the Commission's proposal.[107] This curious formulation is an indicator that the Commission will not have the final say on the matter. Indeed, Article 13(14) Regulation (EU) 2017/1938 provides that if Member States fail to agree or finalise their technical, legal and financial arrangements, they only have to agree on the necessary ad hoc measures in case of a crisis.

Finally, Regulation (EU) 2017/1938 stresses at several points[108] that solidarity shall be a measure of last resort, which applies only in an emergency and is subject to several restrictive conditions. A Member State that is declaring an emergency should first take all available measures to resolve the situation before calling upon the solidarity of other Member States.[109] This emphasis on solidarity as a last resort is a result of the opposition of Member States towards the inclusion of a strict solidarity mechanism. It can also be seen as a final attempt by the Commission to discourage 'free riding' and encourage instead Member States to have robust arrangements in place to save themselves in a crisis.

5. CONCLUSION

The essential theme of the new security of gas supply Regulation is 'solidarity'. The EU has put into place a number of new measures on that basis. However,

---

106 More on this below in the concluding section.
107 Art 13(13) Regulation (EU) 2017/1938.
108 Preambles 38–42, Arts 1, 13(3) Regulation (EU) 2017/1938.
109 Preamble 38 Regulation (EU) 2017/1938.

they also include some 'exit gateways' for Member States that are unwilling to participate to the full extent. Moreover, there is still considerable leeway for Member State discretion, for instance in cases where a number of Member States could potentially provide solidarity. In these cases, the Member State receiving solidarity could 'steer' its choice towards countries with which it has a strong relationship anyway via its interpretation of terms like reliability and diversification of supplies. This might lead to situations where the optimal, most efficient solution is not the one selected. It is also interesting to note that renewable gases, discussed in other chapters of this volume, are not considered by Regulation (EU) 2017/1938.

The fact that there are numerous exemptions and limitations to the solidarity provisions is merely a manifestation in law of an underlying problem. The debates about the composition of risk groups showed that Member States are reluctant to participate in the proposed solidarity mechanisms and are cautiously protecting their sovereignty over energy matters. Against this backdrop, the new provisions constitute a big step and could be deemed a considerable 'win' for the Commission. But as previous gas crises have shown, the words on paper and the top-down obligation imposed on Member States is not worth much if there is no willingness to comply when push comes to shove. The EU still has a considerable task ahead to really change this position.

www.ingramcontent.com/pod-product-compliance
Ingram Content Group UK Ltd.
Pitfield, Milton Keynes, MK11 3LW, UK
UKHW051921100926
8556IPUK00021B/1295

9 781780 686721